Troy H. Middleton

Troy H. Middleton

A Biography

FRANK JAMES PRICE

Louisiana State University Press
BATON ROUGE

ISBN 0-8071-2467-2
Library of Congress Catalog Card Number 73–90869
Copyright © 1974 by Louisiana State University Press
All rights reserved
Manufactured in the United States of America

Designed by Dwight Agner. Set in Linotype Times Roman
by The TJM Corp., Baton Rouge, Louisiana. Printed and bound
by The Colonial Press Inc., Clinton, Massachusetts.

To Lucile

Contents

Illustrations

Preface

IN October, 1964, my son, James Patrick Price, had to write a term paper in a sophomore course in military science at Louisiana State University. In a supper table conversation, my wife, Lucile, suggested that Pat interview a military figure. He chose General Troy H. Middleton, president emeritus of LSU. "Your dad knows him. He'll introduce you and lend you a tape recorder for the interview," Lucile said.

On October 28, Pat recorded the interview in General Middleton's office on the LSU campus. The tape and the typescript were turned in to the ROTC class instructor; they became part of the course of instruction in subsequent semesters.

In the course of conversation with Middleton, I asked who was writing his biography. "Nobody," he replied, "and I'm surely not going to write an autobiography. Somebody asked General George Marshall soon after World War II if he planned, like a lot of other generals, to write an autobiography. Marshall declared, 'I'm not going to write one because if I did I'd have to tell the truth; in telling the truth I might hurt a lot of people.' Well, if I wrote one, I'd have to do the same thing," Middleton said.

Finding it hard to believe that no one was at work on the life story of the university's president emeritus, I said, "How about my writing it?" Middleton said, "Fine. I'm here in my office every Wednesday morning. Let me know when you're ready to start." For the next six and a half years, Middleton and I spent from one to three hours talking most Wednesday mornings in his office. Most of those days from two to ten visitors dropped in. The telephone rang three or four times. The General signed five or six letters his part-time secretary had typed for him.

This book is essentially Troy H. Middleton's own story. Early in our conversations, I provided General Middleton with a tape recorder and instructions for operating it. He provided me with tapes which ran to seventy-two typescript pages, about 25,000 words. These tapes became the framework for the manuscript. I sought supplemental information in interviews. With rare exceptions, these interviews took place in the General's office on the LSU campus. My teaching schedule was arranged to leave Wednesday mornings open for these sessions. In the relatively austere surroundings of his office, Middleton never needed to refer to a book to supplement his recollection. To hundreds of my inquiries for first name and middle initial of a military man or educator, up to fifty years in the past, he responded all but unerringly. On the rare occasions when he could not supply the information, he would say, "It'll come to me." At our next session, he would have recalled it.

Unfailingly, I checked out these items. Unfailingly, the General's recollection was correct. Occasionally, when I sought more information on a battle or the circumstances of an educational problem, three or four years after the original interview, only the slightest prompting was needed. I checked out these recollections against the published record or documentary evidence; they always stood up.

This book is not footnoted, not because I have any prejudice against such scholarly appurtenances, but because many readers find that footnotes interrupt the flow. Middleton read the manuscript after I completed it in May, 1973, having the opportunity to challenge either the information or the interpretation I put on it.

I spent a day at the Pentagon in Washington reading the contents of two thick pouches of typewritten and printed material filling Middleton's 201 file (the army's term for personnel records), beginning with his first enlistment as a private in 1910 and ending with his retirement as a lieutenant general in 1945. My interview with General Eisenhower at Gettysburg was a useful followup to the Pentagon visit.

One note came through in the 201 file and in the interviews with Eisenhower and scores of others: the calm with which Troy Middleton faced every crisis. The more demanding the crisis, the more coolly Middleton operated. "I must have learned this from my mother," he said; "how else could the mother of nine have managed?"

Photographs and other memorabilia of Middleton's childhood do not appear in this book because they were lost in a fire which destroyed the family home and its contents in 1935. Mrs. Middleton faithfully preserved virtually every item dealing with her husband's army service, after their marriage in January, 1915, including most of those Lieutenant Middleton had accumulated in the previous five years. Mrs. Middleton likewise preserved a great many items dealing with her husband's three terms of service at LSU and with eleven years of retirement in which he remained an active public servant.

Unlike some other military commanders, Middleton did not keep a diary while he was in combat. "It was against regulations," he said; "I believe in obeying them."

This book is tightly linked with the contents of the Troy H. Middleton Collection of Memorabilia in the LSU Library, where tape recordings, photographs, military documents, books, and scores of awards won by Middleton are on display or are available.

The Battle of the Bulge runs at considerable length in this book because I found that it was not readily compressible if it was to be treated in the proper perspective. Middleton felt that this was the largest and most involved action in which American military men ever fought. It was Middleton who made the decision to scrap the textbook recommendations, the service school doctrine, and to use armor in small task forces around Bastogne. It was he who made the decision to hold Bastogne against a swarming foe greatly outnumbering the defenders. It was he who ordered small forces to hold, hold, hold. They did, and in the immense confusion of battle they thwarted the German hordes until help could arrive.

George Patton first railed at Middleton for putting the 101st Airborne Division in Bastogne to be surrounded. Later, Patton hailed Middleton for his "stroke of genius" at Bastogne. It was, Middleton told me, just a common sense decision. "I knew the Germans had to have the road net focusing in Bastogne. I decided to deny it to them."

I chose to use an absolute minimum of technical military language because this book is written for the general reader, who may have known Troy Middleton or may want to learn about the former Mississippian who gave nearly half a century to serving Louisiana and his nation.

Middleton read the manuscript in installments. He returned them promptly, usually with a chuckle over some anecdote, and with a recurring comment, "I must have led a pretty eventful life."

So he had. He was the youngest colonel in the American Expeditionary Force in France in 1918. He spent more days in combat than any other general officer in the United States Army in World War II. He retired from the army in 1937, after a distinguished career of twenty-seven years. His years at Louisiana State University were in three installments. First, from 1930 to 1936, he was commandant of cadets for an unprecedented six years, the last two of which he served also as dean of men. After retiring from the army in 1937, he returned to LSU, where he worked until January, 1942, volunteering to reenter the army, where he served with great distinction, rising from colonel to lieutenant general, before returning to LSU in June, 1945. He resumed his duties at LSU as comptroller. In 1951 he was appointed president and served through LSU's greatest growth period until his retirement in February, 1962, at age seventy-two. As president emeritus, in retirement he became an extraordinarily active public servant. Unfailingly, through the eight and a half years I have worked with the General, I have never known a more patient, a more thoughtful, or more responsive person. His phenomenal recollection has brought alive military and educational history of seven decades.

F. J. Price and General Middleton on a Working Wednesday Morning (Photo by Catherine Arnold)

Troy H. Middleton

1　Calm in the Hurricane

SECURE behind its new seawall, Galveston was riding out its second killer hurricane in fifteen years. On this night of August 16–17, 1915, shortly after midnight, Jerusha Collins Middleton, a bride of seven months and eleven days, pushed through the throng in the home of her uncle and aunt, Mr. and Mrs. John Hagemann. Jerusha Middleton was looking for her husband Troy.

As the winds drove toward their peak velocity of 120 miles an hour, the two-story house at 3301 Avenue L flinched, recovered, shuddered, held firm. The Hagemann house had withstood the full fury of the 1900 hurricane. Recalling this, friends and neighbors, black and white, crammed the house. Through them Jerusha threaded, then forced passage. Where was Troy Houston Middleton, second lieutenant, United States Army? Not in the living room, or the reception area at the front. He was not among the throng in the hallway. He wasn't on the curving staircase which led to a landing at the back of the house; it was jammed like the bleachers at the baseball park. Surely Troy Middleton was not in the huge kitchen, quiet and deserted. Jerusha went there next; a first look showed nothing. Then, in the thirty-inch clear space behind the huge coal-burning kitchen range, she saw a familiar figure. Seated, with his arms clasping his drawn-up legs and his head pillowed on his knees, Middleton was sound asleep. "Troy, what on earth are you doing back there! Don't you know there's a hurricane howling outside?"

Put out? "Yes, she was," Troy recalled. "She couldn't understand

1

anyone's not being excited and wide awake at such a time." But, since there wasn't anything he could do about the storm, he chose to rest. There would be work aplenty next day for everyone, especially for a young infantry officer whose troops had been quartered in tents on the Fort Crockett reservation two miles or so away.

Galvestonians had grave reason to fear hurricanes. Fifteen years before, September 8–9, 1900, the deadliest of them all had drowned between six and eight thousand residents in the worst natural disaster in United States history. Without a seawall, the people of Galveston had no place to go and little to cling to as storm tides surged to a depth of fifteen feet or more all over the island. Not a structure failed to suffer some damage.

Because the Hagemann home had borne up in 1900—three fourths of a mile from the open Gulf of Mexico and half a mile from Galveston Bay—the house with its eight spacious rooms drew near and distant neighbors steadily through the day. The wind had freshened and begun to build in the morning. By six that evening Gulf waters overspread the Hagemann yard and sloshed in the oleanders and palms of the neighborhood. Along Avenue L, which paralleled the Gulf, no land showed. On Thirty-third Street, which led straight to the open sea, water raced toward the bay behind the island.

In 1915, Galveston no longer lay defenseless against the sea. A sturdy seawall shouldered all the way across the part of the island on which Galveston sat. No longer could waves, building strength all the way across from Yucatan, smash unchecked up that unprotected beach. When the wind peaked that night at 120 miles an hour, tide heights ranged from 9.5 to 14.3 feet above mean Gulf level in the city and to 16.1 feet at the causeway linking Galveston to the mainland. The business section swirled with water up to 6 feet deep. Though the storm's thrust and killing potential was as great as it had been in 1900, this time only 275 persons died. Damage was $50,000,000. The seawall saved Galveston, the people of Galveston, if not all of their property. Next morning, as the waters began receding, the Hagemann home remained intact, and full of grateful friends and neighbors who had expected it to continue standing.

When he could make his way back to his company area where the Seventh Infantry Regiment was quartered under canvas, Lieutenant Middleton had to clamber past a three-masted schooner the storm had pitched smartly over the seawall five hundred yards east of his tent. The schooner's cargo of sisal wrapped and shrouded the area for blocks around. At his tent, in the lee of a Fort Crockett coast artillery gun emplacement, Middleton found the canvas taut and the guy ropes humming in the dying gusts— as if the shelter had been drenched by nothing more than a benign August shower. Steele's two-volume *American Campaigns*, required reading for any earnest young army officer, stood undampened on a shelf next to Middleton's cot.

The army pitched in with rescue and rehabilitation work. An arms chest containing six rifles from Lieutenant Middleton's company had been swept fifteen miles across the bay and deposited near La Marque. When the storm waters receded the chest was found and its contents returned to the inventory of the regiment.

No army men were lost in the hurricane. All troops in the area had been sent to refuge in the permanent buildings of Fort Crockett or, in some instances, to more substantial structures in the city of Galveston.

At twenty-five, Lieutenant Troy Middleton weathered a crisis, the second great Galveston hurricane, in what was to become characteristic fashion for him. His calm increased as the barometric pressure decreased. He wasted no fears on what might befall his family and friends in the Hagemann house. Hadn't it withstood a sterner test fifteen years before? Why shouldn't it stand up this time, buffered by the splendid new seawall? The House of Hagemann stood. When Middleton left his bride to join in the long cleanup after the hurricane, Jerusha understood a little better the kind of man her lieutenant would turn out to be.

2   Plantation Boyhood and School Days

T ROY HOUSTON MIDDLETON was born October 12, 1889, the fifth child of John Houston Middleton and Katherine Louise Thompson Middleton, on a plantation near Georgetown in Copiah County, Mississippi. Eleven years younger than the oldest and eleven years older than the youngest, Troy stood directly in the middle among nine children. The Houston in his father's and in young Troy's name was derived from Sam Houston, who went on to Texas and a place in history. But the young Troy, then and later, held little regard for the name. "Sam Houston was involved in too many things I have never been able to build any enthusiasm for," he said more than once.

A hike back along the genealogical trace, taken in Troy Middleton's behalf when he was invited to membership in the Sons of the American Revolution, at age eighty-one, identified his ancestry well before the Revolution. His father was the son of Benjamin Parks Middleton and the grandson of Captain Robert Middleton. The first Middleton over from England was an earlier Robert Middleton, 1651–1696, who settled in York County, Virginia.

Captain Robert Middleton had moved from Georgia to Alabama to Copiah County, sometime early in the 1800s. His son and his grandson, Troy's father, had all spent their lives in Copiah County, about thirty miles south of Jackson and a day's wagon ride from Hazlehurst.

Troy Middleton's first American ancestor started with sizable land

4

grants from the crown. Subsequent Middletons were not so favored. From Virginia, through North and South Carolina, they moved with the frontier on into Georgia and Alabama, finally settling on the inviting acres of Copiah County. There crops grew bountifully. The woods yielded deer, squirrel, turkey, and other small game. Streams ran clear throughout the year.

Young Troy's earliest experiences were with the abundance of country living. Before he reached school age and the first large responsibilities of childhood, he roamed the plantation acres with playmates, most of whom were black. They shot marbles and played other games on a grassless yard, the sands of which were vigorously swept each day with a yard broom made of long twigs of the black gum tree lashed firmly together. A row of cedars, planted by Troy's grandfather, led from the road to the Middleton house. Quick-growing china trees shaded the back yard. Chinaberries were ammunition to be discharged from elementary "guns" made by reaming out the pith in a foot-long section of elderberry stalk. A plunger, moving under hand pressure behind a tightly fitted chinaberry, compressed the air in the gun barrel and finally blew out a chinaberry projectile rammed earlier into the muzzle of the gun. A solid hit at ten yards stung smartly. Each year Troy watched flocks of robins get ingloriously intoxicated on frost-nipped chinaberries which had fermented on the tree.

Every child in the Middleton family had at least one quilt, produced at a bee where the neighborhood women pitched in, cutting, trimming, stitching, to produce the star, the Dutch doll, and other beloved patterns. Troy took his turn as a child in shelling peas and butter beans for the table and for canning. He learned to churn, lifting and driving home the crossbladed hardwood dasher in a ten-gallon crockery churn to cause the fat globules to cluster and finally to be skimmed from the surface and shaped into pounds of butter. Having learned how to churn and process butter, young Troy was content to leave this chore to others. On one farm task he drew the line. He never even tried to milk a cow.

Entertainment and amusement in the first six years of Troy Middleton's life were fairly standardized. On a plantation with about four hundred acres under cultivation, there were always neighbors to visit and neighbors visiting. A trip to Jackson required a 10-mile buggy ride to Hazlehurst and then a 33-mile ride on the Illinois Central Railroad to the state capital. These trips were rare. Even rarer were excursions to New Orleans, 150 miles south, the prime shipping point for bananas and other delights of boyhood.

Horseback riding, fishing, and hunting (only in season, his father insisted, to let the young broods be raised and to give the wild creatures a chance to replenish their numbers) engaged every young boy. Troy rode bareback, scorning the saddle, wherever he went. A Hazlehurst livery stable owner kept a pack of foxhounds, and Troy rode a sure-footed mule at night on the trail of the hounds, never taking a serious fall. He did have one brush with disaster. With a chum he had clambered onto the back of a horse-drawn wagon loaded with three long planks, coupled far out. The planks bounced and swung freely. Then the team shied, Troy was thrown, and a wagon wheel passed over his stomach. The driver did not notice. And Troy decided against making an outcry. "For weeks my stomach was sore," he recalled. But whatever damage was done eventually cleared up. Thereafter Troy was more careful about unconventional modes of travel.

Sundays were special to the Middletons. Everyone went to church by wagon or by buggy. Church at Bethel started promptly and early. The typical sermon ran an hour and a half—never less. "You could never remember what the preacher said, but you couldn't fail to hear him," Troy reminisced.

"I was an Episcopalian by birth, but at that time the only church in the area was Baptist. So we became Episcopal Baptists. Either we went to the Baptist church or we didn't go. Not going was unthinkable. So our Sundays were always spoken for. We looked forward to seeing all our neighbors. If the sermon wasn't the kind you could recall all week, it was explicit enough in its warnings about where mortal man was headed and the conditions he'd encounter if he didn't straighten up and live the right kind of life."

Periodically there would be all-day preaching, blessedly broken by dinner on the grounds. This rural church practice, confined to the warm months, persisted through the first quarter of the twentieth century—or so long as the automobile did not penetrate extensively into community life and disperse folks beyond a radius the good Lord had equipped them for, either as far as they could comfortably walk or be borne in a bone-shaking buggy or wagon.

In the last decade of the nineteenth century, most of the plantation population was black. Servants were plentiful. There were no household problems. Almost all the food consumed on the plantation was produced right there. For variety, the young hunter could kick up a covey of quail almost anywhere. If he had the persistence and infinite patience, he could entice a wary wild turkey into gun range. Once, Troy recalled, his father baited an area with corn and they downed seven turkeys. The deer that had greeted his grandfather on these acres had disappeared. But wild ducks moved in from the north early each winter, landing on the clear streams and feeding on oak and beech mast in the flatlands which flooded with each winter's rains.

Two creeks flowed near the Middleton home. The Lick ran into the Strong which emptied into Pearl River. Both creeks abounded in fish: channel catfish, Kentucky bass, white perch, and rafts of smaller panfish gulped any bait dangled before them. Troy's first artificial lure was an imitation shad with triple hooks mounted fore and aft. Catfish were lured to trotline hooks or to set pole lines with rank cheese or chicken entrails wrapped in cheesecloth. Buffalo came up the Pearl to spawn in spring and were taken in quantity, though their coarser flesh was not a favorite with the boys. Through the summer, the boys spent endless hours on the stream banks. They learned to attach a small sheep bell to the set poles to let the catfish themselves announce when they were on the hook. All-night sessions yielded enough catfish for everyone on the plantation.

Humbler game like rabbit and squirrel frisked and darted out in front of the bead on young Troy's double-barreled 12-gauge shotgun. He shot worlds of squirrel for the table, but rarely fired at a rabbit, "which I never ate," he said. "It all depended on the family. We didn't know that rabbits carried lots of disease; it just wasn't thought to be the thing to do to eat rabbit. But squirrel were something else; we ate a great many. And opossum on occasion, done just right by a good Negro cook who banked the opossum in a bed of sweet potatoes. Very good, very rich it was."

At eight or nine, Troy drew his shotgun from among several around the house. The first shotgun he could call his own was the double-barreled 12-gauge. He traded a horse to a neighbor boy for this gun. "That's how cheap horses were," Troy recalled.

He also had a .22 rifle, and he had learned to aim at sitting game and to track moving targets with a slingshot. The shotgun was too heavy for the young shooter. It had to be laid over a fence or held tightly against a tree before it could be fired with any reasonable assurance of being on target. Black powder propelled the shotgun pellets. "The shells I used were named New Club. You'd kick up the birds and shoot into a covey of quail; then you'd have to run out from under the cloud of black smoke to see whether you'd hit any. Smokeless powder came in after I was a pretty good-sized boy."

The house Troy grew up in was cut from virgin pine on the acres surrounding it—from the heart of pine. (It burned in 1935 in a spectacular fire that was like some gigantic torch feeding on the resin and the oils in that prime lumber.) The house was sealed inside with snug-fitting tongue and groove lumber which was never papered. It had one story, with great stretches of storage space in the attic. From the front porch, the Middletons could go down a long hall, open to the breezes, giving on two large bedrooms on the right, and leading on to a dining room and to a detached kitchen, set a little separate from the rest of the house but joined to it by a covered passageway—to keep the smell and the heat of cooking out of the main house and to protect the main house from fire.

Across the central hall, the first room on the left was the parlor, a room little used, set apart for company which would just as soon take the breezes on the long front porch. Behind the parlor was another bedroom. And behind that was the water well with shelves and basins for freshening up and, for the boys, some down-to-earth scouring before they could take their places at the table. Just beyond the well was a small bathroom enclosing a portable tub. The tub stood on legs resembling sturdy lion's paws. Water was poured into it straight from the well in the warmer months. Baths came infrequently during the winter, for the water had to be heated across the hall in large pans and carried to the sheet metal tub with a wooden rim around the top.

Water for drinking, for cooking, for bathing was drawn in a six-inch by three-foot well bucket with a hinged bottom, the container sliding smoothly down a shaft into the bored well. A second well of much greater diameter had been dug by plantation laborers. This all-purpose well, likely perforating the same sands as the other, provided cooling storage for milk and butter and for waterproof perishables before the first iceboxes came to the plantation. "We kept our milk and butter in containers lowered into the well. When we wanted a chilled watermelon, we slung it in a sack and let it down into the well. But we never drank the water from this well,"

Troy recalled. Water for the livestock and poultry came from ponds and springs on the plantation. Perfectly clear water ran from springs the year round.

Since there was no refrigeration suitable for meats, whatever was eaten on the plantation had to be cured in preparation for dry storage or it had to be eaten fresh. Hog-killing time always came with the first heavy frost of autumn. The wash pots, heavy cast iron, three-legged vats in which clothes were boiled in the standard laundering process each week, were filled with water and fired in preparation for the first hog slaughter. After the hog or hogs were shot or clubbed, the carcass was hung upside down and bled, the hair having been removed by a boiling water bath and by vigorous scraping. This left the bleached-looking carcass ready for the cleaning and carving. The intestines were removed and their contents scraped out, leaving the translucent casings to be stuffed later with sausage. Troy regularly took his turn at the stuffer, where the fragrant sausage was extruded into the casings. Troy remembered liking this chore.

Fresh pork—chops and cutlets and savory backbone meat—was served daily while the curing went on in the smokehouse, a light-tight wooden structure apart from the kitchen. A fire was built with oak in an earthenware container on the earthen surface of the smokehouse. Fed more oak, this smudge poured out great volumes of smoke, curing the hams, the sides of bacon and the long chains of sausage. "I can see it now, hanging over those poles high up in the smokehouse. When you'd have to go in there to get something, the accumulated smoke and odor would almost run you right out."

Whereas hog-killing time always came with first cold weather, slaughtering of other animals came at different intervals. "You would kill a lamb for the family; it didn't last very long. But you had lamb, not mutton, but real lamb," Troy recalled. "Beef was a community thing. If the Middleton plantation killed a thousand-pound steer, why they divided it up with the other families around that area—and then another family would do the same thing, and you'd be paid in return, you see. And you didn't have to refrigerate it. We ate a great deal of meat at those times, since it didn't keep without refrigeration.

"We had chickens aplenty, with eggs every day, ducks and guineas. There was a trick to finding the nest of the guineas, sort of a polka-dotted African fowl; when you'd turn up a nest, you'd find a hundred eggs there, out in the woods, well away from where the chickens laid theirs. A flock of geese kept the grass out of the cotton rows; they were plucked for down for pillows, but never eaten. For short-term storage, eggs went to the well along with the day's milk and butter."

Breakfast, year in, year out, was always a stout meal on the plantation, with ham, bacon, eggs, grits and homemade bread, always called "light bread" to distinguish it from the much denser corn bread. Light bread was for breakfast, corn bread was for noon. Many days there were four meats on the table for dinner, the noon meal. Whoever happened to be there or to stop in for a visit was welcomed to the table. Fourteen feet long, the dinner table seated a crowd.

The plantation remained home to more blacks than Middletons. They worked the producing acres. The women contended for the opportunity to work at the big house, which always assured fine food for their tables. The four hundred acres under cultivation produced cotton, corn, peas, and sugar cane. The sugar cane was white, soft, easy to chew. It yielded a syrup that looked like castor oil, heavy and clear, but was a delightful sweetener. Syrup was cooked in a syrup house on the plantation. The extraction of juice from the white cane was accomplished by a mule, walking an eternal circle in the autumn air, putting the cane stalks through the grinder before the juice went to the cooker to be thickened into syrup.

"We did a great deal of canning. Our large peach orchard produced perfect peaches for hundreds of glass jars of peach preserves, pickles, and jelly. And we didn't have to baby those peach trees. I can't recall that the trees ever did need much spraying, as today's trees do. In fact, I can't recall that those trees were ever sprayed. We made pickles and we canned and preserved just about everything that grew wild or was cultivated on the farm. We could go to the pantry shelves any day in the year and pull down jars of something we'd grown in the kitchen garden or out on the bigger acreages," he recalled.

Food on the plantation table was about what the stereotype of Southern food called for: cornbread, grits, collards, turnip greens, blackeyed peas, crowder peas, purple-hulled peas. These were staples, the background foods for the grander things which seized a youngster's imagination. Ice cream was a great Middleton family favorite. It was cranked by hand in a wire-bound wooden bucket surrounding a two-gallon galvanized can.

Christmas was, to the young Middletons, an orange in the toe of a stocking, among other things. But, whereas bananas were great rarities elsewhere in most of the United States, they were not novelties to the Middleton children. "You could always find a bunch of bananas hanging in front of an Italian store in Hazlehurst," Troy recalled. They became popular with the Middletons. When John Middleton went to Hazlehurst he brought back a hefty bunch of bananas, half-green, weighing up to forty pounds. They were hung at the end of the front porch to ripen and to disappear almost magically down the gullets of young Middletons and their friends from neighboring plantations.

The Middletons rarely went into town without dressing up for the occasion. "I very seldom went barefooted," Troy recalled. "My father didn't believe that you should go barefooted because you'd be sure to stub your toe. I wasn't in knickers and long stockings very long. They put me in long pants pretty early. I wouldn't have thought of going to town in blue jeans or anything like that. Even before I went off to Mississippi A & M College, I was expected to wear a necktie. I learned to tie a bow or a four-in-hand when I was quite young."

Troy remembered no special position or esteem enjoyed by anyone in his large family. He, like his other brothers and sisters, did benefit mightily from a custom of families of that day, the custom of sending an older girl off to college with the understanding that she would acquire her education, return home to teach school and to share her learning with the rest of the brood in the summers.

It fell to Emily, seven years senior to Troy, to bring back the word from Blue Mountain Female College at Blue Mountain, near Ripley, Mississippi, 250 miles north of home. Emily learned well, and she found Troy eager for her knowledge. She taught school during the regular session and tutored Troy several summers. His schooling had formally begun at a little three-room school near Bethel, where the Middletons got their Episcopalian Baptist preaching each Sunday. Women teachers, paid perhaps forty dollars a month, ladled out the knowledge at Bethel School, after having, like Emily Middleton, spent at least two years at Blue Mountain or a like pedagogical institute. His first day at school, Troy sat on a slatted form-fitting seat at a hinge-topped desk. "I was swinging my feet, which didn't touch the floor, when my teacher came along and rapped me on the head with her pencil. She didn't mean for it to hurt but it did," he recalled.

"Don't swing your feet," she said. "Dad covered my seat with sheepskin to make it a little more comfortable for a five-year-old," Troy recalled.

School at Bethel involved a lot of recitation. "They'd call you up front and ask to go over a lesson with you. Or teacher would send a bunch of us to the board, giving us more problems than we could work, to be sure we remained occupied. It was a full day, from eight in the morning until four in the afternoon," Troy recalled. A recess broke the morning at mid-point. Another halved the afternoon. Lunch made the day endurable. The scholars at Bethel took lunch in buckets and baskets. No one had ever heard of hot lunches. The youngsters ate cold food and thought nothing of it. Sandwiches, sausage, ham, biscuits were standard fare.

Lunch was a trade fair for most of the Bethel scholars. "Sometimes you might eat your lunch but most of the time you'd trade off at least half of it. Our lunches included a surprising lot of cake, pie, and other sweets—great trading material. If you liked ham, you could swap a dessert for an extra slice of ham. A good biscuit with fried ham made a pretty good sandwich. But a kid at that age, you know, could digest anything," Troy recalled. When lunch had been bolted, the boys headed for the baseball diamond; football was a game most had never heard of.

What Troy learned at Bethel School, supplemented by long hours of tutoring from Emily, gave him a substantial education for the times. When, at age fourteen, it appeared that there wasn't much more he could learn at Bethel and at home, Troy was asked whether he'd like to go up to Starkville to Mississippi Agricultural & Mechanical College, and become the first in his family to consider pursuing college all the way through to a bachelor's degree.

He liked the thought. Late in the summer of 1904 he was driven in a buggy to the Illinois Central depot in Hazlehurst, bidden a grave farewell by his father, commended to the keeping of the conductor of the train, and dispatched north on a trip longer than any he had ever undertaken, 172 miles to Starkville. Through Jackson and on up the line the coal-burning locomotive of the local passenger train rocked and hooted at every crossing, cinders raining in the open windows and sifting into the shirt and jacket pockets of Troy, wearing a necktie, bound for the biggest adventure of his life. At Durant he changed trains, heading east the 78 miles to Starkville. At Starkville, the train disgorged a cindery, smudged Troy. Starkville was not a great deal more town than the A & M College. The arrival of each train on the Illinois Central and the Mobile and Ohio was an event.

With other boys Troy struck out for the college, one and a half miles distant. "We could have hired a horse and buggy for the ride out but nobody did it," he recalled. The college drayman picked up Troy's trunk and dumped it with others in front of the dormitory. "I asked one of the fellows to help me carry my trunk, promising to help with his in turn. That's how I got my first roommate, a boy from Wesson."

Just before he saw Troy up the steps and onto the train in Hazlehurst, John Middleton had renewed one of the pieces of advice he sparingly imparted to his sons. "Troy, if you must drink alcoholic beverages, remember to take them sparingly as a gentleman should; but whatever you do, don't learn to shoot dice, that is not a gentleman's game."

As the train gathered speed out of the Hazlehurst yard, young Troy mulled his father's soft-voiced advice. He resolved—and always kept that resolve—to drink sparingly, as a gentleman should. He could not then—or ever thereafter—shatter his father's innocence by revealing that his black playmates on the plantation had taught him much about dice, early qualifying him as an accomplished crapshooter, but a cautious one who never pressed his luck.

3 Mississippi A & M College: Education and the Military Life

JOHN MIDDLETON wanted his son to become a doctor. No, said Katherine Middleton, his mother; Troy should study the law.

At his first counseling session at A & M, his faculty adviser asked a bemused Troy Middleton, "What do you want to do in life?"

"I don't know, sir," fourteen-year-old Troy responded.

"Then take industrial pedagogy [one of the three curricula, including agriculture and engineering], because it will fit you for nothing."

Thus introduced to college at the preparatory school level, Troy began his higher education, as bewildered as but no more bewildered than any other student from Copiah County or even from Oktibbeha, home county of Starkville and A & M. "As a matter of fact, I didn't want to study agriculture because I came from a plantation and did not like farm life. I knew nothing about engineering except that I'd heard it was rather difficult, and I didn't want to be an engineer. It so happened that the course subject matter I took in college stood me in good stead later because it gave me a reasonably good liberal education," Troy recalled. Industrial pedagogy ("it will fit you for nothing") was anything but what the whimsical faculty adviser had said it would be.

In September, 1904, six weeks short of his fifteenth birthday, Troy entered Mississippi A & M College as a "preppie." His father had made the decision to send him to Starkville. Earlier Troy had moved as his ability qualified him to, in the three-room Bethel school. His handwriting was firm and clear. Emily's tutoring through ages nine to eleven had given him

14

advantages over his classmates. Troy had learned to like school work. He was reading at four, picking his way through the primers and the more advanced books available. The Hazlehurst *Courier*, the Memphis *Commercial Appeal*, and the weekly Atlanta *Constitution* came by mail to the Middleton home. Troy read them all. He reacted to the outrageous antics of cartoonist R. F. Outcault's "Yellow Kid" and to the "Katzenjammer Kids," invented by a competing New York newspaper. "Wish books," the catalogs from Sears Roebuck and Montgomery Ward and the other mail order houses, were the encyclopedias of every household. They lasted and lasted, finally being taken apart in the outhouse in every rural back yard.

Places in the Mississippi A & M student body were open on the quota system. Each county superintendent of education in Mississippi was authorized to test prospective students. Copiah County was assigned a quota of fifteen. Troy took the test, passed it, and was told that he probably could make the grade as a freshman at A & M but that he was really too young for college. Troy and his parents took the superintendent's advice. They sent Troy to Starkville for a final year of high school. For all practical purposes he was an A & M student, taking his place in the dormitory and subjecting himself none too willingly to the military organization of the college.

Before he became a full-fledged student he, like the other four hundred or so residents, formed and marched to all three meals daily—seven days a week. They marched to the delights of Sunday night supper, a stopgap of cold cuts, cheese, canned salmon, preserves, crackers, butter and milk, as well as to the heartier offerings at twenty other meals each week. In the dining hall, a regimental staff table stood on a platform at one end of the hall. Everyone stood behind his chair, awaiting the command, "Take seats." Everyone stayed in his chair until the diners were dismissed, a battalion at the time. Nobody ever left the dining hall without permission. This was the well-disciplined, seemingly happy group Troy joined.

"The food wasn't good but it wasn't so bad," he recalled. Students were waiters. The head waiter held one of the most prestigious positions among working students. The faculty, all males, ate apart from the students. Married faculty ate at home. Bachelors lived and ate at their quarters on campus, the Ranch, where they paid for their own mess facilities.

Relieving the tedium of the dining table at A & M, an assortment of student entrepreneurs made life worth the living in off-hours eating.

Charlie Knost of Pass Christian, Mississippi, was the son of a plumber who thoughtfully shipped Charlie a keg of oysters every once in a while. Charlie made oyster stew which sold briskly at fifteen cents a bowl in a room under the Old Chapel. One night in Troy's senior year, Charlie Knost and his roommate were frying oysters in their room on a gasoline iron. They had taken the top off the iron and put the oysters in a skillet. Somehow the iron exploded, plastering the ceiling with half-fried oysters. Cadet Lieutenant Colonel Middleton heard the noise and went to see what had happened. "I was supposed to report them, but I didn't. They suffered enough," he recalled.

Clayton Rand, later something of a newspaperman and columnist, set up shop regularly in a cubbyhole next to the campus post office and from it dispensed parched peanuts and boiled goobers so profitably that his income probably outreached that of some of the junior faculty. Other enterprisers came and went, enjoying the laissez-faire policy of a benign administration. After all, the dining hall's clientele was 100 percent captive; what harm could come from letting the boys take the edges off their barbarously sharp appetites before they began the big gobble in the mess hall? It might reduce the food bill, running perilously close to two bits a day for each cadet.

Every school day began with a rousing first call on the bugle at 5:30 A.M. The cadets were assembled in the halls of gigantic Old Main Dormitory for roll call. "I often wondered why. There was no place to escape to." After the first sergeant had called the roll, cadets were given time to go to the bathroom, clean up their rooms, make beds, and plunge thankfully into a postponed half-hour of study.

Mess call started the scholars to breakfast at 7:10. After breakfast they marched back to be dismissed and given fifteen to twenty minutes to prepare for the next assignment, chapel call. Nobody marched to this formation but everybody had to go, to sit by classes. A faculty member read a passage from the Scriptures, some with feeling and more without. If there was a visitor on campus, he was usually invited to say a few words to the captive audience. Some of these visitors were misled by the applause, both before and after they had spoken. They weren't told by the cadets that students regularly prayed for a long-winded speaker, who had at least enough to say to carry over into the first class period, thus canceling the next item on the day's long agenda. Thus motivated, the cadets overwhelmed an occasional speaker with relevant and intense questioning, sending him back to the Ivy League where he would shame his apathetic students by telling them of the zeal for knowledge he had discovered in this quaint Mississippi institution, the A & M College.

After chapel, the uniformed cadets formed in class sections and marched to the day's first instruction. Morning classes ended at noon. Each morning class extended just past an hour. Lunch brought an hour break. Afternoon classes began promptly at 1:00 P.M. and were devoted largely to laboratories. Depending on the subjects, some laboratories ran three hours. All classes ended at 4:00 P.M., without having been relieved by a break.

From 4:00 until 6:30 P.M. the cadets were flushed out onto the playing field for intramural sports. Every class fielded a team in the sports in season: football in the fall, baseball in the spring, along with track and field. Tennis was just catching on at A & M, and attracted enough participants to jam the picture on the tennis page in the yearbook. Basketball came to A & M in Troy's last year there, 1908–1909, when a team was scratched together to show how the novel game was played. Baseball was the prime sport; football was gaining but trailed in popularity. Uniforms were discards and leftovers from last year's varsity teams.

At 6:30 P.M. the playing fields emptied and cadets formed for the evening meal. As soon as the tables were cleared, a dance band picked up its instruments and launched into a waltz or a fox trot. "A lot of country boys learned to dance in the mess hall, at a dollar a head a month," Troy recalled. Boys danced with boys, out of necessity, but they were learning their social graces for the times when girls from Starkville and the student body from Mississippi State College for Women, less than twenty-five miles away in Columbus, stood reasonably ready to respond to invitations to A & M.

At 7:30 P.M. the bugler sounded school call, for the start of study hours. Cadets repaired to their rooms and everything quieted down. "You could hear a mouse—even a little one," Troy recalled. Cadet officers inspected every room in the block-square, five-story dormitory. No one slept. Everyone studied or made a good pretense. Visiting other rooms was forbidden. The hall orderly was honor bound to report visitors out without a pass. At 10:00 P.M. the all-clear sounded. Visiting and bathroom missions were permitted. At 10:30 the bugler sounded taps. At 10:40 all room lights were shut off at a master switch. Only hall and bathroom lights gleamed thereafter. To this regimen, Troy subjected himself without strong complaints. But he hadn't cared for it at first, having been brought up in the free and easy life of the plantation, where there was no roll call and no daily accounting for how a youngster spent his time.

If there was a high point for Troy and his fellows in his year as a preppie, it probably came February 10, 1905, when John Philip Sousa brought his band to A & M. Sousa's train was late. Long before he arrived, the mess hall was crammed to its 2,000-seat capacity and standing townsfolk stuffed the corners. The concert started late at 2:30 P.M. and ran overtime, extended by repeated calls for encores, past 5:00 P.M. Trains waited at the edge of the campus, on the Illinois Central and the Mobile and Ohio tracks, to move the band on to its next engagement and to take home Mississippians who had swarmed to Starkville for the concert.

The *Reflector*, a monthly literary publication, provided minimal news coverage to the campus. The yearbook, the *Reveille*, had lapsed in 1898. A & M, nominally founded in 1878, hadn't begun operation until 1880. With a student body of about four hundred, it was a lightly populated campus.

As Troy's preparatory year sped toward a close, with his group going against the college boys in baseball and with impending final examinations competing for attention, he had confirmed that he was ready to join the college ranks but was not unhappy that he had spent a year down the ladder with the other fourteen- and fifteen-year-olds. In fact, if one were to believe the terms of an advertisement for the college, published in the *Reflector*, Troy would not have been eligible for admission to the A & M freshman class in any event in his first year at Starkville. The matter-of-fact advertisement stipulated:

Applicants must be 16 years of age and of good character. To enter the Freshman Class, they must pass an examination in English Grammar, Arithmetic, Geography, and United States History. Those who have not completed these studies may enter the Preparatory Department, provided they are not in reach of a High School.

The average cost of board per month has been $7.60. The cost of uniform, board, books, furniture, etc., for the entire session is about $145. Many students earn enough by labor in the farm and garden and shops to reduce their expenses below $100.

The College has dormitory accommodations for 750 students, and its equipment for literary, scientific and practical instruction is full, varied and excellent.

For the times, Mississippi A & M College offered a fair bargain: three meals a day for twenty-five cents; shelter in reputedly the world's largest college dormitory; and organization enough to keep every mother's son busy from 5:30 A.M. to 10:30 P.M.

When Troy went home early in June for summer vacation, he found that the family now had a source of ice. The ice was brought in periodically from Hazlehurst to be used in making ice cream. Replenishing the supply, squeegeed clear of its insulating coat of sawdust, called for periodic trips to town. Usually, his father laid on a big stalk of bananas, perpetually appealing to the younger Middletons and to Troy. He played a great deal of baseball that summer on the plantation. Though he was still a growing boy, he was beginning to play the game fairly well.

Back at A & M in September, 1905, Troy began reaping the advantages of his year as a preppie. He was at home in Old Main (Old Main it was, though it had stood only twenty-five years, colleges having such a need for tradition). Again, none of the tortures of homesickness seized him, though they did attack seemingly more sophisticated lads away from home for the first time.

Troy wasn't indifferent to military life. After a year he still hated the military, and even asked a senior how he could get out of it. The senior said he guessed the only way out was to resign from the college. Troy wasn't ready for so drastic a move. "How could any fifteen-year-old—still a month short of his sixteenth birthday—know what was good for him at so tender an age?" he asked in recollection.

He toughed it out. As the year ran on, he found the military discipline at first tolerable, then agreeable, and finally, reasonable. On the schedule provided by the military organization, boys got things done—many of which would have been put off forever if they had been left exclusively to the boys to decide.

On a February afternoon in 1906, a professor of chemistry taught Troy one of the most valuable lessons he learned in college. Troy had gone out for the baseball team, having just received the unsettling news that he had flunked freshman chemistry. "Chemistry Professor Hand flagged me down on the way to baseball practice," he recalled. "First he asked me, 'Mr. Middleton, how can you be so stupid?' My mind was on baseball so

I thought to put him off with a solemn promise that I would retake the chemistry course next year. 'You'll start at 4 P.M. today,' Professor Hand declared." Troy did. The class baseball team got along without him that year. "I went back and told my roommate that that old buzzard Hand really meant business. And he surely did, too. I wanted to play baseball. I might have been able to beg off on the chemistry makeup sessions. If Professor Hand had let me off, I'd probably have washed out of A & M. Dr. Hand taught me a lesson that February afternoon; it has lasted all my life: If it has to be done, get with it and do it." While his classmates were extracting bats from the rack on the baseball field, Troy was lifting a test tube from its rack before moving over the ground he'd stumbled on in the fall semester. He knew his chemistry when the term ended early in June.

The baseball itch had developed and spread over Troy before he ever set foot on the A & M campus. He had played pickup games on the plantation or on nearby diamonds on teams half black and half white. He had developed some rude skills as a shortstop on the dimpled infields of Copiah County ball yards. He played two summers as the only non-Catchings on a nine whose other members were all named Catchings. Besides, baseball mattered a great deal more to most youngsters than the cruder sport of football. Baseball required finesse. Football promised bruises and bloody noses. Football ran by the clock. Baseball could be over with in a hurry or stretch deep into the dusk.

Since the senior cadet had answered Troy's September question about how to get out of the military, Troy decided that he might as well enjoy the inevitable. He decided to do what was asked of him on the drill field and to obey all the rules of dormitory life. He went through his freshman year without incurring a demerit. Having gone this far, he resolved to keep his name off the penalty lists. He was graduated without ever having received a demerit, a record equaled by but two or three of his classmates.

Through his freshman and sophomore years, a classmate, Mahlon T. Birch, son of an Episcopal minister, had shown Troy the opposing example. "Birch never even checked the bulletin board to see how many demerits he'd earned," Troy recalled. "He just grabbed his rifle and headed for the parade ground on Saturday, to walk tours from 1 to 5 P.M." No talk was permitted. The erring cadet had to stride along, alone, in a military manner. He paced from Old Chapel to the railroad cut and back. "One day I passed and saw that 'Red' [Birch's nickname] didn't have a bolt in his rifle. As softly as I could, I said, 'You don't have any bolt in your rifle.' He replied, 'I know it; the rifle was getting too heavy. I've got the bolt in my pocket.' "

After three years as the chronic tanglefoot of the cadet body, Birch, a brilliant youngster, was appointed a company commander by the army officer in charge of the military at A & M. "I think I'm going to make Birch a company commander. What do you think?" he asked Cadet Lieutenant Colonel-Designate Middleton, at the end of Middleton's and Birch's junior year. "I said I thought it was a good idea and it turned out that way." Birch edited the yearbook, the *Reveille*, with great flair, pouring out reams of better than passable verse both for the *Reveille* and for the literary *Reflector*. His sketches enlivened as many as a hundred pages of the yearbook. Birch showed, Middleton recalled, "that if you've got brains and will finally decide to use them, you can go somewhere."

In Troy's freshman year, the student body was organized as a battalion. Before the Reserve Officers Training Corps was formed on college campuses in the United States, one resident army officer was in charge of the military. He wore eagles on his shoulders and had the courtesy title "colonel," though his rank was rarely so high. He taught military classes to the seniors, the only students to receive formal instruction in military science and tactics. Major Ludlow of the Coast Artillery was the resident army instructor in Troy's freshman year. The battalion marched to the music of a thirty-member military band. It was an under-strength battalion; a 1905–1906 photograph, showing the cadets drawn up in ranks on the parade ground, counted out to 350 at the most. Captain I. C. Welborn, a former A & M student who had been graduated from the United States Military Academy and had won the Medal of Honor for bravery at Santiago, Cuba, moved to A & M at the beginning of Troy's sophomore year. From Ellisville, just below Laurel, Captain Welborn was known as a fighter. As a boy he had had a fighting mixed-breed dog, from which he was inseparable. As cadets added to the story, "You couldn't tell which one would bite you." Troy served as a corporal in the cadet body under Captain Welborn. Welborn appointed Troy cadet sergeant major for his junior year, months before a dispute with President Hardy sent Captain Welborn back to the comparative safety of regular military duty. Captain Welborn had designated Troy regimental sergeant major in quite informal fashion. Corporal Middleton, toward the end of his sophomore year, had gone to the bulletin board, as did everyone else at least once daily, to find his name posted as the number one junior noncommissioned officer for the 1907–1908 session. He was surprised but not astonished.

Welborn was replaced in the military assignment by a professor of chemistry, I. D. Sessums, who ran out the term in this dual capacity. It was Sessums who made the next key decision in Troy's life, with similar informality. Everybody had to stay on campus through commencement, if for

Sergeant Major Middleton at Mississippi A & M

no other reason than to assure a good turnout for graduation exercises. Colonel Sessums was sitting on the steps of a classroom building when Troy came along. "Come on over here," he called; "I'm going to make you lieutenant colonel next year."

As the principal cadet officer for his senior year at A & M, Troy was the student commander of a military body of more than 700 cadets, organized in eight companies, two battalions, and, in token of the growth of the military, given a regimental headquarters. The college's enrollment reached its high, 740, in the fall of 1908, the *Reflector* reported. The new commandant was Captain George S. Goodale, a West Pointer. Working with him, Troy took on added responsibilities, for which he was paid $25 a month.

While Troy was rising in the cadet ranks at A & M, he was observing the good points and detecting the shortcomings of some of the faculty. A laconic adviser in his preppie year had done him a favor by recommending the curriculum in Industrial Pedagogy, which led Troy into a reasonably good selection of courses which added up to a reasonably good liberal education. Professor Hand had inquired into Troy's stupidity quotient, had detoured him from the baseball practice field, and had convinced him that learning freshman chemistry could be accomplished starting at 4:00 P.M. today—not next year. Troy, day in and day out, watched one faculty member who used a classroom pointer as if it were a baton. Everybody was distracted by the beat, a point which came back to Middleton when he took his place on the podium later as an instructor at the Infantry School at Fort Benning, Georgia, and, for four years, at the Command and General Staff School at Fort Leavenworth, Kansas.

Through his four college years at A & M, a lone girl, Mary Dille, had stood out in the all-male student body. The daughter of the superintendent of buildings and grounds, she wore an A & M uniform with skirt and cap. She was usually last in line, having been shoved back by the none-too-chivalrous cadets, but she marched to all her classes. And she proved to be one of the most devoted members of the class of 1909, through a long succession of class reunions.

Attending A & M was more than just participating in classes, intramural sports, and the military. One of five corporals in the battalion as a sophomore, Troy found his name in print in the *Reflector* as a member of the official party listed in the college directory at the start of the fall term.

In the November issue of the *Reflector*, Middleton's name appeared among twenty-seven admitted to membership in the Lee Guard. Though there was no hint of the significance of the Lee Guard, it was a *sub rosa* fraternity, forbidden by Mississippi law. Later the Lee Guard surfaced as the Order of Kappa Alpha, a Deep South-flavored fraternity still known for its Old South balls and the flourishes of another century. Whether anybody was fooled by the masquerade didn't seem to be important in 1906. The Guard dressed smartly for the yearbook picture and met discreetly, if they had any business to conduct.

Another *Reflector* reported that a derailment delayed departure of a special train which took the student body to Columbus for a football game with Louisiana State University. The game ended, 0–0, but the presence of the girls from Mississippi State College for Women in Columbus was compensation enough for the host team. The *Reflector* noted the "gentlemanly qualities" of the LSU team which, it said, always seemed to characterize the visitors from Baton Rouge whether they were on the road or at home.

Though A & M had two literary societies, the Dialectic and the Philotechnic, it was further enriched by the creation, in October, 1906, of the Hull Debating Club and the Magruder Debating Club. Troy Middleton's name appeared on the charter roster of the Magruder Debating Club, which was named for the head of the English Department. Troy held office as censor (spelled *sensor* in the *Reflector* account of the club's founding) and was listed as the third member among the twenty-three named on the charter.

The 1907–1908 *Reflectors* carried Troy's name in the military organization chart, where he appeared as sergeant major on the regimental staff. A December, 1907, *Reflector* recorded that the junior class football team, with Middleton alternating at end, had won the class championship, 6–2, over the sophomores. Next year, Middleton played harder but his class lost the title. His touchdown gave the seniors a 5–0 victory over the freshmen. Middleton scored when the seniors punted and he recovered the free ball, snatching it up and pounding sixty yards to a touchdown "with footfalls sounding heavier and heavier behind me." In the class championship game, the juniors repelled the seniors' move toward two titles in a row, winning 5–0 on a broken play. Middleton was cited by the *Reflector* for good work, as were half a dozen teammates. At five feet ten inches and

160 pounds, Troy Middleton began to learn the game of football at A & M. He played it with greater skill later in the United States Army.

The *Reflector* for October, 1908, recorded the organization of the Mississippi Sabre Company with a membership of twenty-nine and with Troy H. Middleton as its commanding officer:

> The Mississippi Sabre Company of the A & M College, the only military company of its kind now in existence in the ken of the writer, was organized October 14 of this year. This company is not in any way connected with last year's sword company, but is identical with it, in that the membership is limited to seniors exclusively, men of military bearing and good social, academic and military standing. In the election of officers and members, the company has obtained the best military talent procurable at this college for leadership. Officers—Captain, T. H. Middleton; First Lieutenant, C. J. Rhodes; First Sergeant, M. T. Birch; Second Sergeant, A. E. Mullins; Third Sergeant, O. Black.

The same issue of the *Reflector* reported that A & M's most exclusive club, the Collegian Club, had reorganized and had elected Troy Middleton vice president. The *Reflector* never did make clear the basis for the Collegian Club's exclusiveness (membership was limited to twenty). On another score, however, there could be no doubts about the straightforwardly named Gun Club, pictured in the 1909 *Reveille*. Its officers, led by President Troy Middleton, hefted or stood nonchalantly by their weapons, Middleton's being a gleaming shotgun. No stuffy rules in that day forbade a cadet's keeping firearms in his room, for use in hunting in the Starkville countryside on dull weekends.

The March, 1909, *Reflector* reported in last-minute "locals": "Troy H. Middleton and W. P. Craddock have received appointments to West Point. Though we are sorry to lose these men, we hope them much success in their chosen field." The *Reflector* was premature. The appointments did not pan out, since the principal appointees exercised their selections to the Military Academy. "Losing the appointment was a disappointment to me. I really wanted to go to the Military Academy," Middleton recalled. "But as it turned out, by joining the army as a private I wound up with a commission dating from November, 1912. If I'd entered the Academy I wouldn't have graduated until June, 1914. So I got a two-year head start on the West Point entering class of 1910."

Middleton was president of his junior class. The *Reflector* reported that, at the junior banquet, he gave a short but eloquent speech preceding the three-hour dance "pronounced as the best dance ever given in Stark-ville." Troy Middleton's longest published material written during his student days appeared in a 1908 *Reflector* at the time of the junior banquet:

A REUNION DREAM

One dark and dreary night when the students had about all retired I closed my English Literature, placed my feet on the window seat so as to tilt my chair, and fell to musing on the future. While in this attitude I had a dream, and in this dream I thought that after my graduation I had the good fortune to continue my studies in the University of Oxford, England, where in four years I received my M.D. degree. Upon graduation I made a flying trip back to America, the land of my nativity, to take unto myself a bride, but returned very quickly to Berlin to take a position as court physician to his majesty, Kaiser Wilhelm IV. Here I remained for several years, almost forgetting my American home. One bright May day in Nineteen Hundred and Twenty-Four, while playing on my front veranda with my children, two in number, I was interrupted by a servant, who handed me a telegram bearing the inscription so familiar in my boyhood days. Tearing it open, I read the following: "We will be glad to have you with us from May 31st until June 15th, as that is the time set for the reunion of the class of 1909."

Signed: *Lenoir, Neal, Fuller,* Committee.

What did this mean? It simply meant that once more I would be with those dear fellows with whom I had spent so many pleasant days. After consulting my wife, we decided to leave some day the next week, which would be about May 29th. After completing our plans and the day set had arrived, we set sail at 1:30 P.M., 5–29–24, on the modern Cunard Liner *Samuel L. Foster,* and after a pleasant ocean voyage which was almost too short, we arrived in New York City the next morning about sunrise. My wife and I went to the Belmont, where I found *President of the United States Mullins* and my old friend *Oscar Black,* who was then *Mayor of New York.* They informed me that they had heard of my arrival over *Rhodes' Wireless Telephone.* After a short talk with them I suggested a tour of the city, since we would not leave for Mississippi until the afternoon. We rang to *McClanahan's Garage* for an air-ship, and then proceeded around the city. The first very large establishment that attracted my attention was a magnificent fifty-story edifice, beside which the Singer building looked small, owned by *Gen. G. W. Smith Tobacco Company.* As we passed the northeast corner, I noticed a sign bearing the following inscription: "Star Navy is our specialty."

Returning to the Belmont we prepared for our trip to Mississippi. (The party then composed Mullins, Black, McClanahan, Smith, together with their wives and children; my wife, two children and myself.) Leaving New York at 3:35 P.M. by the *Crow-Hemingway-Graves Traction Company,* forty-five minutes run placed us on the University of Virginia campus. Here we were pleased to see our old friend, *Robert Skinner,* as *Chancellor of the University, Fortune Chisholm,* head of the *Engineering School, Grady Guyton* of the *School of Law, Dan Raney* of the *Medical Department* and *Sexton Morris,* coach of the football team. Leaving here at 4:20 P.M. and after passing through several plantations owned by fellow-classmates of ours, we arrived in Memphis, Tenn., in time for supper. We dined at Floyd's, where we ran across old *Didlake,* who was conceded to be the only *sport* the South has ever produced. He, *Jack Loflin,* and his " 'So Darling' Wife Maud," had just come up from Star to meet the southward bound party. At 9:30 we took the North Mississippi car and arrived in Starkville just as the clock was striking ten. The town was all dried up except the *German Club* building, which was originally owned by the Oktibbeha Club but was now occupied by the College boys. The old *Motor Hotel,* now owned by *Bill Whitten,* retired millionaire, was to be the scene of the banquet, and dance which would follow the banquet, given in honor of the class of 1909. It was a *magnificent ten-story* building designed by my classmate and "old lady," *Red Birch,* and built by *Magruder-Moncrief-Thigpen Construction Company.* We were assigned to our rooms by the *hotel clerk, Nathan Kaplan,* and as we took the elevator for the ninth floor I thought I recognized *Thomas Cicero Kite,* the elevator boy, who was an old friend of mine. After a pleasant night of rest and a hearty breakfast such as Sam E. Oliver used to give, we started for the college and you can imagine my surprise upon looking down the street to see, about a block away, a huge bronze gate bearing the inscription "CAMPUS OF MISSISSIPPI POLYTECHNIC INSTITUTE. *I. P. Carr, President. Jno. J. Hood, Mgr.*"

We passed in and were enthusiastically welcomed by old classmates who had arrived before us. I remember seeing several town girls who had become "blushing brides" of our 1909 fellows. Here I saw *Clinton Dorroh,* who had coached the *Yale* football team the season before; *Russell McCargo, President of the Southern League; Willie Mitchell,* who had just gotten out the *"Cutter,"* a small book on how to pitch the *"Willie Return Curve"*; *Bennie Mitchell* and *George Trotter,* who informed me that their Tech pupils would make a short tour of Europe the next spring to play the various large universities.

Entering the large auditorium I saw seated on the rostrum *President Carr* and, by his side, *Major William Perry Craddock,* U.S.A., who was then Commandant and Professor of Military Science and Tactics. Seated behind them was *Dr. C. A. Knight, Dean* of the *School of Engineering; James Shelton, Professor of Textile Industry; J. L. Mitchell,* head of the *Department of Agriculture; Miss Mary L. Dille,* head of the *Department of Industrial Pedagogy,* and *"Reuben 'Whittle' Boydstun,"* with a long frock tail coat, a stove-pipe hat and walking cane, serving as *assistant steward,* filling the place of Mr. Oliver, who had recently married.

As President Carr was about to address the assembly of about three thousand visitors, together with about two thousand five hundred students, I was awakened by the voice of "Red" saying hurriedly: "Teddy, Teddy, get out of that chair quick and turn off that light. I hear the footsteps of Col. Ward."

T. H. M., '09.

Thus ran Troy H. Middleton's longest published literary effort during his years at Mississippi A & M College. The nickname "Teddy" appeared nowhere else in references to cadet Middleton. Later, Troy could not recall the source or significance of the nickname, though there might have been some connection between his proficiency in the military and exploits of the incumbent United States President Theodore (Teddy) Roosevelt.

Two other times Troy Middleton appeared in Mississippi newspapers in advocacy of Mississippi A & M. During the summer before his junior year, Troy was photographed in wing collar, ascot tie, elegant stickpin, and light vest. He appeared in the Jackson *Clarion-Ledger* with three other college seniors, each representing his school in the Intercollegiate Oratorical Contest. "The Crystal Springs Chautauqua closed tonight in a blaze of glory," the *Clarion-Ledger* reported, "the last event being the Intercollegiate Oratorical Contest between representatives of the four principal male colleges of the State—the State University, Millsaps, Mississippi College, and the A & M College." Middleton's topic was "Mississippi for Mississippians"; and though the Millsaps representative won the contest, the judges declared that all four young men had spoken well.

So ended Troy Middleton's first off-campus experience in oratory. The *Clarion-Ledger* reporter gave no hint of what kinds of Mississippians deserved what kinds of Mississippis. Nor did he supply even an inkling of response to winner Crisler's question, "Is This An Imperial Age?" He left the judges secure in anonymity.

Just the same, the full house at the final Crystal Springs Chautauqua must have got their money's worth. Chautauquas had come to be the prime cultural events in rural and small-town America at the turn of the century. Like other Chautauquas, this one brought in lecturers, concert artists, and others—a sort of cultural consensus—for most of the week. Ticket holders sat on slatted wooden benches or folding chairs and even spilled onto the ground, usually four inches deep in sawdust, determined to absorb all the culture they could. Under the flimsy shelter of brush arbors or the more permanent tabernacles—roofs but little else—lighted by kerosene lamps, the folks flocked in from hundreds of square miles. Some families rode in in wagons and camped through the Chautauqua period. Here at Crystal Springs, Troy performed before what was almost a hometown audience.

As his junior year at A & M had drawn toward a close, the army officer in charge of the military, Medal of Honor winner Captain I. C. Welborn, had differences of opinion with A & M President John C. Hardy, leading to Captain Welborn's return to active army duty. Independent of Welborn's clash with civil authority, the president of the senior class of 1908, a lad named Blanton, had carried to Hardy a growing number of complaints about administrative matters. Finally, Hardy had heard one complaint too many. He dismissed Blanton, the senior president, from the college. The seniors got their backs up over Hardy's treatment of their leader; they became so militant that Hardy cashiered them all.

Some of the senior firebrands urged the whole student body to rise in support of the seniors. Junior class president Troy Middleton was importuned by the seniors. He knew that Blanton had been given an ultimatum by President Hardy after Blanton had gone to the president with a complaint about food in the dining hall. Hardy told Blanton then that he would be dismissed if he came back complaining. Blanton couldn't let the opportunity pass; he was back with a complaint the first thing next morning. Hardy was as good as his word. "You're out," he told the senior class president.

Blanton took the surprising news back to the senior class, which voted to back him and sent a committee to Hardy demanding Blanton's reinstatement. Hardy stood by his original decision. The seniors turned then to junior class president Middleton, who was also sergeant major of the cadet corps. Middleton mulled the matter, and then went to Dr. David Carlisle Hull, professor of industrial pedagogy, in whom he had great confidence, to talk over the seniors' request for support. Following the conference with Hull, Middleton called an assembly and reported to his fellow juniors his decision not to quit in support of the seniors. The juniors concurred with their president. The sophomore and freshman class officers, also importuned by the seniors, turned to Middleton for guidance. They too elected to stay. The revolt ended.

After two weeks, President Hardy called the Board of Trustees into session. The board gave its backing to the suspension order. Once his authority had been established clearly, Hardy said he was willing to permit the seniors to come back. The Board of Trustees agreed again.

Like a good strategist, Lieutenant Colonel-Designate Troy Middleton organized a letter-writing campaign in support of President Hardy in the summer of 1908. He capped it with a letter to the editor of the Hazlehurst *Courier*, September 10, 1908, headlined "Letter From a Copiah Boy," prominently displayed on page one, outlining the difficulties at A & M, tracing the college's impoverished financial circumstances, and pledging his faith in Hardy's ability to bring A & M through its crisis. Middleton wrote in part:

LETTER FROM A COPIAH BOY

Troy Middleton Writes About the A & M College

As a member of the senior class of the Mississippi Agricultural and Mechanical College, I have consented to give people who are interested, my view of affairs in the college the past eight months.

The public press has misrepresented the facts very much and consequently there may be some boys who are refraining from going to the college because of what they have heard.

President J. C. Hardy began his administration as president in 1900. Enrollment for twenty years had averaged about 300 students per year. College property was valued at $270,000. There were only two distinct courses of instruction and the faculty was comparatively small. Enrollment has reached 1,015, the value of the college property is more than $1,000,000, there are more than a dozen courses of instruction, and the faculty, including assistants, has reached eighty-one members.

President Hardy's administration has continued more than eight years, sufficient time for fair and intelligent judgment as to its efficiency. Do any of you believe that such results could have been obtained if there had been inharmony among the president, faculty or student body? I do not give President Hardy any undue share of the credit. Such progress would not have been possible without the faithful and loyal support of the faculty, students, legislature, and the good people of the state. Our friend Captain Welborn says that there has been friction in the college ever since President Hardy came into office. The history of the college will show that during President Hardy's administration it has been free from friction up to the time that Captain Welborn was dismissed. The board of trustees has vested in the hands of the president the power to dismiss any student or member of the faculty whom he deems detrimental to the welfare of the college. Would you say that during his term of office President Hardy has acted in any way autocratically? Captain Welborn and Dr. Crigler were the only two in the eight years. I can say of President Hardy that during my four years in the school, I have watched from my window the midnight oil burn in his office night after night. There is no doubt but what he was neglecting his young wife and children as well as his health. I have never known him to refuse to see a student at any time day or night.

When President Hardy took up his work there was dormitory room for about 350 students and only a few buildings, poorly constructed. Now we have ample room for 1,500 students. The engineering school is one of the finest in the South. The dining hall recently constructed has accommodations for 2,000. It is one of the most modern of any college in the United States.

Are people going to believe what a few enemies of the school have to say, rather than to risk the judgment of such men as Governor Noel, Superintendent Powers, Captain J. M. Coen, of this county, and Hon. T. L. Wainwright, of Stonewall, all members of the Board of Trustees, who saw fit to cast their votes in the direction they did. Quite naturally the gentlemen who were so unfortunate as to be relieved of their duties as instructors in the college have made a great appeal that they were in the right. Together with their friends they have brought charges against the president, one that the faculty was against the president. After examination, out of the eighty-one professors and assistants, only five said a word that was against the president's administration in any way.

I have heard some gentlemen around Hazlehurst say that if they had boys they would not send them to A & M. You will be injuring no one but the boy, for remember A & M is a state institution. You need not fear that your boy will be troubled, for under the supervision of an experienced army officer, a good faculty, and splendid student officers there will be no trouble unless he starts something himself.

Troy H. Middleton

Of all the activities Troy Middleton took part in, he considered the Magruder Debating Club the most valuable. Topics were assigned one week and debated the next week. Critics appointed from the membership were quick to point out the deficiencies in a presentation. Conducted in a lecture room in the YMCA building, the debates were open to all. "You learned to think on your feet—and fast—or you didn't last," Troy recalled.

The A & M campus was about a mile and a quarter from the main downtown section of Starkville, population four thousand. Cadets went to town periodically. "Townies," who didn't live in the dormitory, were only incidentally subjected to the military discipline of the campus. By the same token, they missed most of the flavor of campus life.

Major breaks in campus routine were provided by train trips to the sites of football and baseball games each season. Seniors took on the chore of selling tickets, contracting with the railroad, and hoping some profit would be left to support the class athletic program. For three dollars they arranged a round trip to Jackson on the Illinois Central. The cadets always traveled in uniform, were quick to oblige with a parade wherever they went, and were received as enthusiastically as a circus. The whole student body rode the train to Jackson each year for the football game with the University of Mississippi. The teams never met at Starkville or at Oxford, it being conceded, apparently, that only fools would bid for the privilege of being host to a biennial riot. (Troy Middleton, in fact, never set foot on the Ole Miss campus until May 3, 1967, when he and Mrs. Middleton were invited to Oxford for a special Chancellor's Review of the military.)

While the football teams met each fall at Jackson, the baseball teams spread their favors, with A & M and Ole Miss meeting wherever the ball park was big enough. A chartered train hauled the lot to Kosciusko in Middleton's freshman year, to Meridian in his junior year, and to distant Greenwood in his senior year. The whole student body rode the Mobile and Ohio Railroad to Columbus at least once a year, as much to see the girls at Mississippi State College for Women as to watch A & M competing in football or baseball and track.

It was at Starkville in 1908 that Middleton saw the wondrous Louisiana State University football team pound A & M "something like 48–0." He said, "I've never changed my opinion that Doc Fenton of LSU was the best back I ever saw." That LSU team was undefeated. It bounced the earnest A & M boys all over the hard clay of Hardy Field.

Fenton, like a number of other LSU players, came south from the gridiron breeding grounds of Pennsylvania. "The story we heard at A & M was that Fenton had been ticketed for A & M and that he was supposed to change trains at Durant and catch another train to Starkville. He rode on through to New Orleans and then showed up on the LSU campus in Baton Rouge. The story went that Fenton had been coached, back in Pennsylvania, by Coach Edgar Wingard of LSU or that Wingard had played against Fenton in Pennsylvania. In any event, LSU got Doc Fenton, John Seip, Mike Lally, A. J. Thomas and another Pennsylvanian or two. They surely could play football," Middleton recalled.

4 Middleton Joins the Army

T HE 1909 commencement, with its endless ceremony and its lingering farewells, finally dispatched Troy Houston Middleton, holder of a bachelor's degree, into the none too hospitable social and economic order. While Troy and his schoolmates had enjoyed the security of the Mississippi A & M campus, financial panic had scarred the United States in 1907. The effects lingered.

As Troy and his classmates compared notes more than once in the spring of 1909, it became ever more clear that the world wouldn't miss them if they all flunked and managed to stick around Starkville for another year. One—just one—of sixty-two seniors had a job waiting when the 1909 graduates received their diplomas and hesitantly said their last good-byes around Old Main Dormitory.

Troy Middleton had hopes of landing the appointment to the United States Military Academy mentioned in the *Reflector* item of the preceding March. After commencement he settled down to study for the West Point examination as a prospective alternate. No opening came, however. Since he was only nineteen years old and would have had to be twenty-one to take the examination for an army commission, Middleton acted on the advice of Captain George S. Goodale, given him earlier at A & M, and rode the train halfway across the United States to Buffalo, New York. There, on March 3, 1910, he enlisted at Fort Porter as a private in the Twenty-ninth Infantry Regiment. Why the long trip to Buffalo? Because the commander of Company A, First Battalion, Twenty-ninth Infantry Regiment, Captain

33

Howard Perry, was a classmate of Troy's commandant at Mississippi A & M.

"My battalion was stationed in Buffalo. The Second was at Fort Niagara near Niagara Falls, the Third was on Governor's Island in New York Harbor, also headquarters for the regiment and for the Department of the East. I could have enlisted on Governor's Island and been nextdoor to New York City, but Captain Goodale's classmate's command was in Buffalo. I never regretted going there," Troy recalled.

Captain Perry's first question, after Troy identified himself, was, "What are you doing up here, Middleton? You after a commission?"

"He could tell that I was. He put me to work as company clerk as soon as my enlistment papers cleared. After six months I went to Captain Perry and told him that I was not learning enough as a clerk. I told him I wanted to be a soldier. He said he would help.

"In those days a muster roll for each command was made out once a month, by hand, no typewriters being authorized for army use. Name, rank, serial number, duty were recorded for the whole company. Three copies were painstakingly made. One went to the company file, one to regimental headquarters, and one to the adjutant general in Washington. With these three copies in hand, the first sergeant would round up another sergeant and the three of us would compare those three copies for possible errors. While I was there, use of a typewriter was authorized. I could type fairly well, having learned to hunt and peck at Mississippi A & M where, as assistant commandant, I worked in the office to justify my twenty-five-dollar-a-month salary. Determined to bring Company A up to date clerically, I typed the muster roll with two carbon copies. I explained diplomatically to the old first sergeant that we no longer needed a three-man team to verify that the three copies were identical. Somehow, he didn't get the message. 'We've always compared for correctness; we'll continue to do it that way,' the first sergeant said. I never could get across to him the fact that the two carbons had to be duplicates of the original. His kind of Old Army didn't change," Middleton recalled.

Payday came once a month. On that day, no one performed duty, except for the essential routines. A private's pay was fifteen dollars, payable in gold, one ten-dollar piece and one five-dollar piece, coins so small they could have been hidden under a postage stamp. As gold became relatively scarce in the East, paymasters took to handing out silver dollars. "Next to the pay table was the settle-up table, where we squared accounts with the post exchange representative for laundry, billiards, and other incidentals. In special observance of the day, the PX sold beer to help us reduce our surplus pay. Arrival of the paymaster was never quite certain. He started at Governor's Island, 535 miles downstate, and usually went on to Buffalo, Niagara Falls, Plattsburg, Watertown, and Fort Ontario near Syracuse, assuming the snow was not beyond his depth, as it got to be most winters," Middleton recalled.

Someone had found out that Private Middleton had played football at Mississippi A & M. Shortly, he was pressed into duty as a quarterback. Fort Porter played Fort Niagara each year. Since Fort Niagara caught more than its share of snow each winter, the accumulation had to be removed from the gridiron. The snow usually went, but it left ice patches all around. Quarterback Middleton learned what scrambling meant, on the treacherous footing at Fort Niagara.

Before a late-season game at Niagara, Middleton and another soldier rode the interurban car up to Niagara to reconnoiter. Not really so much to reconnoiter as to gawk. Mist from Niagara Falls boiling up at the foot of the falls regularly froze into an ice bridge strong enough to support venturesome people. Hucksters sold coffee at portable stands. The afternoon Troy Middleton went up to look, the ice bridge collapsed, catching a man and wife on an ice floe. A younger man who saw what was happening jumped back on the floe to aid the couple. Below the falls, people quickly lowered ropes from the traffic and rail bridges. The man caught one of these ropes and, fighting the strong current, tried to tie it around his wife. A piece of ice cracked off, taking with it the younger man. More ice jostled the floe with man and wife on it. Not far downriver was the gorge through which nothing could pass alive. Middleton and his friend half-ran along the banks high above, as did others on the Canadian side. When the three on the floes reached the gorge, that was the end of them. "I had nightmares for a long time after that. On the interurban ride back to Fort Porter I told my friend that I didn't want to see any more damned bridges," Middleton recalled. "I was reminded of that incident lots of times later when I came to a bridge in peacetime and in war."

Pleasanter diversions drew Middleton into the city. He paid five dollars to hear Enrico Caruso sing in a New York opera house, later telling himself he could have done a lot better with his money. At other times, in

Buffalo, he found the theater attractions more inviting and less expensive. "My first year at Fort Porter, I had the opportunity to grow up physically, to mature, to get to know a sizable city, to go to the theater—all this before I was twenty-one."

In 1912 Middleton moved on to Fort Leavenworth, Kansas. He was promoted to corporal in Company A of the Twenty-Ninth Infantry Regiment on June 10, 1912, twenty-seven months after his original enlistment. Promotions came ever so slowly in those days, and only when someone of higher rank was promoted to make room. Corporal William Combs was promoted to sergeant that day—upon the retirement of Sergeant Henderson of Company A. Private Middleton stepped up to corporal.

Shortly after his first promotion came through, Corporal Middleton was ordered to Fort Leavenworth, where he would have an opportunity to compete for a commission in the army. From Washington had come the announcement that the army was going to expand a bit. Some additional second lieutenants would be authorized. At Fort Leavenworth, Middleton joined other selected enlisted men in attending an intensive training course to prepare for the rigorous written examination for a second lieutenant's commission.

Three hundred civilians and a few enlisted men took the examination late in September. Of that number fifty-six passed and were commissioned. Corporal Middleton stood twenty-ninth on the list of the successful fifty-six. With Middleton, at least three of that number went on to become general officers in the army: Edward F. Witsell, Edwin P. Parker, Jr., and Terry de la Mesa Allen.

The army's elite branches in 1912 were: (1) engineers; (2) field artillery; (3) coast artillery; (4) cavalry; and (5) infantry. The infantry was lowest on the army totem pole. Only after World War I did top graduates of the Military Academy apply for infantry assignments. Middleton asked for the infantry because he had served in it and liked it.

Some time after the examination, he found that his average score was 83.2. "I often wondered," he said later, "how twenty-seven fellows could stand between a passing 75 and my 83.2. If you were not a college graduate, you had to take a preliminary exam. If you flunked that, you were out. I thought it was tougher than the exam I had to take. Very few of the fifty-six who succeeded were not college graduates. They came from Harvard, Yale, Virginia Military Institute, Stanford."

Recalling the zeal with which he and his fellows had prepared for their examination, Middleton said he had heeded the advice of a veteran tutor by enrolling in the informal school which helped the candidates prepare, at a stiff thirty dollars a month tuition. He had learned as much as he was likely to learn by the eve of the examination. Instead of cramming, he went to a movie on the post. Next day's test brought a question based on the book which the motion picture dramatized. Middleton shot a bullseye on that question.

In addition to the written examination, all of the three hundred candidates were required to take a horseback riding test. When this test was announced, the candidates were told that the successful ones probably would be offered a commission in the cavalry. To save some wasted motion, Middleton told the officer in charge that he wanted to go into the infantry and that there was no point in his taking the test.

"Young man," the officer replied, "you take the test no matter where you want to go." The riding test was anything but simple. It involved walking the horse, trotting, galloping, changing leads, jumping ditches, taking hurdles, and riding cross country. Of the forty-five or fifty who set off on horseback on that part of the examination, four or five made it back to the stables still in the saddle.

The cavalry captain in charge said to Middleton, "Young man, you can ride; why don't you want to go into the cavalry?" He replied, "Captain, I was practically born on the back of a horse and I just don't like a horse."

The captain never did accept Middleton's explanation. "I met this officer several times later in the service—and he would have to tell me why he could never understand why a boy who could ride a horse did not want to serve in the cavalry. It defied his comprehension that anyone would choose to walk when he could ride in grand style on a beautiful horse," Middleton recalled.

Having passed the written examination, Middleton was recommended for his commission by President William Howard Taft in November. The whole nation paused then for a national election, in which Woodrow Wilson, a former president of Princeton University, was chosen president of the United States. Not until Wilson took office in March, 1913, and the new Congress convened, did former President Taft's nominations of fifty-six second lieutenants go to the Senate for confirmation.

The Senate concurred and Middleton became a second lieutenant in the United States Army on March 3, 1913, with the appointment being effective as of November 30, 1912. His discharge as a corporal and appointment as a second lieutenant were recorded at Fort Crockett, Galveston, Texas, where he had been transferred by the time his appointment was confirmed.

When Middleton moved out of the enlisted ranks at Fort Crockett, the medical officer saw him as a twenty-three-year-old man with blue eyes, light brown hair, and a fair complexion, standing five feet eight and one-half inches. His physical condition was good, and he was single. His military record, as recapitulated on the back of his discharge certificate, showed that he was still serving in his first enlistment period; that he had been a corporal from June 10 to July 29, 1912; that he had reverted to lance corporal while he was at Fort Leavenworth preparing for his examination for a second lieutenancy; that he had been promoted to corporal January 8, 1913, after qualifying as a second lieutenant. He had qualified as a marksman as recently as May 10, 1912.

Nine of Middleton's old friends and former athletic teammates at Fort Porter wrote to him when they received word that he was becoming a second lieutenant:

> It may sometimes be a matter of doubt whether an entrance upon the arduous duties of an army officer is a fitting place for congratulation. We know of nothing of this nature that has been so thoroughly a piece of good news to us, as to hear that your long studied and carefully planned work has proven a success so as to place you on the long list of our superiors. Let us congratulate you. If the fact that your friends also rejoice can add any measure of your happiness, accept the assurance from your former comrades.

At Fort Leavenworth through the summer, fall, and most of the winter of 1912–1913, Middleton played basketball after the football season. At Mississippi A & M in his senior year, the college band director had induced members of the baseball team to play basketball to help get in shape for baseball. Middleton first laid hands on a basketball that winter at Starkville. He didn't touch another basketball until one bounced his way in the YMCA building across the street from Company K of the Seventh Infantry at Fort Leavenworth. Coach Hurley, also in charge of the football team, played with the Company K quintet and taught Middleton what he knew about basketball. "Mainly, I learned that basketball demands en-

durance," he recalled. "You had to keep soldiers busy, with little schooling going on. Indoor sports helped when snow was on the ground."

THE ARMY PLAYS A LOT OF BALL

During Middleton's first year in the service, at Fort Porter in Buffalo,
he found the army just as enthusiastic about sports as his fellows at Mississippi A & M had been. Coach of the Company A team at Fort Porter was
a former West Point quarterback, Benjamin Castle. He went to the office
of Company A's clerk in the fall of 1910 and said to Middleton, "I understand you played football. " Middleton replied that he had, but that it was
"only class football at Mississippi A & M." Coach Castle made a quarterback of Middleton. He played two years, 1910 and 1911, taking the ball
direct from the center in the standard T formation, rediscovered by college
football coaches thirty or so years later.

As quarterback of the Fort Porter football team, Middleton went into
battle with a minimum of equipment. He wore no shoulder pads. In their
place, quilted inserts were sewn on the shoulders of his jersey; they ab-
sorbed about as much impact as a woman's heavy duty powder puff. His
football pants were drill or canvas with a little cotton padding on the hips.
He wore a helmet, a comic contraption which took some of the impact of
a head-on collision with a tackler. He wore stockings, which almost felt
good at chilly Fort Porter. Cleated high top shoes gripped the ground firmly, except when a scrimmage play took the quarterback across an ice patch.
His uniform was topped off by a rubber nose guard, swinging downward
from a strap around his head; his teeth gripped the mouthpiece to keep the
protector in place.

Unfortunately, a quarterback found it difficult to call signals with a
noseguard mouthpiece between his teeth. Quarterback Middleton surrendered this protection. He handled the ball on every play, taking it direct
from the center in the T formation. The forward pass, revolutionizing the
old power game, required some finesse. "My passes were more lobs than
anything. The football was shaped more like a runty watermelon than the
slender ball that later favored the passer. We used the single and the
double wing formations. I ran a great deal, depending on the other team's
defense," he recalled.

"Football at Porter was a great experience. The huddle had developed about my senior year in college, the fall of 1908. Working from the huddle, I learned how to make the quick study and to hope for the right decision. I'd be looking over the defense and somebody would shift position. I compensated by changing the play, checking off, to meet the defender's switches. The drop kick was prevalent then. With that square-ended football, it wasn't so difficult. I also did the punting. It took a lot of practice. The ball was hard to control. My 30-yard average was pretty respectable. With the goal posts on the goal line, field goal and extra point kicking was a little easier than it is now. Football as we played it at Fort Porter, and later at Fort Leavenworth and Fort Crockett, provided perhaps the finest training I got in the army. I never met a good football player in the army who wasn't a good soldier."

The Fort Porter team in Buffalo was one of eight competing in the city league. A team of Poles dominated the league in a city where ethnic ties remained tight. An all-city team was chosen to challenge the Polish supremacy. Middleton quarterbacked the challengers, steel workers from Lackawanna. "They had tremendous hands," he recalled, "to go with their great size. They could reach over and hoist opponents by the pants, hold them up, toy with them. They beat our all-city team but we gave them a good scrap."

At Fort Porter, the army team never had enough members to permit a scrimmage. Consequently, they worked out with teams from Lafayette High School. In 1911, Middleton was carrying the ball on an end run when an opponent cut his feet from under him. A round, chubby end dropped on Troy and smashed the wind out of him. They next saw each other nineteen years later at a party in the home of King Knox in Baton Rouge. The chubby end, W. R. Edmonds, had finished Lafayette High, attended Syracuse University, and transferred to Louisiana State University, where he was a member of the 1915 varsity. When, in 1930, they met at the Knox party, each thought he had seen the other before. They drew back, trying to remember where they had met. Then Edmonds said, "Weren't you the quarterback of the Fort Porter football team in Buffalo and didn't I knock you out when I fell on you in a scrimmage?"

"Yes, I was that quarterback, and I've never been more thoroughly flattened, you big rascal," Middleton told Edmonds. Edmonds had married a Baton Rouge girl and stayed on in the South.

Moving to Fort Leavenworth in 1912 Middleton continued there as a quarterback. Five teams played in the Leavenworth league. The engineers were the heaviest. Coached by Lieutenant John C. H. Lee, the engineers stood between Middleton's team and the post championship. "We lost to Lee and his engineers at Leavenworth, 6–3. We scored with a place kick. They came back with a touchdown, pulling a big lineman out of his regular position to carry the ball. Those big devils were hard to put down. We didn't block with the body those days, sticking to shoulder blocks which weren't too effective," he recalled.

"Courthouse (from his middle initials, C. H.) Lee coached the engineers all over the field. During times out, he'd come on the field with a satchel to administer first aid and do a little illegal coaching. No matter how much I protested, it didn't stop him."

Quarterback Middleton did score one major triumph at Fort Leavenworth that season, however. His coach was off on an assignment when the Saturday game came round. Middleton turned coach and in his dual capacity led his Third Battalion to a 35–0 victory over the engineers team.

Quarterback Middleton Leads Interference at Fort Leavenworth

He thought enough of the feat to have picture postal cards made up showing a scrimmage play in front of a Leavenworth barracks, with quarterback Middleton leading the interference on an end sweep. He mailed one
of the cards to George Shurman, a friend in Boulder, Colorado, to be sure
that the word got beyond the boundaries of Fort Leavenworth.

When the Seventh Infantry was dispatched to Fort Crockett at Galveston, Texas, in February, 1913, Second Lieutenant Troy Middleton remained in the Seventh. This was most unusual. The War Department had
made it a practice not to assign an officer to a regiment in which he had
served as a noncommissioned officer. "I presume that I was retained in the
Seventh because I was the quarterback of the Seventh Infantry football
team and the powers that were didn't want to discard such an important
asset—especially when it appeared that we might be able to handle Courthouse Lee and his big, bad engineers."

Courthouse Lee and his big, bad engineers were also transferred to
Galveston in 1913, as was about half of the United States Army. Troubles
with Mexico had led to this concentration of fourteen regiments in the Galveston area. Five regiments were quartered, mainly in a tent camp, on the
Fort Crockett reservation; six infantry regiments, an artillery regiment, a
cavalry regiment, and an engineer regiment were stationed across Galveston Bay near Texas City.

Here were fourteen of the army's twenty-eight regiments clustered
around Galveston. The football season of 1913 in Galveston brought big
crowds to all the games. Bands turned out. Galveston turned out. Ten
army teams contended for the championship. Middleton again quarterbacked the Seventh Infantry, a relatively lightweight team, averaging 170
pounds. The Seventh put down three opponents before tackling the artillery outfit. The artillerymen were accustomed to leading those fractious
little pack mules around. From the mules the artillerymen had acquired
some less than admirable habits: they kicked and bit in close quarters in
a scrimmage. They were tough and big, too. "They pushed us around for
a while before we finally dug in and stopped them just short of the goal
line. Our one touchdown gave us a 7–0 victory," Middleton recalled.

When the championship game came in the Texas league baseball park
in Galveston, the stands were packed. The Seventh's opponents were their
old friends from the baked-clay playing field at Fort Leavenworth—Courthouse Lee and his big, bad engineers. Courthouse carried the same satchel

onto the field to minister to his engineers, who averaged 200 pounds, and to coach illegally while he dealt out first aid.

Before the kickoff that day, halfback Early of the engineers, who had played football back in Massachusetts, came over to Middleton to warn him that the engineers were out to get him. "Early told me 'I wouldn't run with the ball if I were you.' I didn't know how to take this but decided that I'd have to carry the ball if the Seventh was to have a chance of winning. So I carried the ball. One of their big backs met me. He swung a huge fist, split my lip and knocked me cold. I came to on a table in the baseball team's dressing room. The regimental medical officer was standing over me. It was halfway through the second half. I wanted to get back into the game but the doctor wouldn't let me," Middleton recalled. The game ended 6–3 with the engineers on top, just as they had been the year before at Fort Leavenworth.

Early, the man from Boston who had alerted Middleton to the engineers' plot, had played football and basketball earlier with the Seventh Infantry. His enlistment ran out; he reenlisted with the enemy in the fall of 1913, joining the engineers team that he and his infantry mates never could lick. Old loyalties surfaced long enough for him to warn Middleton but they did not prevent Early's enthusiastic participation in the defeat of the Seventh. Both teams left the baseball park with their skins plentifully punctured by the grassburs which abounded in the outfield of the Texas league's park.

5   Galveston:
Second Home

Troy MIDDLETON had arrived in Galveston in February, 1913, a second lieutenant without a commission (pending Senate confirmation), set up camp with Company K of the Seventh Infantry Regiment on the chilly sands of the beach at the Fort Crockett reservation, and pondered the next mission of the United States Army.

As was mentioned earlier, it was trouble with Mexico which brought so many American troops here. The difficulties had begun in 1910 when President Porfirio Diaz, a dictator friendly to United States business interests in Mexico, was overthrown by a reform leader, Francisco Madero. Madero, supported by General Victoriano Huerta, put down a series of revolts in 1912. However, in February, 1913, Madero and others were murdered by General Huerta, who then took control of the government. American investors thought Huerta offered them a good chance to continue their control over the railroads, mines, smelters, and oil of Mexico, in which they held a majority interest. They pushed for recognition of the Huerta government. President Woodrow Wilson refused, abandoning the established American policy of recognizing a government already in effect, protesting against what he called "government assassination." He hoped to bring about the collapse of the Huerta government and a return to constitutional government in Mexico, represented mainly by Venustiano Carranza and his adherents. In June, Wilson made an offer based on trying to get the opponents to mediate. They declined. Wilson was irritated, especially by Carranza, who offered the better hope for reform in Mexico.

President Wilson thereupon decreed a period of "watchful waiting" to see what would happen in Mexico. Thus the presence of Troy Middleton and half the American army in Galveston, the port of embarkation handiest to Mexico.

While Middleton and his regiment went about the routine of garrison duty, Galveston, on the social side, throbbed with activity. With a population of some forty thousand, Galveston was a principal commercial port and home to United States Navy units; lieutenants and ensigns abounded. The city sponsored a weekly dance at the Galvez Hotel, showplace of the Gulf Coast. Another weekly dance was held at the Garden Verein, a private club. After one of these dances, Lieutenant Stanley Wood, who served in Middleton's battalion, talked all the way through breakfast about two lovely sisters he had met at the dance the night before. Lieutenant Middleton listened half attentively. He knew Wood to be extremely social minded and a little inclined to exaggerate. Wood suggested that the two double date at the next dance. "Though I was a country boy from Mississippi, I was much too smart to go on a blind date. I thanked Stanley for the suggestion and went to the dance at the Garden Verein, stag. Then I contrived to have Stanley introduce me to the Collins sister in the red dress, Jerusha. She was an excellent dancer, though somewhat reserved where second lieutenants were concerned," Middleton recalled.

Jerusha Collins had made her debut in Galveston society in 1911 at the Galvez Hotel. She had attended Southwestern University in Georgetown, Texas. She and her sister Bernice had lived in Galveston with their aunt and uncle, Mr. and Mrs. John Hagemann, following the death of their father when Jerusha was eight. A commission merchant, John Hagemann enjoyed a better than comfortable living. He drove a Studebaker touring car, one of a handful in a Galveston which was geared to buggies, wagons, and surreys.

Lieutenant Middleton met the aunt and uncle and began to call with some regularity at the Hagemann home at 3301 Avenue L, in the heart of Galveston. He managed to live down the minor indignity of having been warned about his dancing on the Galvez ballroom floor. Lieutenant Middleton had broken into a lively Boston—a fast two-step with a dip on the turn—a dance popular in Kansas City (near Fort Leavenworth) but one which hadn't yet been recognized in Galveston. An overzealous chaperon asked him to comply with the regulations limiting dancers to the waltz or the two-step—or to take his place on the sidelines. Middleton subsided into an approved two-step and kept his privileges at the Galvez.

Through the summer of 1913 the Seventh remained in camp at Fort Crockett. Troy's company commander, Captain Alexander T. Ovenshine, didn't put much faith in the current practice of having the troops work only in the morning. While other second lieutenants played tennis, Captain Ovenshine found military tasks for Lieutenant Middleton in the afternoon. "The others said they wouldn't want an assignment like mine; at times I agreed with them. But I also had enough sense to realize that Captain Ovenshine was giving me extra opportunities to learn. His exactness and his attention to duty greatly impressed me," Middleton recalled.

There was time for baseball, however. Troy was playing second base one afternoon when the shortstop asked to trade places with him. "My arm is tightening up and I'm not getting the ball over to first base as I should," said the shortstop. Middleton moved over and Colonel Van Vliet, fit at age fifty-eight, switched to second base. As the game wore on, shortstop Middleton had to make more and more throws to first from deep shortstop, all the way out to the outfield grass. He was nipping the runners, but by ever closer margins. Then two opponents beat the laboring shortstop's throws. After a particularly close play, Colonel Van Vliet said, "Now look here; if you can't get that ball over, I'll go back to shortstop." The remark made Middleton so angry he nearly threw his arm off the rest of the afternoon.

Shortstop Middleton prepared for football as September neared. He played sixty minutes of almost all the football games. A linebacker on defense, he was expected to diagnose plays more than to tackle ball carriers. "I watched our opponents' eye and foot movements to detect where the play was going and focused the defense against the play," Middleton recalled.

Saturday nights, Lieutenant Middleton called on Miss Jerusha Collins for dances, either at the Galvez or at the Garden Verein, which looked like a miniature city park. Their friendship deepened, though Middleton had competition. An ensign from one of the navy vessels based in Galveston kept calling, "but he never offered serious competition," Middleton recalled.

Each military organization in the Galveston area tried to outdo the others in sponsoring dances. Though the army was still committed to horse and mule power for its own movements, alert recreation officers were authorized to rent trucks in Galveston to transport proper Galveston girls to dances as far away as Texas City.

Middleton himself was something of a proper gentleman. He did not smoke (although later he tried cigars in his middle years, only to renounce them when Mrs. Middleton candidly told him how bad they smelled around the house). He took his first drink of scotch whisky on the Fort Crockett reservation, recalling his father's ten-year-old injunction to drink, if he must, "like a gentleman." Military duty, including the extra afternoon sessions scheduled by Captain Ovenshine, athletics, and social life kept Troy fairly busy through the winter of 1913–1914. He was quartered in a tent at Fort Crockett, but more and more of his free evenings found him at the Hagemann house with Jerusha Collins.

At the officers' mess the patterned talk often returned to terms of service and to promotions for officers long in grade. Promotions weren't flying in the ever-blowing sea breezes at Fort Crockett. Everybody knew everybody else's time in grade, from regular study of the *Blue Book*, yesterday's equivalent of today's *Army Register*. One evening, after supper, a grizzled captain addressed himself to Middleton, a second lieutenant for less than a year. "You know, lieutenant, you're going to be in grade thirteen years. Don't look for a promotion before then. That's the normal time in grade at the rate things are going in this man's army." Middleton looked down the table at his company commander, Captain Ovenshine, who was graying around the temples. He was about forty—the age Middleton would have to reach before he'd be able to pin on the silver bar a first lieutenant was entitled to wear. "My, my, that old man; will I be like him when I get that old?" Middleton thought as he studied the features of Ovenshine.

The routine of garrison duty was broken for Lieutenant Middleton one day when he was appointed to defend a soldier in court martial proceedings. A private guarding two soldiers from the post stockade who were out cutting wood had been challenged by one of them. The prisoner told the guard he was walking off. The guard replied that he'd shoot if the prisoner persisted. The prisoner said, "You yellow son of a bitch, you wouldn't shoot me." The guard shot, killing the prisoner. "I defended him," Middleton recalled. "He had given adequate warning. I don't know why the trial was ever ordered. Anyhow, the guard was found innocent. The word got around, and others came seeking me."

Troy's introduction to military justice came from an incident at Fort Crockett, where Major Hanson E. Ely was his battalion commander. "Major Ely held summary courts martial at his tent in informal surroundings. I looked out of the corner of my tent and watched one afternoon when two enlisted men were marched into Ely's presence. The charges and the specifications were read. The first man was asked how he pleaded. 'Not guilty,' he said. Ely responded, 'The hell you say! What did they bring you over here for? Guilty, five dollars, for drunkenness on duty.' That was my introduction to military justice. The man had showed up drunk for kitchen police duty."

Later, when he was at Fort Bliss in 1916, an Ohio National Guard lieutenant asked Middleton to defend him in a novel case. The National Guardsman stood accused of committing a nuisance, under terms of an old General Order. His offense was urinating on a company street at Fort Bliss. "I got him off on a plea that it was either wet the uniform or wet the street. This happened before 7:30 A.M. when the lieutenant's unit started out to drill," the defender recalled.

Middleton put on the robes of justice in one final court martial. In this case, one enlisted man had been charged with beating another. Middleton asked the accused man why he hit the other. "He called my captain a son of a bitch," the soldier indignantly replied; "sir, he's my captain even if he is a son of a bitch." A military Solomon was needed to handle that one.

While Middleton's thoughts were thus engaged, the cause of the strong American military presence in Galveston remained in Mexico. Woodrow Wilson's "watchful waiting" brought little change. In October, 1913, General Victoriano Huerta clamped down with a full military dictatorship over Mexico. President Wilson put the squeeze on, persuading the British, who were buying most of the oil for their navy from Mexico, to withdraw their support of General Huerta. Next, Wilson informed General Venustiano Carranza that he would dispatch troops to support Carranza. But Carranza didn't want American troops. "Let me buy arms and ammunition in the United States," he replied. In February, 1914, Wilson called off former President Taft's arms embargo. Even then the Carranza forces could not prevail.

The American Congress became restive. Republicans made fun of Wilson's Mexican policy which was, they said, "making the United States the laughing stock of the world." All this time, at Galveston, there were no information and education officers keeping the troops posted (these were unheard-of functions before World War I). Wilson was in a spot. He might eventually have to recognize the Huerta government or throw American military force into the contest and risk drawing together all the Mexican factions against "Yankee imperialism."

In April, 1914, the army had been on standby in Galveston for fourteen months. Naval units had been cruising restlessly off the Mexican Gulf Coast for almost a year. Huerta remained in power. Carranza, pulling together the old Madero forces, was being opposed in northern Mexico by the growing numbers which had rallied to General Francisco (Pancho) Villa. Then came the break Wilson had been waiting for. On April 9, several sailors on shore leave from a United States naval vessel were arrested by a Huerta officer in Tampico. A superior of the impetuous Huerta officer quickly opened the brig and turned the American sailors loose, with an apology. The apology wasn't enough. The American admiral in command ordered the Mexicans to fire a twenty-one gun salute to the United States flag. This was too much for Huerta; he refused. President Wilson ordered the mass of the American fleet to Mexican coastal waters. He turned then to Congress, asking for the go-ahead for drastic action. Before Congress could consider the request, Wilson told the navy to take Vera Cruz. On April 21 and 22 the navy moved—but not bloodlessly, as Wilson had hoped. Mexican forces at Vera Cruz lost 126 men and 195 were wounded in the action. Of the Americans, 19 were killed and 71 wounded.

In Galveston the word spread fast. The Seventh Infantry Regiment, four other regiments, and supporting troops were ordered to embark for Vera Cruz. They sailed from Galveston on April 24, with the Seventh boarding the transport *Kilpatrick*. They were escorted by more naval craft than Troy Middleton had ever seen before. He wondered why, because the Mexican navy did not exist. Perhaps it was to deter the Germans, who had a ship loaded with ammunition on the high seas bound for Huerta's forces at the time of the Tampico incident.

Brigadier General Frederick Funston was given command of the American forces. The Seventh Infantry was to take part in the landing and to become part of the occupying force in Vera Cruz. Lieutenant Middleton didn't even know what the other missions were to be. At sea he spent much of the time studying a map of the Vera Cruz area, coloring the roads, coloring the villages, getting it all dressed up for Captain Ovenshine, the company commander.

When the *Kilpatrick* dropped anchor at Vera Cruz, the dramatics were over. The landing party was not opposed. "In fact," Middleton recalled, "our landing was about as tranquil as one could get. We went straight into occupation duty without being fired on."

After the Americans had been ashore outside Vera Cruz for two weeks, about five miles from the harbor, Lieutenant Middleton's first experience "at anything approaching combat," he said, "was to take a squad of eight men, plus a sergeant who spoke Spanish, to see if any Mexican soldiers could be found. We walked at two miles an hour down a sandy road without seeing any soldiers. About dark, Major Hanson Ely, who was commanding the regiment and had sent me on this mission, rode past us, was gone about an hour, long enough to go down to a Mexican village, and came back.

" 'There's nothing down there, Middleton; you can go on back,' he told us. You can imagine how much he went up in the estimate of our squad. He'd gone with only his orderly to accompany him. Of course, he had no business going there. Suppose he'd found Mexican troops and been shot; he'd have been hard to replace.

"We marched on back, arriving about midnight. It was a spooky experience. We encountered Mexicans on burros, frightening both them and us. Fortunately nobody had to fire his rifle on that trip," Middleton recalled.

From late April until late November, 1914, Captain Ovenshine's company was part of the long, arching outpost spread around the outskirts of Vera Cruz to prevent Mexican soldiers from coming into the city and to keep Mexican civilians from carrying arms, ammunition, and other supplies to the open country where Mexican soldiers were scattered. Ovenshine from time to time took over command of the battalion, turning over the company to Middleton. With other lieutenants, Middleton was first quartered in tents under the tall palms surrounding Vera Cruz. Later he moved to more elegant quarters, in a match factory with mosaic tile floors.

The battalion was deployed near a large cemetery. Mexican dead, mostly civilians who would have died in the ordinary course of events, were carried through the American lines to the cemetery. "One of our duties was to inspect all the caskets to see that they were not transporting other than corpses to the cemetery. At the time, epidemics of typhoid and smallpox were killing wholesale numbers of Mexicans in Vera Cruz. Our army doctors immediately inoculated and vaccinated the entire Mexican population, so that when we left in November there were no cases of typhoid and only a few of smallpox in the city," Middleton recalled.

Lieutenant Middleton spent seven months in occupation duty in a foreign country without being fired upon. From May to mid-July, American and Huerta representatives conferred at Niagara Falls, Canada, only a few miles from Middleton's first army post at Fort Porter. Carranza forces moved in on Mexico City, forcing Huerta to give up. Carranza took over as president. Mexico should have quieted down and returned to normal. That it didn't may have been the result of a mistake made by President Wilson and Secretary of State William Jennings Bryan. Pancho Villa had seen an opportunity to fight Carranza and to enlist American support in the effort. In September, 1914, he made friendly gestures to the United States and talked expansively of his plans for land reform in Mexico. By the spring of 1915, Carranza's forces had taken Villa's measure, whipping him and his plunderers decisively.

Their work done at Vera Cruz, the Seventh Infantry had reembarked for Galveston late in November, 1914. From the mild tropics, they were transported back to the grit and chilly sea breezes of Galveston. Troy Middleton came back to a much pleasanter prospect—to Miss Jerusha Collins.

Jerusha had seen Troy off to Vera Cruz in April, and it was now late November. In fact, Jerusha had known Troy's outfit's sailing date before it was communicated to the regimental commander. Her source was the society editor of the Galveston *Daily News*, Miss Josephine Goldman. When Miss Goldman learned of the imminent troop movement she telephoned Jerusha Collins that the Seventh was to sail on April 24. The message awaited Jerusha and Troy when they came in from a brisk walk in pursuit of the hot tamale vendor's cart. They had bought a supply of tamales and put them in the kitchen stove warming oven to hold until supper.

"When Miss Goldman's message was delivered to me," Jerusha recalled, "I lost my appetite for hot tamales then and thereafter. We sat around camp fires all night on the beach, now that a sailing date had finally come." Troy had proposed marriage earlier. Now he renewed the proposal. The Hagemanns, aunt and uncle, thought the couple should wait, although they approved of the match. They waited.

Troy and his regiment returned to the Fort Crockett reservation, where he was the most junior of the four second lieutenants on the post. The units which hadn't gone to Vera Cruz were now out at Fort Bliss in El Paso, or west of there, on guard against Pancho Villa and his brigands. With Troy back at Galveston, he and Jerusha Collins resumed their plans. They set January 6, 1915, as their wedding date. The Galveston *Daily News* recorded the event:

A pretty wedding was quietly solemnized on Wednesday afternoon at 4:30 o'clock at the residence of Mr. and Mrs. John Hagemann, 3301 Avenue L, when their niece, Miss Jerusha Collins, was united in marriage to Lieutenant Troy H. Middleton, Seventh Infantry, United States Army, Reverend Charles S. Aves, rector of Trinity Episcopal Church, officiating.

Lieutenant and Mrs. Middleton left for New Orleans, en route to Georgetown, Mississippi, to visit Lieutenant Middleton's parents, Mr. and Mrs. John H. Middleton, and on returning to Galveston, will be at home to their friends at the Plaza Hotel.

The bride is one of Galveston's fairest flowers, and ever since her debut season, 1911–12, has been a great social favorite. She is the daughter of the late Sidney G. Collins of this city.

Lieutenant Middleton is a member of one of Mississippi's oldest families. He is a relative of Colonel and Mrs. Edmund Molyneaux Blake of Fort William, U.S.A., formerly of Fort Crockett, U.S.A., and is one of the most highly esteemed officers stationed at Texas City.

The timing of the wedding let the couple arrive at the Santa Fe depot in time for the departure of the late afternoon train to Houston. There they changed to the Southern Pacific's Sunset Limited for a honeymoon trip to New Orleans. It wasn't exactly a honeymoon trip, because it was tailored to the schedule of the Seventh Infantry Regiment, but it served just as well. The Seventh Infantry, along with the Fourth Infantry, having fought in the Battle of New Orleans on January 8, 1815, the two units were guests of the city of New Orleans for the observance of the one hundredth anniversary of the battle. The regiment had gone to New Orleans by ship.

The Middletons were in New Orleans about a week. They never got near Georgetown, Mississippi, where Troy's parents lived, Mrs. Middleton eventually meeting her parents-in-law in 1918 after Troy had gone to

France with the Fourth Division. In New Orleans, the regimental adjutant insisted that the honeymooners make the return trip to Galveston by ship, not train. As Jerusha Middleton recalled, "They had Troy and me go up on the ship's bridge while the ship's band, in place for a concert in New Orleans, struck up the 'Wedding March.' I caught both my high heels in the grating on deck and couldn't pull away." Jerusha did her marching in place while Troy marked time beside her.

The Galveston *Daily News* account of the Middleton wedding erred in a second small detail, in addition to the misinformation about the newly-weds' trip from New Orleans to Georgetown. They didn't set up house-keeping at the Plaza Hotel; rather they accepted the Hagemanns' invita-tion to move in with them. The young couple had a huge upstairs bedroom fronting on Avenue L and catching the breezes from the Gulf and the Bay. Officially, Lieutenant Middleton's quarters remained a tent behind a coast artillery gun emplacement down on the Fort Crockett reservation. But he slept on his cot down there only when he drew duty as Officer of the Day or when he had to take the troops of his company on a tactical march. Otherwise he enjoyed the comforts of the Hagemann home.

Jerusha Collins Middleton, 1919   *Lieutenant Troy H. Middleton, 1917*

Troy and Jerusha Middleton lived with the Hagemanns from January, 1915, until October, about a month after the second great Galveston hurricane. That summer, Galveston drew all the best marksmen in the army for tryouts for the army rifle team. Candidates flocked in from all over the United States. Since he was there anyhow, Troy Middleton tried out for the team. He found that he was pretty good but that he wasn't in the expert class. "Take Courtney Hodges," he said. "I met him there. He could hit the bullseye ten times out of ten at two hundred yards, standing. All the men on tryout were put on special duty. All they did was shoot all day for a month and a half. The real experts had an anemometer hooked up to keep them posted on wind velocities. They would consult the wind gauge half a dozen times in half an hour. They may have been fussbudgets, but could they shoot! They were far out of my class."

When word of the impending hurricane came in mid-August, troops on the island were dispersed to safe places. Those who stayed to ride out the storm, did so in sturdy permanent buildings at Fort Crockett or in downtown Galveston. Troy Middleton chose to weather the hurricane with his wife in the Hagemann house.

Shortly after the storm and the cleanup, the Seventh Infantry was put under travel orders again. In October, 1915, the United States acknowledged the Carranza government as the government of Mexico. This displeased Pancho Villa, who vented his displeasure by shooting sixteen Americans he took off a train in January, 1916. He raided Columbus, New Mexico, killing nineteen more Americans in March, 1916. President Wilson, at the end of his patience, on March 15 ordered Brigadier General John J. Pershing to take command of an expedition, with twelve thousand troops under his command, to find and punish Villa.

Villa was a hard one to catch. He drew American forces three hundred miles into Mexico. In two skirmishes, Americans tangled with Mexican troops. Full fighting was averted, however, and President Carranza agreed to appointment of a joint commission in July, 1916, to study the Mexican-American difficulties still further. The joint commission deliberated into January, 1917, breaking up without suggesting how the United States should go about withdrawing its troops. The United States, on the brink of war with Germany, pulled out its troops and gave final formal recognition to the Carranza government.

Under travel orders to deal with the Mexican problem in yet another arena, the Seventh Infantry was reequipped and entrained for Fort Bliss at El Paso, Texas. There it came under the command of Brigadier General Pershing, an extraordinary soldier who had been promoted from captain of cavalry over the heads of hundreds of officers of intermediate rank to brigadier general, for the work he had done in the Philippine Islands. "A great many senior officers didn't care for him because he had jumped them on the way to his first star," Middleton recalled. "But he was a fine field soldier. When the Seventh Infantry arrived at Fort Bliss it ceased performing garrison duties and began training as a field force."

American troops had gone into Mexico late in 1915 after Villa had renewed his troublemaking. Villa had kept it up with raids in January and in March, 1916, the latter at Columbus, New Mexico, about eighty miles west of El Paso and Fort Bliss. Now the Seventh Infantry was ordered to Douglas, Arizona, another 150 miles or so west of Columbus. The Seventh was sent there to guard the border while the Pershing forces were operating deep in Mexico.

On this, his second confrontation with Mexican forces, Middleton finally experienced his first combat. A Southern Pacific train had deposited the Seventh, combat ready, in Douglas early one morning. *Villista* forces were in position opposite Douglas, preparing to attack the Mexican border village of Agua Prieta, just across the international boundary. Middleton and several other lieutenants wanted a better look at the prospective enemy. They hiked over to a baseball park not far from their encampment and the international boundary. They clambered to the top of the grandstand for a better look, expecting to see the developing engagement from ringside. "An old major came running up and chased us out, so we missed seeing the fighting between the *Villistas* and the *Carrancistas*, who were defending Agua Prieta," Midddleton recalled.

When night fell, the *Villistas* were deployed in front of Agua Prieta. The defending *Carrancistas* had searchlights in position to play along the *Villista* line to keep track of the enemy movements after dark. The right and the left of the *Carrancista* defensive line rested on the international boundary. On the right, where a large copper smelter stood, it was feared that the *Villistas* might come around onto United States territory and outflank the *Carrancista* line, using the copper smelter as a screen. To prevent this, two companies of the Seventh Infantry, under Lieutenant Middleton's company commander who was acting as battalion commander, were sent to dig a trench linking with the *Carrancista* trench and extending over to the copper smelter. This would keep the *Villistas* out. As the junior commander, Middleton was placed with one company over near the *Carrancista* line. He ordered his men to dig in. The ground was hard and full of rocks. Middleton's company dug with all the enthusiasm of a flock of arthritic armadillos. They couldn't see the sense of entrenching since they were fairly sure that no Mexicans would try an end run on them.

By mistake, one of the *Carrancista* searchlights swung beyond its prescribed zone. It illuminated the Americans in stark silhouette. The *Villistas* began firing at this target of opportunity. Eight of Lieutenant Middleton's men were hit; none were killed. As soon as the *Carrancistas* realized their mistake, they switched off the searchlight. The firing ceased. Middleton's company fell to digging. "By daylight they had dug so deep, I had to stand well over a trench and peer down in it to find a soldier," he recalled.

That was Middleton's first combat experience. The casualties were lighter than they might have been. Middleton was untouched. The *Villistas* gave up at Agua Prieta and moved west. It appeared that they would attack next at Nogales, Arizona, about a hundred miles west of Douglas. The Seventh moved again to protect the border there and to oppose the *Villistas* if necessary. The Americans encamped on the outskirts of Nogales. The *Villistas* came along on the other side of the border but made no threatening gestures. Middleton remembered Nogales as an ideal rest and recreation area, after the mild combat at Douglas.

"Nogales was a beautiful little city in a crater. The quail-hunting around it was spectacular. Mountain quail abounded; they wouldn't flush like our bob whites back in the South. They could outrun a horse. I had a great time trying to chase those birds down so that I could get a shot at them," Middleton recalled.

Shortly before Christmas, 1915, the Seventh was moved back to Fort Bliss at El Paso, to resume intensive field training under General Pershing until April, 1917, when the regiment moved to Gettysburg, Pennsylvania, in preparation for overseas duty in Europe in 1918.

"While we were at Fort Bliss, I had command of the company from time to time when Captain Ovenshine took over for the major. I drilled the men, trained them, took them to fire on the rifle range. A company then had only about sixty-five men; we trained it as you'd train a platoon today.

The sixty-five included clerks, cooks, everybody. The only time we were all together was when we went to the rifle range. Officers fired with the enlisted men every time.

"We knew war was coming just by reading the El Paso papers. My battalion commander, Major Ely, had toured Germany on a bicycle. He was much impressed with the Germans and admired them. He had graduated from the Command and General Staff School, commanded a Philippine Scout battalion in the Philippines, and come back home by way of Europe. The declaration of war in April, 1917, switched off Ely's admiration for the Germans."

Mrs. Middleton had stayed on in Galveston a while after the Seventh was first sent west to oppose the *Villistas* while General Pershing led his larger force deep into Mexico. In the winter of 1915–1916, after the Seventh's return to Fort Bliss, she joined Lieutenant Middleton. That winter they acquired their first home. For five hundred dollars they bought the materials for a house, "some place we could put our things," Mrs. Middleton recalled. "We lived in tents while the house was being built by a man and a helper. Lumber was cheap; so was labor. Some other officers decided to build, too. The Fort Bliss post force would do the plumbing and install lights at cost to the officers. We had them put on a tarpaper roof. And before long we were sung against the elements. We had an agreement with the post permitting us to sell the house and allowing the buyer to move the house off the military reservation if he wanted to."

When the Middletons were ordered to another post, a cavalry sergeant inquired about buying their house. "Make me an offer," Middleton said.

"Eighty dollars," said the sergeant.

"Sold," said Lieutenant Middleton.

Lieutenant and Mrs. Middleton not only owned their home on the post, they became one of the first Seventh Regiment families at Fort Bliss to own an automobile. It was a Model T Ford. Delivered to the purchaser's new home, it cost $404.44. It came with the standard hand crank, but Lieutenant Middleton would have none of that action; he bought and had put on a Fisher Brothers self-starter, costing $115. The Ford Model T had coil shock absorbers, demountable wheel rims permitting removal of the tire without removal of the wheel, electric lights, and a radiator which was the first without gaudy brass trim around it. The Middletons went out in style thereafter, with their huge airedale dog Loopie accompanying them in cruises around the countryside. When Lieutenant Middleton was ordered away from Fort Bliss in April, 1917, he turned the car over to the Ford agency in El Paso. That same afternoon the dealer called to say that he had disposed of the car for $650, more than offsetting the original cost plus $200 in added extras and refinements. The threat of war had driven up the price of automobiles as it did with everything else. The check for the car, which was to have been mailed to Mrs. Middleton in Galveston, was laid in her hand in El Paso.

At Gettysburg, the Seventh Infantry settled down to preparation for its most rugged assignment, the war in Europe. It had been going on since August, 1914. Congress had just acceded to President Wilson's request for a declaration of war, four days after the president made the impassioned request. Now it was up to the relative handful of Americans who had been in uniform—like Troy Middleton—to build an army which could survive the brutal combat conditions in France.

Second Lieutenant Troy Middleton had put on the silver bars of a first lieutenant July 1, 1916, well short of the thirteen years in grade solemnly predicted for him by the older captain at the dinner table at Fort Crockett three years before. The silver bars of the first lieutenant were, in fact, the only ones Middleton or any other man in his circumstances was qualified to pin on. Second lieutenants didn't wear gold bars.

After three years as an enlisted man and three years and seven months as a second lieutenant, Middleton was to spend only ten and a half months as a first lieutenant. After an extraordinary battlefield performance, he would rise from major to colonel in four months.

First Lieutenant Middleton was detached from the Seventh Infantry at Gettysburg National Park, where the regiment went on training. He was sent to Fort Myer, Virginia on June 10, 1917, to become adjutant of the Reserve Officers Training Camp (not to be confused with today's campus-connected Reserve Officers Training Corps).

Since the army had few officers, in preparation for the great buildup in strength, large numbers of junior officers had to be trained. Officer training camps were organized all over the nation, to turn out officers in the grade of second and first lieutenant, captain, and major—all in three months. Middleton spent the summer at Fort Myer in suburban Washington. He had been promoted to captain on May 15, 1917. As adjutant, he directed the flow of increasingly complicated paper work for 2,700 candidates for commissions.

By November, 1917, it appeared that the United States Army had swallowed about all the civilian officer material it could digest. The Reserve Officers Training Camp at Fort Myer commissioned its last class of "ninety-day wonders."

Now, thought Captain Middleton, maybe I can get on with the war. He asked the War Department to assign him to a combat division scheduled for early departure for Europe. The War Department obliged. Go to the Fourth Infantry Division, now training at Charlotte, North Carolina, Captain Middleton's orders read. On December 21, 1917, he reported to the commanding general of the Fourth Division at Camp Greene, Charlotte, and was assigned as the commanding officer of Company A, First Battalion, Forty-Seventh Infantry Regiment. As he took over command of Company A, he looked out on a training area that was about half land and half water. Winter rains left part of the camp afloat and the rest bogged down in muck that clung with equal affection to private and captain alike. Camp Greene had been hacked and graded out of the Carolina pines. A pleasant training ground it was not, but a combat-worthy division the Fourth was becoming.

Captain Middleton had stowed his foot locker and shelved the contents of his barracks bag and was ready to join his command in the Camp Greene mud bath. He arrived on Friday, December 21. The night of December 23–24, he received a telegram from the War Department ordering him to proceed immediately to Leon Springs, Texas, twenty-four miles northwest of San Antonio, where he was to take command of yet another training company in yet another Reserve Officers Training Camp. Mrs. Middleton was preparing to catch a train in Washington, headed for Charlotte, when Captain Middleton received the telegram sending him back to Texas. He told her to come ahead, but to buy a ticket to San Antonio, not Charlotte. He joined Mrs. Middleton aboard the Pullman for New Orleans. On Christmas day, they were on a Southern Pacific train leaving New Orleans and headed for San Antonio.

Captain Middleton remained in command of the training company until its mission was completed in April, 1918. One of the earnest young officers there was Second Lieutenant Fred C. Frey who would later become dean of Louisiana State University and acting president as well. In the dry, bracing climate at Leon Springs, Middleton missed—without one regret—the muck of Camp Greene. As the last of the trainees departed for San Antonio and new assignments, camp commander Middleton wondered about the futures of the camp staff, without a discernible future since this training group was the last to be processed.

6   This Time, Real War

I WENT over to headquarters and asked the commanding general if he would send me back to the Fourth Division since I was merely detached from it—on loan for the training mission at Leon Springs. He wired the War Department and it replied, "Yes, return Middleton to his division." Believing that the Fourth Division was still training at Camp Greene, I wired Camp Greene and received a reply saying that the Fourth Division had departed. I assumed that they were on their way overseas. So I caught a train for New York. When I arrived there, April 28, 1918, I found the division about ready to load on transports for Europe. They were in tents at Camp Mills on Long Island. I got a second lieutenant to put my name on the sailing list of the Forty-seventh Infantry.

If Captain Middleton's cross-country movements without formal orders seem unconventional—they were. He was bent on getting to where the fighting was. The Fourth Division was his sure ticket to France. He first made the acquaintance of Captain Hurley Fuller, who had taken command of Middleton's old Company A, First Battalion, on March 31. Middleton resumed command of Company A and took over the battalion also, as the regimental commander had decreed. Fuller was transferred to Company L in the Third Battalion, with which he remained a captain through his service in France. "Fuller was a cantankerous fellow, but a good fighter," Middleton recalled. Fuller served briefly on the ROTC staff at Louisiana State University in the late 1930s.

Middleton's regiment sailed from Camp Mills on the *Princess Matokia* on May 11. "We had fourteen ships in our convoy. We dodged sub-

61

marines and dropped off all escort ships but one scout cruiser until we were three days out of Brest. A flock of destroyers met us and took us into Brest on May 23."

When the Fourth Division marched down gangplanks in Brest, the new arrivals were not met with applause and band music. They stepped off their ships into a thicket of gloom. The Germans had mounted their spring offensive of 1918 and were knocking holes in the French and British defenses. "We were at Brest five days unloading and organizing before we loaded into forty-and-eights, those tiny French boxcars, on May 29. I'll never forget a particular Britisher there. We looked at each other for a long time. Finally, he said, in a Cockney accent, 'Oh, Sammy, going up?' 'Yes,' I said, 'I'm going up.' He waited a minute and said, 'They're raising 'ell up there.' The Germans were doing just that. I thought they'd drive the English and the French into the Channel," Middleton recalled.

"Our train went to Calais, arriving at 3 P.M. on May 30. We were loaded onto British trucks and trundled out to join a much-depleted British brigade which had had hell shot out of it. German air raiders flew over twice that night but inflicted no casualties. We became a reserve unit for the British at the village of Samer, just south of Calais, on June 3."

In the British area, the Americans were required to give up their Springfield rifles in exchange for British Enfields. "Matter of ammunition supply, old chaps," the Americans were told. The infantry received French machine guns and automatic rifles, none too dependable Chauchats. The Fourth Division's artillery units were issued French 75-millimeter guns. After being rearmed, the division was broken into smaller units and placed in reserve of the British in the north of France. In these positions, they received some training from the British. While this training was going on, the German drive in the Aisne-Marne sector north of Paris began. The Fourth Division was pulled back together, loaded on trains, and sent to a location near the small town of Meaux, on the Marne River twenty-five miles west of Chateau Thierry. There the division unloaded early in June and moved in as a reserve to the Forty-second (Rainbow) Division which had been badly mauled by the Germans. Middleton recalled that his train headed for Meaux took him within clear sight of the Eiffel Tower in Paris. He wondered if he would ever get to see the fabled city.

Late in July, two battalions from the Forty-seventh Infantry were ordered up to join the 167th Infantry of the Forty-second Division. Middleton, a major as of June 7, commanded one battalion, the First. Major James Perry Cole commanded the other, the Third. Cole later became a professor of mathematics at Louisiana State University.

The two American battalions marched all night to reach an area where the 167th Infantry was supposed to be, arriving shortly after daylight. Middleton found an officer of the 167th, who gave the reinforcing battalions their orders. Middleton was to take his First Battalion in and join the 167th Infantry. Cole's Third Battalion was to link up with an infantry regiment originally from Iowa—off on Middleton's right.

Information came hard. Middleton did ascertain that the 167th had an advanced command post about a mile and a half to the front up a draw. He left his battalion in concealment of a wood, took a few men, and went up to the headquarters of the 167th. There he found Lieutenant Colonel Baehr, a National Guardsman who knew the score. Baehr advised Middleton to hold his battalion in concealment through the day and to bring it in that night. Colonel Baehr's regiment had no continuous front line; small groups of a few soldiers each stretched across his front. Baehr told Middleton that his First Battalion would attack the next morning. Middleton's battalion, moving up in darkness, would pass through elements of the exhausted 167th and into position to attack the Germans. The date was July 28, 1918.

This was the situation which faced the two battalions from the Fourth Division. They were moving to the relief of the Forty-second Division units whose effectiveness had been shot out of them by the Germans. The opponents were contending for possession of Sergy, a tattered village two hundred yards from the banks of the Ourcq River. That Sergy had survived forty-five months of war was remarkable. The village had been overrun by the Germans in 1914. It had been retaken by the French in the first Battle of the Marne. The Germans, in their spring offensive of 1918, had seized Sergy again and pushed beyond it, dangerously near Paris. In late July they were pushed out of Sergy again. The Germans counterattacked on July 28, pushing out the American defenders from the Forty-second Division's 168th Infantry. The Americans threw the Germans back once more. They held through the night of July 28–29. At daybreak the Germans came storming back and retook Sergy.

Middleton's and Cole's battalions moved toward their battle positions. Cole's battalion moved up through tall wheat covering the slope leading to a thin belt of woods fringing the Ourcq River. The Ourcq was no obstacle; it rose about five miles to the east and could be cleared by an energetic jumper. Middleton's battalion marched just over a mile to the cover offered by the Foret de Fere. Under the trees, the battalion moved eastward through a wooded ravine. There it halted while the company commanders went forward to reconnoiter the approaches to the banks of the Ourcq. What was left of one battalion of the 167th was holding a position on the north bank of the stream. Using its concealment to full advantage, Middleton's battalion worked its way two hundred yards north of the Ourcq. The remainder of the 167th withdrew. Middleton's First Battalion, Forty-seventh Infantry, submerged its identity to become, for this battle only, the Third Battalion of the 167th Infantry. Middleton disposed his Companies B and D on a front line resting on a dirt road which paralleled the Ourcq and ran to the village of Fere-en-Tardenois. Companies A and C were in support. The men they replaced supplied the battalion with maps showing the boundaries of the area they would be responsible for attacking—and defending if necessary.

Middleton's initial objective was the Foret de Nesles, in which the Chateau de Nesles was of first priority, just over a mile distant. Battalions on each flank were being held in place by German machine gun and artillery fire. At 9 A.M. the battalion began its move against the Germans entrenched on the hillside. Companies B and D dug the Germans out in bayonet fighting. By nightfall the advance elements of the battalion had carried to the top of the hill. They dug in for the night of July 29 with Companies B and D on the flanks and A moving into the point. Water supplies ran short. The battalion's casualties were heavy, and evacuation of the wounded grew difficult.

While Middleton's First Battalion had taken its objective at considerable cost, Cole's Third ran into even more determined opposition. It came under a heavy artillery concentration, and it had to fight its way uphill through fields of wheat, over which a German airplane flew, strafing the attackers. More artillery poured in. German machine gunners cut down both wheat and Americans. Cole was shot through the knee, just as he entered the village of Sergy; this injury took him out of action permanently and left him with a lifelong limp. The man who took over command was severely wounded by an artillery burst. Finally, another captain assumed command. The Third Battalion held Sergy, though ammunition ran low. They picked up food and ammunition from the dead. More than a hundred wounded made it through to Sergy.

Middleton's battalion remained under heavy fire from machine guns and artillery all day July 30. The Germans had control of the air and sent planes over regularly to reconnoiter and deliver harassing fire at the Americans on the ridge. Late that afternoon the Germans counterattacked after heavy artillery and machine gun fire. The battalion threw the Germans back. On July 31, Middleton's battalion moved ahead again in coordination with the 167th Infantry on the left. That night the First Battalion was relieved, after four days of steady fighting and serious losses. Relieved by elements of the 167th, the First Battalion marched back to the Foret de Fere.

Middleton's and Cole's battalions and their fighting companions had taken on the Prussian Fourth Guard Division, fresh from a month's rest at Metz. The veteran Germans fought exceedingly well. They penalized the Americans heavily for the gains they made. But they were forced to give ground, never to be regained, in some of the bloodiest infantry engagements of the war. The First and Third Battalions lost 27 officers and 462 men; 6 men were reported missing in action. More than 1 man in 4 was a casualty.

After the First and Third Battalions were relieved, they rejoined the other elements of the Fourth Division. The Fourth Division then shouldered its way forward into the area the Forty-second Division had held. The Germans, just before this transfer, had pulled back to the Vesle River, ten to twelve miles from the Ourcq. They needed time to lick their wounds.

The Fourth Division followed the Germans to the Vesle, more of a stream than was the Ourcq, and much better for the defense. When the Fourth began its move at the Vesle, the Germans put up a tremendous defense. The Fourth lost a great many men in the effort to dislodge the Germans. After a week here, the Fourth was relieved and sent into the St. Mihiel Salient in preparation for the St. Mihiel offensive, in which they played a small supporting role. Though his battalion did little fighting in the St. Mihiel sector, Middleton gained some valuable experience on the move from the Vesle River to St. Mihiel. All the Fourth Division transport, entirely horse and mule drawn, was organized into one unit for the move. This brought together the Forty-seventh Infantry, the Thirty-ninth Infantry and brigade headquarters, and their transport. Middleton was given the task of directing the movement. Everything had to go by night.

I studied the maps, got some second lieutenants, and procured myself a motorcycle with a driver and side car. I got no sleep. My days were spent in reconnaissance at the head of the column looking for the next overnight stop areas where we would be hidden in woods. At dark, we'd creak onto the road, move all night to the next bivouac, being sure to leave time to be under cover before daylight. We moved without lights, and by all accounts the Germans didn't detect our movement of all this transport.

Using secondary roads, the vehicles were a week on the way. They began moving about 10 P.M. when the last daylight faded and had to be under cover before 4 A.M. We didn't rest, but pulled right on through at night. I was out on my feet when the move ended. We were exhausted from having to plot every inch of the move on the map, advise people where we'd be all the time, notify them of every smallest change in plan. The Germans had planes in the air every day but we were always hidden away by dawn.

All the planning and nighttime travel from the Vesle to St. Mihiel was to prove valuable to Middleton at Avranches another night in another war.

After St. Mihiel, the regiment was moved north of Verdun for the Meuse-Argonne offensive. Preparation for the attack required extensive planning. Hundreds of thousands of French and Germans had died on the slaughter grounds around Verdun. No American commander wanted a repetition. Middleton's battalion was one of two in the Seventh Brigade (of the Fourth Division) designated to lead off in the attack on September 26, 1918.

Middleton's battalion was designated a leading element in the attack. He had repeatedly demonstrated his competence as a commander and had just received word of his promotion to lieutenant colonel. With the promotion came an order to move to a regimental headquarters position. He had trained his battalion so well, and the men responded so well to his leadership, that he asked the commanding officer of the Forty-seventh Infantry to let him stay with the battalion through the attack. The commander gave his permission. The Fourth Division, together and on its own for the first time, was assigned a front of slightly more than a mile at its narrowest and no more than two miles at its widest, between French divisions long in combat. The field of battle lay no more than eight miles from Verdun.

At first light on September 26, Middleton's battalion and one other stormed into the trench area held by the Germans. That day they covered five miles, smashing the German defenses and bursting into the open. Lieutenant Colonel Middleton saw his men into position for continuing the advance, turned the battalion over to his second in command, and reported to regimental headquarters to become the executive officer of the Forty-seventh Infantry. The Forty-seventh remained busy holding onto its gains of September 26, having moved from a line between the villages of Haucourt and Bethincourt, past Cuisy, Septsarges, and Nantillois. The regiment remained in combat until the Armistice came on November 11.

Soon after midnight on October 11, one day before Middleton's twenty-ninth birthday, Colonel Parsons and the entire regimental staff of the Thirty-ninth Infantry were gassed by the Germans. The commanding general, George H. Cameron, who had returned to command of the Fourth Division just the day before, reached into his recollection and came up with Middleton as Colonel Parsons' replacement. General Cameron sent for Middleton, just two weeks in his job as executive officer of the Forty-seventh Infantry, to move over and take command of the Thirty-ninth Infantry and all the troops adjacent to the regiment in the Bois de Fays, a roughly rectangular wooded area about a half mile deep by three quarters of a mile wide. The Bois de Fays lay shoulder to shoulder with the Bois de Malaumont directly to the north, from which the Bois de Peut-de-Faux poked east like a hitchhiker's thumb. The three joined woods gave and promised concealment ahead but also offered the well prepared Germans concealment of their own.

The transfer of command would not have been especially difficult except for the fact that Colonel Parsons and his regimental staff had gone under the choking fumes of German gas shells less than six hours before the regiment was to lead the attack northward. At 1 A.M., division headquarters informed Middleton that he had a new command, the Thirty-ninth Infantry, a regiment shorn of all its top command. He received the call in a wet, muddy dugout. Middleton asked if anyone could show him the way to the Thirty-ninth.

"One soldier said he could," Middleton recalled. "It was the darkest night I'd ever seen. It was raining. We had to go through the woods about three and a half miles. The volunteer guide knew what he was talking about. He pointed out the bodies of dead soldiers along the path we were following. We got to our destination before daylight and found the Thirty-ninth under orders to attack at daylight."

Attack the Thirty-ninth did, under a new leader who had little time for conferring. At 7:28 A.M., after a barrage had been laid on the German defenders, the Second Battalion led out in the assault with the First Battalion echeloned to the Second's right rear for protection. Their objective was the Bois de Foret, long used by the Germans as concealment for weapons, ammunition, and food dumps.

The Germans responded to the Thirty-ninth's move with heavy machine gun and *minenwerfer* fire, holding off on the gas. In the first hours of the attack, the Americans were held to short gains in the dense wood. Then Middleton decided to try something different. Against an enemy well dug in throughout the Bois de Foret, he ordered a resumption of the attack. "I gave orders that everybody should shoot—in what is commonly known today as marching fire—under the theory that if we were shooting, the defending Germans would naturally conclude that we could see them, or at least this would force them to keep their heads down."

For more than a mile through the dense wood, the soldiers of the Thirty-ninth advanced in a skirmish line, shooting low so that the "thwack, thwack" of passing bullets would keep the Germans in their holes. "You never heard such a racket in your life," Middleton recalled. "We walked right on through the wood to its northern edge. This was the farthest advance of Fourth Division troops into enemy territory, putting us right up on the edge of the Meuse River beyond Brieulles. I don't recall how many Germans we captured, but it was a sizable number. Among our captives was a young German officer who told me that he had never been under such small arms fire as he'd been under that morning. I had studied German at Mississippi A & M. I hadn't learned much, but I thought I'd try out my German on this young officer. He stood at attention and I launched into my Mississippi German. He replied to me in better English than I spoke, saying: 'Colonel, if you will speak English I can understand you better.' That was the end of my Mississippi German."

Three days after he took command of the Thirty-ninth Infantry, on October 14, Middleton became a colonel. He had been promoted to lieutenant colonel on September 17, and to major on June 7. At twenty-nine, he became the youngest wearer of eagles in the American Expeditionary

Force. For the Bois de Foret action, Middleton later received the Distinguished Service Medal.

At the end of the fighting around the Bois de Foret, Colonel Oliver P. M. Hazzard, a cavalryman in his sixties, came over to take command of the Thirty-ninth. Colonel Middleton went back to the Forty-seventh, now in a reserve position. Shortly after his arrival there, an order came to Fourth Division headquarters, transferring him to command of the Eleventh Infantry in the Fifth Division. General Cameron, who knew a natural regimental commander when he had one, shuffled the transfer request around his headquarters and said nothing to Colonel Middleton about it. The original request had come over from Troy Middleton's former battalion commander back at Vera Cruz, now Major General Hanson Ely. The general had heard of Middleton's promotion to colonel, had a vacancy, and wanted him in the Fifth Division.

Later, Middleton was informed, General Cameron sent a message to the army commander that Middleton was not available. He did, however, happen to have on hand a colonel, now commanding the Forty-seventh In-

Middleton as Colonel of the Forty-seventh Infantry, France, 1918

fantry, who would be available. That colonel went over to the Fifth Division to take command of the Eleventh Infantry, finishing out the war most capably. Command of the Forty-seventh Infantry passed to Middleton, who had joined it originally at Camp Greene, North Carolina, on December 21, 1917, and had remained with it for all of three days before he was dispatched to Leon Springs, Texas.

On October 19, the Fourth Division was withdrawn from the battle line. It had been in continuous contact with the enemy for twenty-four days, the longest unbroken period any American division was in action in World War I. Early in November, the Fourth Division was in the process of relieving a Negro regiment near Metz, before preparing for an attack on the German defenders down the Moselle River toward the Rhine. Middleton's regiment was designated to lead the assault, as his battalion had been chosen when he held a lower command. The exact date of the attack had not been set. On November 9, Middleton's regiment was moving into the front line, having completed the relief of the black regiment.

The next day, November 10, confidential word came to Middleton that an armistice was coming. He was ordered to continue his troop movements as if no change were contemplated. At 6 A.M. on November 11, a messenger from division headquarters brought word that there would be no more firing after 11 A.M. When that time came, Middleton recalled, "The first thing I did was to get my regiment out of the woods and into the sunshine to enjoy not being shot at. Brief though the sun's appearance was, it was timed perfectly for the Forty-seventh Infantry and the rest of the Fourth Division; they had spent almost all their combat time in the rain, fog, and unending mud of northeastern France."

There were no Germans around to watch the Fourth Division emerge into the sunshine. They had pulled out. Shortly, orders came to turn in live ammunition. That made the war's end as sure as anything could. "Our joy was tremendous," Middleton recalled.

The Fourth Division did not luxuriate long in sunshine. It was designated as part of the occupation forces to move into Germany. Middleton soon had an opportunity to repractice all the detail that went into the transport move from the Vesle to the St. Mihiel sector. This time, however, the move went on in daylight. "What I'd learned on that move made the move from Metz, France, to Boppard, Germany, relatively easy. We encountered no problems that I hadn't already solved."

7   After War, Occupation

FROM METZ, the Fourth Division was to move to the area of Koblenz, a road march of at least 125 miles. There it would become one of several reserve divisions in the Army of Occupation. The division began its march at the end of November, through Metz and straight north to Thionville, then northeast through Trier and Simmern, with their destination Boppard, where the Lorelei sang from the rock guarding the Rhine River there, about ten miles upriver from Koblenz.

The Forty-seventh stayed off the main highways, which were in full use supplying divisions ahead of the regiment. Progress was steady and relatively smooth. Short of Simmern, orders came rerouting the Forty-seventh to another destination, Adenau, about thirty-five miles due west of Koblenz. The Forty-seventh was assigned an area in this mountainous hinterland with Adenau among fourteen other smaller German towns.

The regiment was fifteen days on the road and beginning to weary when the advance elements creaked into Adenau in a driving snowstorm on December 15. The last twenty miles of the march went uphill in the snow. All the vehicles were drawn by horses or mules. Through the early days of the march they pulled their loads in incessant rain. Preparing hot meals each night and morning put the cooks to a test almost as stern as they had experienced in combat, but they came through.

Middleton authorized a first-class mount, forgot his anti-cavalry feelings and spent most of each day in the saddle. He rode from head to tail of the long column, which moved for fifty minutes and rested ten in each

71

hour. On one of these rest breaks, Middleton had dismounted and was walking along the line of transport. He came to a wagon driven by a fine looking soldier driving a four-mule team. "He didn't look like a mule-skinner to me," Middleton recalled. "I stopped and said, 'Soldier, in civilian life, what did you do?' He said, 'I was a certified public accountant.' That may give you some indication of how poor our classification system was in World War I. I said, 'What are you doing here driving these mules? You should be in the Quartermaster Corps or the Finance Department where your training could be used.' He said, 'Colonel, I just want to do something different.' Well, he was really doing something different, driving those mules."

Once in Adenau, the Forty-seventh dispersed among the villages for which it was responsible. Middleton was billeted in a substantial home in which the German owners continued to live. The regiment remained in Adenau and surroundings until March, 1919. While they were there, army issue rations sometimes palled on the palates of both officers and men. The occupying forces were under strict orders not to draw on the civilian populace for food. From time to time inspecting officers came around to see that the restriction was being obeyed. Captain Betts, the regimental adjutant, inspected messes. He found the remnants of eggs on the plate of Captain Thomas J. Sheehy of the regimental supply company. Betts remonstrated with Sheehy: "You know better, Tom. I'll have to report you to the Old Man." Sheehy replied, "But I didn't buy the eggs from the Germans." "No?" Betts rejoined. "Then where did you get them?" Sheehy responded, "I rented the hens." Betts couldn't think of either answer or remonstrance. Later, Middleton told Captain Sheehy that he should have been court-martialed, but he said so with a smile.

Along the route of march, Middleton had insisted that the horses and mules be given the best of care, fed well, and rested as much as possible. On the way, the foot soldiers and the drivers had to get up, roll their packs, be fed, tend the stock, organize the column, and get on the road. They halted ten minutes each hour and a full hour at lunch, feeding on canned beans, canned tomatoes, canned salmon and corned beef. French bread, by the wagonload, accompanied every meal. "I'm glad I liked all these," Middleton recalled. "After the war I met a fellow who said he had learned to hate everything that came out of a can in France or Germany. I not only liked the canned stuff, I thrived on it."

Once they were in permanent quarters, Middleton's German cook turned out palatable meals, always accompanied by French bread. The bread, baked at a central bakery, was hauled round to the messes in wagons, like so many heads of cabbage. "Our cook," Middleton recalled, "had a trick of peeling the big round French bread loaves like thick-skinned apples. He would dampen the inch-thick slices and put them in the oven. They always came out delicious."

Later, when he was billeted with another German family at Remagen, on the Rhine, Middleton was treated royally. Again, when he was transferred, the nuns at a school at Vallendar, near Bierdorf, insisted on feeding their best cooking to Middleton, who was billeted on one floor of the school while scores of girls, aged ten to twelve, were housed on the second floor and regimented as tightly as any military force.

The move from Adenau to Remagen came March 9, 1919, when the Forty-seventh was ordered there to relieve another unit. Colonel George C. Marshall, aide to General Pershing, had spent the night in Adenau and had breakfast with Middleton. "I remember that we had hot cakes," Middleton said. "As we got ready for the march some twenty miles up to Remagen, one of our soldiers was having a hard time falling into ranks. He had imbibed a lot the night before and was in poor shape. His buddies were steadying him and keeping him pointed in the right direction. George Marshall asked why I didn't put the man in an ambulance. I told him that the company's morale would suffer if we let the man with the hangover ride. The soldier walked off his unsteadiness. Marshall laughed and agreed that I had been right. I saw sergeants carrying privates' packs along the way rather than have anyone drop out of their platoons."

At Remagen, the Americans guarded the bridge over the Rhine, and continued to train. (The Remagen bridge, incidentally, was captured intact by the American Forty-seventh Infantry in World War II and offered quick, almost uncontested passage to the east bank of the Rhine in March, 1944, twenty-five years after Middleton's unit stood duty there.) Training continued, as it probably would have anyhow, because the Germans had not signed the terms under which the November armistice was granted. "Along about May, 1919, we were ordered to extend the bridgehead at Remagen as a threat to get the Germans to take action," Middleton recalled. "My regiment was moved across to the east bank of the Rhine. This convinced the Germans that we meant business; they signed. We were

Middleton and his Regimental Staff Officers, Germany, 1919 (U.S. Army Photo)

pulled back into reserve, this time with my headquarters in Vallendar."

From December, 1918, through February, 1919, the Forty-seventh went on with its training program, as if it might be called to combat any day. The regiment built a rifle range, ran combat problems, and practiced what it had learned in combat back at Sergy, on the Vesle, and especially in the Bois de Foret.

Though he had been out of touch with a football since he last played at Galveston in 1915, Colonel Middleton was recruited for one more go at the game early in March, 1919. He received an order from Fourth Division headquarters, directing him to turn over command of the regiment to his assistant and to report to the division commander. When he did so, the division commander informed him that he had been ordered down to play football. Captain Hamilton Fish (a former Harvard team captain) had organized a division team. Each division in the Third Army was to be represented. The division commander told Middleton, "We understand that you played on army teams back in the States as a quarterback; we need a quarterback. You start training tomorrow."

"Well, there wasn't much I could do about that," Middleton recalled. "I told the general that I hadn't played football in nearly four years and that I was pushing thirty years of age. I didn't need to remind him that soldier football is rough. But I was stuck with the assignment. We had several West Point graduates on the team, one or two players from the University of Oklahoma, and another from Oklahoma A & M. The squad came from all over the country. And like myself, they were getting old. I was practicing with the team for the coming schedule when a fumble back at Adenau put an end to my football playing in the army. General Charles H. Muir, the corps commander, came around for an inspection visit. He found something wrong with my regiment and asked, 'Where is Colonel Middleton?' The reply, 'He's down at division playing football,' was too much for General Muir. They told me that the general blew his top. He got hold of General Hersey and said, 'You get Middleton back up here right away. I don't want any regimental commander playing football.' That ended my football career for good."

The Fourth Division team went on to become champion in Germany, where teams representing the First, Second, Third, Fourth, and Forty-second Divisions played. The Eighty-ninth Division, champion in France, defeated the Fourth in the American Expeditionary Force's title game.

If Middleton couldn't play, he could watch his team. "I'll never forget the Second Division game at Koblenz," he recalled. "Half that division were Marines commanded by John A. Lejeune, from Pointe Coupee Parish, Louisiana. Many Second Division players were Marines. When the Marine band came on the field playing the 'Marine Hymn' I thought those gyrenes would tear up the wooden bleachers, but our team won in a struggle."

Colonel Marshall's aforementioned visit came on the heels of Middleton's involuntary retirement from quarterbacking. Middleton had no time to brood. Marshall brought news that the Forty-second Division, which the Fourth had relieved at Sergy, was again to be relieved by the Fourth, this time at Remagen. Middleton's Forty-seventh Infantry was to take over the prime duty of guarding the Rhine bridge at Remagen. The regiment stayed there until it received orders home in August, 1919.

Before those orders came, Middleton was summoned to report to the chief of staff of the Third Army at Koblenz. There he was informed that he and several other senior officers in the Third Army were being ordered to Camp Benning, Georgia, to form the first faculty of the Infantry School which was being organized at that place. "I knew that my regiment was going home in only a month, so I requested that my orders be delayed, permitting me to return with the regiment," Middleton recalled.

"The chief of staff looked at me for a little while and then said, 'Colonel Middleton, we have an order that you will be at Camp Benning, Georgia, on August 1. Now if you can tell me how you can take a regiment home and be at Camp Benning on August 1—if you can do that, it's O.K. with me.'"

Major General Mark L. Hersey wrote Troy Middleton in farewell from Niederbreisig, Germany:

1. We are in receipt of your orders sending you as an instructor to the Infantry School in the United States. Realizing full well that no better selection could have been made by the War Department, and appreciating the high compliment that is paid to you and to the Fourth Division thereby, we none the less regret beyond measure the orders that take you from us, even though the great work that has been given us to do has been done, and well done. From all quarters inquiries as to the correctness of the rumor that you have been ordered home are heard, and profound regrets expressed at your departure.

2. Added to the military efficiency which has made us all proud of you and your record and your regiment, is that personal charm that counts for much in

the leadership of men. Nothing that I could say would add to the estimate of your Brigade Commander on your own rating card; namely, 100. It is the only rating card I have ever seen or known of so filled out, and your Division Commander takes pride in having forwarded the same without change or revision.

3. The citation with your Distinguished Service Medal but feebly expresses our appreciation of what you have already done and our faith in your future.

The enlisted men of his regiment joined in the farewell from Vallendar in a letter signed by the three battalion sergeants-major and the headquarters company first sergeant:

1. On the eve of your departure from the Forty-seventh United States Infantry, we, the enlisted men of that regiment, desire to extend to you our most hearty and sincere appreciation for the great interest you have, at all times, shown in our welfare.

2. It has been, we feel, largely through the just treatment you have accorded the men of this regiment, that it has developed its high standard of efficiency, and well known "esprit de corps." We will indeed lose a friend.

3. Our heartiest wishes follow you to your new field of endeavor; may the same success be yours in the future that has attended you in the past.

Middleton left for Camp Benning on schedule. In mid-July, 1919, he sailed from Brest, where he and the Fourth Division had landed in May, 1918. He had sent the good word to Mrs. Middleton, at home with her aunt and uncle in Galveston, where she had spent most of the war. Mrs. Middleton met him in New York. After two days there they departed for Camp Benning by way of Washington and Atlanta.

Colonel and Mrs. Middleton boarded a Southern Railway train in Atlanta bound for Columbus, outside which lay Camp Benning. The run should have required five hours or so. Though it was due at 6 P.M., the train struggled into Columbus at 2 A.M., after a hotbox had immobilized it for half the night.

8   Back to Schools

COLUMBUS, Georgia, at 2 P.M. was not among the livelier Southern cities. But at 2 A.M. no sign of life showed on the streets or at the Southern Railway station. A lone Negro sat sleeping, his back against the station wall. Colonel Middleton looked up the street and saw a sign: RALSTON HOTEL. He tapped the sleeping Negro on the sole of his shoe and inquired about the accommodations in the Ralston Hotel. "Boss," he was assured, "that's the best hotel in Georgia."

The best hotel it wasn't. But it became home to the Middletons, whose registration was extended again and again. They lived in the Ralston more than a year. There was nowhere else to go in Columbus, a city of 31,000, overflowing with student officers being trained out at Camp Benning, nine miles southwest of town. Middleton was assigned as one of the instructors in the school that was being organized.

"Benning was a horrible place," Middleton recalled. "You rode a train out there and back each day or traveled nine miles on a dirt road." To soldiers used to the relative comforts of posts like Fort Leavenworth, Fort Crockett, and Fort Myer, Camp Benning could hardly have been more primitive. A few frame buildings remained on what had been an old plantation. The school troops and one infantry regiment, the Twenty-ninth, Middleton's old regiment at Fort Porter, lived not in barracks but in tent camps. If Fort Crockett and Galveston had been sandy, at least they had been swept by breezes from the Gulf of Mexico the year round. Benning was sandy, too. Marching troops had to take three steps to gain two.

78

In summer's heat, after a mile on the march, troops at Benning looked as if they had been lightly stuccoed; sweat bonded sand to their uniforms.

With every other officer promoted in 1918, Troy Middleton reverted several grades upon return to peacetime duty. From youngest colonel in the army, he became captain, his permanent rank. The same stepping down took away eagles and oak leaves from hundreds of others.

Captain Middleton spent a year at Benning as a teacher and member of a new organization called the Infantry Board. The infantry had been the army stepchild until the World War. The Infantry Board was set up as a research organization, to hear, review, and accept or reject ideas about warfare. Some were good, most were not. But anyone who came along with a suggestion was given a hearing.

"One of the most productive things I did with the Infantry Board was to work with a civilian ordnance man named J. C. Garand," Middleton recalled. Garand was working on a semiautomatic rifle which became the standard infantry weapon of Americans in World War II. Middleton fired hundreds of rounds from what was to become the M-1 rifle. The weapon was fired in the rain, in heat and cold, after immersion in water and deep dunking in the gritty Benning mud.

Other branches of the service had long had their schools: the cavalry at Fort Riley, Kansas, the field artillery at Fort Sill. Before the World War, the best the infantry could claim was a so-called weapons school (School of Arms) at Fort Sill. The Infantry School, whose faculty Middleton joined at Camp (later Fort) Benning, soon became the best of the lot and remains the best of the branch schools in the army. Here, after seeing officers from other branches mishandle the infantry in France, combat-veteran infantry commanders taught combat lessons rather than school doctrine.

When he joined the Infantry School faculty in July, 1919, the school was a notion and little more. For the first month, the faculty chewed the fat, finding little or nothing to do. "Brigadier General Harold B. Fiske, something of a martinet but a good school man, asked me for some recommendations for the faculty. I gave him some names from among my comrades in the Fourth Division. Every man he chose served well. These men had come home with the division in August. So many Fourth Division men turned up on the faculty that the word got round that 'This is a damned Fourth Division school.' Maybe it was," Middleton recalled.

The Benning "campus" covered 100,000 acres, taking in a number of small farms along with the old Benning plantation on the Chattahoochee River. Government condemnation proceedings brought all the acreage together before the end of World War I, but only the commanding general's quarters would have reminded anyone of the southern plantation heritage. Set in beautiful oaks and gums, the commander's home emphasized the squalor of the rest of the raw camp.

Once the faculty knew what was wanted of it, the work began to flow. They devised a curriculum. Where were the textbooks? The faculty wrote a shelf full of manuals. They called for a move away from too-heavy dependence on the rifle and pistol to the use of automatic weapons and the employment of combined arms to support the infantry, the ground winner and ground holder without which all the other branches would lose their protection.

The commandant of the Infantry School was charged with the administration and housekeeping details of the operation. The assistant commandant had charge of instruction. With a great flurry of ideas coming in, the Infantry Board kept busy all the time. Middleton was the junior member of the board. When J. C. Garand learned of the creation of the board he brought his rifle over for evaluation. Other, less successful weapons were proposed to the board. Since many of the Infantry School faculty had attended schools in Europe in preparation for American involvement in combat, the cross-fertilization was valuable. Foreign officers shortly began seeking the opportunity to attend the Infantry School at Benning.

First, though, there had to be a school. Classes for the first nine-month term began in September, 1919. Some of the students had been in combat and had pointed comments on their experiences. The school was set up to meet the needs of three groups: field grade officers, company officers, and basics, largely second lieutenants fresh from the Military Academy.

"We gave everybody a refresher course in infantry weapons to start. Then we served up tactics for units from company through division size. We gave them a little on the company, more on the battalion and the regiment, and some on the division—all of this emphasizing employment of combined arms. We had little in the way of air power to show, but we flew a few planes to show the students what they could do. I was reminded of what had happened to the adjacent regiment back in France one day when a lone German flyer went over, strafed our men in the open, and, on a lucky hit with his bombs dropped blind into a wood, killed or wounded hundreds of Americans. We couldn't ignore the air arm after what we saw in France," Middleton recalled.

The company officers' curriculum put each student in turn in command of a platoon, a company, a battalion. The basic curriculum put every infantry weapon in the hands of every student. He had to qualify on the range and become proficient in the tactics of platoon and company. He had to take his turn as a scout and a patrol leader and member, and at least become familiar with night operations. (Night operations were to become much more standard in World War II; little fighting went on involving the infantry at night in World War I.) The student learned how to use the mortar to stick a little high-flying bomb down the throat of an enemy as close as one hundred yards or half a mile away. He was taught how machine guns, positioned so they could deliver enfilading fire, could stitch up an enemy patrol or cut down a hostile company. The rifle became something more than a weapon to be fired when an enemy was sighted. Middleton recalled how devastating the rifle had been in the Bois de Foret, when it seemed to the German defenders that the noise of grazing rifle fire would drive them out of their minds. The young German lieutenant who had interrupted Colonel Middleton's "Mississippi German" to ask him to speak English, after the lieutenant and scores of others surrendered, came back to Captain Middleton at the Infantry School. The retelling of this experience made a deep impression on his students and, with other qualities, marked him as the ideal teaching man.

No student or faculty member at the Infantry School in 1919–1923 could have made it through without meeting "Calculator." Calculator was a black and white, mixed breed, pot hound, privileged to go where he pleased, leave when he wanted to, and to confer his friendship on a select number. One of Calculator's legs had been hurt when he tangled with an automobile on the post at Benning. He walked on all four feet, but when he was in a hurry he put down three feet and carried one. It was inevitable that a soldier would remark this peculiarity with a name as appropriate as "Calculator." He rode the narrow gauge train which transported students and school troops from the barracks area to the wide open expanses where their field problems were run off. Calculator walked over the problem areas with the instructors when they were setting up tactical problems.

"Watch Calculator," students were advised by other students; "which way did Calculator go? Envelop that flank if he went that way."

"He was the smartest dog I ever saw," Middleton recalled. "A shuttle train ran from Columbus to Benning. When the train left for Columbus at noon on Saturday, Calculator was aboard. He spent Saturday afternoon in Columbus but at five o'clock he'd be there at the station to ride back to the post. He also learned to bum automobile rides at the Benning post office. He alternated between cars and the train. After we acquired quarters on the post, he would scratch at our back door two or three times a month. I'd let him in the kitchen; he'd eat, then scratch on the door to be let out. He slept in his choice of the school buildings."

When old Calculator had made his last run at Benning, word of his death went round in a circular inviting his officer friends and acquaintances to contribute to a monument in his memory. That monument stands in front of the Infantry Building on the main post at Fort Benning. Many an officer owed gratitude to Calculator for his having pointed the way to the correct tactical decision out on the banks of Upatoi Creek or the Chattahoochee River.

On the train between Benning and Columbus, some officers played bridge, a game which Middleton never played with much eagerness. Major Franklin C. Sibert carried a lap board onto each train in expectation of promoting a game. If sight of his board did not bring contestants, he'd go down the coach aisle recruiting them. Major Sibert had commanded a machine gun battalion in the Fourth Division in France. When he was stationed in Remagen with Middleton during the occupation of Germany, he wouldn't play bridge with the junior officers but would drive ten miles to Adenau for a game. But Middleton didn't care for bridge, "particularly playing for money." Characteristically he said, "My mistake could affect others. I wanted to pay for my mistakes but not to have others pay for mine or to pay for theirs. Besides, I saw too much time wasted on bridge, which was just a game."

At the Infantry School, Middleton was in charge of night operations. General Fiske went out regularly with him. "Anyone who could look ahead to air developments knew you'd have to go under cover," Middleton recalled. "The only way to do that was to operate at night." He recalled two incidents illustrating the threat of air power. One involved an American whose name he remembered as Luke Lee. Lee was looked upon by groundlings as either a brave man or a monstrous coward who remained above ordinary infantry combat. Lee had shot down a German plane in Middleton's sight, landed his plane, and cut the insignia off the German plane in a clearing north of Verdun in the Meuse-Argonne area. This convinced the men on the ground that Lee was indeed a brave man. He later received the Medal of Honor and was subsequently killed in action. The other incident involved a German pilot in July, 1918, on the Vesle River between Soissons and Reims. "That pilot in his little black plane came down the line, weaving over and under, shooting at American artillery observers in their baskets under balloons. He missed them all, but several observers bailed out rather than risk being targets on a second run. The other balloons were quickly winched back to the ground. That convinced me that planes were more than just nuisances."

The Infantry School acquired its own modest air detachment. Most students had never been in an airplane. Some didn't relish the prospect, but everybody took at least one ride. Planes were used in connection with various firing problems. And there were no plane accidents while Middleton was there, perhaps because they flew only in good weather.

"After I had been at Benning on the faculty from September, 1919, through June, 1921, it looked as if I'd be leaving there without having a chance to earn a diploma. I prevailed on the commandant to let me enroll in the advanced course in September, 1921. In the advanced course Middleton was joined by other former faculty members. The class totaled ninety-five officers in grades from captain to colonel. Middleton had become a major again as of July 1, 1920. He saw himself as a very junior major among mostly older officers. The ten-month course covered not only the infantry but the combined arms, tactical principles and decisions, military history, and economics. In addition, everyone had to write a thesis— to some extent paralleling graduate work in a good college. Middleton was graduated with an overall average of 95 percent in all his work and with the rank of number one in his class. "I believe it was the first time I'd ever been number one, except for the fact that I had been the youngest colonel in the army in the World War," he recalled.

At Fort Benning, Captain Middleton's efficiency report (the army's form of grading), prepared by Major Fiske, scored Middleton superior in every capacity. Major L. M. Nuttman appended a note: "Believe he should be rated as average in physical energy and endurance. Agree with other ratings as he is a remarkably fine officer."

Middleton had come to the Infantry School with even more note-worthy efficiency ratings, prepared in September, 1919, by Colonel Robert H. Peck of the Eleventh Infantry and by Brigadier General B. A. Poore of the Fourth Division. General Poore wrote of Middleton: "The best all-around officer I have yet seen. Unspoiled by his rapid promotion from captain in July to colonel in October; and made good in every grade. He gets better results in a quiet unobtrusive way than any officer I have ever met. Has a wonderful grasp of situations and a fine sense of proportion."

Colonel Peck wrote: "Although this officer is not a graduate of the service schools, he got results in every task he undertook that showed great ability to grasp situations. I recommended his promotion from junior major to lieutenant colonel to colonel. This officer spent most of his time inspecting the front lines, and insured the proper performance by our less experienced officers and men." It might be inferred from Colonel Peck's concessive clause—"Although this officer is not a graduate of the service schools, he got results"—that this represented a deficiency in Middleton's preparation for duty as a combat leader. It is more likely true that combat leader Middleton "got results" because he had not attended the usual service schools. He had not learned the older doctrines. His decision in the Bois de Foret to order his regiment to deliver steady marching fire that overwhelmed the Germans, safe though they were in their holes, wasn't taught in any service school.

Major Nuttman's reservation about Middleton's physical energy and endurance showed up in a World War II general's rating of Middleton. Apparently the second writer, too, expected an officer to be always on tiptoe. He'd have earned a quick rebuttal from the American commander in World War II, who valued Middleton's calm as one of his great assets. Dwight Eisenhower only wished Middleton's calm could have been communicated readily to some of his fellow corps and division commanders who reacted with great energy but considerably poorer military sense at crucial times in 1944 and 1945.

Before he left the Infantry School, after three years there as an organizer, first faculty, and star student, Middleton reviewed the lessons he had learned in France and had tried to transmit to his students after the war.

He dwelt on the necessity of careful reconnaissance and regular visits to the front lines. He recalled his unit's first action at Sergy, during which he and his men watched the 165th Infantry launch a parade ground attack, advancing in a line, "with the result that the Germans shot the hell out of them." He recalled seeing his first combat aircraft there, too, Germans who dropped small bombs on his unit in a wheat field without doing any damage.

He summarized for himself and his students these lessons:

1. You can't advance against enemy ground troops with machine guns and mortars, without covering fire. You move one unit, then you must cover it with fire from another unit.

2. You must use all cover. Infiltrate forward. Find the enemy's weakness; move in. Hit him from the flank or rear of his strong points; the object is to kill or capture men.

3. Always seek the observation. Take the enemy-held ground from which he is looking down on you.

4. With the untrained troops we Americans had, officers had to be up front directing or risk bogging down at the start. Officers learned only if they got out and looked around.

5. I learned the tremendous value of fire power. Marching fire demoralized the Germans in the Bois de Foret. I never forgot that. The 37-millimeter gun and the mortar proved extremely useful.

6. I learned that you can't count heavily on artillery. It is good for support but your own infantry weapons have to be used well. Fire and movement has to be worked out. No soldier should be moving forward unless he is covered by fire. Look for enemy weak points. Try never to take an enemy position in frontal assault. It demoralizes an enemy when he hears that "the enemy is in our rear." I had never heard the word "infiltration" before the World War. If you can move your troops back among the enemy, you'll confuse him. We didn't do much of this in the World War. We had been taught to move a squad forward in a rush, to have them fall down, then to have another squad rush forward. It proved much better to have the men wriggle into position.

7. There's absolutely no substitute for experience. I found that untrained American soldiers were overly brave. We had a lot of unnecessary casualties. Instead of finding a hole and hiding for awhile, Americans would take chances and often suffered the consequences.

8. If the method you're using doesn't work, try something else. The fellow who wrote the book couldn't think of everything.

While Middleton was still a student in the advanced course at the Infantry School, on Friday, January 25, 1922, Troy Houston Middleton, Jr., was born at the Middleton's apartment in Columbus. Shortly after graduation from the course in June, Middleton received orders to proceed to Fort Sam Houston, at San Antonio. When he arrived there he was told not to unpack but to turn around and head for a Reserve Officers Training Camp at Fort Logan, Colorado, where he would be senior instructor. The three Middletons found Colorado's climate delightful that summer.

General Benjamin A. Poore, who commanded the Seventh Brigade of the Fourth Division in France, put in the call for Middleton that sent the family to Colorado for the summer. Middleton drew part of his faculty from the Command and General Staff School at Fort Leavenworth. A National Guard unit came in for instruction. Reserve officers, most of whom had had war service, rounded out the student body.

In September, the Middletons returned to Fort Benning, where he spent a year as a member of the Infantry Board, doing more research into infantry weapons and better uses of the combined arms of the army. Many of Middleton's classmates who had been graduated with him in June had been sent to the Command and General Staff School. He wasn't happy at seeing them go while he moved into his fourth year at Fort Benning.

Major General Walter H. Gordon had taken command of Fort Benning. Major General C. S. Farnsworth had been appointed Chief of Infantry in Washington. General Farnsworth made several trips to Benning, out of his interest in the Infantry School. He and Middleton became friends. Farnsworth asked Middleton to come to Washington to tell students in the Army War College about the school's operations at Benning. In his lecture at the college, March 7, 1923, Middleton described the current state of "Infantry and Its Weapons."

If conducted properly, the Special Service Schools will send intelligent teachers to the next war. In order that the lessons learned in the past war may be carried to the army of tomorrow, that the lives expended may not have been expended in vain, but expended in teaching lessons that will save lives hereafter, it behooves those teachers to make careful and thorough studies of past wars. Nothing demands a higher class of personnel than does teaching at our service schools. Foundations, the soundness of which only a war can test, are being laid in these schools today. If in laying these foundations, we make mistakes, these mistakes will not be discovered until lives have been expended. Men responsible for improper leadership are guilty of a serious crime. None but officers of unusual and proven ability should be entrusted with the teaching of others at these schools.

In a war of any magnitude we will find the battalion and lesser units composed of and commanded by young men. The efficiency of the divisions will be greatly dependent upon the efficiency of the small units. They are the ones that will largely determine where the front line will rest at night. One cannot do better than to resolve that all effort will be constantly directed toward the improvement of these units. Let none go poorly clad, hungry, or improperly equipped so long as a wheel can turn in the rear of the line. The accomplishments of the small units will be written in history as the accomplishments of the superior; the senior officers will largely depend upon the efforts put forth by the junior.

While he was in Washington as a guest of the Farnsworths, Middleton confided to Mrs. Farnsworth his disappointment at being held on at Fort Benning—perhaps for as long as another three-year term. Mrs. Farnsworth agreed. She went further and volunteered to put in a word for Middleton with her husband.

"General Farnsworth took me to the train next day for the return trip to Georgia. Standing there in the deep snow at the station, he turned to me and said, 'Middleton, I think I'll send you to Command and General Staff School.' He was as good as his word," Middleton recalled.

The year went along more pleasantly after the winter lecture at the Army War College. The Middletons were moving to the next school in the army's ladder climb. The three of them went to Fort Leavenworth in September, 1923. Troy had been there before, in the summer of 1912 to prepare for the test that led to his being commissioned as a second lieutenant, to play football against Courthouse Lee's rugged engineers, before the whole post was all but buttoned up while everyone was sent off to Galveston.

While the Middletons were at Benning, living at the Ralston Hotel in downtown Columbus, they did their banking on the post at Benning. "When we'd been in town about a week," Middleton recalled, "a fat man came up to me in the bank and invited Mrs. Middleton and me to a party the bank was giving at the Muscogee Club, right up the street from our hotel. We went to the party, arriving at the specified time. We were the first couple there, not having become accustomed to the fashionability of being late. As we stood around, along came another fat man. I told him, 'I'm looking for a fat man who invited us to this party.' 'Oh,' he said, 'you aren't looking for that fat man, you're looking for me. I'm giving the party. Name's Rhodes Brown, president of the First National Bank.' He really was fat, but a good host. At the party we met Mr. and Mrs. Ernest Dismukes, owners of the largest insurance business in town, as well as widespread textile mill interests. We became fast friends. The Dismukes became godparents to Troy, Jr., when he was born."

Before they left Benning, Middleton recalled that an acquaintance asked, "You got any money?" Middleton said, "No." The acquaintance said, "Go borrow some." "What for?" Middleton asked. "To buy Coca-Cola stock," he was told. "I didn't have the money—even the few hundred it would have taken to buy enough stock to make us rich for life," he recalled.

At Benning, the Middletons acquired their second automobile. It was a Sayers Six (manufactured by Sayers-Scovill, a company which also built hearses). Inflation had jacked up prices, all right. The Sayers cost $1,800. A Ford now went for $1,100. "Cars were hard to find in 1920. We looked at an Oldsmobile, but it had a wooden body," Middleton recalled.

They bought a third automobile in 1922. After receiving orders to report to Fort Sam Houston, the Middletons decided to sell their Sayers Six rather than drive it to San Antonio. "The roads were so bad, the trip would have ruined the car," Middleton recalled. "Rather than ship the car to San Antonio from Columbus, we sold it for $1,200. The Middletons were sent to Fort Logan, Colorado, for the summer and then sent back to Benning for service on the Infantry Board. They bought another Ford touring car, which gave good service at Benning and around Columbus. Then came the orders to Command and General Staff School at Fort Leavenworth.

They shipped the Ford by rail to Leavenworth. In the box car en route another automobile broke loose from its fastenings, rolled back and forth much of the journey, jamming the back seat of the Middletons' Ford almost up under the dashboard. The Ford people in Leavenworth fixed it up. The railroad and the government made good the damage to the car. The Middletons drove it several years.

At Leavenworth, Middleton almost lost this car for the winter. After he became a faculty member at the Command and General Staff School, one night he had to go from his residence to a classroom building in a heavy snow. "I drove six blocks to the building, parked, and went in. Hours later I left, forgetting the car. Next morning it wasn't in the garage. Finally I remembered where I'd left it. After twelve hours of blizzard, it was all but out of sight in a snowbank. That was the first time I was ever accused of being an absent-minded professor—and I suppose I must have deserved it," he recalled.

9 First Student, Then Faculty

ONE OF the youngest majors in the army, Middleton found himself among majors, lieutenant colonels, and colonels from ten to fifteen years his senior in the student body of the Command and General Staff School in September, 1923. As the youngest colonel in France he had found that older officers were reserved in his presence, as if they resented great competence in a man twenty to twenty-five years younger than they.

The scorekeepers on the Command and General Staff School faculty were not so much interested in a man's age as in his ability to do the demanding work of the ten-month course. The students here were qualifying to move on to higher commands. Most of the 1923–1924 student body did move to higher commands.

Middleton met one classmate again and again later—George Patton. After Command and General Staff School at Leavenworth, Middleton saw Patton next in Hawaii, then in North Africa, Sicily, France, Belgium, Luxembourg, and Germany.

George Patton and Troy Middleton became friends. They regularly went for walks together. Leaning into a snowstorm one day, Patton said, "Troy, I'm going to be an honor graduate in this class." Middleton, several years younger, kept his predictions to himself. In a class which usually had about two hundred students, the top 25 percent were designated honor graduates; the next 25 percent, distinguished graduates; the remainder, graduates. They represented all the arms of the service. Patton guessed right. He ranked fourteenth. Middleton stood eighth in the class.

Patton, born to wealth and married to a wealthy woman, cut something of a figure at Leavenworth. "He was always turned out perfectly and, being a cavalryman, rode the finest mounts when he had the opportunity. In fact, he rode better horses than the army could afford to supply him. George liked polo, so he bought enough ponies for a team. After giving the matter a little more thought he turned around and bought enough ponies for another team, since few army officers were well off enough to afford any kind of horse. George played polo with great confidence, just as he had confidently predicted a high rank for himself in the school at Leavenworth," Middleton recalled.

Most important of the courses at Leavenworth was Tactical Principles and Decisions. Working from the Gettysburg map, the student was required to make a decision and write an order supporting it. One of Middleton's fellow students had been graduated first in his class at West Point. His first grade on a problem in Tactical Principles and Decisions was an F. He studied it for a long minute, then turned to Middleton and said, "Well, I'll be damned; I'd better study, hadn't I?" He did, graduating third in the Leavenworth class.

"The infantry had arrived by this time," Middleton recalled. "From last preference among second lieutenants in 1915, the infantry had climbed to the top. In my class were three who had ranked number one in the Infantry School; two of them were honor graduates at Leavenworth, and the other a distinguished graduate. In earlier classes, infantrymen had done reasonably well; now they became pace setters."

Graduating from Leavenworth in June, 1924, Middleton was invited to stay on for another four years as a member of the faculty. "I didn't even know I was under consideration and I certainly wouldn't have sought an appointment to the faculty," Middleton said. With half a dozen classmates he moved over from student officer quarters to a comfortable, two-story home of his own, where he and Mrs. Middleton and Troy, Jr., found life on the post agreeable and busy.

Middleton was good at teaching. He had been on the faculty for two years at the Infantry School at Fort Benning. Beyond that, as commander of a platoon, company, battalion, and regiment, he had taught—and helped his students to learn—lessons which would mean survival or death for the attentive or the inattentive—and the fortunate. In one of his classes he came to the inevitable student who goes off to sleep immediately after overeating at lunch. Middleton's attention was drawn to an officer whose chin had settled slowly to his chest. Calling the student by name—and enunciating in an exaggerated drawl to give the fellow time to be awakened and to gather his wits—Middleton was met with "Uh, uh, I was about to ask you that same question, sir." The laughter awakened anyone else who might have overeaten that noon.

Dwight D. Eisenhower was a student in the 1925–1926 class at Leavenworth. Like Middleton, he was something of a maverick, who had not been to the usual service schools; in fact, Ike had not even been through the usual branch schools. He had been off in Panama serving as aide to General Fox Conner, a sage Mississippian who had coached Ike exceedingly well.

"Ike used to come to my office (we were always available to students). He would sit on a corner of my desk and pump me for information. He always asked the most practical questions. And he wasn't after information about tests; he wanted to know what a commander should do in combat situations—knowing that I had led a regiment in hard fighting in France," Middleton recalled. Eisenhower was graduated number one in his class.

Through the four classes Middleton taught from 1924 to 1928 came almost all the men who were to command divisions in Europe in World War II. At one time in World War II, every corps commander in Europe had been a student under Middleton at the Command and General Staff School.

With another faculty member, Middleton was in charge of instruction in employment of the infantry. In addition to being experts in the principal teaching field, every faculty member took a turn at other assignments. The instructor teams wrote complete problems and an approved solution for each. After the student submitted his solution to the problem, he found an approved solution in his box, to let him know how he'd done.

"I gave some students a better grade when they made a wrong decision but wrote better reasons for the decision and for the execution of it—better than I gave those who came up with 'right' decisions and poor execution. We put the emphasis on logic—and the punch behind it. I've seen some terribly vacillating executions. I can't recall any place where so much emphasis was placed on thinking. This country owes that school at Leavenworth a great debt; I can't think of any great military leaders who did not go through the Command and General Staff School," Middleton recalled.

"You hear there's nothing to the business of class standing. Well, don't believe it. You had to be good to stand high. General George Marshall, every time he had a choice of men to make, went to the roster of those classes. It didn't always follow that all the choices made good; poor health hurt the effectiveness of some. I wish we had an educational system in which we could develop thinking—teaching how to think a situation through to the likely end result," Middleton recalled. "Outside the military," he said, "I'm a great devotee of the generalist approach in education, of exercises in the powers of thought. With such a background the student can go out and do almost anything."

In every problem written for the course at Leavenworth the student was expected to come up with his recommendations for supply during the operation. Middleton recalled for his students how supply difficulties had hampered operation after operation in France. Rations, artillery support, ammunition had to move behind horses and mules if an operation was to be successful. (Though the motor truck and the automobile were becoming commonplace in civilian life, the army remained committed to four-footed beasts for most of its moves through the four years Middleton was on the faculty at Fort Leavenworth.) He remembered the great competitive spirit among units in keeping their horses and mules in prime shape. When elements of the Fourth Division moved from Meaux to combat at Sergy in 1918, a splendidly groomed and fed horse drew the battalion medical cart. Each company had a baggage wagon and a mess cart, each battalion had two carts, and the battalion commander rode a handsome iron gray mount.

He could have amplified his lectures at Leavenworth with other examples of the problems of supply. He recalled drawing gas masks from the British while his battalion was being broken in. The masks were big awkward things. But they were nothing compared to the trouble they made for a battalion commander who had to talk on the field telephone while wearing a gas mask. He was supplied with a large wooden box which he had to carry on his back to permit use of the telephone while he had his mask on.

Middleton recalled the difficulties which led the British to take away all the American-made Springfield rifles and to issue the Fourth Division the British Enfields. "Matter of ammunition supply, old chaps," the Americans had been told. And, he recalled, there were compounded difficulties when the Fourth Division was brought back together, turned in the British rifles for the American Springfields and ammunition—but kept the British-provided horse-drawn kitchens and medical carts.

Since the subject of automotive transport was occasionally being brought up in the classroom, Middleton could refer his students to his experiences with the automobile in France and Germany. His battalion was authorized a Dodge open touring car, which survived combat experience. As a regimental commander, he had problems with his car. A German artillery round, landing close by, knocked out the back end of the car, but didn't affect its riding qualities. Colonel Middleton had his doubts about the car, but his driver, Davis, reassured him: "Colonel, this car drives just fine. And we surely ought not to turn in the only car in France that carries its own wound stripes." They kept it.

Instructor Middleton could reach back into his own experiences for additional illustrative incidents, recalling how, after the Armistice, American commanders at regimental and higher levels were issued Cadillacs, price-tagged $1,800 and still in their wooden crates. Artillerymen at division level drew the top prize, however. They acquired a four-wheel-drive ammunition truck. "If you didn't know how to operate it, you got the front end going one way and the rear end going just the opposite way," he recalled.

Halfway through his second year on the faculty at Leavenworth, at noon on Thursday, January 21, 1926, the Middletons' second child, Bernice Collins Middleton, was born in the station hospital, right behind the Middleton home. Both Middleton and another member of the "marking committee" assigned to grade tactical problem papers, became fathers of daughters that day. After spending the morning at home with Troy, Jr., Major Middleton went back to grading papers that afternoon. Troy, Jr., four, had protested being left behind with a sitter when his mother went to the station hospital that morning. Mrs. Middleton solved the problem by asking Major Middleton to remain with Troy, Jr., while a private first class and his wife took her on to the hospital. Bernice was born at noon. When Middleton went to the hospital that night he found that Mrs. Middleton was identified as another soldier's wife; he told the attendants and they got the record straight.

Since his return from Germany, Middleton had spent two years on the Infantry School faculty, a year as a student, another year on the Infantry

Board at Benning, a year as a student and four years on the faculty of the Command and General Staff School at Leavenworth. One more year of school would give him a straight run of ten.

The War Department now had its eye on him, issuing orders February 15, 1928, that his next assignment was to attend the Army War College in Washington, as a student. At the War College, Middleton was again a quite junior major. Most of the officers on the climb up the army ladder were years his senior in that grade, and much his senior if they were lieutenant colonels or colonels. Here he spent ten months in the upper hierarchy. Most of the work, except for the thesis each student was required to write, was done by committees. There was no class standing. Assignments dealt with the larger problems of military command. Middleton was appointed commander of an army for the concluding problem of the year.

"This was a very satisfactory year," he recalled, "for the man who would really work. I spent quite a bit of my time in the library and particularly in the Library of Congress." As an instructor at the Infantry School he had been invited by the commandant, General Charles S. Farnsworth, to lecture to the War College on "Infantry and Its Weapons" in March, 1923. The lecture left a sharp and lingering impression. Middleton's thesis, submitted near the end of his term in the War College, likewise made a deep impression. Major General William D. Connor, the commandant in 1929, informed Middleton that his staff memorandum (the designation for a thesis) showed thoughtful study, careful analysis and preparation. The memorandum, by direction of the Chief of Staff, had been forwarded to the War Department for reference to the Operations and Training Division, the Supply Division, and the General Staff. Middleton was commended for work of exceptional merit.

What had the young major said to earn this commendation? His subject was "Proposed Reduction of Equipment and Transportation in the Infantry Division." In the covering memorandum, General Connor had noted that "Major Middleton's experience lets him speak with authority and his good judgment and common sense merit thoughtful consideration of his opinions." For a soldier who didn't like horses, who had passed up a crack at a cavalry assignment when he became a second lieutenant, Middleton, from the time he landed in France in 1918, had to work with horses and mules. It fell his lot to move the transport of the whole Fourth Division cross country by night from the Vesle River to the St. Mihiel sector. He brought if off without a hitch, though with great loss of sleep. He had to move a regiment 130 miles from Metz to Adenau, Germany, in fifteen days and did it, on horseback, to take up his occupation duties in Germany after the Armistice. Now his War College memorandum cut to the heart of the army's continued use, and overuse, of horses and mules. He recommended that each infantry division divest itself of—put out to pasture—655 riding horses, 1,053 draft and riding mules, 235 escort wagons, 61 bicycles, and 12 rolling kitchens. In place of these he prescribed 4 motor cars, 1 motorcycle, 103 trucks, and 8 trailer kitchens.

Long live the horse and his cannier companion the mule—in retirement!

In a review of changes since the World War, Middleton's thesis noted that though the World War division strength was 28,059 officers and men, the division on the move occupied 29.6 miles of road space. Ten years later, in 1928, division strength had been reduced by 8,284 officers and men to a total of 19,775. The road space requirement shrank but 1 mile. Middleton noted that the World War division required 6,636 animals to the much smaller division's 6,657, a gain of 21. The World War division had been fed from 104 rolling kitchens; the new division required 108. The World War infantry regiment had 3,832 officers and men and 390 animals. The new regiment, down to 3,106 officers and men, was allotted 492 animals.

"The question now arises," he wrote, "whether or not the transportation and equipment provided for the World War division was sufficient. Having served through our participation in the war in a combat division I was convinced that transportation and equipment was ample and that more would have been wasteful. I heard no complaint from officers and men on the insufficiency of equipment and transportation and I find nothing in the records to the contrary. It therefore follows that there is too much equipment and transportation in our infantry division; that we can dispense with some and that we can serve the ends of efficiency by replacing some of the remaining transportation by the motor. By a further reduction in equipment and transportation we can increase the flexibility and mobility of the division, releasing men for the firing line, and reducing the ever-increasing cost of maintenance."

He declared, in his conclusions:

The War Department has realized that the infantry division adopted in

1920 contained a surplus of equipment and transportation. Studies, recommendations, and approvals for the reduction of equipment and transportation in the infantry division have only begun to solve the problem; much remains to be accomplished.

The tendency of the various services appears to be that of one who zealously guards non-essentials: this is exemplified by the retention of mounts in the machine gun companies and the two mounts per officer in the artillery brigade. (Emphasis supplied by the author.)

The desire to reduce the road space of the infantry division by reducing the personnel more than eight thousand has been defeated by the lavish assignment of animal transportation and the failure to provide for the motor where it could be used with safety.

These were reasonable recommendations—worth adoption by the next fiscal year. Eventually they penetrated all the way to the top—but not until unridden mounts and surplus mules had eaten enough hay to carpet Nebraska and enough oats to roll a two-inch cover over Iowa.

While he was a student in the Army War College, Middleton once more found time for athletics. He had been retired from football in Germany in 1919, by order of the corps commander. At Fort Myer, he took up a more sedate sport, softball. The game was relatively new. Middleton saw his first softball game at Fort Myer. He promptly volunteered and became involved in competition among teams representing the War Department and the Fort Myer permanent party. They played with the usual complement of nine men plus two—not one—short fielders, using softballs and bats which were about the same as those in use four decades later. At age thirty-eight, Middleton found softball a satisfactory game for a man approaching his middle years.

10   Back to Benning, Then ROTC

AFTER writing his commendation of Troy Middleton's thesis on transportation of the infantry division, General Connor said farewell to Major Middleton with an efficiency report which rated him as "superior in all regards as a student at the Army War College."

Having completed the army's top school, where was Middleton to go next? The army at that time required an officer to spend part of his service with troops. By the summer of 1929 Middleton had been away from regular troop duty since he left the command of the Forty-seventh Infantry Regiment in Germany in mid-1919. If he had to go back to a battalion command, for which a major qualified, why not with the Twenty-ninth Infantry, the School Regiment, at Fort Benning?

Middleton requested this assignment. The War Department granted it. "Mrs. Middleton and I liked Columbus. We had a lot of friends there. Our only son was born there. His godparents lived there." Farewell then to Washington; hail, Columbus. The Middletons had been to a reception at the White House in December, 1928, with President and Mrs. Calvin Coolidge as their hosts. Troy, Jr., had entered the second grade. Life at Fort Myer had been pleasant. The major had had the opportunity to work with other prospective higher commanders. He had spent endless hours in the cool confines of the Library of Congress.

Fort Benning had matured and ripened in the six years since three Middletons had departed for a student year at the Command and General Staff School. Now four Middletons were returning to Benning. Columbus had grown from 31,000 past 41,000 and was reaching out toward Fort Benning. Automobiles stirred the dust and sand between town and the post where shuttle trains had previously run. The narrow gauge train still transported students at the Infantry School to and from problems on the banks of Upatoi Creek and the Chattahoochee River.

Middleton had wanted to return to Benning because he liked the school atmosphere. And, finally, he told himself, the Twenty-ninth Infantry as the School Regiment would be experimenting with anything new. He was assigned as commander of the First Battalion, the unit he served with as a newly enlisted private at Fort Porter back in 1910–1911. Lieutenant Colonel Thorne Strayer commanded the regiment at Fort Benning. As the school year drew toward a close, Middleton was informed that he would be going back to Washington to join the General Staff in the War Department. General King, who had been commandant of the Command and General Staff School when Middleton was on the faculty there, had requested Middleton's assignment to the G-3 Section. The assignment was confirmed. "Duty with the Twenty-ninth Infantry had purified me as far as service with troops was concerned," Middleton recalled. Then somebody in the War Department came up with another regulation, applicable to and unmet by Middleton: he hadn't had duty with a civilian component of the army, such as the National Guard, the Organized Reserve Corps, or the Reserve Officers Training Corps. He could not, he was told, take a General Staff assignment until he had met this requirement. "You might be a general someday and be handicapped without civilian contacts," he was told.

He was asked to state a preference. Make it ROTC duty, preferably with a college or university in the South, he requested. He had heard of three vacancies for professors of military science and tactics and commandant of cadets coming up at the University of Florida, Louisiana State University, and far out west at the University of Wyoming. He chose Louisiana State University, even though, as he said, "I knew nothing about LSU except that their 1908 football team beat Mississippi A & M about 48–0. I made the usual inquiry and apparently I was acceptable at LSU."

(Recalling that the current commandant at LSU was a Mississippi A & M man, he had written to LSU and asked the advice of the incumbent, who suggested that Middleton visit the LSU campus and call on the president, Thomas W. Atkinson. The Middletons took this advice. They stopped in at LSU on a trip to Galveston. President Atkinson welcomed this show of interest and assured Middleton that he would be pleased to have him join the LSU faculty.)

Middleton prepared to leave Fort Benning, where Colonel Strayer, his commanding officer, had written on his efficiency report: "The placidity and even-temperedness of this officer at all times serve to accent the initiative and force he possesses and mark him as a leader one wants to follow."

"On July 1, 1930, I loaded my wife and two children in a Ford car and reported to headquarters at Fort McPherson in Atlanta, as I had been instructed, en route to Louisiana State University. The commanding general there was General Frank McCoy, a distinguished, statesmanlike man. He said, 'Middleton, I'm delighted that you're going to Louisiana State University. The officer who preceded you there has not hit it off very well with the governor. I'm not saying whether I'd want the governor for my governor or not, but nevertheless he is the governor and he must be treated as such; therefore I expect you to recognize that fact when you get to Louisiana.' General McCoy could see that I was curious enough about the

Middleton as LSU's Commandant of Cadets, 1933

necessity of our taking the side trip to Atlanta instead of going straight from Columbus to Baton Rouge. He told me more about the Louisiana governor, Huey P. Long, who had received a German ship captain while he, the governor, was wearing pajamas," Middleton recalled.

What McCoy did not know was that Middleton's predecessor at LSU, Major William E. Brougher (who was graduated from Mississippi A & M a year after Middleton), was a first cousin of Charles P. Manship, publisher of the Baton Rouge *State-Times* and *Morning Advocate*, a strong critic of Governor Long and his dictatorial ways. Brougher, identifying with his cousin the publisher, went so far as to sign a letter to Governor Long, with " MOST RESPECTFULLY YOURS (not for the man you are but for the office you hold)." McCoy said, "You know, the governor didn't like that." Middleton replied, "Hell, I wouldn't have liked it, either."

The Middletons drove to Baton Rouge from Atlanta in two days, arriving on the LSU campus on the afternoon of July 3, 1930, and being assigned to the commandant's house at the heart of the campus. Brougher was not, however, in any great hurry to leave, so the Middletons had to wait several days to occupy their quarters.

After they moved in, Middleton, his curiosity somewhat stirred by General McCoy's briefing in Atlanta, decided to have a closer look at this Governor Long. He telephoned the governor's office in what is now called the Old State Capitol, telling his secretary, Miss Alice Lee Grosjean, that he would like to see the governor. Miss Grosjean said, "Come on down."

Middleton said, "Wait a minute, ma'am; this is just a social call. I don't want anything from the governor and I'm sure he doesn't want anything from me. I merely want to pay my respects."

"Oh," said Miss Grosjean, "come on down; he'll see you."

So Middleton went down to the capitol, through the rotunda, and into the secretary's office. Miss Grosjean said, "Just sit down out there; the Governor will see you in a little while; he's busy right now."

"I'd never seen Governor Long, but while I sat there waiting a gentleman in shirt sleeves passed through the rotunda in a hurry several times, with a hand in one pocket. It turned out that was Governor Long. Finally, the secretary said, 'The Governor will see you.' As I entered the door there were four gentlemen sitting in front of the Governor's desk. I thought that was a most unusual way to receive a man on a social call. But anyway, Governor Long jumped out of his chair, rushed toward me, put his arm around me, picked up a chair with his other hand, and said, 'Major, I'm awfully glad to see you here. I didn't like that fellow you're relieving.' He put my chair in line with the other four, which made five of us. Well, I could hardly say a word, because he did most of the talking. After four or five minutes, I stood up and said, 'Governor, I see you're busy. I merely dropped in to pay my respects.' He laughingly said, 'Oh, hell, Major, sit down. These are just four sons of bitches trying to get something out of me.' So, out of deference to him I sat down, but I made a mental note to find out who those other four men were. I was never able to identify two. One, it turned out, was the mayor of New Orleans, Robert Maestri, and the other was a minor politician from Winn Parish, O. K. Allen, who succeeded Huey as governor when Long became a U. S. senator. Anyway, that first meeting started a friendship with Huey Long," Middleton recalled.

Middleton had, in keeping with protocol, reported first to President Atkinson. He was received warmly by Atkinson, who was at the end of a three-year tenure in the presidency, during two years of which he had been acting president. After his visit to Atkinson's office, Middleton headed across campus to the military building.

On his way, he came abreast of a classroom building. In a ground floor classroom sat a teacher and some fifteen students in varying attitudes of somnolence. The teacher, seated at a small table at the front, read in a monotone from a book. Middleton entered the building, started down the hall, and was somehow drawn to the back door of the classroom. Here, he told himself, he was in the big leagues. What was big-league teaching like? Temptation took him nearer to the door. Then it overwhelmed him. He sidestepped neatly through the door, without, he thought, being detected by the teacher or the students. Taking a seat, he noted quickly that no education was going on. Those who weren't asleep gazed vacantly out the window or busied themselves at tasks unrelated to the instruction that was not being accomplished. A short sample was all Middleton needed. If this was big-league instruction, what minor leaguer was that pitching from the table at the front? He eased out the back door and continued on to the military building.

Several days later he was in conversation with Professor Charles W. Pipkin, a distinguished political scientist and scholar, who told Middleton that it had been reported to him that the major had committed a cardinal sin on the campus. Middleton asked what the sin was. Pipkin told him, "You entered a classroom without invitation or without permission of the instructor. That is never done on a university campus."

This perplexed Middleton. He admitted as much. Pipkin enlightened him about this curious folkway of the campus. Middleton apologized for his ignorance, both to Pipkin and, later, to the offended instructor. He had not, he assured both, intended to commit any offense. Nevertheless he remained puzzled. He could not remember ever having taught a class in the army or having been a student in a class in which there were not one or more officers monitoring the proceedings, whether they were evaluating the instructor or learning from a superior teacher. Standards of instruction were expected to be high in the Infantry School, at the Command and General Staff School, at the Army War College. They were high. Why, then, should a civilian classroom stand in such stark contrast? Who could call that higher education?

The Baton Rouge of 1930 to which the Middletons came was a city considerably smaller than Columbus, with a population of less than 30,000. This figure was misleading, however, in that the city limits were tightly drawn, with perhaps another 10,000 living within two miles of Third Street, the principal shopping area at that time. Louisiana State University had just completed its move from the old campus, where the state capitol now stands, to a 1,944-acre tract three miles south of the original downtown area. Between the new campus and downtown lay open country, with Highland Road linking campus and town. The first buildings were going up on Chimes Street, adjoining the campus on the north. Highland Road snaked through the campus and on out into open country to the south. A dormitory for women and the Pentagon Barracks for men students were the extent of campus housing. The commandant's house stood at the heart of things.

College campuses in 1930 and 1931 were reacting to the preachments of pacifism. Politicians were talking about how Uncle Sam had been made Uncle Sucker in the World War, about how the munitions makers had maneuvered the United States into a war it had no business joining, and other simplistic doctrines. The Reserve Officers Training Corps had come under attack on other campuses. Middleton arrived at LSU in time to meet this challenge. It came in the form of a letter, written by a corporal in the LSU

ROTC unit, W. Willeroy Wells, and addressed to Governor Long. Corporal Wells had brought the letter to Major Middleton's office, where he told the commandant, "I thought I owed you the courtesy of seeing this letter before I mail it to the governor."

Middleton read the letter, "hot enough to scorch the stationery," he recalled, demanding freedom from the involuntary servitude of compulsory ROTC. Middleton thanked Corporal Wells for his courtesy. He took a copy of the letter to President James Monroe Smith. The president read it and asked, "What do you want me to do about it?"

Middleton said, "Nothing. All I want is your support of my action. I'm going to call this young man in and let him out of the ROTC by resignation. I will approve his request and post it on the regimental bulletin board."

Corporal Wells came in response to Major Middleton's invitation. He wrote out his resignation. Middleton approved the request and posted it. In three days the former corporal came back.

"You have put me in a terrible position," he told Middleton.

Middleton replied, "You did it; I didn't."

"That cured that," Middleton said, recalling the incident some forty years later. "No more resignations were offered. Some seniors in the Cadet Corps were up in arms, wanting to ride Wells off the campus on a rail. Wells was a smart youngster, but handicapped by the impetuousness of youth. He complained further, 'You took unfair advantage of me.' I said, 'I gave you what you said you wanted—in writing.' I think that one incident with Corporal Wells did more than anything else to strengthen ROTC at LSU in my time."

Concurrently, Wells had written to the *Reveille*, signing it only with his initials:

The editorial appearing in the *Reveille* of December 19, and aimed at the popularization of military training fell somewhat short of its mark. Last week "War Made Easy" hit a little closer to it. But we haven't scored a bullseye yet. Let's get the correct range, aim at the little black spot, and fire away. Ready! Aim! Fire!

Compulsory military training should not be tolerated at Louisiana State University for the following reasons:

1. It is utterly medieval and a blatant denial of the ideals of democracy.
2. It is entirely foreign to the education policies of America.

3. It (the two-year compulsory course) does not adequately train men to serve in time of war.

4. It does not develop citizens who can live creatively by their own initiative.

5. It offers no courses in citizenship.

6. It is practically worthless as physical training.

7. It makes the youth of this nation look upon war as a normal part of life, in which they expect to take part; and this in the face of national legislation condemning war.

8. Its discipline is based upon the dominance of one will over the will of another.

9. It nurtures attitudes among students which are negative to absolute harmony between student body and authority.

10. It is a waste of time to those who do not intend to take the full four years and are not interested in it at all.

11. It is not, as many people think, made compulsory by the national government.

12. And LSU would not lose a nickel if it were made elective.

Is this bolshevism? If bolshevism is taking a stand against those elements of society which undermine American democracy, free education, constructive initiative, and international good will, then this is bolshevism. But we have always been taught by those who have given of their life's blood for the founding of this nation that to stand against these elements is not bolshevism, but patriotism! Patriotic students and faculty members, take your stand; the issue challenges you.

W. W. W.

Appearing in the February 27, 1931, issue of the *Reveille*, the letter's opening references were to editorials by editor Henry Grady Spencer dealing with the honorary military organization, Scabbard and Blade, and with girls in sponsors' uniforms who had taken to the drill field with the cadets. Letters on the subject kept coming until Spencer called a halt with the issue of March 27.

That was the end of the protest against involuntary servitude in the ranks of the ROTC at LSU in 1930 and 1931.

Middleton let it be known that he would be willing to talk to University classes, on invitation, on the role of the military in world affairs. One of his first invitations came from Charles Pipkin. Middleton, the *Reveille* reported, told the class in international relations that a military doctrine of preparedness was not advocacy of war-mindedness. He made a strong case for ROTC service. He was invited to other classes. Civic and other organizations in Baton Rouge invited Middleton to interpret the military to them.

Having learned the game of softball so well at the Army War College in 1928–1929, Middleton introduced the game at LSU, playing himself at age forty-two. W. I. Spencer, a sports writer for the Baton Rouge *Morning Advocate*, wrote disparagingly of the new game. "They'll be playing mumblety-peg next out at LSU," Spencer said.

When school opened in mid-September of Middleton's first year at LSU, another of his immediate problems was the Cadet Band. "LSU had a band of about 30 pieces and some of those were salvaged from the instruments discarded by the army when they were worn out. The university had a fine old gentleman in charge of the band, but he was also the groundskeeper. That was enough to keep him busy, the way things grow in Baton Rouge.

"Not long after the semester started I was sitting in my office in Thomas D. Boyd Hall with my back to the open window. Someone tapped me on the shoulder and said, 'How are you doing, Major?' I looked around and it was Governor Long. So I said, 'I'm doing all right.' Then I asked him, 'Are you alone?' He said, 'Oh, yeah, I travel alone; I just slipped out the back door.' So I said, 'Come on in and sit down.' And he replied, 'Oh, no, I'm too busy.' So we stood there and talked at the window. He asked, 'Can I do anything for you?' I said, 'Yes, how about giving me a band?' Just to have something to say; it had been on my mind."

Long said, "You know, that's not a bad idea. When I was campaigning, I had an 8-piece band that would make more damn noise than the one you've got out there." He said no more and moved on. Two or three days later he came into Middleton's office with a stranger. Long said, "Major, here's your new band leader."

"Why," Middleton replied, "Governor, does President Atkinson know anything about this?" Long answered, "The heck with the president —you and I are going to have a band out here. This is your new band leader." It was A. W. Wickboldt. "He was a good band leader," Middleton recalled; "he'd been a band leader in the Regular Army at one time."

Middleton went over to see President Atkinson. "He'd been having some heart trouble. He gulped another pill from his heavily supplied desk drawer. I said, 'Mr. President, I'm sorry that I got you into this. I did start it by just saying, 'How about giving me a band?' but I didn't have any idea he'd follow this up!"

"Well," said Atkinson, "go ahead and let me see what you come up with."

"So Mr. Wickboldt and I worked up a list for a band of 75 pieces. As money went those days, the cost of 75 instruments was rather staggering. I took the list over to the president. He took another pill and said. 'I don't know whether I can go along with that or not; I'll let you know.' So I went on back to the office."

"In a day or two Governor Long called and asked, 'How are you and Mr. Wickboldt getting along with that band?' I said, 'Oh, pretty well.' He said, 'You don't talk very enthusiastically.' I said, 'Well, the president's considering it.' He said, 'How large a band are you going to have?' I said, '75 pieces.' He said, 'Oh, no, that won't do! I want 250 pieces.' So I went back and told President Atkinson that, while he was puzzling over the 75. He had to take another pill. But anyway, we finally came up with a band with approximately 250 pieces. I doubt that some of the band members could really play their instruments, but at least they went through the motions and on parade you couldn't tell whether they were playing or not. But the uniforms and the instruments and all were something. It was a fine band. Mr. Wickboldt did a splendid job; it added a great deal to the Cadet Corps," Middleton recalled.

"Governor Long was not only interested in the band, but he loved the cadets—he liked the show. As everybody knows, he was somewhat interested in football, but the band and the cadets came first. The Reserve Officers Association of the United States was going to hold a convention in New Orleans late in the fall of 1930. Long called me and said, 'There's some kind of military organization going to meet down in New Orleans and they've asked me to make a speech. How about taking the Cadet Corps?' "

Middleton said, "Governor, that's quite an undertaking." Long replied, "Oh, don't worry; that's no undertaking. We'll load them on out at City Park on the L & A Railroad." Middleton said, "Well, you handle it with the president."

Apparently the governor didn't have much trouble with the president—a new one by this time, named James Monroe Smith. Middleton marched the cadets a mile over to City Park and loaded them on the train for New Orleans. Pete Couch was the ranking railroad official in charge. He had the private car of the Louisiana & Arkansas Railroad for the governor's use. Long invited Middleton and others to come back and sit with him. He read a magazine on the way to New Orleans. "He was," Middleton observed, "as sober as could be." The train arrived in New Orleans. Middleton formed the cadets and they paraded—with Governor Long at the head of the column. "He'd fuss at streetcar conductors and wave to this fellow and that along the line of march. He had a grand time," Middleton recalled. "We finally reached the disbanding point of the parade. The cadets had an order to be back at the L & A station by a certain hour. I went with the governor over to the St. Charles Hotel where he made an excellent speech to the Reserve Officers Association. By the time he finished, it was time to go back to the train. "Some time later I was in New Orleans and one of my friends I met on Canal Street said to me, 'That was a fine parade you had down here the other night, but wasn't old Huey drunk!' I said, 'You know, that's a funny thing. I was with that man every moment, and he didn't take a drink.' 'Well,' the friend said, 'if he wasn't drunk, he should have been.' That's how rumors get out on a person."

For Troy Middleton, "life at LSU was a fortunate thing. It gave me an insight into how civilians live. I had not been a real civilian since I went off to college as a preppie at age fourteen. In college I was a cadet. Then I went right into the army after graduation. It was quite a revelation, living on a metropolitan campus."

Serving as commandant, he was also professor of military science and tactics on a campus with a strong military tradition. LSU had begun as the Louisiana State Seminary of Learning and Military Academy; its first president (superintendent was the original title) was William Tecumseh Sherman.

Middleton alone taught the senior class until he was joined by Captain Lawrence (Biff) Jones in 1932. The commandant knew how deadly the straight lecture could be. He asked a great many questions, drawing his seniors into discussions that grew quite lively. He was able to deal with just about any problem involving combat decisions, thanks to his months in France. The seniors could see that here was a man who would always

"level" with them. In addition to teaching seniors and handling administrative chores, Middleton headed a staff of seven, including four other
officers.

In 1930–1931, LSU enrollment was 2,100. ROTC regimental
strength was 768 cadets. Walter Sullivan Richardson was cadet colonel.
Nine understrength companies and an undermanned military band answered roll call at drill periods. All able-bodied males, excepting former
Corporal Wells, were required to enroll in the ROTC for their freshman
and sophomore years. Juniors and seniors volunteered to continue if they
wanted to become candidates for commissions. During the year, thanks to
Governor Long's efforts, the Cadet Corps marched to the music of a greatly enlarged band.

Middleton not only commanded the military element, he was in
charge of campus discipline. He was responsible for the operation of the
campus police detachment. "I was pretty much father confessor; people
who wanted a job would come to me," he recalled. "The commandant in
that day had a great deal to do, and the authority to do it. At times I
thought I was also dean of women. I still had time to enjoy the friends
whom Mrs. Middleton and I and our children made, on the campus and in
Baton Rouge."

With Governor Long leading the interference, the Cadet Corps took
another trip in the fall of 1930. This was the customary excursion to the
State Fair in Shreveport for the Arkansas football game. Arkansas had
beaten LSU three years in a row and was confident of doing so again. Middleton marshaled his ROTC forces for the overnight run to Shreveport by
way of Vicksburg on the Yazoo and Mississippi Valley Railroad. The
cadets marched behind their augmented band down Texas Street with
Governor Long leading the parade. Arkansas scored first, but LSU won,
27–12. "I'll never forget that Arkansas team, the first I'd seen. They had
an enormous tackle, weighing 320 pounds, who made exaggerated arm
motions, as if he would destroy the man in front of him. He didn't do anything; he was so big and awkward he couldn't get out of his own way,"
Middleton recalled.

As the year moved along, the image of ROTC at LSU improved considerably. "At registration in September, 1930, the line at my desk was the
longest one in the building, made up of people wanting excuses from
ROTC. They said they had to work and do other things. I didn't give many

excuses. Instead, I sent excuse seekers to Dr. J. A. Tucker, the University physician, after I'd talked to him. He handed out few excuses. Some students thought they couldn't make the three drills weekly because they had jobs on campus; I talked to their deans and found them cooperative about rearranging work schedules, especially Dean J. G. Lee of the College of Agriculture.

"No football players were among the advanced cadets in ROTC. Coach Russ Cohen had been an artillery officer in the World War. Somehow he had soured on the military—or that was the impression that I got. I talked with him and told him it would be helpful if athletes went ahead into advanced ROTC.

"Later, Dean Frederick Beutel of the Law School said that he didn't want his students in the military organization. I had begun a practice of talking to sophomore military classes about advanced ROTC, telling the sophomores that they weren't wanted in the advanced course unless they really wanted to get in. Sophomores in pre-law, having been advised against entering the advanced ROTC, showed no great interest in signing up for the advanced course. So I took none of the pre-law group. They didn't like this. They protested so strenuously that word got around to Dean Beutel. He came to see me the next morning, wanting to know what was up and why his pre-law students were being discriminated against. I told him that if he advised his prospective students not to go into the advanced military course, we didn't wish to recruit against his advice. He changed his tune after that," Middleton recalled.

On the parade ground one day, Middleton noted that the cadets wore wrap leggings left over from the World War. He moved to get rid of the wrap leggings as quickly as the army could do so and put the cadets into trousers. Getting rid of the atrocious-looking leggings improved the looks of the corps. Not one cadet in ten could spiral the long khaki wool strips from knee to ankle with any degree of skill. Someone in every squad was soon trailing up to eight feet of legging moments after the band struck up for a parade.

To set the seniors properly apart from the rest of the cadets, Middleton authorized them to wear the elegant high boots which characterized the cavalry and were the envy of many enlisted men. The seniors jumped at the opportunity. Middleton recalled that Alfred Glassell, in a later class, sent to London for his $80 handcrafted boots. Glassell became Middleton's aide when he rejoined the army in 1942 and eventually took command of the Forty-fifth Division.

From time to time during his first year, Middleton let the seniors know that the quality of the ROTC depended on them. "I stood aside and let them run the show. 'It's your regiment, your battalion, your company, your platoon, your squad,' I told them. 'If you want the worst squad in the Cadet Corps, then it's your funeral.' Those seniors deserved all kinds of credit," he recalled.

Middleton saw a great deal of evidence of this rise in self-esteem among members of the Cadet Corps. A characteristic example was supplied later by Oma Bates, first sergeant of a company. With his fists, Bates whipped a troublesome cadet who had cursed a sergeant who put the troublemaker on report for visiting outside hours and for other infractions. First Sergeant Bates checked the condition of the offending cadet, found him little the worse for wear, then reported to Middleton what he had done. "I remonstrated mildly with Sergeant Bates, but didn't take any action against him," the commandant recalled. Perhaps he was remembering a soldier back in his days as a lieutenant, whom he had defended against a charge that he struck another soldier for calling the first soldier's captain an S.O.B. "Later, when I was trying to decide among four or five prospects for cadet colonel for 1933–1934, I remembered Bates's action. I chose him for cadet colonel. He became an outstanding combat commander in World War II."

Discipline was seldom perfunctory under Middleton. C. W. Kennedy, a student in September, 1934, recalled an incident which might have resulted in his being shipped home. "I had been working at the dairy, earning my meals, and living in the dairy barn on campus. Word had been put out that hazing on campus would cease. Several of us had been to Pender's (a popular restaurant where beverages were also served) and we came back pretty happy. We decided to discipline a double first cousin of mine for some reason. We whacked him right vigorously with a broomstick. Then the word got around and we were summoned to a meeting of the disciplinary committee, composed of President Smith, Dean Lee of the College of Agriculture, and Major Middleton. They punished us by having us trot along the legs of a large triangle for ten days. Major Middleton told me, 'If you'd had just one demerit you'd have been gone.' I'd been so busy at the dairy I hadn't had time to earn any demerits."

Middleton worked some variations on old themes, coming up with, "If you don't want to have to lick them, get them to join you." First Sergeant Richard Cadwallader, in charge of the Pentagon Barracks, ran into difficulty with a group of freshman football players who didn't take to military discipline. They were giving their cadet officers trouble. George (Gee) Mitchell, a stalwart guard on the freshman football team, big and rough, set in motion retaliatory action by the freshmen against their sergeants. Word of what was brewing was leaked to Middleton.

"I had Gee Mitchell summoned. He came to my house and we sipped lemonade together. I said I'd heard that trouble might be shaping up. Mitchell said he'd take care of it. Mitchell gathered the freshman football players, canceled their fight plans, and promised to take any objectors behind the barracks and beat the hell out of them," Middleton recalled.

Later, Mitchell asked for a bouncer's job at the Gym-Armory, where student dances were held. (They didn't speak of bouncers, preferring instead to refer to them as dance committeemen.) Perry Cole, dean of student affairs, declined to give Mitchell the job. Middleton intervened in Mitchell's behalf, telling Cole that, at five dollars a night, Mitchell was a great bargain. So he proved, intimidating even the most troublesome at the Saturday night dances.

Since Middleton's home was only a block from the Pentagon Barracks, he often walked over to the barracks in the evening for visits with the cadets. One evening as he strolled across the lawn outside the easternmost building of the Pentagon his attention was drawn to bobbing heads and what looked like an occasional brandished fist—although the fists were never tightly clenched. He moved in closer, then stepped up to the window, the ledge of which just came to eye level. Then he went round to the entrance and stepped quickly across the little foyer and into the room. The back of the current brandisher of a fist was turned to Middleton. "Jesus Christ!" exclaimed the brandisher. He bolted straight across the room and dived through the window, taking the screen with him. He left the dice on the floor and forty cents in change beside them. The student with the dice had looked back under his arm as he made ready for his roll and spotted the major. "Since I hadn't seen the fellow's face, because his back was to me, I couldn't say that I recognized him. And since his path of departure took him straight out the window, I couldn't make the identification. For all I knew, the dice might have belonged to the shooter, along with the few coins on the floor. Recalling my father's early admonition about crap-shooting not being a gentleman's game, I left the scene without further comment," Middleton remembered. The participants in the crap game heard nothing further about the incident.

Hair cutting—really, it was head shaving—of incoming freshmen had been a problem when Major Middleton arrived at LSU. President Atkinson asked Middleton to help him enforce an order forbidding the cutting of freshmen's hair. President Smith, coming in a few months later, turned over the full responsibility to Middleton. "I took care of it by issuing an order that all freshmen would have haircuts with the length not exceeding one inch. This took all the fun out of cutting their hair and ended our problem," Middleton recalled.

General Melvin Zais, who in 1973 commanded the Third U.S. Army area, was another LSU student whose military future might have been eclipsed in his freshman year, but for the intervention of Commandant Middleton.

Zais, an athlete from Massachusetts, had been recruited as a freshman football player. He got into disciplinary difficulties and appeared before Middleton. "I got him a job in the cafeteria after he said he'd just as soon be dismissed from school since he knew he'd lose his football scholarship. Zais took the cafeteria job and stayed the year. Then he went on to the University of New Hampshire, nearer home, was graduated and received a Regular Army commission," Middleton recalled.

General Zais remembered Middleton and recalled what a fortunate turn his life had taken in his freshman year at LSU, when Zais and the author met at the Army War College at a National Strategy Seminar in June, 1967.

General Zais again recalled his freshman year difficulties in a letter to Middleton in March, 1973, expressing his disappointment at being unable to attend dedication ceremonies for the Middleton Collection of Memorabilia.

Toward the end of Middleton's fourth year at LSU, when his tour of duty would normally have ended, he was visited by President Smith, who said, "I would like to have you stay another year. If you stay, would you be dean of men in addition to your other duties?"

"I said, 'I can't do that. In the first place, I couldn't stay without War

Department permission and second, I couldn't be dean of men without War Department permission,' " Middleton recalled.

Smith wouldn't be denied. "Would you stay if I get it fixed?" he asked.

Middleton replied, "Well, you've been good to me and the university has been good to me; I can't say no."

Smith put in the request to the War Department, getting Middleton's tour extended a year and gaining approval of the extraordinary request to have him serve also as dean of men "They got me cheap," Middleton recalled, "paying me $1,000 a year to serve as dean of men in addition to my other duties.

As Middleton's fifth year began to run out, Smith came back with another request. He told Middleton that he understood that officers with Middleton's length of service who served in the World War were eligible to retire.

"How about you retiring and staying in the house that you're in and becoming permanent dean of men?"

Middleton replied, "Dr. Smith, I can't do that. I'm an army man. I like this place, but I'd better go on back to service."

"Well," Smith said, "would you mind serving another year if I can get your term extended again?"

Middleton said, "That's almost unheard of—six years."

Smith came right back with, "I just don't want to make a change right now (he gave a good reason). Middleton agreed, and Smith persuaded the War Department to extend the tour one more year.

Middleton was promoted to lieutenant colonel on August 1, 1935. He went into his sixth year at LSU. As that year approached an end, Smith was back with one more suggestion: "Now, how about retiring and staying with us?"

Lieutenant Colonel Middleton said, "Doctor, let's not discuss that, because I'm going back to the service."

Smith asked, "Where are you going?"

Middleton replied, "I don't know yet; but it would be unfair to you and all concerned if I made this decision now."

So Middleton notified the War Department that, since he hadn't had any foreign service since 1919—and here it was July, 1935—it was time for him to be sent to foreign duty. He asked if he had a choice as to where he might go. Told that he did, he asked for the Philippine Islands, "because I'd never been there." He received orders to the Philippines, with an assignment as an assistant inspector general and headquarters in Manila. "This was a good area for an officer because it gave you an opportunity to find out something about all areas of the service," Middleton recalled.

The six years (a normal four plus two one-year extensions) at LSU were drawing to a close. Troy, Jr., was now nearly fourteen; Bernice was almost ten. Lieutenant Colonel Troy Middleton could look back on the satisfaction of having brought the ROTC unit back from the low point it had reached before his arrival at LSU.

Not all his work, however, had turned out so pleasantly. In his capacity as dean of men, he had had to sign letters of dismissal addressed to most of the staff members of the *Reveille*, who in November, 1934, became involved in a dispute with Senator Huey Long over the propriety of Long's having ordered the Louisiana senate to meet (the legislature was in one of Long's special sessions) to name Abe Mickal, the star quarterback on the football team, a state senator.

A student, D. R. Norman, wrote a letter to *Reveille* editor Jesse Cutrer, critical of Long's cavalier attitudes and especially his action in ordering the Louisiana Senate to make Mickal, a much embarrassed youngster, a state senator. The letter was polite. It made a good point. A copy of the editorial page of the *Reveille*, printed in the first run on the flatbed press at Ortlieb Press on St. Ferdinand Street, was taken from the print shop to the state capitol by a sophomore, Frank Cayce. Cayce took the half-printed pages to a senior, Dave McGuire, on duty at the special session of the legislature, where he represented the International News Service.

McGuire looked over the Norman letter with considerable interest. He and Cayce were talking about it when another reporter, Helen Gilkison, an admirer of Senator Long, came over to see what had excited their interest. She read the Norman letter and went running to Long with what she had seen. The senator was displeased and relayed his displeasure to President Smith at LSU. Smith in turn passed along word from the senator to Jesse Cutrer, the editor. A close relative of Cutrer was politically at outs with Long, so Cutrer diplomatically listened to reasons why the Norman letter should not be published, rather than involve the *Reveille* in a political dispute. He permitted its withdrawal from the editorial page. The page was remade and was reprinted so that that issue of the *Reveille* could appear on schedule.

The incident might have excited no great additional interest had not Long prevailed upon Smith to appoint Miss Gilkison to the journalism faculty at the university as a special lecturer with the responsibility of keeping a close eye on the *Reveille* and any possible further mentions of Long. Miss Gilkison let it be known to editor Cutrer that she would be inspecting the *Reveille's* columns before it went to press. Here, the patient Cutrer drew the line. He told Miss Gilkison that if she persisted in prereading what was to go into the *Reveille*, he would publish in bold type the fact that she had been appointed censor of the newspaper. Miss Gilkison backed away from so damning a label and agreed not to do what Smith had appointed her to do, at Long's urging.

A number of journalism students complained about the attempts at censorship of the *Reveille*. As the case heated up in discussions and in print in the Baton Rouge and New Orleans newspapers, the students went before a notary public and swore to a number of assertions of fact. It was for swearing to these assertions that the students were dismissed from the university, a disciplinary board having ruled that false swearing was occasion for dismissal. (The university's Board of Supervisors, after the scandals of 1939, on March 11, 1941, formally restored the dismissed students to good standing and apologized for the action of dismissal.) The dismissed students were offered academic shelter at several other universities and took up the offer of the University of Missouri, where they transferred with full credit and earned bachelor's degrees in journalism the next spring. LSU got a deserved black eye out of the incident. Troy Middleton, dean of men, had to sign the dismissal papers as a function of his office, but he did so, he said, "with great reluctance."

Other assignments were more pleasant. As LSU football fortunes turned upward, under the coaching of Captain Lawrence (Biff) Jones, also of the ROTC staff, Senator Long determined to show his Tigers the world, and the world, his Tigers. He proposed that the Cadet Corps accompany the football team to Nashville for a game with Vanderbilt University in October, 1934. The Vanderbilt coach was retiring that year after a long and highly successful career. Middleton was in Long's room the day the senator began negotiations with the Illinois Central Railroad for a bargain round trip fare for transportation of some 1,500 members of the Cadet Corps to Nashville. "I heard Huey say, 'I'll give you $6 a head.' Then the conversation abruptly ended. Huey paced back and forth, then went to the telephone and asked the operator to get him the man he had originally been talking to. Reconnected, they argued. Huey said, 'You haul gravel for the Highway Department, don't you? Well, you're through.' He banged down the telephone. Next morning he called me and said, 'We got the $6 rate; I guess the railroad wanted that gravel-hauling job.' "

"I later asked the Illinois Central man if his railroad had lost or made money on the trip to Nashville. He said they'd made a little but would have lost if there had been an accident or a delay," Middleton recalled.

The movement to Nashville involved four trains of fourteen cars each. One car carried the ladies, Mrs. Middleton, Mrs. Long, Mrs. Smith, and two or three newspaper reporters. Huey was offered a Pullman but declined, saying he'd ride like the boys. He didn't smoke and didn't permit smoking in the ladies' car on the round trip.

"I told Huey earlier that we could have trouble if liquor were permitted aboard the trains. He said there'd be none. There wasn't any. We had an officer in charge of each car on the four trains," Middleton recalled.

"We left Baton Rouge at ten-minute intervals, starting about 4 P.M. on Friday. The first section arrived in Nashville at 8 A.M. on Saturday.We went by way of Vicksburg and Memphis, stopping several times en route. At our Vicksburg stop, a number of people tried to board the trains. They were repulsed. Word must have gone up the line ahead of us, for no one tried to get aboard at our other stops. Refreshment cars in the middle of each train dispensed sandwiches, soft drinks, candy, and hot coffee."

Senator Long and the LSU Cadet Corps excited about equal comment as they paraded through downtown Nashville before the football game. LSU soundly whipped the Commodore football team, 29–0.

Troy Middleton's last trip with the Cadet Corps took them on five trains to Athens, Georgia, in November, 1935. Huey Long did not make this trip, having been assassinated at the state capitol in September. Of this man, about whom no one knowing him could remain neutral, Middleton said in recollection:

"Huey Long was one of the most unusual men I have ever known. He was quite advanced in his thinking. He could predict what was going to happen next year. There was no question about his love and desire for power. He was a terrific worker. I doubt that he ever just sat down. He was always talking or reading. I never saw him idle in six years of contact with him while I was commandant at LSU.

"He loved cadets, showmanship, bands, parades, marching—and football. He did not—as some thought—interfere with the educational mission of the university. I doubt that he knew a dozen faculty members. The incident of the dismissal of the *Reveille* staff could have been prevented, if I had been asked to go down and talk with Huey. Professor James Broussard, chairman of the LSU Athletic Council, simply went along with Huey. I could have talked Huey out of making that mistake with the *Reveille* if I had known what was going on.

"Louisiana was ripe for a man like Huey. He was a doer when this state needed a doer. Sometimes a doer will be wrong, but nevertheless he awakens in people something that is necessary to carry a state forward. LSU certainly was ripe for someone to move it forward. Huey gave it a building program that it needed. He had great vision. The times in which we now live prove the correctness of Huey's stands on so many questions.

"There is no question but that Huey Long would have sought the presidency of the United States. And he might have won it. I don't say that he should have been elected—but he could have been. I don't think anyone could have predicted Huey Long's future. He quit drinking and smoking. He went more heavily to biblical quotations in his private and public utterances. He was changing. Huey Long not only liked power but he displayed it. Though he became a United States senator, he continued to control the affairs of Louisiana. Governors who served while he was senator were merely carrying out his instructions," Middleton observed.

In Middleton's opinion, Governor O. K. Allen, under whom he completed his tenure as commandant of cadets at LSU, "was not well equipped for the governor's chair. He was put in by Huey. A nice man, a gentleman, he did no one harm. As an administrator, he was a man of quite limited ability. I didn't have much to do with Governor Allen, however, and these opinions were formed largely from sideline observations."

In the six years he served as commandant, Middleton saw the ROTC ranks swell from 500 who completed the 1930–1931 session to 1,711 in the 1935–1936 session. These figures, given in the *Gumbo* for those years, were appreciably more modest than the fall enrollments in the military, given in news stories in September, 1930, and September, 1935, as 768 and 2,502. The shrinkage was attributable not so much to the rigors of ROTC as to academic flunkouts and the normal attrition which reduced a student body by as much as 25 percent over the academic year.

The army complement at LSU increased from five officers and two noncommissioned officers in 1930 to six officers and three noncommissioned officers in 1935. The *Gumbo* noted that "The Corps of Cadets boasts of its largest enrollment this year, with a total of 1,711 cadets, as compared to 1,335 last year. The corps includes 85 seniors, 106 juniors, 561 sophomores, and 959 freshmen." A photograph made from the top of the Memorial Tower showed the corps in formation on the parade ground, stretching more than two blocks. The parade ground, bounded on the east by Highland Road, was framed in 1936 only by the Episcopal Student Center and Chapel at Highland and Dalrymple Drive and by great open spaces to the east. ROTC was a genuine focal activity for students. Under Middleton, it became a desirable, almost fashionable, activity.

The student cadet colonels of that era, along with the student officers under their command, produced some sterling combat commanders in World War II. The cadets were: 1930–1931, Walter Sullivan Richardson; 1931–1932, Claude O. Stephens; 1932–1933, J. B. Heroman, Jr.; 1933–1934, Oma R. Bates; 1934–1935, George S. Bowman, Jr.; and 1935–1936, Abe Mickal.

The 1936 *Gumbo*, in a page of tribute facing a full page picture of Middleton, said:

For six years Lieutenant Colonel Middleton has given outstanding service to Louisiana State University as Commandant of Cadets and Dean of Men. He has been with the University through the most important years of its existence and has labored unceasingly to aid in the tremendous expansion during this time. Under his guidance the military has almost tripled in size and has constantly maintained a national rating of "excellent."

The countless improvements that have come about through the direct influence of Lieutenant Colonel Middleton will insure his memory at LSU. Physical evidences of his worth are many. But like a beacon-light shining forever as a guide to the youth who have felt its glow is the personality of the man himself. More than a soldier he is a leader with those characteristics that bind his followers closely to him. More than a teacher, he is a friend to whom the students can turn for advice in any problem. His rare gift of understanding, his unending patience, and his ability to inspire others to greater achievement are traits that will always endear him to the students of Louisiana State University.

11   Back to LSU
by Way of the Philippines

$\mathbf{T}$ROY MIDDLETON and his family had been in Baton
Rouge six years, longer than he had stayed in one place since he left the
plantation near Georgetown for Mississippi A & M. Since Troy, Jr., was
born in Columbus, the family had lived at Fort Leavenworth, where Bernice was born, at Fort Myer in Washington, back at Fort Benning. Now
the four were heading east to go west, halfway around the planet to Manila,
Philippine Islands.

The family departed August 15, 1936, in a Dodge sedan bound for
New York City. Army transportation experts had figured the costs closely.
The government would save money by sending the Middletons to New
York, where they would board an army transport. They would go through
the Panama Canal and up the Pacific coast to San Francisco and on to the
Philippines by way of Hawaii and Guam. Following their leisurely drive to
New York, the Middletons were aboard the transport forty-two days. They
stopped two days in Panama, a week in San Francisco, two days in Hawaii,
and one day in Guam.

In Honolulu their transport had just been made fast at the wharf
when a couple looking like burned Indians came aboard. It was George and
Bea Patton, greeting the incoming passengers. Middleton said, "George,
you sure look weatherbeaten. What's happened?"

George was on duty with the Hawaiian Department headquarters
there. He pointed to a sailing sloop moored nearby and said, "Bea and I,
with my boy and a beachcomber, sailed it out here." He had sailed this

119

small vessel from San Diego to Hawaii. He said, "I'm going to sail it down to the Marshall Islands before I leave here."

"When we came back through Hawaii the next year, I asked about George and whether he had gone to the Marshall Islands, and the reply was 'No, the general wouldn't let him, but he did sail back to the States at the end of his tour. He ran into a storm and they were delayed several days. At one time it was thought they were lost.' That was the sort of fellow that George was."

Middleton's service in the Philippines was quite pleasant. Having arrived early in November, after public schools had started, the Middletons enrolled their children in an American private school. Troy, Jr., entered his last year of junior high school; Bernice was tested and placed in a class advanced for her age.

Finding living quarters in Manila was not the simplest chore. The Inspector General, Colonel Dowell, lived in the old walled city portion of Manila. The Middletons had to look around before they found a house for rent. After they moved in and Middleton reported for duty as one of two assistant inspectors general, Dowell told him that he and his wife were about to go on leave. "How about you, Mrs. Middleton, and the children occupying our quarters while we're gone?" Dowell asked. The Middletons moved in for a month, from mid-November to mid-December. While they were there, Mrs. Middleton recalled, "a Filipino houseboy was overheard complaining that my dog slept on a bed. How did he know that? He peeped through the keyhole. I stopped up the keyhole and took care of that."

The Middletons moved back to their rented quarters when the Dowells returned from leave, remaining in these quarters until February. Army accommodations became available then. These were quite pleasant, with isinglass push-up windows to let the breezes play through. In Manila, hot the year round, breezes were always welcomed. Mrs. Middleton recalled that mosquitoes were a constant problem. She remembered the iguanas, big climbing lizards, always stretched out on the window ledges. Best of all, she recalled, were the servants, plentiful, accommodating, and inexpensive.

Middleton's duties took him away from home from time to time. His hours were sometimes irregular. The United States Army had forces at Fort McKinley. The Philippine Constabulary had passed from American sponsorship into the Philippine Army. Previously, as the Philippine Scouts, they had been under the direction of the United States Army. Most of these Scouts, totaling about 10,000, had been stationed at Fort McKinley.

One of his assignments took him to Corregidor, where he spent two weeks inspecting troops and the housekeeping of the fortress, and making himself available to hear complaints, as do all inspectors general. Corregidor became the last stronghold of Philippine and American forces in the Philippine Islands after the Japanese overran the islands in December, 1941, and January, 1942.

The Middletons had been in the Philippines less than six months when in April, 1937, President Smith of LSU renewed his invitation to Middleton to retire and become a member of the LSU staff—this time as dean of administration at $5,400 a year. Middleton was in the army hospital in Manila when he received President Smith's cablegram. He had reported in January for the required annual physical examination, in the course of which physicians had detected what they said was an irregularity in his heart beat. In April, he was hospitalized for further testing.

He was in his hospital room one night when the cablegram was delivered. Two fellow lieutenant colonels had dropped in to see him. He handed the cablegram to Jimmy Ord, asking him what sort of response he would make were he in Middleton's place.

Ord didn't take long to decide. "Take it," he said. "Here we are, all lieutenant colonels. We might get to be colonels before retirement. That $5,400 salary is good money."

Middleton passed the cablegram to the other lieutenant colonel. He studied it, then said, "No, Troy, I'd pass it up. A war is coming. With your record you ought to become a general. I'd turn it down." That lieutenant colonel was Dwight D. Eisenhower, who had been a student at the Command and General Staff School under Middleton ten years before.

General Eisenhower, in an interview with the author at Gettysburg in 1965, recalled the reasoning behind his answer to Middleton in Manila in April, 1937. "I served," Eisenhower said, "for three years in Panama as the aide to a very wise soldier named Fox Conner, a general from Mississippi. He was little known by the public, but he was a great philosopher. A student and especially a student of military and political affairs, he regularly reminded me that the Treaty of Versailles assured another war. I began to believe Conner implicitly. So, unquestionably my advice to Troy was based on what Conner had told me so often—that already Europe was uneasy, Hitler had come to power, the Treaty of Versailles had been broken. Everything was happening just as Conner had predicted. No, I told Troy Middleton that April, 1937, was no time for him to be thinking of retiring from the army."

Middleton, however, gave the matter more thought. He was far down the list of lieutenant colonels, having been promoted August 1, 1935. A general's star or stars looked extremely remote to him. He decided to apply for retirement and to inform President Smith at LSU that he was ready to become a civilian at last. He wrote the necessary letters and began the process of retiring. The salary at LSU, the opportunity, the rewarding nature of campus living beckoned more strongly than the army—finally.

Approval of the request for retirement came through, to take effect October 31, 1937. Middleton would take up his new duties at LSU in the fall, replacing Paul M. Hebert as dean of administration. He took on the added assignment of director of student personnel. Dean Hebert, a brilliant scholar of the law, was moving to the deanship of the Law School. With leave and travel time, the Middletons could take a good long vacation together.

They left the Philippines in May, 1937, on a Canadian liner, the *Princess of Asia*, traveling as civilians, paying their own way. Their first port of call was Hong Kong, where they stayed nights aboard ship and spent their days ashore as tourists, riding the ferry from their ship to Hong Kong. Then they sailed to their first Japanese port, Nagasaki.

As they passed through customs at Nagasaki, a woman official studied Middleton's papers, then looked up and asked, "Colonel, have you a camera?" Though nothing on the papers indicated that Middleton was a military man, the Japanese knew precisely who he was.

"I wanted to go to Japan because I could see troubles coming, and I wanted to see the country. The Japanese had already begun showing their strength on the Asiatic mainland. I was told that I probably would be watched while I was in Japan. We stopped at Kobe for a day and finally at Yokohama. As we went through customs there I noticed a man down the table, eyeing me. He stayed with me and got into the same compartment on the train going to Tokyo. When we left the train he followed. When we registered at the Imperial Hotel he was at the desk. After we went up to our rooms and freshened up, we went downstairs to go out on the street. He was there and followed us. He stayed with us a day and then disappeared. I saw no more of him. Later, I was telling a friend about the incident. He said, 'Why didn't you introduce yourself? There was one following me; I introduced myself and we went along together. He made a pretty good guide.'

"While we were in Japan I saw no evidence that a war was just around the corner. I was free to travel just about anywhere I wanted to go, except near military installations. We left Japan and went back to China to spend a month before we had to catch an army transport in late July to sail to San Francisco.

"We sailed on a Japanese ship to Tientsin. One of the remarkable things on this crossing of the China Sea we observed was where the blue water meets the muddy water—ocean and river water. The Chinese fish in the edge of this blue-muddy water. There were so many fishing junks that Troy, Jr., and I decided to count them. We counted up to a thousand, then stopped. We went on up to Peking (Peiping, they call it now), where we spent most of our time.

"When we left, it was on the last train out of Peiping. The Japanese were moving in. The last two or three days we were there, I saw considerable Japanese air power over that part of China. As we went down the steps out of the railroad station to the train, Japanese guards were on one side of the stairs and Chinese on the other—a most unusual situation. Those who didn't come out on our train were caught in there for some time," Middleton recalled.

The Middletons saw enough in China and Japan to convince them that Japan was on the move in the Far East. Middleton's eye for detail noted that the trains departed and arrived precisely on schedule. Many of the locomotives had been manufactured in the United States. Japan itself was a delight to the traveler, with fine restaurants, in one of which the Middletons were impressed by the gold-plated table ware.

Their army transport arrived in San Francisco early in August. The Middletons, in the Dodge they had driven to New York from Baton Rouge and had taken to the Philippines with them, toured the West and returned to Baton Rouge in time for Middleton to report to the office of President Smith at 9 A.M., August 16, 1937. Middleton had been away from LSU a year to the day.

Middleton, civilian-to-be on October 31, settled immediately into work in his new position as dean of administration. The duties were comparable to those of later deans of the university, or chief academic officer. He had few dealings with the business office of the university. In fact, President Smith was quite specific in saying that he would have no dealings whatsoever with the business office. Instead, he would assist the president on matters dealing essentially with academic affairs. His office was in the same building with Smith, in David F. Boyd Hall. That service, he recalled, brought him great pleasure. It did not, however, yield Middleton any understanding of the financial and business affairs of the university.

Less than a week after he officially became a civilian on October 31, Middleton received this letter written November 3 by General Malin Craig, Chief of Staff, the War Department:

My dear Colonel Middleton:

Your retirement from active service, upon your own request, having recently become effective, I wish to express the appreciation of the War Department for the valuable service you have rendered your country.

In reviewing your record I note the many commendatory remarks of the officers under whom you served relative to your ability and attainments. In recognition of the exceptionally meritorious and distinguished services you rendered to the American Expeditionary Force you were awarded the Distinguished Service Medal. You were also awarded a Silver Star for gallantry in action in the Bois de Fays, France, on October 10th and 11th, 1918.

Your entire record is one of which you may well be proud. You have been a valuable officer and I feel your retirement is a distinct loss to the Army.

The Middletons rented a home at 2330 Kleinert Avenue and spent the next eleven months there. Knowing that Baton Rouge was to be their permanent home, they turned their thoughts to a permanent residence. They looked around for building sites. Two lots at Lakeshore Drive and Stanford Avenue caught their eyes. They were owned by Harry Nelson and O. K. Allen. The asking price was $3,600. After they had looked them over, Nelson told Middleton, "Come on, let me show you a lot on Highland Road."

"What do you want for it?" Middleton asked.

"Twenty-two hundred dollars," Nelson replied. "And I can get it," he said.

"I told Mrs. Middleton about the Highland Road site. She said she liked the site on the lakeshore. I told her she couldn't have a backyard on the lake. So we went out to see Vernon and Jane Porter, friends of long standing. We told them we couldn't agree on a home site. Vernon said he'd take the lake. Then Jane said, after she'd seen both sites, she'd buy the acre on Highland Road," Middleton recalled.

They bought the Highland Road lot in January, 1938, paying $2,200. The blacktop surfacing of Highland Road ended at the Middletons' new property. Beyond that, travel to the south was on gravel. The only house on Highland on the Middletons' side was a chateau built by Dean James F. Broussard of the LSU faculty at 4512 Highland.

Before building, Middleton turned to Dr. Henry Howe, director of the School of Geology, for advice. He had heard that there were prospects for oil in the area. Howe, a distinguished geologist, could be counted on to know if experts thought there was indeed oil underneath the property.

"Dr. Howe," Middleton said, "I propose to build a home in the 4700 block of Highland Road, and I understand there's a possibility of oil in that particular area."

Howe replied, "Well, I'll tell you; if you want to build a home in the center of an oil field, you go on and build that house."

The house at 4782 Highland Road eventually stood in the geographical center of what became known as the University Oil Field.

Once they had decided to build on Highland, helpful people suggested how Middleton could save money on the construction. President Smith suggested that Middleton have George Caldwell, the university superintendent of buildings and grounds, do the job. He was an experienced and excellent contractor. Despite the temptation to save money by having Caldwell do the work, Middleton had misgivings. He decided that it would be bad business to have another university official building his house for him.

Instead, he talked to J. A. Moore, a former head of the Mengel Company, who had started building houses. They agreed that Moore would build the house, cost plus. "I'll give you a fixed price," Moore said, "but I might be able to save you a couple of thousand dollars." He did the job well and saved the money he had said he might. Moore laid down a heavy undercourse of cinders and gravel for drainage, poured a thick slab and laid mosaic tile floors. The house is one of few in Baton Rouge not plagued by troubles with termites.

The Middletons moved into their new home July 31, 1938. Just before they did so, they bought 2.2 additional acres just behind the house, from a neighbor, T. N. Farris, a professor of economics. Their home site and surrounding grounds now extended 208 feet along Highland Road and 624 feet back to Bayou Fountain.

Before the house was completed, the University Oil Field came into being with completion of a producing well, to be followed by numerous others. The investment of $2,200 with Harry Nelson and a larger sum with Farris was repaid many times over with royalties on the oil drawn from beneath their land.

With the Middletons' return to Baton Rouge, the choice of schools for the children came up again. This time, Troy, Jr., was sent to Georgia Military Academy at College Park, from which he was graduated in 1939. Bernice, who had skipped a grade on the basis of tests in the Philippines, skipped another grade after their return to Baton Rouge and was well into high school.

The university seemed to be running smoothly. Enrollments had be- gun to climb in 1938. LSU football fortunes, under Coach Bernie Moore, had been extraordinary for three years in which the Tigers won twenty- seven games, lost two, and tied one in regular season competition. The for- tunes fell off in 1938 when the team won six and lost four. The *Southern Review*, founded three years before, was receiving international acclaim as a leading critical quarterly published by the university. Grand opera was performed each spring in the university theater, under the coaching and direction of former artists from the Metropolitan Opera of New York and the Opera Comique of Paris. Recruiters from the Music School went scour- ing the country for basses and baritones, sopranos and contraltos, as reso- lutely as football coaches went out in search of quarterbacks and bulky, agile guards. The university had celebrated its seventy-fifth anniversary in 1935, while Middleton was in his fifth year as commandant and his first as dean of men, with a great flourish in the performing and the graphic arts. One observance in 1935 had brought to the campus a representative of Premier Mussolini of Italy, among dignitaries from other countries, at the time when the Southwestern Journalism Congress, made up of faculty and student journalists from Oklahoma, Texas, and Louisiana colleges, was meeting on the campus. At a dinner, the Italian representative had spoken glowingly of his country's premier's most recent achievements. Out of the crowd of diners came the voice of Walter Harrison, managing editor of the *Daily Oklahoman*, an Oklahoma City newspaper, inquiring about some of Mussolini's harsher practices. President Smith and others of the host group

Professor of English John E. Uhler and Dean of Administration Middleton, Breaking Ground for LSU Faculty Club, 1938

professed shock at editor Harrison's barbarism. (The Forty-fifth Division, in which Harrison served as a lieutenant colonel and which Troy Middleton commanded in 1943 in Sicily and Italy, spilled considerable blood making the same point Harrison had raised on an April evening in an LSU banquet hall.)

To this university, in which the right emphases were being encouraged, there came a great shock in June, 1939, when the New Orleans *States* ran a front page photograph of an LSU truck on a building site in suburban New Orleans, from which workmen were unloading assorted building materials. They had, it developed, come from Baton Rouge, illegally. The picture and story accompanying it led to far more sensational developments, climaxed when President Smith left town after it was revealed that he had stolen almost a million dollars from the university by forging bonds left in his keeping and using the money to cover his losses in speculation on the wheat futures market in Chicago. Shock after shock jolted the campus. An academic Richter scale would have registered an intensity of 10, the highest mark. Smith changed his mind about fleeing, later stood trial, and was sentenced to the state penitentiary at Angola. There he atoned in part for his transgressions by organizing instruction to teach reading and writing to many illiterate fellow convicts. Governor Richard Leche resigned; he was tried, convicted of federal offenses, and sent off to an Atlanta penitentiary. George Caldwell, superintendent of buildings and grounds, was tried and convicted of failure to report as income and to pay income tax on the 2 percent he was taking off building contracts on the campus. (Here, Middleton's sensitive nose had warned him against taking Smith's advice to have Caldwell build his house on Highland Road.)

When Caldwell had done his time at Atlanta penitentiary, he returned and paid Middleton a visit at the university, asking if his bids would be considered if he went back into the contracting business and bid low on a university building contract. Middleton assured him that his low bid would get the same consideration as anyone else's. Caldwell, a highly capable contractor, later built the LSU Library and Graham Hall, a men's dormitory, two of the sounder buildings on the campus. Caldwell, Middleton recalled, was a dedicated builder. When he received word in the Atlanta penitentiary that his sentence had but a few days to run, he protested that he couldn't leave then; he was needed for several additional weeks to oversee completion of a building project there.

The university was in trouble with a capital T. Middleton had been serving as dean of administration, in a relatively sheltered position. He at once recalled how Smith had told him, quite positively, that he was to have nothing to do with university business affairs and finances in his position as dean of administration. Perhaps he knew why, now.

The Board of Supervisors met in special session and called Middleton before it in late June, 1939, to tell him that he was to take over the business management of the university. "It shocked me that so much had transpired that I could hardly believe. But LSU had been good to me; we were in trouble now; this was no time for anyone to run out," he recalled. "I told the board that I would accept the new position, but only if certain conditions were met. They asked what the conditions might be. I said: 'One, that I be given a free hand, and that I be permitted to select my own personnel.' The board members agreed. 'The finances are yours; you do as you see fit,' they said." Paul M. Hebert, dean of the Law School, had been named acting president. He concurred heartily in the board's decision to put Middleton into the new position of acting vice president and comptroller.

Middleton moved at once to pick the people he needed to help restore the university's financial integrity. He chose Dr. Daniel Borth and Dr. Mack Hornbeak, both professors of accounting. Then he went to Dean J. B. Trant of the College of Commerce and told him why he needed the two. Trant was understandably reluctant, but said, "Well, I hate to lose those men; they're two of the best; but if we can help in this situation, go ahead and take them." Borth and Hornbeak were not overjoyed at the invitation but agreed to take the jobs. Borth became auditor, in charge of accounting and auditing. Hornbeak became purchasing agent. With their aid, Middleton set out to restore some sort of order to the university's finances.

"It was pure chaos at first. The university had been operating on a cash basis. We didn't know whom we owed, if we owed anyone. As I recall, we ran an advertisement in Louisiana newspapers saying in essence, 'If the University owes you, come talk to us.'

"We had to establish a proper business organization. Checking around, we heard from the University of Tennessee that it had had some experience with a New York firm, Franke, Hannon, and Withey, which was experienced in institutional accounting. It took some doing, but we finally persuaded the Board of Supervisors to employ this firm at $40,000, a fee that was shocking to some people. The firm set up a business procedure which is still in use at the university. The recoveries we made as a result of what they found and did, compensated many times over for their fee. They were on the campus regularly for a year, setting up those procedures," Middleton recalled.

"Those were trying days—days that I would not want to relive. They are days that some twenty-five or thirty years hence we should try to forget. I will say, however, that after the first year when the unpleasant things had been dealt with, my service as the head of the business organization, my association with Dean Hebert, the acting president, and my work with Dan Borth and Mack Hornbeak—all were quite satisfying and rewarding. The Board of Supervisors was most cooperative.

"In my long years with LSU, perhaps my service in heading the business organization from June, 1939, until I reentered the army in January, 1942, represented the greatest contribution I was able to make.

Daniel Borth recalled the task faced by Middleton, Hornbeak, and himself:

"Little did Colonel Middleton or I realize the full extent of the financial mess in which the University found itself. The books of account were conducted on a hash—or stewpot—basis with funds from all sources—that is, regular appropriations, trusts, deposits, bonds, and athletic and other auxiliary enterprises thrown into the same bank account. All bills, regardless of the purpose of the expenditures, were paid out of those same bank accounts. The bond indentures of the university were violated, and funds which should have been in the sinking fund had been thrown into the stewpot.

"Faculty and staff had been accustomed to ordering their needs direct from business firms without the benefit of purchase order, without full knowledge of the status of the budget, and without bids. Bonuses were paid to favored deans and other administrative officers at the end of the year if the bank balances seemed to dictate.

"Enrollments were inflated in extension classes in order to favor members of the instructional staff who were paid on a per-student basis. Accounts with students were not collected except in the most haphazard manner. At the time of the bank holiday (imposed by President Franklin D. Roosevelt in 1933), President Smith and some of the members of the business office cashed checks in the university in order to circumvent the restriction on bank withdrawals.

"The university had to advertise in Louisiana newspapers to determine whether business firms were owed by the university. While we were straightening up affairs and getting funds to operate the university, firms not having been paid for an extended period would send in duplicate invoices, often more than once. Four auditing agencies were concerned with the university at the time: the state auditor; the federal Internal Revenue Bureau; F. W. Lafrentz and Company, CPAs of New Orleans; and Franke, Hannon, and Withey, CPAs from New York City, specialists in financial operations of higher education. All these firms and agencies were critical of the university's financial and business operations.

"One of our first jobs was to get the requisition and purchasing processes under control. Lacking a budget at first, all requisitions and purchase orders were scrutinized by the office of the auditor, to determine whether we could finance the purchases. This meant that the purchasing agent could not issue purchase orders without coincidental approval of the auditor as to the availability of funds. Every check was signed by hand in those days. The auditor signed these checks after ascertaining whether they were properly documented, for duplicate invoices were submitted without being so identified.

"Faculty and staff frequently would sign invoices without checking to see if they had been authenticated earlier. Lacking funds, the payments of bill were held up; creditors were literally on the doorsteps of the auditor's office, requesting their payments. The problem was one of being fair to as many creditors as we could. This did not satisfy the more aggressive ones. We sent notices out with every check, informing business firms not to take additional orders of any kind from the university without the benefit of a formal purchase order. Many firms violated these warnings and we had to withhold or delay payment to those who did not choose to cooperate."

Further delving into the tangled finances revealed that some favored faculty members employed on a twelve-month basis and paid twelve monthly salaries had been illegally paid summer session compensation. They howled when they were billed for these overpayments, but they paid back the unearned *lagniappe*.

Borth recalled that the auditor's office worked sixteen to eighteen hours a day, six days a week through the summer of 1939, and only slightly shorter hours six days a week until mid-1941. By then things were straightening out sufficiently "so that we could depend upon the knowledge of the faculty and staff and the business community. We ceased reviewing requisitions and purchase orders and reviewing each invoice about that time. Check-signing machines came into vogue about that same time, reducing considerably the time required for the auditor to do his work," Borth said.

Through this period Middleton led in bringing a real measure of confidence and integrity to the business office. Borth recalled, "I checked my proposed, and actual, major actions with him frequently. He often advised certain practices which I followed with extreme care. Once having taken an action based on what I thought was the policy, I was never reversed by Colonel Middleton. We spent many a night in Alumni Hall (the business offices were here), reviewing the budget with all the deans and academic directors. The meetings frequently went far into the morning. The Colonel was always ready to give advice as to actions which brought harmony to the group. He always gave considerable independence to his subordinates; he looked after the broad issues and left the details to them.

"Once when I found that the president's office had violated the accepted business procedures in a major case, I refused to pay the bill until I had been assured that it would not happen again. I took the entire case to Colonel Middleton, who supported me fully in my stand. He believed in conforming to his own rules, not that rules were made for the other fellow," Borth recalled.

It required regular overtime work from June, 1939, to about June, 1941, to straighten out all the university's finances and to educate many faculty and staff members, for the first time, to the accepted business procedures by which the rest of the world must live.

So much for the business reorganization of the university. In June, 1939, when the Board of Supervisors was just beginning to realize the enormity of the university's troubles, it had, of course, to choose a successor to President Smith. The board selected E. S. Richardson, president of Louisiana Polytechnic Institute. Richardson accepted, came to Baton Rouge, got a disturbed night's sleep, and next morning telephoned his son Leland, a Baton Rouge attorney, to say that he was having second thoughts about accepting the LSU presidency. Then third thoughts. And finally, as the size of the new burden began sinking in, Richardson thanked the board and all concerned, and returned to Ruston after serving less than two days in the LSU presidency.

After choosing his two chief aides, Borth and Hornbeak, Middleton did more to earn his $9,000 salary (the president was being paid $10,000). Middleton fired the two principal business officers, one of whom he described as nothing more than a check writer. He brought George Schwab over from the Athletic Department to become manager of the bookstore, replacing the son-in-law of President Smith.

Governor Long was, during this period, offering such help as he could to the university. He served out former Governor Leche's term, Leche having resigned after the scandals broke. Governor Sam H. Jones, who ran on a reform ticket, succeeded Long. Jones kicked out the entire Board of Supervisors after he took office in May, 1940. "He should have left some good men like Lewis Gottlieb and Fred Ratzburg," Middleton recalled. Jones's board consisted "largely of his own cronies—some good, some indifferent. They came in to do wonders. But they didn't disturb the business office. One especially good thing that board did was to install Colonel Monnot Lanier as chairman of the board's finance committee. Lanier knew his business. I never worked with a more considerate man."

Paul Hebert, dean of the Law School, was the board's second choice for president. "Hebert should have been made permanent, instead of acting president," Middleton recalled. "Dean Hebert's qualifications were excellent. He almost certainly would have been made permanent president had he not been a Roman Catholic. He was strongly opposed on this point by Tom Dutton, an influential member of the Board of Supervisors, who was almost rabid on the subject of religion."

Acting President Hebert served through 1939 and 1940. In the spring of 1941, the board finally made a permanent selection. It chose a retired major general, Campbell B. Hodges of Bossier Parish, to take office in June.

"President-elect Hodges called me in the day they elected him," Middleton recalled, "and said 'I understand that you were opposed to my becoming president.' I said that was not the case, but that I hadn't worked for his selection. I told him, 'I know that you were retired from the army for physical disability and that you ought not to take on such a demanding job as the university presidency,'" Middleton recalled.

Hodges said, "I don't want you to leave."

Middleton replied, "I have no intention of doing so."

Middleton and President Hodges got along. During Middleton's last year on the faculty at the Command and General Staff School, Hodges had written to him asking if he would like to be invited to become a tactical officer at the United States Military Academy, where Hodges held the number two position on the academy staff.

Middleton declined the prospect of a tour at West Point, with thanks. "Hodges couldn't quite understand. He thought I'd be greatly complimented. I was on the list to go on to the Army War College. I asked the commandant at the Command and General Staff School for his advice on the offer from Hodges, since I didn't want to offend Hodges. The commandant told me bluntly, 'Hell, go on to War College. You don't want to go to West Point.' "

Middleton's recollection also provided one of the few lighter incidents to come out of the scandals of 1939. As chief business officer and vice president of the university, he had custody of the minutes of the Board of Supervisors. He was called by Judge Charles Holcombe of the District Court in Baton Rouge and asked to bring the board minutes down to the court. "When I arrived, Judge Holcombe was reading something in the courtroom. George Caldwell, already serving a sentence in the federal penitentiary in Atlanta, was in the courtroom as a witness in yet another trial. When I went up to the bench to tell Judge Holcombe that I had brought the minutes, Caldwell jumped up, grabbed my hand, and said that he brought me greetings from a couple of my friends in Atlanta. The lawyers in the courtroom cracked up at that (as much as they could under the gaze of Judge Holcombe, as stern a jurist as ever frowned on laughter in the courtroom). In fact, Judge Holcombe didn't even look up. Caldwell explained, after the laughter subsided, that the two friends he had mentioned were prison mates, one being in for having killed his wife. Both had known me in the army, he finally explained."

As 1941 wore along, the manpower draft began to cut into enrollment at the university. National Guard units had been called up.

The war which had been going on in Europe since September, 1939, seemed more certain to draw in the United States. Middleton had given this so much thought that back on July 5, 1940, he had written his old World War friend, George C. Marshall, now chief of staff:

The situation with respect to enlargement of our military and naval forces prompts me to address this letter to you.

On October 31, 1937, at my request, I was placed upon the retired list as a Lieutenant Colonel, and was subsequently carried as a retired Colonel.

I feel that if my services are required at this time, I should voluntarily state my willingness to return to the active list of the Army in such capacity as the War Department may desire and be placed on the promotion list in keeping with regulations which may govern such cases.

During the period of my retirement, I have established a home in Baton Rouge, Louisiana, and at present am serving as Chief Business Officer and Acting Vice President of the Louisiana State University. Resignation from my present position in order to return to the Army would be made at a personal and financial sacrifice. However, my military training and experience prompt me to offer my services. If there is a need at this time for those who have been trained in the military service, I feel that personal sacrifices should, of course, be considered as secondary.

General Marshall responded on July 11, 1940:

I appreciate most sincerely your willingness to return to active service, particularly in view of the personal and financial sacrifice involved. Although we are recalling a few retired officers under recent legislative authority, the present laws limit their employment to duties such as ROTC and recruiting. Until you are needed for an assignment appropriate to your outstanding record as a battlefield commander, I do not intend to take advantage of your offer, much as we would like to obtain your services.

George Marshall had written across the top of Middleton's original letter, the author noted later in a study of General Middleton's 201 files at the Pentagon in Washington, this notation: "This man was the outstanding infantry regimental commander on the battlefield in France."

Troy, Jr., had entered LSU in September, 1940, after graduation from Georgia Military Academy. He was a sophomore. Bernice, thanks to her high scores on placement tests whenever she changed schools, had finished high school and had enrolled at LSU in September, 1941, at age fifteen. Three Middletons were now in LSU.

12 "What Are You Doing Here?"

THROUGH the morning of December 7, 1941, their luck had been good. When the hunters started across LSU-owned Ben Hur plantation soon after eight o'clock a skin of ice lay on each water trough. The temperature had risen slowly from thirty-one degrees as they continued their hunt for doves. The birds flew up repeatedly from their feeding on coffee weed, goat weed, and beggar weed seed, as well as the remnants of corn planted on Ben Hur.

As noon approached the temperature rose to near fifty. "Let's go get some lunch," Middleton said to Troy, Jr., and George Bowdon, fellow members of Kappa Alpha order. Their hunting coats plump with doves, the three walked back across the plantation, then drove two miles to the Middleton home. Troy, Jr., a sophomore at LSU, and George, a freshman from Alexandria, had been on target as the doves hurtled through their erratic flight. Troy's double-barrel 20-gauge shotgun, Troy, Jr.'s 16-gauge automatic, and George's gun had knocked down two dozen doves, comfortably short of the bag limit of twelve each. They would, they agreed, hit the limit after lunch.

As they walked into the house, Mrs. Middleton greeted them with, "The radio just said the Japs have bombed Pearl Harbor!" The hunters stowed their shotguns, dumped their doves on the kitchen table, and went to the radio for details. "We didn't go back hunting," Middleton recalled.

The next day, Monday, at the university, Middleton went to President Hodges and told him that he intended to offer his services to the army. "I don't blame you," Hodges said, "You should become a general." Colonel Middleton, in retirement from the army just four years, wired the War Department that day, saying that he was in good physical condition and available for any service the department might choose for him.

Excitement ran through the campus all day Monday. Students formed in a body and went to the home of the president, chanting, and wanting some kind of direction. Hodges came out and told the students the best thing they could do was to go back to their studies, that the war would go on a long time, and that they would have their chances to fight their choice of enemies.

In a day or so, the War Department replied to Middleton's telegram, informing him that he would be ordered to active duty as a lieutenant colonel January 20, 1942. This was to give him time to get his affairs in order at LSU. Middleton cut into the military grapevine, as a retired officer, and discovered that, in all probability, he would be ordered to some stateside service, in command of a station complement in an area like Atlanta or San Antonio.

None of that kind of service was for Troy Middleton. He had had as much combat time as any man in the World War. He had been the youngest colonel in the American Expeditionary Force. He had excellent training, as student and teacher, in the army schools between wars. He was in good physical condition. He wouldn't settle for anything less than field service. This time he directed his telegram to the Chief of Infantry. After a short delay, the response was more to his liking. He would be ordered to an Infantry Replacement Training Center at Camp Wheeler, Georgia, where he would be given an opportunity in command of troops, "presumably to prove that I was in fair shape," Middleton said.

While he waited for January 20, Middleton worked hard. Hornbeak, the purchasing agent, was a bachelor. He wanted to get into the army and not wait to be drafted. He came to Middleton for advice. Paul Hebert, Law School dean, and J. Denson Smith, a law professor, came with questions. Borth didn't want to be left behind. On January 12, the Board of Supervisors promoted Borth from auditor to comptroller, replacing Middleton.

On January 20, the *Reveille* reported Middleton's departure that day for Camp Wheeler. It noted that his family would remain in Baton Rouge. Bernice was now a freshman in LSU. Troy, Jr., a sophomore, wanted to enlist, but his parents persuaded him to stay in school. "This war is going to run a while," Middleton told his son. Troy, Jr., said, "Yes, and if I stay in school, it'll be just my luck to get drafted. Now, how would that look?" Nevertheless, he stayed in LSU.

Though scores of faculty and staff members sought Middleton's counsel on how to get into military service, he noted wryly that they didn't come up asking how they could join an infantry company to be assured of an early opportunity to grapple with the enemy.

Eleven days after Middleton's departure, the *Reveille* reported that Borth, veteran of nearly three weeks as comptroller, had been commissioned a major in the army and would leave February 12 to take charge of instruction in the revising of accounting systems in army depots over the country. Borth said he "hated like the devil to leave the university, but the work is in my line and they need me." He was to travel over the nation, visiting army depots, helping quartermasters keep track of the avalanche of equipment and material that would be needed in a long war. Arthur G. Keller, university purchasing agent, was given Borth's duties. Middleton, hearing the news of Borth's commissioning as a major, could recall no parallel. He had never heard of a civilian taking so high a first step in the army.

At Camp Wheeler, Middleton took command of a training regiment. He put on the required high top shoes. "I won't forget how those things chafed my ankles," he said. From January 21 until March 10, he shepherded several thousand novices through the routine of training for combat. (During this period, on February 1, he was promoted to colonel.) On March 10, he received orders sending him to Camp Gordon, Georgia, for duty with his old World War division, the Fourth.

"What are you doing here?" he was asked when he reported to the Fourth. He showed his orders. "Fine, I'm glad to see you," the commanding general said, "but I don't know what to do with you. I have a full complement of colonels." Middleton remained at Camp Gordon several weeks —after he had solved the general's dilemma by suggesting that he be attached to a regiment, the Twenty-second.

His next orders directed him to Camp Blanding, Florida, to take command of the 142nd Infantry Regiment in the Thirty-sixth Division, the Texas National Guard. He reported there early in April.

A parade was called, to give visiting higher commanders a look at the division. As a regiment passed the reviewing stand, its colonel would turn out of the column and join the reviewing officers until the tail of the regiment passed. "My regiment came abreast and I climbed upon the stand. There was General George Marshall. He looked at me and asked, 'What are you doing here?' I told him I had been ordered here. He said nothing further. When my regiment had passed, I rejoined it. I heard no more from Marshall for the time being," Middleton recalled.

A few days of training passed. Then Middleton received a call from the War Department. He was to proceed at once to a specified room in the Munitions Building. "I caught a night train, rode to Washington, and reported to the specified room. There was Ike Eisenhower. He told me that General John C. H. Lee, who was going to command the Services of Supply in England, had selected me for his staff. I was to report at once to another room to receive instructions from Lee.

"I reported to Lee. He told me, 'We're going to fly to England shortly and we've got to land in Ireland; therefore you'll have to have a passport to land in that neutral country. The picture will be in civilian clothing. We have made arrangements with a photographer here in the building to take the pictures. We have only one civilian coat, so all of you will have to wear the same coat.' I got my picture taken.

"Next, I had to go down—for what reason, I don't recall—to the War College where General Lesley McNair, who had been a classmate of mine at Leavenworth, was in command. General Mark Clark was his chief of staff with the Army Ground Forces. When I got down to the War College I ran into Clark," Middleton recalled.

Clark asked the question that Middleton was growing accustomed to hearing: "What are you doing here?"

"I told him I'd been ordered up from Camp Blanding and that Lee was taking me to England as his planning officer."

"You're not going to England," Clark said. "Lee grabs every good officer we get our hands on. You're pegged for the Forty-fifth Infantry Division up at Fort Devens, Massachusetts. You get on back to Florida and get your stuff together. An order will await you there; then you go on up to Devens."

Middleton thus escaped the grasp of his old friendly adversary, the same Courthouse Lee who coached the engineers on and off the field at Leavenworth and at Crockett, where his football teams had vanquished the teams quarterbacked by Troy Middleton. Lee, Middleton discovered later in England, was the only officer of his acquaintance who wore stars both fore and aft on his helmet. "Old Courthouse wanted to be sure that GIs knew that he was a general, coming and going." Again in England, Middleton was at a meeting planning the invasion of France when Lee's special train wheeled into the station. "For an engineer, Courthouse knew how to travel in style," Middleton recalled.

Middleton went back to Florida and the Thirty-sixth Division. When he arrived, he found himself to be a brigadier general with an assignment as assistant commander of the Forty-fifth Division at Fort Devens—just as Clark had said.

His orders specified that he was to have time off to visit his family in Baton Rouge. Early in June he caught a bus in Starke, Florida, for the ride home. Confirmation of his promotion awaited him in a telegram. Troy, Jr., and Bernice were still students at LSU. Mrs. Middleton had an added interest, having decided that she would raise turkeys, to give her something to do and, equally important, to put meat on the family table. Food rationing had been imposed on the nation. Everyone was issued books of ration stamps, entitling him to just so many pounds of meat and so many cans of vegetables and strictly limiting the purchase of sugar. Gasoline and tires also were restricted.

About this time, Selective Service gave notice to Troy, Jr., that he would be drafted in July. "See," he said, "now they've gone and done it—drafted me."

"He didn't like it a bit," Middleton recalled, "after he'd almost pleaded with me to let him enlist back in January when I went back to duty. Later, Troy, Jr., felt that he missed chances to move up in the army because he wasn't graduated from Officer Candidate School at Fort Benning until late 1944." After his induction into the army in July, 1942, Troy, Jr., remained in LSU. In the spring of 1943 he was sent to Fort Ord, California, for seventeen weeks of training. Then he was returned to LSU for studies mostly in engineering, in the Army Specialized Training Program (ASTP). He remained at LSU from November, 1943, until early in 1944, going then to Fort Benning and Officer Candidate School, from which he emerged a second lieutenant in October, 1944.

When his father returned to the states from Sicily and Italy in January, 1944, and was home on leave before taking the VIII Corps command, the ASTP students turned out in a parade in honor of General Middleton. Troy Middleton, Jr., commanded the parading ASTP cadets.

Brigadier General Middleton reported to the Forty-fifth Division at Fort Devens in mid-June. He was greeted by Major General William S. Key, the division commander, "a fine gentleman" in Middleton's book. Shortly after his arrival, Generals Middleton and Key were chatting one day when Key surprised Middleton by saying, "I'm not the man to lead this division into combat, since I've had no fighting experience myself." He told Middleton he had reason to believe that Middleton had been sent to the Forty-fifth to take his place. No one had troubled to tell Middleton, if this was the case.

Late in the spring the Forty-fifth had been ticketed for a part in the invasion of North Africa. Other outfits were found for this chore and the Forty-fifth went back into training. Middleton took elements out onto Cape Cod for endless practice in shore-to-shore operations, involving boarding ship and leaving ship, ready to shoot. After the summer on Cape Cod, the division went back to Devens. There, Middleton was given another star and command of the division. Key had been right.

Bill Mauldin, the cartoonist, in his book *The Brass Ring*, recorded the National Guardsmen's reactions to Middleton's assumption of command:

> Even the good-natured General Key, who hadn't minded being kidded in cartoons, was relieved by Troy Middleton, a professional, who was called from retirement for the job. This purge upset the division at first—after all, a National Guard unit gets to be a sort of social club—and there were mutterings about "The West Point Protective Association," but it all turned out to be justified by the Forty-fifth's combat record. Indeed, Middleton himself, after eventually leading the division through a distinguished beginning in combat, went on to become a corps commander.

What Mauldin did not know was that Middleton was not a West Pointer, and that although he might have been retired from the army, he had left a demanding civilian job at considerable sacrifice at age fifty-two.

Mauldin, at twenty, was developing the cartoon style which made him famous, earned him a Pulitzer Prize, and brought him the gratitude of all infantrymen in World War II. He had enlisted in a National Guard unit which was a component of the Forty-fifth, in Phoenix, Arizona. The unit

was sent to active duty with the division when President Roosevelt proclaimed a national emergency in 1940. Drawn from Colorado, Arizona,
New Mexico, and Oklahoma, the Forty-fifth consisted mainly of Oklaho-
mans, among them numerous Indians, better educated than the majority
of their fellows.

Mauldin's cartoons, drawn for the *Forty-fifth Division News*, poked
gentle fun at the brass during this period. They took on an edge, with
Willie and Joe wryly commenting, late in the Sicilian campaign, and grew
more pointed during the long, back-breaking, man-killing fight up the
peninsula of Italy.

Like his predecessor, General Key, Middleton knew the value of a
good newspaper in which readers have confidence. He left the newspaper
to the enlisted men who ran it, under the direction of Sergeant Don Robinson. When a complaint came his way about the irreverent character of the
News, Middleton paid little attention. Better to have the men work off their
complaints vicariously through a Mauldin cartoon, than to have them store
up their grievances.

Cape Cod had been breezy, almost like the vacation resort it was for
civilians, and relatively pleasant for the men of the Forty-fifth that summer
and early fall. Middleton took over the division in time for its next move,
to Pine Camp, New York, for winter training. Without scaling the highest
peaks in the Rocky Mountains, it would have been hard to find more arctic
conditions in the continental United States. On a December morning, Middleton looked out at the thermometer on the screened porch of his cottage
and read 36 degrees below zero. Snow drifted head high and kept piling
up. Soldiers who were ordered to dig foxholes in the Pine Camp terrain
dug their picks into solid ice and chipped out holes without disturbing the
earth underneath. "For winter training, the army couldn't have found more
demanding terrain and conditions than we encountered at Pine Camp,"
Middleton recalled.

Mauldin's cartoons in the *News* took note of conditions. A sergeant
on the firing range gave these instructions to a prone GI, aiming his rifle in
a snowstorm: "Ceiling zero; visibility zero; range 200 yards." A soldier on
KP, inside the kitchen door, gestured toward a bucket of slop frozen to the
head of a column of ice descending into a garbage can outside the door,
saying "Awright—come out an' look for yaself if ya don't believe it." A
soldier, foot braced on the coils of a tuba, tried to free the mouthpiece from

the lips of the tuba player in the division band while another soldier poured water onto mouth and mouthpiece to aid in the endeavor. "Yes, it got that cold—and colder—at Pine Camp," Middleton recalled.

The Forty-fifth trained in cold storage at Pine Camp on into February, 1943. Then it was moved to Camp Pickett, near Blackstone, Virginia, for mountain training in the Blue Ridge of West Virginia and western Virginia, and for ship-to-shore operations from Norfolk, Virginia, to Solomons, Maryland.

On the trip from Pine Camp to Blackstone, Middleton and his aide, Captain Alfred Glassell, stopped for the night in Allentown, Pennsylvania. In the hotel elevator going up to their rooms, they were greeted by a man who appeared to be about forty years old, who turned to Troy Middleton and said, "I sure like to see you boys in uniform. I was too young for World War I and I am too old for World War II."

"I surely did want to hit that bird," Middleton recalled.

Glassell, Middleton's aide, had been a major in the ROTC under Middleton when he was commandant of cadets in 1930–1936.

Early in April, Middleton, still at Camp Pickett, received orders to take part of his staff and proceed to North Africa, with no indication of what they were to do there. "We flew to Natal, Brazil, in an old transport plane. At Natal we took a converted B-24 that carried extra gasoline. It took us all the way across the South Atlantic to Dakar in West Africa. From there we flew to Marrakech in the Atlas Mountains and on to the headquarters of General Patton in Morocco," Middleton recalled.

In Morocco they learned that Patton would command the Seventh Army in the landing in Sicily that summer. They also were told that the Forty-fifth's role would require that it be the only one coming out of the United States to be combat-loaded. It would come off the ships ready to fight, without preparation. The other divisions in the operation would come out of North Africa, among them the First Division, commanded by Terry de la Mesa Allen, with whom Middleton had been commissioned and later had gone through Command and General Staff School. After an inauspicious start in combat in North Africa, American troops had been turned over to Patton, who showed what he had learned about tank warfare.

Middleton remained at Patton's headquarters almost a month, preparing for the part the Forty-fifth would play in the landing scheduled originally near Palermo, Sicily. Middleton returned with his small staff party

to Camp Pickett, where he was told that the invasion orders had been
changed and that the division would sail for the Mediterranean about June
5. Furthermore, Middleton would have to return to North Africa ahead of
the division to prepare another plan for landing on Sicily. Mrs. Middleton
came to Camp Pickett for a brief visit with her husband before his second
departure for North Africa.

Middleton got his division ready to sail from Norfolk. Radio network
men came to shipside, recording all the sounds of arrival of trains, marching men, martial music from the band, each man's response to roll call as
he started up the foot of the gangplank, plus a dramatic reading of a message explaining to the men what a momentous assignment they were em-
barking upon. Later, transcriptions of the occasion were sent to Mrs. Middleton and the children.

Lieutenant General Lesley J. McNair, commander of the Army
Ground Forces, inspected the Forty-fifth at Hampton Roads, Virginia,
Port of Embarkation. What he saw prompted him on June 3, 1943, to
write to Middleton:

Commendation of Quality of Forty-fifth Division.

Personal observation and recent reports of officers from this headquarters
who visited the Forty-fifth Division indicate that your division will leave the
control of the Army Ground Forces better prepared than any division that has
left our control to date. I was particularly impressed by the most favorable reports I received upon the condition of the divisional equipment and the efficiency with which the division solved the many situations arising in connection
with their activities within the last two months. I wish to take this opportunity
to commend you officially and through you the officers of your staff, who
through supervision, leadership and untiring efforts contributed in a large measure to the state of preparedness attained.

Perhaps General McNair knew of a small problem involving the
Forty-fifth Division News. When Middleton took his division from frigid
Pine Camp, New York, down to Camp Pickett for mountain training, the
commander of Camp Pickett said that the camp newspaper was the only
one authorized to publish at Pickett. Publication of the *News* would com-
plicate matters unnecessarily. No one had ever heard of publishing two
papers at one base. Middleton thought the *News* was too good a paper not
to continue to be published. It came out regularly while the Forty-fifth was
at Camp Pickett.

Middleton himself had to leapfrog ahead of the convoy surrounding and including the Forty-fifth Division, to take care of the unfinished business of planning a landing on a hostile shore. He flew back to North Africa, where part of his staff had stayed to work on plans, took additional staff with him and reported to the headquarters of Omar Bradley near Algiers. Middleton had not known or served with General Bradley before. On the Sicilian mission, Bradley was subordinate to Patton. The entire operation was under British overall direction.

At Algiers with Bradley, the planners worked out a mission for the Forty-fifth, as yet untested in battle. The division would have responsibility for a forty-mile front with its center falling a few miles to the left of the village of Scoglitti. The nearest town of any size was Vittoria, eight miles inland. Airfields near Biscari and Comiso, eleven and twelve miles inland, were early objectives. Middleton planned to land all three of his infantry regiments abreast, holding out a small reserve.

By the time the division arrived at Oran, Algeria, the plan was complete. The division ran through one rehearsal, landing on the beaches near Oran, in far western Algeria, a good six hundred miles from Sicily. The men didn't perform so well. Perhaps it was because they were still feeling shut in, after the long trip across the Atlantic, bunking three layers deep on canvas sheets lashed to pipe frames deep in the hold of their transports.

13   Sicily Next

THE FORTY-FIFTH Division sailed from Oran the afternoon of July 4, with only subdued notice of the fact that it was America's birthday. The division was headed for the invasion beaches, sandy and relatively smooth, where its men would begin landing shortly after midnight July 10.

The ships carrying the Forty-fifth were combat loaded in Norfolk. Units would come off their craft ready to fight. The small fleet bearing the Forty-fifth was joined on July 5 by transports which had taken on the veteran First Division at Algiers. Later, transports bearing the Third Division would put out from Bizerte to join the swelling convoy. Finally, a combat command of the Second Armored Division, initially scheduled for reserve duty, came along from Oran. It was a sizable fleet when it finally turned north late in the afternoon of July 9, to move on Sicily.

In anticipation of what might be rough riding on the Mediterranean all hands were issued a small bottle of brandy to help combat seasickness. It measured about one drink. One of the newspaper men accompanying the division was Clark Lee, who had begun to make a name for himself as one of the few reporters present in Honolulu when Pearl Harbor was attacked by the Japanese. "Lee was a kind of Jack London," Middleton recalled. He had known London and Richard Harding Davis at Vera Cruz, Mexico, when the two adventuresome writers came in looking for far more dramatic news than they ever succeeded in uncovering.

The division had a fairly uneventful crossing most of the way. Then

146

the weather kicked up and most of the men aboard the infantry transports got seasick. The men in the landing craft got even sicker. Barrage balloons which were supposed to ride a thousand feet or so above the invasion fleet, to keep off German dive bombers, swung down and back in the gale. Some broke loose. The rest were reeled in. By nightfall on July 9, however, the wind let up. The sea kept on kicking at the American and British invasion fleet.

As the fleet moved into the rendezvous area, twenty miles off Scoglitti, Middleton was on the *Ancon*, command ship of the naval force commanded by Rear Admiral Alan G. Kirk, whose Naval Task Force 85 included one light cruiser and sixteen destroyers in support of the transports and lighter craft bearing the men of the division. "As soon as we arrived in the rendezvous area, the weather changed and the sea was much like a millpond," Middleton recalled. They saw searchlights and heard some firing. "I was positive that we had been discovered because the enemy lowered the beam right onto the command ship. But we were twenty miles offshore and, come to think of it, all the enemy could have seen would have been the top of the ship's superstructure."

He chose to land the division in an area four miles and more to the west of Scoglitti. Along this beach extremely high sand dunes reached almost to the water's edge. They offered almost perfect protection against Italian and German defenders who might fire from inland positions. If the enemy came down to the dunes, he couldn't squeeze many troops onto the beaches. Fire from the ships' guns would take care of defenders who came so far forward.

At 2 A.M. the small landing craft went into the water and were quickly loaded with infantrymen. There had been no preparatory naval fire. The matter had been thrashed out by the army and the navy in warm discussions weeks before. Since paratroopers were to be dropped behind the beaches along with the attacks across the beaches, the army wanted to take no chances with naval gunfire reaching all the way back to where the paratroopers were to drop.

The Forty-fifth went in in waves, at 2, 2:10, 2:25, 2:35, staggered so their arrival couldn't be predicted precisely by the enemy. "I went in with the fourth wave because the Forty-fifth had never been in combat and I didn't know how they would act. I went with the center regiment so I'd have a regiment on either side of me, which would simplify communications. We had an order that we would not fire as we went ashore unless we were discovered. Well, I assumed that we were going to be discovered when we were ten minutes offshore with the first of the landing craft. I asked Admiral Kirk to open up with everything he had, ten minutes before our first landing craft hit the shore. He complied. I don't know whether we were discovered or not, but in talking to some of the enemy troops that we captured, after the action, we were told that the naval gunfire on the beaches was terrific," Middleton recalled. If these captives were Italians, their accounts were predictable since almost all of them wanted it thought that they resisted much harder than they did.

The primary mission of the Forty-fifth was to capture two airfields needed for Allied planes. The British Eighth Army, under General Bernard Montgomery, had attacked in an area from Syracuse, a third of the way up the east coast of Sicily, around to the west to a junction with the 505th Parachute Infantry, an American unit fighting on the Forty-fifth's right. The First Division went in on Middleton's left, minus the Eighteenth Regimental Combat Team. The Third Division went in on the far left of the invasion front.

One of Middleton's battalion commanders, Lieutenant Colonel William Schaefer, was known throughout the division for his vigorous lectures to his men, warning against taking foolish chances and getting themselves captured. "A captive can't fight," he told his men repeatedly. One of the first units ashore, the battalion was led by its commander. He was seen to head off fast to the right flank. Then he was seen no more. When Middleton went ashore, he went over to check on the progress of the battalion and inquired about the commander. It appeared, his troops said, that the commander had been the first to break his cardinal rule. "After the war, when prisoners were released, I got a note from him, written on brown paper, saying simply: 'Dear General, I'm sorry I got captured. Schaefer,' " Middleton recalled.

Comiso airfield, about eleven miles from the shore, was a primary objective of the Forty-fifth; it was needed for American planes. The planners allowed two days for the capture; the division took it in one. Biscari airfield, about twelve miles inland, was an objective of the third day; it fell on the fourth. American planes were using the Comiso airfield the second day after the landings.

Two regiments of the Forty-fifth landed at the appointed places and moved inland in good order, without meeting heavy resistance. The navy placed a third regiment ashore well to the west of where it was supposed to have landed. The regiment was almost completely disorganized. "It took a couple of days before we got that regiment back on its objective. That was one reason why we took an extra day to capture Biscari airfield," Middleton recalled.

"The invasion plan called for the Eighty-second Airborne Division to drop on the left in front of the First Division. The planes got in the wrong area and dropped a lot of paratroopers in front of my division. We didn't know it, of course, until we got ashore. That first night ashore—it's cold in Sicily, even in July—we had nothing but the clothes on our backs and our guns. We dug foxholes, and late into the night we rolled up in some of the parachutes the paratroopers had left after their jump and turned in for the night. Along about midnight, the navy got the wrong deflection and began shelling our area. The moon was shining and I looked over to the next foxhole, where I saw Clark Lee, the war correspondent, sitting up. I said, 'Get down, Lee; you'll get your head shot off. What are you doing, sitting up like that?' He replied, 'I'm drinking this brandy; you don't think I'm going to die with it in my pocket, do you?' "

The second day the Forty-fifth pushed farther inland, after overcoming problems of congestion on the beaches where inexperienced beach crews weren't able to move supplies smoothly. The beach crews had had no training in what they were doing; they were not connected with the Forty-fifth Division.

On the second night, a second airlift of the Eighty-second Airborne Division was scheduled. The paratroopers were directed to a specific area so as not to pass over the ships of the division's convoy or over the troops of the Forty-fifth, either. Despite the plan, near midnight the troop-carrying planes came in over the division and went out over the navy ships. Some German planes got mixed in with them. Somebody yelled "Aircraft" and somebody else yelled "German," and ground troops started shooting at the planes. "I doubt that any were hit by our troops but as they went out over the navy, the antiaircraft guns knocked down several of the planes—a very unfortunate incident. But the fault lay with the aircraft traveling in the wrong direction," Middleton recalled.

Middleton's only close shave with the enemy occurred his first day ashore in Sicily. He had his driver take their Jeep over a lightly traveled trail, following the footprints of what he thought were some of his own force. The footprints played out. Middleton thought they might be running out of friendly territory. At that moment a German Stuka dive bomber came skimming along just above the trail. The General and his companions abandoned their Jeep in a rush. The Stuka's machine guns kicked up the sand but didn't come perilously close to the Americans.

On the third day of the Sicilian campaign, the 157th, the 179th, and the 180th Regimental Combat Teams (RCTs) were moving steadily ahead, leapfrogging battalions and keeping a careful eye to their flanks. The 157th was moving along the boundary between the Forty-fifth and the British Eighth Army, with the Canadian First Division immediately on Middleton's right. Middleton warned Colonel Charles M. Ankcorn, the 157th's commander, to keep close liaison with the Canadians since the 157th would be operating in part across the boundary between the armies, Highway 124, one of four main roads in Sicily.

While this was going on, General Montgomery at the British Eighth Army headquarters, without waiting for approval by his superior, General Harold Alexander, decided that he would have to have Highway 124 west of the town of Vizzini for the prospective use of his forces moving up the east side of the island. Word of Montgomery's decision didn't get to Middleton.

At daylight on July 13, the 157th was advancing on Vizzini. It moved within a few miles and had halted momentarily when, shortly after 5 P.M., Ankcorn was surprised by the approach of elements of the Fifty-first Highland Division, from the British side of the boundary, also on its way to Vizzini. The original boundary between the armies ran north and south; Highway 124 ran west from Vizzini. Ankcorn watched the British proceed on toward Vizzini, supposing they would continue northward along the boundary. He assumed that Highway 124 surely would remain in the American sector and would still be his objective. To be sure, however, he radioed Middleton of the complications.

Alexander, overall commander in Sicily, had visited Patton the morning of July 13. He had given Patton permission to use other troops to take a port and a town farther west, at Patton's urging, but nothing had been said about an assignment of Highway 124 to the British. Shortly before midnight, Alexander, apparently finding that Montgomery had already made the move, radioed the American headquarters that Highway 124 was passing to British control along its length and was not to be used by the Forty-fifth or other American divisions.

Omar Bradley, commander of the II Corps, in which the Forty-fifth was operating, was sharply disappointed. Patton, the Seventh Army commander, though irritated, did not dispute Montgomery or Alexander. Bradley asked Patton for at least temporary use of Highway 124 to do what he had to: move the Forty-fifth from the far right of the American effort all the way around to the left of the First Division. Patton answered, "Sorry, Brad, but the changeover takes place immediately. Monty wants the road right away."

The Germans had been falling back, hoping to regroup and make a defense across the narrow neck of the Messina peninsula. They needed time. Now Montgomery's preemption of Highway 124 assured them some time—the time lost in having to move the Forty-fifth from right to left. It looked to Bradley as if the British were more intent on taking Messina by themselves than on any joint effort. By the switch in boundaries, the Americans were being shunted off to the west where there was little glory.

After four days of action, it appeared to Alexander that the British were moving well enough in the east and that the inexperienced American divisions might better be brought along with limited assignments to help build up morale and experience. Besides, they seemed capable of protecting the British left flank against counterattack. This feeling seemed natural enough to Alexander and Montgomery. It infuriated most of the American higher command.

While the effects of the changed boundaries were sifting down through the American command, the British were getting nowhere at Vizzini. The British Fifty-first Highlanders asked Ankcorn for help. He sent a battalion to their assistance, but the combined attack was repulsed. The German Hermann Goering Division fought tenaciously.

By early morning on July 15, Middleton's Forty-fifth had pushed within two miles of Highway 124. Orders had come down from Bradley stopping the division there. Furthermore, the Forty-fifth's artillery was not to fire within an area of one mile of the highway, to make sure it didn't shoot at British forces.

Middleton's 179th and 180th RCTs might have proceeded to take the towns of Grammichele and Caltagirone on Highway 124, west of Vizzini, on July 15, but their orders were clear, stopping them short. When a Canadian brigade moved toward Grammichele early on July 15, it was held up by a German rear guard with tank and antitank guns. The Forty-fifth Division artillery was sitting in perfect position to fire in support of the Canadians but was prevented from doing so, by the order from Alexander.

In six days the Forty-fifth had fought well and then found itself in a dead end of British manufacture. To get back into the fight—without ever stopping fighting—the Forty-fifth would have to drop back, sprint out, and make a long end run such as old quarterback Middleton had never contemplated, nor ever confronted at the Command and General Staff School or Army War College.

At daylight on July 16, Middleton began moving his combat teams from the far eastern position of Seventh Army where they had been facing north, to the center of the Seventh Army sector where they would face west. Moving from the right, back to the south, he swung the 157th RCT first. The men rode trucks borrowed from other outfits throughout II Corps. They went down Highway 115 through Gela, where the First Division encountered rough going on invasion day, then northwest toward their new sector. At midnight the same day, the 157th RCT pulled into Mazzarino, after a ninety-mile detour of Montgomery's making. The 753rd Medium Tank Battalion and two battalions of division artillery moved right on the heels of the 157th RCT. After four hours rest, at 4 A.M., the 157th jumped off in the attack, passing Pietraperzia and moving up to the Salso River where a wrecked bridge stopped the advance on the afternoon of July 17. Reconnaissance parties found places to cross; at 1 A.M. on July 18 the 157th was over the river and on its way to Caltanissetta as its intermediate objective and Santa Caterina, ten miles farther along, its final objective.

Without meeting serious opposition, the 157th took Caltanissetta at 4 P.M. and Santa Caterina by 7 P.M. Patrols reaching out from Santa Caterina ran into trouble at a roadblock in a narrow cut at Portella di Reccativo, where a rare side road led off through the desolate countryside to Highway 120.

Following the 157th RCT's interference, the 180th and the 179th swung left and rearward, passing through the rear area of the First Division again, and moved up into line with the 157th on July 18. It looked as if the Forty-fifth was now in position to head for Palermo without much trouble ahead.

In anything but a textbook maneuver, the Forty-fifth had swung its three regimental combat teams out of combat and moved them ninety miles through a companion division's rear area. In theory it couldn't be done. Middleton moved the Forty-fifth, but "I wouldn't have given a nickel for the grade any student would have received if he had proposed such a move at school at Leavenworth," Middleton recalled.

As it turned out, the British had no need for and did not use Highway 124, over which so much ill feeling developed. But knowing that they might have had a use for the road seemed justification enough to Montgomery. It made the situation tidier. Montgomery liked his situations tidy, his maps tidy. And he wasn't worrying about the feelings of the Americans, chaps who were really just getting into the fighting in the European theater. Montgomery would have been genuinely puzzled had he heard one of the American commanders speak his name with such vehemence.

Ankcorn's 157th RCT, having led the way in the switch from east to west and having done most of the fighting on July 18, moved over to let the 180th RCT pass through it and take the lead in knocking out the roadblock at Portella di Reccativo. The Forty-fifth was now cleared to head for the northern coast of Sicily, eighty miles away. At first it had been expected that the Forty-fifth would head for Palermo, but another American corps, the Provisional, had been brought up to make the move on Palermo, using the Second Armored Division and the Eighty-second Airborne Division.

Middleton's Forty-fifth, with the 180th RCT out front, broke up the roadblock at Portella di Reccativo during the evening of July 19. It rolled nineteen miles up Highway 121 on July 20. The 180th pushed into Villafrati, twenty-two miles from Palermo, and put patrols all the way up to the outskirts of the city. Then came the word that the Provisional Corps was to have exclusive use of Highway 121. This sent the other two RCTs, the 157th and the 179th, off the highway and heading north to the coast.

The 157th broke through to the coastal Highway 113 at midmorning of July 23, at Station Cerda, five miles east of Termini Imerese. From Scoglitti to Station Cerda, it had taken the Forty-fifth just a few hours more than thirteen days to make the transit from south coast to north coast of Sicily. The airline distance was just short of eighty miles. Thanks to Montgomery, the distance was extended to something more than two hundred miles.

At Termini Imerese, the 157th split and sent teams left and right to clear the highway. A battalion went east ten miles, taking Campofelice after a sharp tank fight with a part of the Twenty-ninth Panzer Grenadier Division. Heavy artillery and small arms fire stopped the battalion just east of Campofelice.

The First Division, on the right of the Forty-fifth, moving northward much more slowly over rougher terrain and against more tenacious opposition, reached Petralia, about fifteen miles from the north shore, about the same time the 157th RCT of the Forty-fifth reached the sea. Alexander had called for another change of direction, which now sent the First Division east instead of north. The Forty-fifth was to move along the north coast to roll back the Germans toward Messina.

After being halted near Campofelice, the 157th renewed its attack and moved five miles beyond Cefalu, where it was stopped by a blown bridge and a river bed heavily mined by the Germans. The same day, the 179th, following a road six miles inland, took Castelbuono, eight miles north of Petralia, where the First Division had halted. Now the Forty-fifth and the First were on line together.

Under instructions from Bradley to keep moving up the coast road, Middleton put the 180th through the 157th late on July 24. The 180th crossed the Malpertugio River that night, catching heavy artillery, mortar, and machine gun fire from the Germans. Then the 180th ran into a defense based on 3,000-foot-high Pizzo Spina. Vertical cliffs pinned the coast highway to the sea. The 180th had to fight its way almost straight up before breaking the German grip on the heights. Just after this battle, fourteen unidentified naval vessels were sighted off Campofelice, between Cefalu and Termini Imerese, causing Bradley to tell Middleton to stop his advance and be prepared to defend against a possible amphibious attack. Coincidentally, the Germans to the east braced for an American amphibious assault. As it turned out, the ships were American destroyers and mine sweepers, having nothing to do with another invasion.

On July 26, the 180th came to another river, the Tusa. The Germans left the bridge across it undamaged, hoping for some good shooting. The 180th feinted at the bridge and sent a battalion to the top of a high hill inland. The Germans were ready for this move. The rest of the 180th spent the day trying to cross the bridge, managing to get a company over, where-upon the bridge collapsed. The company was pulled back that night. On the morning of July 28, Middleton sent the 157th back to the lead, leap-frogging it over the 180th. It was slow leapfrogging. The Germans had blown out a section of coast highway at the base of a cliff. It took until 5:45 P.M. for the 157th's lead elements to reach the Tusa River. They promptly sent a company across on the coastal flat and another up on the hill, and additional elements across the river well inland. In hard and bloody fighting, two battalions of the 157th fought through to another ridge commanding the division's objective, Santo Stefano.

At 4:30 A.M. on July 30, the Germans, without their usual prepara-tory artillery fire, came storming at the First and Third Battalions of the 157th. The Americans gave a little ground to the surprise attack, then dug in and stopped the Germans. The Second Battalion poured fire into the German flank. Three battalions of artillery joined the serenade. At 1:30 P.M. the Germans stopped and backed off. The 157th took Motta that night and pushed the German rear guard out of Santo Stefano on the morn-ing of July 31.

Santo Stefano was the end of the active fighting for the Forty-fifth in Sicily. In twenty-one days of combat, the Forty-fifth had suffered 1,156 casualties and captured 10,977 prisoners.

The Third Division moved up to replace the Forty-fifth, which was ticketed for the next, and harder, step toward defeat of the Germans, the assault on the Italian mainland. The Italian government had folded and Mussolini had fled; Italy was out of the war as of July 29. But the Germans had taken over Italy and promised a long, bitter battle.

Middleton felt that his National Guardsmen had performed well for the most part. As he looked back over the three weeks in Sicily, he recalled the effectiveness of night fighting, for which the Forty-fifth had been well prepared. "We found a letter on the body of a dead German soldier, saying 'I am terribly tired. I fight all day and I run all night. When daylight comes I'm all mixed up with the Americans.' "

"After we got off the beach the Germans and the Italians didn't have organized positions from which to oppose us. We pushed them too hard. We finally encountered an organized position at Santo Stefano. They knew we had to take that coastal road to Messina, and they made us pay for it," Middleton recalled.

"I was an advocate of night fighting. Our training doctrine back in the states called for it but troops were never given enough of it to get them ready for combat. We found night attacks quite workable. Defenders were sighted in on a relatively small area. When we broke through we could keep going without taking big risks. We took a great many prisoners after breaking through positions at night. There was a great deal more to it than saying, 'Get going!' We had to assign clearly recognizable phase lines, a road or a village. If our attack caused the enemy to try to withdraw under cover of darkness, the withdrawal would turn into a rout. In three weeks, my division got to where it was doing well in night operations," Middleton recalled.

The *Forty-fifth Division News*, an excellent rumor-killer and a publication of the enlisted men for the enlisted men, began overseas publication July 13, the fourth day the division was in Sicily, in a print shop in Vittoria. The editor was still Sergeant Don Robinson, and the cartoonist still Bill Mauldin. No cartoon appeared in the first issue because there were no photoengraving facilities in the town. Before the Italian printers finished handsetting the type they ran out of twelve-point *w*'s and had to throw in six-point type. The staff, in an explanatory item on the back page of the single sheet, six-by-nine inch, newspaper, wrote:

IL POPOLO DI 45TH

This, so far as we know, is the first United States Army newspaper to be published in the European invasion. We hope it is. The *Division News* was the first paper of the "National Emergency" and this new "first" was our ambition.

Don't blame us if it isn't our best effort. We, like you, have been bombed, strafed and sniped at. We're printing in a Sicilian print shop where the printers don't know a word of English, and the press must be run, temporarily, by hand.

We'll print as often as we're able.

The second issue of the *News*, produced on a mimeograph machine, appeared four days later, July 17. It was also datelined Vittoria. Distribution must have been something of a problem, since the 157th Infantry had been displaced ninety miles from its location of the day before, it being the first unit to move in the division's long end run caused by British preemption of Highway 124. A barely distinguishable cartoon by Bill Mauldin occupied half the back page of the single sheet measuring eight-by-thirteen inches. News, as it had been in the first issue, was of men of the division, augmented by news coming in on navy ships' radios.

"PASS IT ON," one headline urged. "Only one *Division News* can be printed for each twenty-five men right now, so please pass on your copy. Don't rat hole it as a souvenir until everyone's had a crack at it."

"MAIL GOES," another headline said. "Mail will go out as often as possible and you may send letters back now, postal authorities said. Censor the mail before it goes to APO. No word of incoming mail yet."

A final filler item said, "Sorry we couldn't print this paper. The printer's sick."

The *News* came out again in Vittoria on July 19, a single sheet, with an excellent quality mimeograph reproduction of Mauldin's cartoon showing two Germans in a foxhole with one saying, "Vot good iss it for Der Fuehrer to tell us God iss on our side? Der Americans haff got all der Indians!" (This was a reference to the great number of Indians from Oklahoma in the National Guard division.) Distribution of the paper was again a problem since the whole division had completed the move over to the left of the First Division and was a long way from Vittoria.

The *News* published again at Caltanissetta on July 22 and 29, miniature four-pagers. Then four issues—five-column tabloids looking like the work of professional publishers—were printed in Palermo and dated August 11, 17, 25, and September 1. The next issue, September 8, was datelined Sicily. When the *News* next appeared on September 29, the dateline was Salerno, Italy, as it was October 4 and 7. By October 14, the *News* was being printed in Naples, where it continued to be published through November.

Throughout the five months the *News* put its emphasis on what the enlisted man was doing, not on the officers. It did note, in the July 22 issue: "PATTON APPROVES: Lt. Gen. George S. Patton, commander of the Seventh Army, has this to say about us: 'The Forty-fifth Division, a green outfit, went into combat with two veteran outfits, and asked for no favors, made no excuses. They kept up with the other outfits. I'm damned proud of every officer and man in the division.' "

Cartoonist Mauldin's wry writing style was developing along with his drawing. He wrote in a column headed "Quoth the Dogface" on July 22:

We've been picking up occasional German broadcasts, and find the Forty-fifth is winning backwards. American forces in the south and west have been driven into the sea, but have lost some 200 tanks in the middle of Sicily. Nazi torpedo boats have successfully blockaded the entire coast, yet nearly 100

Bill Mauldin Cartoon

ships have been sunk in port. Our air force in this theater has been wiped out, and we are brutally bombing churches and cemeteries. Yanks are deliberately starving civilians, but have had to be ordered not to give away their rations.

The programs are usually ended with an ancient Bing Crosby record of "Home Sweet Home," and some bag with a Carolina accent tells us it ain't our fault we were sent here to loot and pillage and rape. Then she tells us she's in Berlin and hopes to meet us all sometime. Coy little thing.

Middleton made it a policy not to interfere with the *News*. He recognized it for its value as a safety valve for men who had no spokesman in their foxholes or on their mountain slopes. Willie and Joe, Mauldin's cartoon characters who grew scruffier as their outfit moved up the Italian peninsula, were invaluable to American morale.

Mack Hornbeak, Middleton's purchasing agent at LSU, had become a member of Middleton's headquarters staff back at Fort Devens. Of him, Middleton said, "You know, some people like war. Hornbeak did. He was always wanting to get out and see what was going on. He was riding through a narrow Sicilian street with his hand on top of the Jeep and got his hand caught between the windshield post and the wall of a building. He had to spend six or eight weeks in the hospital for restorative surgery."

Hornbeak was a lieutenant in the Quartermaster Corps in the Pentagon when Middleton rescued him from Washington. "I was at Devens in July, 1942, when I had to go down to Washington. I invited Hornbeak, Dan Borth, and Paul Hebert to lunch with me at the Willard Hotel. I had just put a star on my shoulder and was ready to stand treat. I got Hornbeak a transfer and he went with me to Devens and stayed with me till the end of the war," Middleton recalled.

In Sicily, Middleton made it a policy to visit his forward units daily. They needed to know that their division commander cared about their problems. "I needed to know what kinds of problems they were confronted with. I never took foolish chances, but I had to make those trips or risk going ignorant of some essential information."

Middleton found it necessary to relieve his assistant division commander in the Forty-fifth when he found his assistant giving all his time to paper work. "He could handle administration, but I needed something more," Middleton said. An assistant also needed to get out and to go forward to battalion level if he was to help in the decision making.

Middleton expected his subordinate commanders to know what was going on up front, too. "I had one colonel commanding a regiment in the

Forty-fifth, who had graduated near the top of his class at West Point. I never found him any place except in his command post. I'd run him out and tell him to go find out what his men were faced with. I saw him at Walter Reed Hospital in Washington after the war and greeted him. He wouldn't even shake hands. He said, 'You ruined my career.' Later, the president of Clemson University asked me if I had known this fellow. I replied that I had but made no further comment. The Clemson president volunteered that he had had to get rid of the man as professor of military science and tactics at Clemson, because he wanted to run the university."

Middleton's friendship with George Patton was put to the test by Middleton's defense of Mauldin, the *Forty-fifth Division News* cartoonist and columnist. Patton developed an intense dislike of Mauldin because the cartoonist "set such a damned bad example with his unsoldierly Willie and Joe," he said. When it was known that Patton was coming around the division in Sicily, Middleton suggested that Mauldin make himself scarce— though it should not be inferred from this that Mauldin was any kind of hanger-on at division headquarters. Middleton didn't want anything untimely befalling the *News*'s prize cartoonist with Patton on the warpath. More than once, Middleton defended Mauldin as an essential to division morale, worth more than several troupes of entertainers.

Regardless of how many times Patton brought up the subject of Mauldin and his "damned unsoldierly Willie and Joe" Middleton always defended Mauldin. Finally, in one such conversation, Patton overstepped himself.

"I order you to get rid of Mauldin and his cartoons," Patton said. Patton wore three stars to Middleton's two and additionally was his superior as head of American forces in Sicily. Middleton weighed his reply.

"Put your order in writing, George," he told Patton. The subject was dropped. Shortly, Patton was to have a problem of his own far transcending his dissatisfaction with Mauldin's cartoon characters.

It was in Sicily that Patton lost control of himself and slapped two men he, with his hair-trigger judgment, suspected of malingering in hospitals. Patton was dead wrong and was sidelined by General Eisenhower after news of the indignities leaked out to newspapers back in the States. Patton told Middleton he guessed that he'd blown his chances of further command with the bad show he'd been involved in at the hospitals.

Newspaper reporting of the Sicilian campaign was good, Middleton said. Ernie Pyle never erred in his writing; he was up front too often. Mauldin did a fine job with pen and typewriter. Clark Lee was given to the kind of dialogue that made lively reading, but he supplied some of it himself. He was with the Forty-fifth all the way through Sicily and usually datelined his columns, "With the Forty-fifth Division." The number of correspondents wounded and killed indicated their nearness to combat, Middleton noted. In Sicily the correspondents attended all the news briefings and got an excellent picture of what was going on and what was contemplated.

"The best man to write military history," Middleton said, "is not a military man. He puts his own interpretation on things. The writer should find out how it happened; the military man might say it couldn't have happened that way because that wasn't good tactics. In the Sicilian action, we had a Harvard historian with us. He was not a military man, but he knew what was going on during his stay with the Forty-fifth.

"Perhaps the attitude of the higher-ups had something to do with the emphasis on getting unbiased accounts of military action in World War II, as opposed to World War I. George Patton liked history; he read it omnivorously. He wanted an accurate record of the action. Perhaps he had much to do with bringing nonmilitary men to the task, as the American commander in Sicily," Middleton recalled. "In any event, *U.S. Army in World War II*, the multivolume history, has been a tremendous improvement on the sketchy accounts we have of World War I."

14   Salerno, Then the Mountains

WHEN THE Forty-fifth completed its combat role at Santo Stefano, Middleton heard that the division probably would be transferred to England to prepare for the invasion of France. But as August wore on, he was told that his division would go to the mainland of Italy for a landing at Salerno, two hundred miles north of Sicily.

While his troops were resting and the next invasion plans were being polished, the division received and the *News* printed a cablegram of congratulations from Will W. Hair, mayor of Abilene, Texas, and Frank Grimes, president of the Chamber of Commerce. Abilene looked upon the Forty-fifth as its own, since the division had trained at nearby Camp Barkeley before moving on to Fort Devens. The Forty-fifth also received fan mail from another of its adopted homes, Watertown, New York, where the infantrymen had practiced digging foxholes in snow and ice. The Watertown *Times*, commenting on the difficulties the British Eighth Army was having before it broke the defenses around Catania, said: "The Eighth Army has run into difficulties in the taking of Catania. We suggest the Forty-fifth Division be sent into action in that sector. That outfit can take any city. They may muss it up a bit, but they'll take it."

During the Sicilian campaign, Middleton was amused and embarrassed by his slowness in assessing the educational attainments of his clerk, Sergeant Paul Cundiff, who traveled with the general and his driver in their Jeep. It was Cundiff's job to record in writing the substance of Middleton's conversations with subordinate commanders in their daily

162

rounds, reaching down to battalion levels. While they were waiting one day, Middleton asked Cundiff where he had gone to college and then asked what the sergeant's plans for peacetime might include. "Teaching," the sergeant said. "If you're going to teach, then you'll have to have a master's degree," the general said. Their conversation was interrupted by the arrival of a colonel. The next lull in action came several days later. Middleton, recalling the earlier conversation with Cundiff, said, in all earnestness, "Sergeant, if you're going to teach, you will need that master's degree."

"I have it, General," Cundiff said.

"Then I really put my foot in it," Middleton recalled. "I asked Cundiff if he contemplated going into college teaching. He told me he did. I told him that he might as well face up to the realities of college teaching and go ahead and earn his union card, the Ph.D. degree.

"And what was Cundiff's reply? He said that he knew what would be required for college teaching. 'I've already earned my doctorate, General Middleton,' Cundiff told me. "And there I'd been using all my less than perfect English on a genuine Ph.D."

Cundiff stayed on as Middleton's clerk through the Italian campaign, until Middleton went to the hospital in Naples in November. George Patton, hearing this story from Middleton, had chuckled and said something about getting a lieutenant's commission for Cundiff. Later, in France, he asked Middleton about Cundiff, saying that he really ought to be a second lieutenant. "I'll give him a battlefield promotion," Patton said.

Reminded that battlefield promotions weren't given for proficiency as a clerk, no matter how valuable the sergeant's contribution, Patton said he'd work something out. He did. Sergeant Cundiff became Lieutenant Cundiff and was assigned to the historical section where his talents could be put to even more profitable use.

Cundiff went into college teaching and became chairman of the Department of English at the University of Delaware, Newark, where later he chuckled over Middleton's recollection of the interrupted conversation which ended in Cundiff's exposure as a genuine Ph.D.

Before the invasion of the Italian mainland, another efficiency report went back to Washington to Middleton's 201 file. This one, signed by Dwight D. Eisenhower, read: "General Middleton's performance to date in active operations as Commanding General of the Forty-fifth Division has been superior. He is apparently living up to the fine reputation he has always had as a combat commander."

For the invasion of Italy, seven plans were drawn. Three were carried out. The British executed two: Operation Slapstick, landing the First British Airborne just under the heel of the Italian boot; and Baytown, putting the Eighth British Army ashore directly across the Strait of Messina. Avalanche, the only operation involving Americans, took the Fifth Army in at Salerno, about halfway up the Italian shin toward Rome.

The British started the move on mainland Italy by crossing the Strait of Messina and moving ahead with relative ease, since the Germans had decided not to cluster out on the toe of the boot where they might be isolated and cut off. The British and American invasion below Salerno gave each about equal responsibility for taking a portion of a crescent-shaped plain about thirty miles along the front, with its points toward the invaders, and with its greatest depth about ten miles. Steep hills fringed the plain below Salerno. Two British divisions went in early in the morning of September 9, in the northern half of the crescent. The American Thirty-sixth Division made the assault in the American half and established a firm foothold. Somehow a ten-mile gap developed between the British and the Americans and was not closed.

On September 10 Middleton took ashore his Forty-fifth Division, which had been in reserve afloat. The 179th Infantry and most of the 157th had sailed from Palermo earlier and had been offshore since September 8. The 179th went ashore north of Paestum. Middleton set up a command post and received as attachments to the 179th, the 645th Tank Destroyer and the 191st Tank Battalion, both already ashore. Middleton's forces were given responsibility for a strip between Sele and the Calore Rivers. They moved inland during the night. Shortly after daybreak, they were hit from their left and rear by a German attack, supported by tanks. Middleton's combat team was forced into an all-around defense. Two battalions of the 157th were put ashore the afternoon of September 10, prematurely, because of a mixup within the naval command. The other battalion of the 157th remained back in Sicily for lack of transport.

Put down on the beach south of the mouth of the Sele River, the 157th, with some quick help from an engineer outfit, built a bridge to replace one destroyed by the Germans and moved to the north side of the river, where it was supposed to have been landed by the navy.

Things grew sticky for Middleton's troops on September 11. They were supposed to plug the ten-mile hole between their left and the British to the north. The Germans were giving them their warmest attention. Recalling that day, Middleton said, "I stopped a battalion of motorized artillery. I asked the lead driver where his outfit was going. A lieutenant colonel came up to see what the holdup was."

"We are displacing to the rear, General," the colonel said.

"You aren't," Middleton replied. "Get your guns out into that wheat field." The battalion deployed in the wheat field, dropped the trails on their guns, and began firing away.

"We had 155-millimeter howitzers firing directly on the Germans after they detected that ten-mile gap between the Americans and the British. The original plan had called for the American Thirty-sixth Division and the British to converge. The British hadn't converged. I was responsible for ten miles of beachhead, without any reserve. I put all my tanks up on line in the hedgerows. The Germans could have broken through us and gone right down to the beach. Why they didn't, I'll never know," Middleton recalled.

"During the defense of the beachhead, I received a confidential message from Mark Clark, the American commander of the combined forces in the Salerno invasion. He told me he was contemplating taking the troops back off the beaches. I told my staff that we weren't leaving. I wasn't having any Dunkerque here in Italy. Without telling my troops what Clark had said might be necessary, I passed around the word that this was a good time to do some hard fighting," Middleton recalled.

The 157th and the attached 191st Tank Battalion fought their way inland September 11, coming cautiously to a large tobacco factory comprising five imposing stone buildings arranged over three fourths of a circle. A panzer battalion had dug in and was waiting; it stopped the Americans, who dug in. They had to pull back the next day under heavy German pressure. The American corps commander, Major General Ernest J. Dawley, told Middleton to do some shifting of his forces back along the Sele River. Parts of both the 157th and the 179th moved over to where the Sele and Calore Rivers joined, about five miles from the sea. Finally the Americans had a line, instead of a string of strong points, to oppose the Germans.

At 8 A.M. September 14 the Germans, misreading what they could see of American and British troop dispositions, thought that the invaders were ready to withdraw and leave the beachhead. The Germans threw in a strong attack on the tobacco factory area. In doing so, they ran straight across the front of the Second and Third Battalions of the 179th Infantry, which had been realigned during the night. The 179th's infantry was joined by tanks, tank destroyers, and artillery in some prime shooting. Quickly they knocked out seven German tanks, immobilizing another, and watched the German infantry back off. Other German units punched at the First Battalion of the 157th and again at the Third Battalion of the 179th. They were knocked back by heavy fire, with the navy joining in for some effective shooting.

All this action was occurring within five miles or less of the sea. From the start the Germans had had the advantage of observation, and their bigger guns on the heights behind the beachhead could reach any point on the beachhead.

General Clark visited the front on September 14, especially the Sele-Calore sector where things had been touch and go. After a careful look, he was convinced that the crisis was past and his army was ashore to stay. The British divisions on the north had been joined by another. The 180th Infantry, third regiment in the Forty-fifth, had been brought in from Sicily, landed and assembled in army reserve near Mount Soprano, the commanding terrain feature at the right rear of the invasion area.

General Eisenhower visited the beachhead the afternoon of September 17 and observed that the battle appeared to be won. At the same time the British corps commander to the north of the Forty-fifth's two regiments found one of his divisions growing "very tired" under steady German pressure. He asked for the 180th Infantry, to help out. Clark was still holding it in reserve, against some unforeseen emergency. The British worked out their problems, then asked Middleton to put his two regiments to work against the Germans at the tobacco factory.

Before there was need for further American attacks, the Germans obliged by pulling out. "When morning came on September 18, there was nothing in front of us," Middleton recalled. The Germans had gone.

"From then on until we got to Venafro we didn't run into any really strong German forces. We worked our way up the center of the Italian boot. Of course, we ran into countless blown bridges, mined roads and villages we had to shoot up to root out the German rear guard."

A five-foot-long panoramic photograph taken at the site of a German observation post in use at the time the Americans and the British landed on September 9 might have been fine propaganda material for the Germans to drop on the Americans and British as they prepared in Sicily for the Salerno invasion. The photograph showed, from the Germans' high vantage point, an almost perfectly flat plain stretching to the sea. There weren't enough woods in sight to hide a flock of geese. A battalion of German heavy artillery on top of Mount Soprano, from which the photograph was made, should have been able to pinpoint any target on the plain. That the Allies made their landing, hung on, and punched their way to high ground in eight days was remarkable, considering the photographic evidence.

After the Germans disengaged and pulled away into the hills backing the Salerno invasion crescent, the Forty-fifth shortly moved out in pursuit. On the far right of the Fifth Army, the Forty-fifth maintained liaison with the British Eighth Army, which had the responsibility for the eastern portion of the Italian boot leg.

By September 24 the division had broken the German defense of Oliveto and Quaglietta in hard fighting. Reconnaissance forces reached the Calore River on September 27. Benevento was taken by the Forty-fifth on October 3, as the autumn rains set in with a vengeance. Heavy fighting carried the 179th Regiment into Piedimonte d'Alife on October 19 and the 180th Regiment into Alife on October 20. The next day the Forty-fifth went into corps reserve, after six weeks of unbroken action.

Along the way in the upper Volturno River valley, Middleton once more encountered the frustrations of having and yet not having air support for his troops. On six occasions between October 11 and 17 he asked for planes to bomb targets of opportunity detected by his forward observers. Once it was enemy artillery positions. Next time it was road traffic. Then it was a column of German vehicles creeping along bumper to bumper. Middleton's requests were denied once because "all fighter-bomber airfields are unserviceable"; then because the targets were not spotted in time for the planes to get to them; and again because "weather in area is reported impossible."

Twenty German planes materialized over a highway near Faicchio and bombed and strafed forces of the Forty-fifth on October 14, deferring the division's advance for a day. The division tried its luck with air support six more times between October 14 and 18, asking for a well-placed bomb or two on enemy positions opposing the Forty-fifth's forward elements. Though six missions were prearranged, none came off because of the weather.

American forces crossed and recrossed the Volturno River as they slogged northward. Having caught its breath, the Forty-fifth was given the honor of fording the Volturno again, along with elements of the 180th Infantry crossing the night of November 2. They were unopposed until morning. Further upstream the 179th Infantry waded over on November 4, finding almost no opposition in the grainfields and vineyards. German machine gunners began firing as the Americans closed on Venafro. A rifle company worked its way through town and onto a hill to the north. After dark the remainder of the regiment moved ahead. And on November 5 the regiment moved onto high ground behind Venafro and secured the town.

With the taking of Venafro, there came a lull as the Allied higher command studied German troop dispositions. The gains were coming slowly. Rome was still a hundred hills away. The hill climbing, the endless rains, the deepening mud had begun to exact a physical toll on Middleton. His left leg had been giving him pain. Now it gave him torture. He had damaged his right knee in intramural football at Mississippi A & M, later learning to punt and drop kick with his left foot.

As he searched his recollection for an explanation of the pain in his other leg, he recalled a march of the whole division back at Fort Devens, where every man, cook, clarinetist, and division commander was required to cover five miles in an hour. Middleton wouldn't require what he couldn't accomplish himself. He had limped in at the finish. Now, high in the hills of Italy, his left leg became all but useless, especially if he had to ride any distance in his Jeep. He decided to let the medics have a look. They studied it, h-m-m-m-ing appropriately over the knee and asking solicitous questions. The pain persisted. Arthritis it wasn't. No one was quite sure what it was. Rest was prescribed.

Other plans were in the making, which involved Middleton and a higher command. This meant farewell to the Forty-fifth, his battle-proved Thunderbirds. He turned over command in a downpour at the forward command post in an olive grove near the town of Presenzano. Major General William W. Eagles, assistant commander of the Third Division, took over. Middleton and Eagles shook hands in the rain. Middleton climbed into his staff car and was driven off.

"No formalities. Middleton was like that. He just drove off," a witness reported. In all likelihood, Middleton saw no occasion to bring his troops out into the rain just to see a general take leave of them. If they had to get wet, let them be fighting the Germans, an assignment that they would take up again shortly, after having fought longer than any other outfit in the Sicilian and Italian campaigns.

Middleton had come ashore at Paestum early in September and set up his command tent under a fig tree. He hadn't been ashore long before he had cause to tell Mark Clark, who had begun to doubt that his force could maintain its hold on the Salerno beaches, "Mark, leave enough ammunition and supplies. The Forty-fifth is staying."

Next Middleton went to the army hospital in Naples. He was there from late November well into December, giving the doctors something to guess about. When he came out of the hospital he was assigned to a board with Major General Maxwell Taylor and another general to decide what to do with four divisions of the Italian army cut off in Corsica. Italy had surrendered and dropped out of the war early in September. The American generals decided to leave the four divisions where they were. In Corsica they surely couldn't become half the liability they might be back on the mainland.

The knee still pained him, but he could get around. One of the doctors at the hospital asked Middleton if he had ever played football and injured his knee in that sport. When Middleton said yes, the doctor exclaimed, "That's it. That's the old knee damage showing up again."

"It couldn't be," said Middleton. "It was the other knee—my right—that I damaged in football. No, I've got it all figured out now. It was that hike at Devens with a pack on my back."

From Naples, Middleton flew back to North Africa to Eisenhower's headquarters. There, Eisenhower asked him to look over plans for an Allied landing at Anzio, Italy, in mid-January. Middleton studied the plans with Major General Lowell W. Rooks, G-3 at Allied Forces Headquarters. "I told Rooks, 'You need more men. You can get ashore but you can't get off the beachhead. You can't fight your way out without risking dangerously exposed flanks,' " Middleton recalled. "Two divisions weren't half enough there, where the Germans could run in far superior forces from their positions around Rome."

Anzio proved to be a near disaster. Middleton's old division, the Forty-fifth, was shortly called upon to help maintain the toehold on Anzio after the landings January 22, 1944. The American forces, opposed by Germans on dominant high ground, found it touch and go for weeks.

At Eisenhower's headquarters, Middleton was given his next assignment. Go home, he was told, and see what develops. "If I'd stayed in Italy in command of the Forty-fifth, I would probably have been relieved. I couldn't buy those plans for the Anzio invasion, giving the invading corps commander, John Lucas, a split mission: to land and establish a beachhead, and to march on Rome. With only two divisions, the American Third and a British division, with the Forty-fifth in reserve—that was a foolish plan for Anzio," Middleton recalled.

With his aide, Alfred Glassell, Middleton remained in the relatively mild climate of North Africa before heading for the United States in mid-January, 1944. "We traveled home in style. There was a big, fancy plane at Allied Forces Headquarters, which had brought some very important people over. It was about to make the return flight. We found out about it and were invited by the pilot and crew to enjoy their hospitality. Each of us had a stateroom to himself. We were flown all the way back to Miami."

They arrived in Miami the way VIPs were expected to arrive and were offered luxury quarters for a day and a night there. From Miami they flew on, less spectacularly, to Washington. Middleton reported to General Marshall at the Pentagon. Marshall, after inquiring about Middleton's health, told him he was ticketed for command of the XII Corps at Atlanta.

"I thought this was that stateside duty I'd successfully avoided so far, so I told Marshall I didn't want any such duty. Marshall then told me to go out to Walter Reed Hospital to be examined. He said that I was certainly eligible for retirement. I wanted retirement even less than I wanted command of the XII Corps at Atlanta, and I told General Marshall so," Middleton recalled.

Out at Walter Reed Hospital, the doctors gathered again, h-m-m-med, and diagnosed arthritis. "They told me I could remain inactive and it wouldn't hurt. While I was in the hospital, General Eisenhower asked General Marshall for me. Ike wanted me to command an army corps. Marshall told Ike of my physical condition. Ike said he wanted me anyhow. So Marshall agreed that I should go to England. I arrived there March 4, 1944, and took command of the VIII Corps."

More than one version of the trans-Atlantic conversation between Marshall and Eisenhower has appeared in print. General of the Army Omar N. Bradley, in his *A Soldier's Story*, wrote it this way: "During the war Major General Troy H. Middleton, commander of the VIII Corps, also suffered an arthritic disability in the knee, and it was suggested to General Marshall that he be sent home rather than given the command of a corps in the field. 'I would rather,' General Marshall said, 'have a man with arthritis in the knee than one with arthritis in the head. Keep Middleton there.' "

After the war, former President of the United States Eisenhower recalled the incident to this author, on August 19, 1965:

"I was wiring to General Marshall from England and I said 'I wish you'd send me Troy Middleton right back here.' And General Marshall wired back, 'Fine, I agree with you in his value. But he's in Walter Reed Hospital with his knees.' I replied, 'I don't give a damn about his knees; I want his head and his heart. And I'll take him into battle on a litter if we have to.' "

That, said Eisenhower, was how he'd told Marshall how much he needed Middleton for the VIII Corps command.

Early in February, Middleton left the hospital with a split diagnosis: arthritis and football knee. Marshall had an assignment for him more to his liking, thanks to Eisenhower. A series of orders sent Middleton to six army installations in Tennessee, Colorado, and finally Washington, D.C., with a brief stopover in Baton Rouge.

Middleton walked into his home in Baton Rouge unannounced. Mrs. Middleton let her turkeys go untended for hours. Bernice, in her senior year at LSU, skipped some homework. Troy, Jr., took advantage of the opportunity and served as commander of the Army Specialized Training Program troops at LSU in a surprise parade for his father. Troy, Jr., had returned to LSU for specialized engineering training after completing his training at Fort Ord. Shortly after his father's visit, Troy, Jr., went on to Officer Candidate School at Fort Benning, where he had been born. Bernice went on to graduate from LSU later that year, at age eighteen.

Having said goodbye to his family and having been joined by his aide,

Glassell, Middleton had a pretty good idea of where he was going next. It had to be overseas.

"When I got to Washington, General Marshall said, 'You get on over to England. Ike Eisenhower is asking for you. I'm sending along a sergeant who's a physical therapist in civilian life, to take care of that knee.' The sergeant went with me. He was very good; he massaged the knee every morning and every night for a year. 'In the final analysis,' the sergeant told me, 'that's not arthritis; that's an injury. You had a calcification as a result of the injury.' So it was nice to know at last just what was wrong with the old knee," Middleton recalled.

All the round-about travels prior to his visit home had been designed to mislead German spies. "Whenever a commander is withdrawn from combat and another comes in, the enemy always wants to know where the first commander is headed," Middleton explained. The Germans should have been thoroughly confused by his travels from Washington to Chattanooga to Lebanon to Memphis to Colorado Springs to Leadville to Shreveport to Baton Rouge to Washington—if they really tried to follow him.

"You're taking over the VIII Corps in England," Marshall said. "What staff members do you want to take with you?"

"None," Middleton said. "I know that Dan Sultan organized the corps staff. He was number one in his graduating class at the University of Mississippi (I can forgive him that). He was number one in his class at the United States Military Academy. Any staff good enough for Dan is good enough for me."

"Are you sure you won't take somebody?" Marshall persisted. "It's customary, you know, for a corps commander to pick his own staff."

"There is one man," Middleton said. "I'd like to have Mack Hornbeak, who was with me all the way from Devens through Sicily and Italy. He's on Anzio right now. I know things aren't pleasant at all there. Could I have him?"

Hornbeak greeted Middleton when he arrived at VIII Corps headquarters a few days later. "Was I ever glad to get orders out of a place!" Hornbeak exclaimed.

Middleton left his aide in Washington, telling him that he was too good a man to go through the whole war as flunky to a general. "Go to Command and General Staff School and prepare yourself for a combat command," he told Glassell, giving a fond goodbye to the aide who had amused him at Devens by asking, "General, when are we going to get ourselves that other, junior, aide we're entitled to?" Middleton had answered, "Why, Alfred, I have enough trouble looking after you, without taking on another man."

"Somebody at the Pentagon shortstopped Alfred," Middleton recalled. "He never got to Fort Leavenworth, serving out the rest of the war in splendor at the Pentagon." Glassell, coming from a family which enjoyed more than a little wealth from its petroleum holdings, could afford to live in glamorous Washington in 1944 and 1945.

Having made his request for the assignment of Hornbeak to his VIII Corps staff, Middleton was reminded of a conversation between Hornbeak and his aide, Glassell, on a cold night in Sicily, when Glassell had called from his foxhole to Hornbeak in his foxhole, "What's a good investment, Mack?"

Hornbeak, busy with the business of survival, answered, "What in hell are you hollering about?"

Glassell responded, "I've just got news of this $400,000 I've received on some oil properties at home. With all that surplus money, I need a good place to invest it. You're an economist and an accountant. You ought to know."

"Hornbeak's reply shook half the olives off a nearby tree," Middleton recalled.

15   Up to VIII Corps

GENERAL John C. H. Lee's plans for Troy Middleton would have taken him to England nearly two years earlier, Middleton mused as his plane winged over the North Atlantic. He was glad to have been fighting rather than working in the Services of Supply for the past nine months. His plane set down at Prestwick, Scotland, then flew on to London.

A young officer walked up as Middleton walked down the steps from the plane, accompanied by his physical therapist.

"Are you General Middleton?" the greeting officer asked. "We have a car waiting." The driver headed for General Eisenhower's headquarters in London.

Middleton was ushered in to see his old friend. Ike stepped back for an appraising look as Middleton strode across the room. He appeared satisfied that his new corps commander's knees were functional and that Middleton did not limp. They talked.

"Ike told me that the VIII Corps was not far out and that my car was waiting. Somebody showed me to the car. The driver was a young English woman. On the way out we stopped for lunch—not a bad lunch for a country long at war—in a little town," Middleton recalled.

Middleton's woman driver wheeled briskly up to VIII Corps headquarters at Kidderminster in midafternoon. Headquarters was in a new, largely unoccupied hospital which had been built to accommodate the wounded who would be coming back from France once the invasion began.

Kidderminster was a pleasant town about 15 miles southwest of the heart of Birmingham and about 110 miles west by northwest of the heart of London. VIII Corps had come to Kidderminster from Camp Bowie, Texas, arriving in England on December 16, 1943. Its commander was Major General Emil F. Reinhardt, whom Middleton had known for years.

As the man who was to become Middleton's new aide told the story, Reinhardt lost the VIII Corps command solely because he had no combat service. When George Patton, who had been in Eisenhower's doghouse for months since the soldier-slapping incidents in Sicily, was returned to good graces as commander of a potential army in the north of England, he asked about the VIII Corps commander. He was told that his name was Reinhardt.

"Reinhardt?" Patton said. "Never heard of him. What's his combat record?" Told that Reinhardt had none, Patton said, "Get rid of him. I want a man who knows how to fight. Get me Troy Middleton. Thus it was (perhaps) that Patton's request went down to London, to be relayed by Eisenhower to Marshall in Washington.

In any event, Middleton thanked his driver and inquired about accommodations she might need at Kidderminster for the night. She would require none, she said, but would be driving back to London at once. And off she went.

General Reinhardt came out to greet Middleton. They exchanged greetings. Then Middleton said, "Ducky, I had nothing to do with this." Reinhardt smiled at the old nickname. "I know you didn't, Troy," he said. "Patton and Eisenhower want a man with combat experience. They know yours is the best."

Reinhardt left for the States the next day. "Next time I saw him," Middleton recalled, "was outside Koblenz, where his Sixty-ninth Division was in an adjacent corps command. Reinhardt and young Perry Craddock (son of a classmate at Mississippi A & M) flew over and had lunch with me. Craddock piloted an artillery spotter plane for the Sixty-ninth. Reinhardt had done a fine job training his division and getting it ready for the combat he didn't have and that cost him his corps command."

Just before Eisenhower had said goodbye to Middleton in London, he asked Middleton for his views on bringing Patton back to command an army. "Ike was wary. I said I thought it would be a good idea to bring

Georgie back because he's such a fighter. Ike agreed with that but remained leery of Georgie's big mouth," Middleton recalled.

Middleton took over the VIII Corps on March 4, 1944. The corps staff he had inherited from Reinhardt had originally been chosen by Dan Sultan, who formed the VIII Corps and had been sent to a command in the Pacific area. With Hornbeak as his only selection, taking over as headquarters commandant, Middleton got ready to settle down to work. Hornbeak was the only corps staff member who knew anything about Middleton's combat record.

Colonel Gainer Jones, in civilian life a banker in Houston, Texas, and corps G-4, asked Hornbeak, "What kind of man is this fellow Troy Middleton?" Hornbeak replied, "He's different. He might put corps headquarters right up there with corps artillery." Jones was incredulous. "My God, man, I never heard of such a thing." Neither, for that matter, had Hornbeak. But he went on to get a bit more mileage out of his yarn. "General Middleton seldom digs in," he told Jones. "He parks his trailer and lives in it." The word went ricocheting around corps headquarters. "They must have figured that I was some tough soldier," Middleton recalled.

To replace Glassell as his aide, Middleton went into the G-3 section and picked John Cribbet. The young officer from Illinois had been graduated from the University of Illinois and had completed one year of law school there before being commissioned at Fort Benning. He went from Benning to VIII Corps at Camp Bowie and went with the staff to England. In Cribbet, Middleton found a man who knew all the corps staff and knew a great deal about plans and operations through his work in the G-3 section.

"Our relationship was close and friendly," Cribbet recalled later. He soon found that Middleton wanted his aide to be the general's auxiliary eyes and ears, not an errand runner or a personal attendant. When the corps moved into combat just three months after Middleton took over, Captain Cribbet observed, "I have never known a man who had such equanimity under stress and who had the ability to master all the details with such apparent ease. At the same time he was a warm, friendly individual who was adored by all members of his corps staff, and everyone had complete confidence in his ability." A corps commander adored? Yes, said Cribbet, the word fitted perfectly.

Middleton had not been long in England when he met Patton again.

Patton had been given command of the Third Army in the north of England; the VIII Corps was assigned to Third Army. Patton stayed in northern England, as did most of the troops assigned to his command, as part of a great ruse, intended to keep the Germans thinking that Patton would take his army across the English Channel in the Calais area, well to the east of the intended invasion beaches.

One of Middleton's neighbors was Lord Dudley, who had a large estate outside Birmingham, to which Middleton was invited. Lord Dudley, soon after their first meeting, offered Middleton a cigar, with the observation that, "You Americans surely smoke green cigars; I put them up for a year and find them at their best about the time you Americans would throw them away."

Lord Dudley invited Middleton to attend a meeting of the Rotary Club with him in Birmingham. It was the only Rotary meeting loyal Rotarian Middleton was able to squeeze into his busy schedule overseas. He hadn't found any Rotary Clubs in Sicily or Italy but had taken time out in July, 1943, to write congratulations to the Baton Rouge Rotary Club on its selection of an old friend, Arthur Choppin, as president. The Birmingham Rotarians ate lamb and briskly ran off their meeting much as the club in Baton Rouge would have done.

At dinner at Lord Dudley's one evening, Middleton was told that a late-arriving guest was a young lady from one of England's most prominent families. "She might have to come in work clothes; she's running the family dairy," Lord Dudley said. No traces of the dairy clung to the young woman, who arrived smartly dressed. She left the gathering early to be ready for early morning milking chores back at the family estate, from which all the males had gone off to war.

Middleton was impressed with the attitudes of British civilians, who never complained. "We Americans were advised never to purchase food in English shops since to do so was to deprive some Englishmen of the opportunity to buy it. They ate lots of lamb—not one of my favorite foods, but always attractively served."

Another neighbor, Mrs. Beecham, invited Middleton and several of his staff to her home for luncheon and a walk through the beautiful gardens of the estate. The main course was a 30-inch-long salmon, beautifully done and sharply contrasting with the army issue foods served at the corps mess. The guests took along tinned foods in keeping with the wartime custom followed by Americans in food-short Britain. Mrs. Beecham's husband, in his forties, was a captain in the British ordnance forces.

Middleton's corps staff at this time never exceeded seventy-five officers. He was asked at Kidderminster, and on several occasions later, why he had such a small staff. "I never was much for using more men than were needed to get the job done. It was surely fortunate that General Marshall had asked me if I didn't want to take *somebody* with me when I went to VIII Corps. Hornbeak was the perfect choice for two reasons: he was a good man, and the headquarters commandant turned out to be something of a dud. The chief of staff of the corps soon told me, 'One of the unfortunate things you will have to do is to replace the headquarters commandant.' In Hornbeak I had the perfect replacement. I promoted him from captain to major, and later in Europe, to lieutenant colonel," Middleton recalled. The corps G-1 cleared the way for the change by declaring the original headquarters commandant surplus. He went back to a cadre somewhere in the States.

Hornbeak's job was routine and not so routine. He was concerned mostly with housing and feeding the corps staff in training and in combat. In addition, he did the same for the headquarters company which guarded the corps headquarters. In combat a corps commander might have under his direction a minimum of one and a maximum of five divisions of infantry or armor—as few as 20,000 and as many as 110,000 men.

It was up to Hornbeak to go ahead when corps headquarters was displacing forward. He had to find parking areas for all the corps vehicles. He had to place all sections of headquarters where they could do their work most efficiently. He had to find a satisfactory water supply and to see that enlisted men's and officers' messes were close by. With the corps signal company he arranged for lights and telephones and other communications requirements. "With his slow drawl and his deliberate movements, old Mack would always have everything set up just right," Middleton recalled.

After the corps staff had had an opportunity to observe Middleton in action around headquarters at Kidderminster for a week or so, their impressions began flowing back up the grapevine to their commander. "I found out that they were impressed when I arrived in an old British limousine with a woman chauffeur, instead of in one of the two Cadillacs I was entitled to. They also liked my eating with them, instead of off in my quarters. Maybe I didn't know any better then. I preferred to get around in my

Jeep, anyhow. All the way through Sicily and Italy, my driver had been the same man, Sergeant Francis E. Briscoe, a high school graduate from Oklahoma. I used to tell him he ought to go to college and get a degree, whether he wanted to or not. He did, and after the war, drove to Baton Rouge with his wife to see me," Middleton recalled.

Though his taste ran to Jeeps and less pretentious vehicles, Middleton regularly was driven down to London and back each day in a big old town sedan for the invasion planning sessions that began in March and continued well into May. With him went his planning staff to an elementary school building, where the movements for D-day were plotted. The planning party always included his G-3, Colonel John P. Evans, and officers from the G-3 section; his G-4, Colonel Gainer Jones; his assistant chief of staff, Colonel Walter C. Stanton; and the corps artillery officer, Brigadier General William C. McMahon, and some of his staff. At times the party was enlarged by more officers from G-4; sometimes the G-1 participated; rarely the G-2 sat in; occasionally the chief of staff was needed. "I was there all the time," Middleton recalled.

To throw the Germans off on where the VIII Corps would go in the invasion, Middleton moved his headquarters from Kidderminster to a spot near Liverpool, another seventy-five miles or so to the north. From this point it would seem much more logical to deliver the VIII Corps forces to the east coast of England for movement down to a channel crossing from a point opposite Calais, France. This ruse succeeded remarkably, keeping the German forces badly split through the first week of the invasion when they were in a perfect agony of indecision, waiting for Patton to bring his army across the channel's narrowest point from Dover.

"Joe (J. Lawton) Collins, commander of the VII Corps, was in on the planning with me, as were several division commanders during this time. Prime Minister Churchill came down twice to visit with us during our planning sessions," Middleton recalled. Collins worked with Middleton in operations on the Cotentin Peninsula, looking to the capture of the port of Cherbourg and the cutting off of German forces on the peninsula.

General Middleton had no problems with his corps staff's intemperate consumption of inexpensive British whisky. "It was available at $1.50 a pint instead of the $6 or $7 it cost back in the States," he recalled. "But in view of an experience I had back in Sicily, I routinely informed all my officers that if I caught them under the influence of alcohol I would send them

home, adding a somewhat ominous 'And you know what that means.'
They would have lost their temporary rank and the fact would have been
noted on their efficiency reports."

In the division mess in Sicily one night, the division G-4 had fallen
over his plate, drunk. "I had to send him home. Fortunately, he straightened up and runs a successful business back in his Texas home town. He
was one of those who couldn't afford to drink—he couldn't stand alcohol,"
Middleton recalled.

This incident reminded him of what had happened to two senior
cadets at LSU during his tenure as commandant of cadets in the 1930s.
Officers both, they had tanked up on near-beer (a low-alcohol product
available during the prohibition era), had made nuisances of themselves,
and had been the subject of complaints. They were called on the carpet by
Middleton, who asked the two if they had ever heard of seniors in ROTC
being privates. They hadn't. "I told them to go get rifles and to join the
rear ranks of their company. They did. The father of one of the miscreants
came to see me, terribly fearful that his son would lose his chance at an
appointment to attend West Point. The reduction had to stand, of course.
The young fellow received his appointment just the same. When we were
in New York in 1936, on our way to the Philippines, we went by West
Point. I looked up my former cadet. We recalled the near-beer incident. He
assured me he would never try such a stunt at the Military Academy."

Middleton had several green divisions in his corps and a lot of
green artillery. Very few officers or men had ever been in combat. He had
worked hard trying to whip his forces into shape, from early March to the
end of May. Two weeks before the invasion, Middleton's forces were
pulled out of Patton's Third Army and assigned to Omar Bradley's First
Army on a special mission. First Army troops were to make the D-day
landings. After the Allies were established on shore, the VIII Corps was
to go over.

The corps and its troops were transported by night to Southampton
and put under wraps. "We were shut up in our compound. The only man
I let out was Hornbeak, to carry a written message to First Army headquarters near Bristol. Mack came back with a pint bottle of Johnnie Walker Black Label Scotch whisky, for consumption some time after a successful invasion. I gave it to my striker to keep and thought no more about it,"
Middleton recalled.

16   Cotentin Peninsula and Beyond

THE VIII Corps and divisions under its command sat in Southampton from D-day, June 6, until late on June 11. They began the move across the English Channel in good order and completed the crossing about daylight on June 12, in not so good order.

One of the Landing Ship Tanks (LSTs) transporting part of the corps staff struck a German mine and sank. Lifejackets buoyed the officers, who were fished out of French coastal waters and taken back to England by their rescuing vessel. "When they rejoined me about ten days later in France, they looked like brand new soldiers in new uniforms, with new equipment. We lost very few craft in our crossing, but half my headquarters complement had to be aboard one of them. Hornbeak and Cribbet were on my ship, which was undamaged," Middleton recalled.

"Wherever I looked at daylight the channel waters were speckled with craft the way flies are drawn to flypaper," he recalled. "We had no problems with German planes attacking us. I was on Cotentin Peninsula fourteen days before I saw a German plane. (I heard some at night.) If the Germans had had half the air power we had, we could not have stayed on the peninsula."

The VIII Corps headquarters went ashore near Carentan, in an area which Joe Collins' VII Corps troops had cleared on D-day. Headquarters was set up between Carentan and Ste. Mere-Eglise, where the Germans had sharply opposed American paratroops their first day in France. Middleton's corps, building up gradually, included the Eighty-second Airborne

Division, the heavily depleted 101st Airborne, the Seventy-ninth and Ninetieth Divisions.

First optimistic plans from Supreme Headquarters had projected much faster movement inland by American and British forces, attacking side by side—after the predictably difficult first week ashore. The countryside took care of that. A tenacious enemy used every landscape feature in the defense. The planned timetable for outward movement of American forces on the Cotentin Peninsula called for their arrival at Granville, near the base of the peninsula, by June 23, and at Avranches, the gateway to Normandy and Brittany, by June 26. They were just halfway to the first objective after fifty days of fighting, on July 26, and were far short of Avranches, the objective of June 26 in the original optimistic timetable drawn up in England.

Middleton's divisions, moving in behind Collins' VII Corps, which was assigned to take the port of Cherbourg at the northern tip of the Contentin Peninsula, heard that VII Corps troops had captured Cherbourg June 29 and picked up the last German defenders at the northwest tip of the peninsula on June 30.

"One of the first Americans I saw in France," Middleton recalled, "was a Baton Rougean, B. W. Wax, who came roaring up on a German motorcycle festooned with two or three German helmets and P-38 pistols as souvenirs. He was with an airborne outfit. He told me, 'I've always wanted to give you something. Here's a motorcycle.' Then he got off and hurried on.

"I had to put a ban on taking over German transport. We did keep some German trucks we captured. But I wouldn't let soldiers have them because they'd always be working on them. A man might even neglect his duty and go riding round in a captured vehicle. Souvenir hunters would pick up anything—even a machine gun—carry it for awhile and then drop it when it got too heavy. Then they'd pick up something else. They especially liked the Luger pistol, which had an attachment for making it into a shoulder weapon," he recalled.

The Ninetieth Division, originally assigned to the VIII Corps, had been turned over to VII Corps as a backup force during the invasion. It crossed early, then reverted to VIII Corps after it moved across the channel. With the fall of Cherbourg to the VII Corps, the VIII Corps was done with its blocking assignment and could begin to move south against the Germans in the middle of the Cotentin Peninsula. Three German divisions, the Second SS Panzer, the Seventy-seventh Infantry and the 353rd Infantry, were well established on the highest ground around, surrounding La Haye du Puits. Middleton's troops had to knock the Germans out of their high perches before they could roll to the south.

Here the character of the countryside channeled the American movements. The bogs of the Prairies Marecagueses de Gorges were on the corps left. In this *bocage* country, individual farmer's fields and pastures were broken into a latticework. Small units fought from compartment to compartment, separated by walls of earth up to six feet high, supporting dense shrubbery and small trees effectively separating each compartment from all the others. Fields of fire were narrow. Firing lanes were short. The German defenders had every advantage, being able to lay as many ambushes as they had the troops to man.

By July 7, Middleton's forces had wrapped their lines in a near strangle hold around La Haye du Puits. They included the Seventy-ninth Infantry Division, the Eighty-second Airborne, the Ninetieth Infantry, and the recently arrived Eighth Infantry Division. It took eight days of the hardest fighting to push the Germans off the heights and to move ahead five miles, with the Seventy-ninth alone taking more than 2,000 casualties. Steady rain complicated matters, depriving the Americans of air support.

The VII Corps, under Collins, had now moved down from its finished task at Cherbourg and was attacking south on the left of the VIII Corps. It, too, ran into the stubbornest German defenses. Hedgerows eight feet thick permitted the Germans to burrow halfway through and then offset the burrow so that it couldn't be seen through by attackers, but would permit defenders to move quickly from one field to the next without detection.

"We finally put some devices on the front of our tanks that permitted them to cut straight through these hedgerows instead of being tipped up with their bellies exposed, making them easy prey to antitank weapons," Middleton recalled. The devices, invented by Sergeant Curtis Culin, welded to tanks just above the ground, looked like giant shark's teeth and enabled tanks to shear straight through the barriers separating fields. The Germans used mines extensively, requiring that American engineers precede every operation, looking for the inevitable explosives. With water

covering much of the peninsula, every movement, it seemed, had to proceed through a narrow funnel neck before the next step could be undertaken.

In England, in preparation for the invasion and subsequent campaigning, the VIII Corps staff had worked on at least five plans for exploi-
tation of the early invasion gains, in coordination with others in the invasion forces. In addition, when all their other work had been caught up on,
the corps staff was given hypothetical situations to cope with. What if, for
instance, the enemy didn't react in his characteristic way in a given situation? What should the American force do? As it developed, none of the
original five plans and none of the hypothetical exercises proved of any
use on the ground of the Cotentin Peninsula. The enemy didn't react by
the book. "The plan the VIII Corps used in finally breaking out of the
peninsula was played by ear—strictly off the cuff. Our action depended on
what the enemy had done and was doing," Middleton recalled.

When the breakout came, the VIII Corps rolled nearly fifty miles
from its positions near Lessay and Periers on the western flank of the
American forces all the way down past Avranches to Pontaubault in seven
days. Middleton's divisions covered fifteen miles the first four days and
swept the last thirty-five miles in a little more than two days.

In preparation for the attack, starting July 24, American air commanders were asked to lay a carpet of bombs on the opposing Germans to
soften them up for the American onslaught on a wide front. The planes left
their bases in England and were over France when their commander, British Air Chief-Marshal Sir Trafford Leigh-Mallory, found the sky overcast
and visibility poor. He ordered the attack called off. But his order came too
late. Three hundred bombers laid their eggs, killing 25 American soldiers
and wounding 131 others. The bombing also alerted the German defenders
to what they might expect in the immediate future.

Try again, the air attackers were told, on July 25. It was suggested that the planes, both high-flying strategic bombers and the ground-
skimming fighter bombers, should fly parallel to the American front rather
than perpendicular to it, using such well-defined terrain features as roads
to be sure there were no more short drops. The air commanders said they
couldn't carry out the mission in this way. Finally, the "safe distances"

Among the visitors drawn to Middleton's headquarters to witness the
were agreed upon and the attack was scheduled for 11 A.M. on July 25.

carpet bombing was an old friend, General Lesley J. McNair, chief of the Army Ground Forces. Middleton had warned him against going forward from VIII Corps headquarters so much as one yard. McNair chose to go much closer. One stick of bombs caught McNair and his party. A careful search of the bombed area later yielded a portion of McNair's ring finger bearing his class ring from the Military Academy. The short fall killed 111 other soldiers and wounded 490.

The bombing also took a lot of the starch out of the German defenders. Generalleutnant Fritz Bayerlein, commander of the Panzer Lehr Division, had placed his tanks where he hoped they would be protected by the hedgerows. He later said, "The planes kept coming over, as if on a conveyor belt, and the bomb carpets unrolled in great rectangles. My flak had hardly opened its mouth, when the batteries received direct hits which knocked out half the guns and silenced the rest. After an hour I had no communication with anybody, even by radio. By noon nothing was visible but dust and smoke. My front lines looked like the face of the moon and at least seventy percent of my troops were out of action—dead, wounded, crazed or numbed. All my forward tanks were knocked out, and the roads were practically impassable."

Did the Germans collapse under the impact of the bombing? Unfortunately they did not. Many of them popped out of their foxholes, just beyond the bomb-carpeted area, and fought the advancing Americans, themselves hampered at first by the churned-up terrain.

It seemed clear, however, that the Germans were about finished on the Cotentin Peninsula, and that the breakout into Brittany would be achieved soon, not twenty days after the invasion began on June 6, but perhaps by the fiftieth or the fifty-fifth day. The Third Army, under command of George Patton, was to become operational when the breakout occurred. It would include the VIII Corps. Omar Bradley, in anticipation of the change, informally asked Patton to take control of the VIII Corps for the run down the west coast of the peninsula. Bradley was to take command of the Twelfth Army Group, comprising the American First and Third Armies, for the move down into western France. Patton's command would include the VIII Corps, the XV Corps, the V Corps, and the XII Corps. He did not yet have the command but he was eager to get back into fighting harness and did so with the VIII Corps move.

"The plan was to break out through Avranches and cross the bridges at Pontaubault and turn into Brittany with two corps. Avranches was important because it was on high ground commanding the terrain for miles around. We had to have the bridges at Pontaubault to break out into the clear, where tanks could roam," Middleton recalled.

"I would go first and run down to Rennes where, we had decided at the planning tables back in England, the greatest battle of World War II would take place. The VIII Corps would be followed out by the XV Corps under Major General Wade Haislip, which would turn toward Brest and follow the north shore of the peninsula. The VII Corps would cut across the peninsula and follow the south shore," Middleton recalled.

Before the final steps of the plan could be executed, there were some small hitches. At Patton's direction, the infantry spearheads of the VIII Corps were replaced by the Fourth Armored Division under Major General John S. Wood and the Sixth Armored Division under Major General Robert W. Grow. The Sixth led out in the attack with the Fourth coming down on its left. The Fourth then took the lead for the move on Avranches. The city fell with only a token struggle by the Germans.

Middleton ordered Wood to push on through Avranches to Pontaubault to secure the bridges there. While this was going on, a column of German soldiers, some of them in trucks marked with red crosses, came down the coastal road from north of Avranches. Since it appeared that the column was transporting wounded, the Americans let it through. After it passed, the Germans cut loose with a blast of rifle fire from their trucks. The Americans returned the fire. The Germans promptly surrendered, along with truckloads of ammunition and supplies. Another group of Germans came along later, fired until they saw the futility of it, and then surrendered.

The VIII Corps' move through Avranches and over the Pontaubault bridges was accomplished in one night. Two armored divisions moved down a single narrow highway in about seven hours of darkness, when they would escape the attention of German planes. Moving the two armored divisions on such a schedule was a manifest impossibility. "You couldn't work it out on paper; you could never have gotten by with saying that it could be done at any of the service schools—an automatic F would have resulted. Time and space factors simply would not permit it. But we did it. We did it by placing officers at critical points and simply shoving the vehicles on through. They went out of Avranches and into Brittany without much confusion," Middleton recalled.

During this transitional period, the VIII Corps remained technically under the command of the First Army, headed by Bradley. In fact, however, Bradley had informally yielded the VIII Corps to Patton, who was shortly to come into the picture as commander of the Third Army. Lieutenant General Courtney Hodges was taking command of the First Army. Bradley was becoming commander of the Twelfth Army Group.

"In such a situation, you'd always run a chance of getting an order from one man to do this and shortly thereafter an order from another to do something else. This happened to me. I'd get an order from Bradley to do something and Patton would come along and say, 'No, let's do this.' The confusion lasted for several days," Middleton recalled. "For instance, Bradley told me, 'When you get out through Avranches to the south, be sure to guard the south flank very heavily because it's wide open not only to the south but in the direction of Paris.' There was a town named Fougeres; I was ready to send the Seventh-ninth Division there to block when Patton came along. 'Hell, no,' George said, 'we're going to Brest.'

"I also had an order from Bradley, immediately after the breakout, to capture the port town of St. Malo. After you make the turn to the west, St. Malo is the first large town on the north coast. I was preparing to attack that town when Patton came along and said, 'No, pass it up; there's nothing there anyway; there aren't 500 troops in there.' 'Well, George,' I said, 'how many German troops are there on the peninsula between here and Brest?' Patton replied, 'Oh, about a thousand.' " As it turned out, Middleton recalled, the VIII Corps captured 10,000 Germans on the way to Brest.

"As we passed St. Malo, the Germans were shooting at us so heavily, we couldn't pass them up. I had to turn the Eighty-third Division loose on the town. It was quite an undertaking. The Eighty-third captured 14,000 Germans in St. Malo; I don't know how many they killed. There was a little island in the St. Malo harbor which we didn't capture for a couple of weeks. The Germans stayed out there; we would bomb them and they'd shoot back," Middleton recalled.

Middleton didn't put much stock in Patton's estimates. He tempered them greatly with his own common sense. Patton insisted that the Sixth

Armored Division, under Grow, "just get in the middle of the road and barrel on out to Brest, 150 miles or so from St. Malo, and capture the fortified port before the Germans can get ready." This was not only foolish, it was dangerous nonsense. The Germans were ready. They had been ready for years. "I never thought any armored outfit could capture Brest because it was an important port city which housed the pens for the German submarines that operated in the Atlantic. I knew from the maps and aerial photographs that it was heavily organized not only to shoot toward the sea and into the air but to shoot to the rear. The Germans weren't going to let the city go by forfeit. They had 90-millimeter guns dug into the ground and set in concrete pillboxes," Middleton recalled.

"At any rate, the Sixth Armored, under orders from Patton, did get near Brest. And there I was, back some 150 miles, fighting in front of St. Malo, which finally fell August 17. The Fourth Armored got to Rennes and didn't find much there. It had orders to go on to Lorient on the Atlantic coast and to St. Nazaire. The Fourth was commanded by a very fine general, John S. Wood, who was a bit obstreperous. John called me one night on the radio link and in an urgent voice said, 'I've got to see you,' " Middleton recalled.

"I asked him, 'Where are you?' He replied, 'I'm just outside Rennes.' I asked, 'How are you getting along?' And he replied, 'I've got to see you; I can't tell you.' I said, 'When?' He said, 'Right now; get in your Jeep and come on down here.' "

"Well, it wasn't like driving out to pay a call on a neighbor. It was enemy country, and there were Germans everywhere. So I got a couple of halftracks, a couple of Jeeps and a few soldiers. We got to Wood's headquarters about daylight. Wood was stripped to his waist, near a little trailer with his maps all out on the ground. He came over and threw his arms around me. I said, 'What's the matter, John, you lost your division?' He said, 'Heck no, we're winning this war the wrong way; we ought to be going toward Paris.'

"I said, 'Where is your division?' He said, 'I've got one combat command here south of Rennes and another in Chateaubriand (about twenty miles in the direction of Paris).' He had no orders at all to go in that direction. So I had to get him back on the track and get him started toward Lorient—much to his disgust. Maybe he was right—I am inclined to believe that he was—but those weren't the orders we had had from Bradley," Middleton recalled.

This part of the war had been so easy, it was decided that Haislip's corps wasn't needed and that the VIII Corps should have full responsibility for the cleanup of Brittany. "My real problem was to try to keep some degree of organization of my troops. I had two armored divisions, one near Brest and one near Rennes; a cavalry group near St. Malo; and three infantry divisions, one near Rennes, one at St. Malo, and one guarding the south flank.

"When the Sixth Armored got over near Brest, late one afternoon I had a call from the division commander, Bob Grow. Bob was a man who, when you told him to do something and indicated how he could do it, would always tell you a better way. Now I had this call from Bob. He told me, 'I'm in front of Brest; I've got a German division in front of me and one in the rear of me. What shall I do?'

"Well," I said, "Bob, you've always wanted to use your own judgment; now's your chance to use it," and dismissed it at that. I knew that unless he butted his head against the defenses of Brest, the enemy could do him little harm. They had no transport and didn't have very much armor, while he had that big armored division. He came out all right; he didn't take Brest and didn't get anyway near it. If he had tried to go on to Brest with that armored division, he'd have lost most of it, because the way those 90-millimeter guns were dug in, they'd have destroyed every tank he had," Middleton recalled.

"I had asked Patton for his estimate of the German force in Brest at the time he was hell-bent on sending a single armored division out to take the city. He told me, 'I don't know exactly how many there are in Brest, but there aren't more than 10,000 Krauts in the entire peninsula.' Whether he was just guessing or whether his G-2 had estimated for him, I don't know. In the final capture of Brest, we took something like 38,000 prisoners. There were 20,000 down in Lorient. I don't know how many escaped to the south. Around Rennes, where the biggest battle of the war was supposed to take place, there were very few troops. We captured 400 or 500 prisoners and killed a few there."

Grow had arrived in front of Brest on August 7. His Combat Command B had reached the outskirts of the city in the morning and had been greeted with stiff resistance. Later in the day, Grow tried to bluff the Germans into surrendering, sending in a party under a flag of truce. The Germans declined to give up and sent Grow's emissaries back to him. Grow began an attack; it failed against the city's strong defenses. At this point, Grow put in his call to General Middleton, far back at St. Malo.

(A British author, David Mason, in *Breakout: Drive to the Seine*, wrote in 1968: "Grow's operation in reaching Brest so quickly and clearing most of the interior of the peninsula was carried out with great skill and panache. Grow, perhaps with some justification, later described it as the greatest cavalry-type operation of the war. He, like Wood and like their superior Patton, had proved himself a bold and farseeing commander who reveled in being given assignments deep into enemy territory. And he, like Wood, had been frustrated by the dictates of caution on the part of one of his superiors. The one question which remains open is whether, had he not been diverted to Dinan, he could have reached Brest one day earlier, taken the Germans completely off their guard, and captured the city. It is a question which can never now be raised above the blurred realms of speculation. It should be recalled, however, in fairness to Middleton, that he was constantly dealing with the problems of an entire corps and was constantly expected to see the role of that corps in relation to the circumstances of the Third Army, even of the entire invading force. Had the fortunes of the Sixth and Fourth Armored Divisions gone wildly wrong, Middleton would no doubt have gone down in history as an irresponsible commander who recklessly sacrificed his divisions or ignored true objectives. For while gambling always afterwards looks brilliant if it is successful, the gambler is generally blamed if he fails. There is every place in the conduct of a war for the counsel of caution.")

The commanders of the Fourth and Sixth Armored Divisions were unquestionably competent fighting men. But it would not have mattered if Grow's Sixth Armored had materialized in front of Brest in one day, instead of nearly the week that was required. A fortified city defended by three German divisions could not be surprised. An early surrender was unthinkable for troops of the quality of those in the defense of Brest. Some of Patton's dash showed in the armored commanders, but a head-on crack at the city's 90-millimeter guns would have cost every tank in the Sixth Armored Division.

Siege operations called for infantry. "As soon as I got some infantry at Brest, the armor left me; I couldn't use it there. The armor was released and joined Patton. The Second Infantry Division came in. It was a fine one, commanded by a man I was on the Leavenworth faculty with, Major General Walter M. Robertson. I knew what he could do. The Eighth Division came up, commanded by Major General Donald A. Stroh, a fine combat soldier who had been in North Africa and in Sicily. My third infantry outfit was the Twenty-ninth Division, a National Guard unit from Pennsylvania, commanded by Major General Charles Gerhardt, who had been a quarterback at West Point in 1916. I also had a cavalry group and two Ranger battalions commanded by Lieutenant Colonel Earl Rudder, later to become president of Texas A & M University, one of the finest combat soldiers I ever saw," Middleton recalled.

"After watching Rudder at work in the siege, I resolved that if the fellow stayed around me long enough, I would give him an infantry regiment. I did in the Battle of the Bulge, where he took over the 109th Regiment of the Twenty-eighth Division. At Brest, he almost single-handedly captured some big 16-inch guns.

"I knew something about Brest besides what I learned from our aerial photographs. I'd spent nearly a week there in July, 1919, waiting for a ship to take me back to the States. When I was there earlier the city was down under the hill, most of it along the waterfront. By World War II much of the city had climbed to higher ground. Most of the land defenses of the city were there on the high ground. In a siege, you just have to blow the defenders out of their positions. One of the German divisions was paratroopers, commanded by Generalleutnant Hermann Ramcke. All the defenders were under Ramcke's command. He had led the airborne invasion of Crete and knew his business," Middleton recalled.

"General Eisenhower had told me not to lose too many men taking Brest. We didn't. We went at the job methodically. I never saw a place so well organized for defense. They had 90-millimeter guns in bunkers in concrete no more than thirty inches higher with the guns having 360-degree traverse. Ramcke was a pretty decent sort. One day he sent me a map under a flag of truce, showing where several hundred American prisoners were being held in Brest. The old devil did another thing, though, putting Red Cross flags at several points most advantageous to us. He could have had an aid station at each of these places, but I doubted it. I told him he'd have to get some of those flags down or I might risk violating

the Geneva Convention. He had one on an ammunition dump. When
you're interdicting with artillery, you have to pick your targets. Ramcke
was slyly trying to deny us some good ones."

While he was directing the siege early in September, General Middleton heard heavy small arms fire not far from the headquarters of the
Twenty-ninth Division. He investigated and found that General Gerhardt
had a battalion practicing on an improvised rifle range—within three miles
of Brest. He told Gerhardt to have his men get back into the siege line and
do the remainder of their practice shooting on the Germans. Ammunition
was always short of needs during the siege of Brest.

Eisenhower and Middleton Confer in Belgium, 1944 (U.S. Army Photo)

Middleton had a considerable exchange of written messages, amounting almost to regular correspondence, with Ramcke in the course of the siege. The exchange opened on August 19 with a protest in English, German, and French, addressed to General Grow of the Sixth Armored Division, the English version of which follows:

Der Kommandant der Festung Brest   19 August 1944

To the Commander of the
Sixth U.S. tanc devission
Sire Generalmajor GROW

We are understood by liberated prisoners that german prisoners have been surrendered by american troops to the so called "Forces Francaises de l'Interieur". –

Opposite to the law of nations these "FFI" took them off all their decorations of the war as well as their personally goods. –

Additionally they have been treated badly according to the Daily War Book dated 11.8.44 from the french bataillons "Rene Caro" and they have been threatened to be killed by shooting dead. –

Y myself and my troop keep absolutely to the Genfer Convention and hope you will do the same. –

Y must protest against the shameless and unworthy treatment opposite brave soldiers and beg you to give to the porter of this letter an obliging declaration for changing these conditions of the "FFI". –

Jf you; Sire, d'not want to do so, Y am obliged to change my conditions particularly against the french Terroist Y have as prisoners. –

RAMCKE
Generalleutnant

To Ramcke's protest went this reply, signed "The American Commander":

20 August 1944

TO: The Commander of the German Forces, Brest

The American Forces follow the provisions of the Geneva Convention in the handling of Prisoners of War. We do not mistreat them, nor do we permit same. It is the policy of the American Forces to take prisoners from the F.F.I. wherever possible. It must be borne in mind that this cannot always be done, due to the large number of Frenchmen now bearing arms.

I do not know of any mistreatment on the part of the French of German prisoners. I shall, however, use my influence to prevent mistreatment, if such is found to be the case.

The American Commander

By now the American siege forces were applying steady pressure to the German defenders. Ramcke renewed his complaints about American observance of the Geneva convention. He turned over some Americans taken prisoner to go with a protest written August 27:

Commandant Fortress Brest   Brest, 27 August 1944
To the Commanding General of the VIII U.S. Army Corps
Brigadier General Troy H. Middleton.
Dear General:
1. With the bearer of this letter I am sending
        Medical Captain Markle
        2 Officers of the Medical Administration
            Corps and
        8 EM, medical personnel
back to you, who have all fallen into our hands, as I assume that you will need this personnel in the present situation. Fortress Brest is so well staffed with medical personnel that also wounded American soldiers, captured by us, are receiving excellent medical care and attention.

2. The naval hospital in Brest has been hit several times by artillery. This field hospital as well as its immediate surroundings are clear of any military installations. I assume that this shelling may be attributed to an error and am therefore enclosing two small plans, outlining the medical installations in the Fortress sector, presently occupied by wounded. These hospital installations are clearly recognizable and buildings are marked with the Red Cross. Calling attention to the Geneva Convention, to which I for my part strictly adhere, I beg of you to instruct your subordinate units, as well as the Air Corps and Naval elements operating under you, to afford these installations the protection of the Geneva Convention.

3. To eliminate at least the wounded from the effects of the bitterness of this warfare, I have designated the community of LE FRET (see sketch) on the Crozon Peninsula as a hospital village. I have cleared this point of all military installations in an area one kilometer wide. All installations, including the docks, serve only the care of wounded. No military traffic is being transacted through this village. This spot is clearly marked as a neutral zone. All wounded capable of being transported, including Americans, are being evacuated to LE FRET.

4. In the vicinity of this protected village, I have arranged to hold all American prisoners of war which we have taken up to date, in order to spare them the effect of their own guns. Only a prisoner of war collecting point is being kept by me in the city of Brest.

5. The ships, marked with white paint and Red Crosses, which circulate across the bay between the Armorique and Crozon Peninsulas, as well as city

and mainland, serve exclusively for the transport and supply of wounded. They bear the Red Cross flag.

6. In the interests of a humane warfare and particularly for the protection of the wounded and prisoners, I beg of you, esteemed General, to also give protection to the installations designated by me in paragraphs 4 and 5. As Commander of Fortress Brest I give you my assurance that all American installations under the sign of the Geneva Convention will be meticulously respected by me under all circumstances.

7. Kindly confirm your agreement with my proposals by a statement over your personal signature.

> With the assurance of my high esteem
> RAMCKE
> Major General, Commander Fortress Brest

Addressing Troy Middleton as Brigadier General Middleton rather than by his correct rank, in the translation of General Ramcke's message, was probably not an attempt at insult to the VIII Corps commander. *Generalleutnant* in the German army is the equivalent of a major general in the American army. A German *Generalmajor* is the equivalent of a brigadier general in the American army. *Generalobersts* are full generals. Lieutenant generals in the German army are designated with their branch specialty, e.g., *General der Infanterie*. General Middleton replied promptly to General Ramcke:

> BRITTANY
> 28 August 1944

Lt General Ramcke,
Generalleutnant und Kommandant de Festung Brest.

Sir:

I have your letter of 27 August 1944 in which you enclose sketches of hospital installations in the Fortress Brest. There has been also returned by your officers certain officers and enlisted men of the Medical Corps. While the services of these persons are not necessarily required by the American Command, nevertheless I appreciate your courtesy in releasing them.

I have studied your sketches of hospital installations. I can assure you that it is the policy of the American Army to respect the provisions of the Geneva Convention and to observe and respect the display of the Red Cross. In a study of the sketch of Fortress Brest, I note that the hospital installations are so widely dispersed that I feel it would be an impossibility to prevent endangering some of them with unobserved artillery fire and by bombing from aircraft, both day and night. If such should happen, it would be entirely unintentional. The installations now so widely dispersed might be placed in more compact areas. I further request that the Red Crosses be large enough and so displayed that they can not be mistaken from the air.

With respect to the shipping, it is not the desire nor the intent by members of this command to fire upon a ship which is clearly marked with the International Red Cross. The cross, however, must be large enough and so displayed that it can be easily recognized by aircraft and ground observation.

With respect to Le Fret, shown on your sketch, the American command will endeavor to respect your wishes in this area so long as combat troops are not transported to and from that locality.

I desire to assure you that your wounded have received the best of care and are evacuated from the battle zone without delay. Furthermore, your prisoners of war are being well cared for and evacuated immediately to safe areas.

If during the battle for Brest any of your hospital installations are fired upon or are bombed by American or British aircraft, I can assure you that it will be purely accidental. I am sure you realize that in a combat area such as Fortress Brest and with the large amount of artillery and air available to the American forces that such accidents may occur. I, therefore, suggest that where possible, these installations be placed so that accidents may not occur.

The location of medical installations, shown on your sketches, will be transmitted to all members of this command, with my desire that they be not fired upon.

If in the future you desire to transmit information to me, I assure you that your officers will be given as safe passage through the lines as the accidents of war permit.

TROY H. MIDDLETON,
Major General,
Commanding.

In his prompt reply to Ramcke's letter of August 27, with its needling reference to the Americans' prospective need of the medical personnel liberated by the Germans at Brest, Middleton took note of the needling. He replied in kind with a reference to the "large amount of artillery and air available to the American forces," which might lead to an occasional artillery round or to an aerial bomb's falling outside the precise target area. He also indicated that he was onto Ramcke's trick of dispersing hospital installations among prime target areas.

After two weeks of intensive day and night attacks, Middleton's forces were squeezing the Germans into ever tighter positions. Middleton decided to give Ramcke an opportunity to stop the bloodshed. He sent a courier to Ramcke with this proposal:

HEADQUARTERS VIII CORPS

U.S. Army,
12 September 1944

Lieutenant General Ramcke,
Commanding German Forces at Brest and on Crozon Peninsula.
Sir:

There comes a time in war when the situation reaches a point where a commander is no longer justified in expending the lives and destroying the health of the men who have bravely carried out his orders in combat.

I have discussed with your officers and men, who have served you well and are now prisoners of war, the situation confronting the German garrison at Brest. These men are of the belief that the situation is hopeless and that there is nothing to be gained by prolonging the struggle. I therefore feel that the German garrison at Brest and on the Crozon Peninsula no longer has a justifiable reason for continuing to fight.

Your men have fought well. Approximately 16,000 of them from this area are now prisoners of war. Your command has suffered casualties. You have lost much of the necessary implements of war and your men are encircled in a small, congested area. Therefore, it is the consensus of all that you and your command have fulfilled your obligation to your country.

In consideration of the preceding, I am calling upon you, as one professional soldier to another, to cease the struggle now in progress.

In accepting the surrender of Brest, I desire that your men lay down their arms and be assembled in proper military formation and marched under command of appropriate commanders to locations agreed upon by you and by my representative who has handed you this communication. At the designated point, transport will convey the officers and men to the prisoner of war assembly point. For you and such members of your staff as you may designate, proper transportation will call at such place as you may select.

I am sure that you realize the futility of continuing the battle. I am also of the opinion that you would prefer to surrender to the Americans who have opposed you in this siege. And that by so doing, at this time, save the remnants of your command who have served you so well. Furthermore, you must realize that the Port of Brest has lost its significance since so many ports are now in Allied hands.

I trust, as a professional soldier who has served well and who has already fulfilled his obligation, you will give this request your favorable consideration.

TROY H. MIDDLETON,
Major General, U.S. Army,
Commanding.

Having dispatched his courier to Ramcke, Middleton turned over a copy of the letter to war correspondents at his headquarters. The next day,

Middleton circulated copies of his letter to Ramcke to all subordinate commands in the VIII Corps. Along with his letter to Ramcke, he distributed the German commander's reply. It was terse and to the point:

"General: I must decline your proposal. Ramcke, Major General and Commandant, Fortress Brest."

All right, Middleton said. He ordered distribution of the exchange to go to every soldier in the Second Infantry Division, the Eighth Infantry, the Twenty-ninth Infantry, his cavalry Task Forces A and B, and VIII Corps Artillery. Then he wrote:

"General Ramcke has been given an opportunity to surrender. Since he has declined what is believed to be a humane and reasonable request, it now remains for the VIII Corps to make him sorry for his refusal. Therefore, I ask the combat soldiers of this command to enter the fray with renewed vigor—let's take them apart—and get the job finished."

On September 19, Middleton wrote an end to the siege of Brest:

HEADQUARTERS VIII CORPS

APO 308, U.S. Army,
19 September 1944

TO: All Officers and Enlisted Men who form a part of the VIII Corps

In the capture of Brest and adjacent territory by the officers and enlisted men who form a part of the VIII Corps, a chapter in history is made. By the elimination of approximately forty thousand troops from the German Army, our future task has been made easier. By securing Brest, an important Atlantic seaport is made available to the Allies.

To single out the achievements of one unit in the task which has just ended would be difficult. The performance of all units has been magnificent. There has been no shirking of duty or responsibility. Each organization has shared in the undertaking. In the Second Parachute Division of the German Army, you met the best. You will meet no better troops in your future battles. We are better soldiers today than we were when we entered this engagement because of the fact that we have met and eliminated the best Germany has to offer.

We have paid a price in casualties for the job we have done. Many of our comrades have died in the struggle for Brest, in order that we who live can share in the satisfaction that the job has been well done—we regret their passing—it is the fortunes of war that they should die while we carry the torch to other battlefields.

I desire to take this means of thanking all who have shared in this campaign for their fine work. It has been a privilege to command and work with you. Each officer and enlisted man should take pride in the fact that, as a result of your work before Brest, three German divisions and many other German troops have been erased from the troop list of World War II.

> TROY H. MIDDLETON
> Major General, U.S. Army,
> Commanding.

Thus ended the siege of Brest and with it, ninety-nine unbroken days of combat for Middleton and most of his staff. The ninetieth day was logged by those members of the VIII Corps staff whose LST had been sunk as they neared shore the morning of June 12 and who had been fished out and hauled back to England for reoutfitting.

Middleton arranged for ceremonies in which he gave the city back to its mayor, Jules Lullien, with brief remarks about his first arrival in Brest in May, 1918, his departure from the city in July, 1919, and his return for a visit in August, 1944, which had just been ended with the German surrender and the city's deliverance after four years of occupation by the Germans.

George Patton came over and pinned a Distinguished Service Medal Oak Leaf Cluster on Middleton, for his outstanding conduct of the campaign in Brittany ending in the capture of Brest. William Simpson, Ninth Army commander, had written the recommendation. The battle for Brest lasted twenty-six days. It went on night and day. Captured with Ramcke were two other generals and a colonel who had succeeded Ramcke when he became fortress commander, and 36,389 other prisoners. The Americans evacuated 2,000 German wounded and counted 800 German graves in the city after the surrender at 3 P.M. on September 19.

Morrow Davis, reporter for *Stars and Stripes*, the army newspaper, said that General Ramcke when taken captive by Eighth Division troops on the Crozon Peninsula opposite Brest, "asked the U.S. general for the latter's credentials. The general pointed to the M-1s carried by his GIs and said those were his credentials.

"This Ramcke was some guy," reporter Davis wrote. "Middleton characterized him by saying that no matter how ruthless, he was nevertheless a soldier. Ramcke had refused surrender terms after the Sixth Armored poured up through Brittany past Rennes and contained the German garrison in Brest—a garrison composed of three Nazi divisions plus navy and marine personnel and Todt Organization labor troops. Ramcke again refused surrender terms offered by Middleton the week before the finale. Reporters encountered this fantastic German general at Middleton's head-quarters (we waited while Ramcke had breakfast). When he appeared with his adjutant he was carrying a cane and leading a beautiful Irish setter. He wore a camouflaged jacket, field-green paratroop trousers, and black para-troop boots. Around his neck hung the Knight Cross over a shirt collar of pale blue cambric. It was the only decoration he wore; his only insignia were his lieutenant general's epaulets, to which he pointed in explaining his promotion, during the siege, from major general.

"Ramcke posed for the photographers willingly enough. The kindly Middleton urged him to where the exacting photogs wanted the group—Middleton, Ramcke and Ramcke's adjutant, Col. Moller, attired in dress uniform of field blue with pink trouser seams. Ramcke was clean shaven; frequently he smiled during the process of posing. Apparently he under-stood some English. 'I feel like a film star,' he announced once. Middleton

Middleton and Brest Fortress Commandant Ramcke, 1944 (U.S. Army Photo)

retorted that posing was little enough for Ramcke to do, seeing that his military job was finished. The American general added that his own work was not finished," the *Stars and Stripes* reporter wrote.

Ramcke shortly was on his way to a prisoner of war camp in south Mississippi in the United States little more than fifty miles from Middleton's birthplace. After the war he was transferred to England, where he spent time in a prison camp, and later to France, where he was tried for alleged offenses committed during the occupation of France and was sentenced to five years imprisonment. He was given credit for the time he had served in the United States and in England and was freed by the French. He went back to Germany and entered the concrete business. He wrote regularly to Middleton for some fifteen years after the war, relaying his letters to a son in Detroit who translated the original German into English. Middleton replied as would a warrior respectful of a worthy foe. Their letters went back and forth regularly at holiday times.

Looking back on the Brittany campaign, Middleton said there likely will be a question why the American army spent a month on the capture of Brest. "Yet," he said, "it was the principal port in that part of France. It was much better than Cherbourg. When we began the campaign Cherbourg was the only port we had. The submarine pens were there and as far as we knew were still operational. When the city fell, I found that the harbor had silted up from the flow of the rivers. Our air and artillery through the months and years had sunk ships in the harbor—it was full of sunken ships. They had ten or eleven submarine pens—the only submarine there was one that had been sunk when a pen had been hit. The prow of that sub was sticking up out of the water. For all the bombing and all the shelling, only one of the pens had been hit. They were well concealed up against a high precipice. The Germans had tremendous machine shops at Brest; they were well organized for submarine warfare.

"We couldn't have afforded to leave so many troops in Brest. I was also ordered to capture Lorient, but I suggested that we let it alone; there were only 20,000 Germans in the city. From time to time new divisions arrived from the States. I suggested that when a division arrived, it should be sent down to Lorient for seasoning by letting it watch those Germans. When the next division came in, it could relieve the first. My suggestion was adopted. The Germans stayed in Lorient to the end of the war. They didn't have any transportation, so they couldn't go far. We would have lost a lot of men if we had decided to attack Lorient. And of course we would have killed many of the 20,000 if they had decided to fight it out," Middleton recalled.

Just before the surrender of Brest, on September 11, control of the VIII Corps passed from Patton's Third Army to Simpson's Ninth Army, newly activated. The First and the Third Army had chased the Germans all the way across France after killing a great number and taking 50,000 prisoners in the Falaise pocket in action ending August 21.

With new divisions getting their orientation down at Lorient, where they could keep an eye on the Germans shut up in the city, western France was finally quiet. The VIII Corps was ordered to move to Belgium, with the Twenty-ninth Division of the corps going to the Ninth Army and the remaining divisions joining the First Army on a line along the Moselle River extending up beyond St. Vith. As he prepared to make the trip all the way across northern France and Belgium, to the German border, Middleton could reflect on the nonstop events since he came ashore near Carentan with half a headquarters staff.

The divisions which came under his command shortly after he landed on the Cotentin Peninsula were of uneven quality. Some fought magnificently; others stalled repeatedly. Among the best was the Eighty-second Airborne Division, commanded by Major General Matthew B. Ridgway. On July 7, Middleton issued a commendation to the Eighty-second, on the eve of its departure from the corps: "The division has fulfilled, in an admirable manner, every requirement asked of it. Furthermore, during the current campaign, the division has acquitted itself in a manner such as to mark it as one of the outstanding units in the United States Army."

Ridgway replied in kind, "Throughout their participation in the operations of the VIII Corps from 3–9 July, they are gratefully conscious of the consideration shown them by the Corps Commander and his staff in the assignment of missions, in providing all the necessary means to accomplish these missions, and in his unfailing support which left nothing to be desired."

On July 9, the same day he received Ridgway's glowing acknowledgment of the division's commendation, Middleton found it necessary to issue a set of mimeographed instructions intended to help commanders and their troops in the extremely complicated business of fighting in hedgerow country. After four weeks on Cotentin Peninsula during which progress was regularly impeded by the next hedgerow, Middleton spelled out his recommendations in his memorandum to division and separate unit commanders. A note at the end of the memorandum said, "This memorandum will not be taken into front lines."

1. In the employment of infantry and artillery in hedgerow fighting, it is suggested that when the infantry has reached a hedgerow, and the enemy occupies the next hedgerow in front, artillery, rifle, machine gun and mortar fire be placed on the hedgerow occupied by the enemy, and the infantry follow this fire closely by going in shooting. Unless the infantry takes advantage of this covering fire it is next to useless to expend ammunition. Having captured the hedgerow the process is the same in attacking the next enemy position. Furthermore, the enemy withdraws along hedgerows which prolong our axis of advance, therefore artillery and mortar fire should be placed along these hedgerows when lifted from the one being assaulted. It is believed that by closely coordinating this step by step method of advance, marked improvement in our attack will be noted.

2. Interrogation of several prisoners of war, including officers, reveals the fact that our artillery fire is very effective and that in general, our infantry is too slow in taking advantage of it. One German officer indicated that after our artillery lifted from a target it was fifteen minutes or more before any infantry appeared. The fact that our infantry must follow closely on the artillery fire needs no comment. Many lives will be saved and the job accomplished quicker if our infantry will take full advantage of fire and close with the enemy as soon as the artillery lifts.

3. It is evident that many of our tanks are too timid in combat. One German officer stated that he and twelve enlisted men threw hand grenades at three of our tanks which resulted in the tanks turning about and running to the rear. Since other statements made by this officer have been verified I have reason to believe that his statement concerning the tank incident is correct.

4.There have been instances where our infantry withdrew to the rear when confronted by an enemy tank. In this type country a tank has both trouble in moving and securing a field of fire. Therefore, it should be an easy matter for infantry with bazookas and anti-tank rifle grenades to destroy or disable an enemy tank.

5. When an enemy tank is accompanied by infantry our infantry must kill or capture the infantry and leave the tank to the mercy of our anti-tank defense. Do not give ground, if so you expose yourself and will be doing just what the enemy would have you do.

6. When enemy artillery or mortar fire is placed on your position go forward out of it and not to the rear; the enemy will seldom shorten his range, especially so if his troops are following his fire.

7. While contact with adjacent units must be maintained this does not

mean physical contact. In this close country if units expect to maintain physical contact the forward movement will be slowed down. A battalion for example must lay stress on capturing its assigned objective. If some depth is maintained in its formation there should be no special worry about its flanks. It may be expected that from time to time the enemy will infiltrate through our lines or that we will bypass him. By pushing ahead we cut him off and he can then be cleaned up from the rear. Patrols should be employed to watch gaps between units.

8. In the employing of Tank Destroyers in depth it must follow that some must be well forward to knock out enemy tanks before they reach our front line, while others are echeloned to the rear. In firing on an enemy tank strive to hit the tank on its side.

9. When not advancing, a unit, no matter what its size, should be capable of all-around defense. Furthermore, security groups should be well out and alert. No excuse for a unit being surprised can be accepted.

10. Some of our units are still timid in action. This must be corrected. We must be both bold and aggressive. Even when not attacking there must not be a no man's land—the front must be ours.

The memorandum couldn't have been clearer. But strong leadership was not always there. Middleton had had to relieve a regimental commander in Italy for spending all his time in his command post. On July 12, he informed the commanding general of First Army that he had relieved the commanding general of the Eighth Infantry Division. The Eighth had come in from the States recently and replaced the Eighty-second Airborne. The contrast between the two was great. He sent the Eighth's commander to the headquarters of General Bradley, commander of the First Army, explaining to Bradley his reasons.

Under a new commanding general, the Eighth began shaping up.

Other commanders had their problems, too, not always with timid leadership. While he was on Cotentin Peninsula, Middleton was appealed to by an old comrade in arms in the Fourth Division in World War I. Colonel Hurley Fuller, regimental commander of the Twenty-third Infantry in the Second Division, was relieved of his command by General Robertson. "It wasn't for any timidity," Middleton recalled. "Hurley was a real fighter. But he was also an opinionated fellow, given to telling higher commanders how to fight an action. I guess he had told Walter Robertson one time too many. Hurley liked the old Springfield rifle used by the army in World War I. At one time in World War II he managed to equip his regiment with

Springfields—just how, I don't know—but that may give you some idea that Hurley was fairly headstrong.

"Anyhow, Hurley came to my headquarters in VIII Corps and told me he had been relieved. 'I need your help,' he said. 'I don't want to go

Bradley and Middleton in Brittany, 1944 (U.S. Army Photo)

back to the States.' I told him that he was, as usual, his own worst enemy. And he agreed. Then I told Omar Bradley, First Army commander, what had happened to Hurley and asked if he couldn't find a place for a fighter whom nobody ever accused of timidity. Brad kept Fuller around First Army headquarters and eventually gave him command of the 110th Infantry Regiment of the Twenty-eighth Division.

"The next time I saw Fuller was just before the Battle of the Bulge. I went up to his headquarters near Skyline Drive and had lunch with him. We went over his plan. He had a pretty good one, with his key points well covered on an impossibly wide front of twenty-eight miles. When the Germans hit, they hit Hurley's outfit hardest, capturing his headquarters and all but destroying his regiment. But Hurley put up a real fight," Middleton recalled. Fuller's visit came just before the breakout at Avranches.

Coincidentally, Middleton had just had to relieve another division commander, whom he replaced on July 29. The Ninetieth Division had come into the Cotentin Peninsula early—and failed. Its first commander was relieved. Its second, relieved by General Middleton, had made something of a record for himself as the commander of troops which defeated the Japanese in the Aleutian Islands. He was, as it developed, not quite up to his clippings.

The Ninetieth's commander on July 14 asked General Middleton to send him an assistant division commander to replace a brigadier general. The Ninetieth's commander asked for an officer "of a more optimistic and calming attitude, which would be more beneficial to this division at this time."

Middleton granted the request of the Ninetieth's commander on July 16. On July 17 he wrote Bradley at First Army that the Ninetieth needed officers of proved ability at the top. He wrote also that he was unwilling to take on the brigadier general for an assignment at the VIII Corps headquarters and suggested that the brigadier be returned to his temporary grade of colonel and sent to an appropriate assignment in which he would not be associated with troops in combat.

The Ninetieth continued in action with indifferent results. Finally, on July 29, Middleton gave up on its second commander. He wrote Bradley recommending the relief of the Ninetieth's commander without prejudice to him. "The Ninetieth Division has given me much concern," Middleton wrote. "I have, therefore, watched it closely in order that I might determine the basic reasons for its failure to perform up to standard." A detailed report followed.

It should be noted that the Ninetieth found the leadership prescribed for it by Middleton in the person of Raymond S. McLain, who had been artillery commander of the Forty-fifth Division under Middleton in Sicily. McLain straightened out the Ninetieth and went on to command the XIX Corps in fighting in Germany.

When he was faced with the necessity of relieving a commander, Middleton did not hesitate. He wrote as charitably as he could of the commander's deficiencies.

Through June, July, August, and September of 1944, the VIII Corps headquarters was never far from the firing lines. The corps staff had its chances to see whether Mack Hornbeak's description of Middleton was off the mark. "The Germans shelled my headquarters on the Cotentin Peninsula," Middleton recalled. "You should have seen those fellows digging in. I sat out the shelling in my van. The van looked like a cattle truck. Later I was given what they called an ordnance repair van. It was armored, self-propelled, with a map board down one side. It had electric heat. The windows were covered by heavy rods, so spaced that they probably would have stopped a shell fragment. If I had listened closely, I probably would have heard some comments about my damn foolishness, but I had learned by experience and knew what the risks were.

"Later, the Germans shot out the rear end of my command car. My driver wanted to keep it just to be able to show how close to the front we operated. [In World War I, Colonel Middleton's driver had been just as insistent on keeping a shot-up vehicle with its own wound stripes.] The German shell really tore the hell out of the car's rear end."

On the daring and theoretically impossible breakout at Avranches and Pontaubault, Middleton could now look back and say, "I might have been sent back to the States if I had failed at Avranches. I talked to George Patton about my proposal and he said, 'Hell, go ahead.' We had speculated that the Germans might attempt to stop us with aerial bombing. They did try, but hit the road we were using in only a few places. We got through with good officers pushing, showing the way, pushing. Theoretically there was no way to put so many vehicles over the road so fast, but we did it just the same."

After the breakout at Avranches, when Middleton had been ordered to head for Brest and to clean up Brittany, and additionally to protect up to 150 miles of the south flank of the Third Army in western France, he was asked by Eisenhower how the VIII Corps flank looked. "Recalling what one of my resourceful, just-awakened students at Command and General Staff School had said in reply to my question, I was tempted to tell Ike the same thing: 'I was just about to ask you that question.' " His was, said Middleton, the longest flank he had ever heard of. Fortunately, the Germans were more intent on getting away than in standing to fight more than a brief rear guard action.

As Middleton prepared to leave Brittany and head for the Ardennes, he was taking along another Baton Rougean with his corps staff. That the newest addition finally made it overseas was testimony to his remarkable persistence. B. B. Taylor, Jr., son of an old friend, B. B. Taylor, who had been the LSU attorney when Middleton was comptroller, had incurred an injury to his neck while he was a wrestler at Davidson College. The army had turned him down when he tried to enlist. He had turned to Middleton for help in getting a waiver which would permit his joining the army. When Middleton was at Camp Blanding early in 1942, along came another letter from B. B. Taylor, Jr., saying "I want to get with you." Now in the army, Taylor, a lawyer, was assigned to Washington. At Fort Devens, Middleton received three more letters from Taylor. He heard from him again at Pine Camp. By now, Middleton was telling Hornbeak that Taylor was getting to be a "real nuisance." He was still asking for an opportunity to go to Europe with the Forty-fifth Division. In Sicily, Middleton heard from Taylor. When he came back to Washington in January, 1944, Taylor heard that he was back. Finally, while he was busy reducing the German fortifications at Brest, yet another letter came from Taylor.

"An officer at my headquarters on a visit was going back to Washington. I gave him B. B. Taylor, Jr.'s name, told him to read Taylor's letter, then told him where to find Taylor in Washington. 'When you get there, go to the Adjutant General and tell him either to send Taylor to my headquarters or to have him shot,' " Middleton recalled.

Taylor came by the first flight. He was landed far from Brest, but hitchhiked to VIII Corps headquarters. Middleton made him a liaison officer between corps, subordinate, and adjacent commands. "He was an unlikely soldier, with no training for combat, but he would have made a good infantryman. He flew almost every day in a Cub plane, taking a great many risks and turning into a valuable supplier of information. During the Battle of the Bulge he came in one night with his trench coat glazed with ice. He stood the coat in the corner and came over to report his findings. Taylor acquired a dog which he kept in his tent at corps headquarters. Hornbeak had not only a dog but a huge Belgian rabbit. The two frolicked together.

With France cleared of the enemy, Middleton could make a leisurely trip to his next assignment on a quiet front in the Ardennes Mountains. He drove across France, visiting the battlefields where he had served with great distinction as a battalion and a regimental commander in 1918. "To show you how little France had changed in some fundamental ways," he recalled, "I went by a farm I remembered most vividly. There beside the well was what looked exactly like the manure pile that had sat there in the autumn of 1918, twenty-six years before."

17 The Bulge Takes Shape:
Poor Boys' Front

Ｔ HE GERMANS had been driven all the way across France in August. Early in September they turned at bay just west of Metz, France, and on a line up through the heart of Luxembourg, just east of Bastogne, Belgium, up through Malmedy, just east of Liege and on a westering curve into Antwerp, Belgium. The Allies were outrunning their supply lines. As they slowed down to resupply, the Germans used the time to form battle lines well to the west of Germany's West Wall. The Siegfried Line campaign, from September 11 through December 15, saw the Canadians and the British on the north and the Americans in the south push to the German borders and across them at Aachen, on the Schnee Eifel just east of St. Vith and at Saarlautern. The line ran roughly north and south. The Germans held their westernmost positions across the Roer River in the far southern tip of Holland and in the high country of easternmost Belgium.

Middleton's VIII Corps was assigned custody of a fifty-mile front when he completed his move across northern France and Belgium. Charles B. McDonald, author of *The Siegfried Line Campaign*, referred to this front as "at once the nursery and the old folks' home of the American command," to which came either green or badly battered divisions—either needing time to learn the first lessons of combat or time for rest and for replenishment of their heavily depleted ranks. The VIII Corps headquarters was trucked to Bastogne, Belgium, about twenty miles west of the porous front manned by the Second and Eighth Divisions. The two divisions settled into position with each responsible for a twenty-five-mile front, early in October.

Middleton's area of responsibility extended from Losheim, on the German-Belgian border, at the north end, to central Luxembourg. His corps went to Hodges's First Army while the Twenty-ninth Division was again under Simpson's Ninth Army. The corps's assigned mission was to defend in place, to attempt to deceive the Germans by active patrolling, and to prepare for an eventual attack to the Rhine River. On October 11 the Eighty-third Division was shifted from Third Army control to the VIII Corps, bringing along with it the responsibility for covering another thirty-eight miles of lower Luxembourg's border with Germany. Now the VIII Corps was charged with maintaining a lookout, carrying on a deception and planning an eventual attack for an eighty-eight-mile front.

Middleton put in long hours checking on his subordinate commanders' troop dispositions and plans for dealing with an attack. When the brand new Ninth Armored Division wheeled up on October 20, he decided not to stretch it along a fourth division front but to hold it as a corps reserve. Additional help came when the Fourteenth Cavalry Group moved in with two squadrons. Middleton attached a squadron to the Second Division and another to the Eighty-third, calling upon the armored cavalrymen to screen a gap in the line. Gap it was called—though all of five miles long.

"On the Schnee Eifel, I wanted soldiers to know that I was interested in their welfare and that I was aware of their exposed position. I regularly visited regimental headquarters, occasionally making a suggestion about defensive alignments. There was plenty to do on a front so long. Usually at noon I'd stop and eat with the troops. We took our mess kits and insisted on getting in line for our food. Usually a mess sergeant would say, 'Wait a minute, General; we'll fix you something special.' I'd reply, 'No, I'm in a hurry. Thanks just the same.' Once the next man in line was a Negro artilleryman from Ponchatoula. We had a visit and remembered the good strawberries grown back in our Louisiana home," Middleton recalled.

On one of his visits forward, he was at a battalion command post when Major Philip Neri Cangelosi, the battalion executive officer, came up, walking down the middle of the road. "I told him not to move around so casually, that the enemy had him in plain sight. He was killed less than a week later." A West Point graduate, Major Cangelosi was the brother of

Theo Cangelosi, a Baton Rougean who became a member of the LSU Board of Supervisors.

With November came the autumn rains and the first penetrating cold foreshadowing winter. The Germans put second-class troops from their infantry divisions in the line opposite the VIII Corps. They had a pretty good idea that the Americans weren't really planning an offensive any time soon. They could operate their patrols through the American lines, just as the VIII Corps forces regularly sent out night patrols hoping to net a prisoner or two and find out more about the defenses opposite them.

The Eighty-third Division in November took 201 casualties, with 25 dead and 176 wounded in the relative inactivity, while 550 men were injured, fell ill, or suffered trench foot. The Germans laid heavy artillery attacks on the Second Division area. Finally, General Walter Robertson told his troops to blow up some of the West Wall pillboxes through which the Germans infiltrated, and to set up in new positions a mile to the rear.

Middleton, working with Major General John W. Leonard, commander of the Ninth Armored Division, placed armored units in the line to relieve battalions of the infantry divisions, to give the infantry a rest, and to acquaint the novice armored units with combat in a quiet sector. He concentrated most of the Ninth Armored's artillery with the Eighty-third Division on the south end of the long, long front.

To carry out his mission of attempted deception, Middleton had the Eighty-third put on three river-crossing demonstrations on the Sauer and Moselle Rivers on October 20. Object: trick the enemy into firing and revealing his gun positions. The Germans fired, but not much. On November 11 the Second Division cut loose with a demonstration by fire without drawing a response from the Germans. That day, the twenty-sixth anniversary of the signing of the armistice ending World War I, Middleton wrote Mrs. Middleton: "In 1918, on this day, I was south of Metz on the Moselle River when the Armistice was signed. Little did I then think that I would be somewhere in Belgium in 1944 and at war with the same enemy."

The continued attempts at deception of the Germans led to a special effort in early December. At the request of the First Army, VIII Corps put the Twenty-third Special Troops to work imitating a buildup indicating that the new Seventy-fifth Division was coming into the line. The special troops put on Seventy-fifth shoulder patches, marked their vehicles and made a show of occupying command posts, organized assembly areas, and used sound effects in place of great numbers of vehicles. They transmitted fictitious radio and telephone messages. And—for a while—the Germans were confused if not deceived. They placed question marks on their intelligence maps, but removed these after a few days.

The four divisions in the VIII Corps through October and most of November thoroughly familiarized themselves with the terrain they were defending. They organized defenses to absorb a heavy punch without letting the enemy all the way through. They prepared withdrawal and counterattack plans. Had the three infantry divisions been in the line when the Germans attacked December 16, they would have slowed the attack much more effectively than did their replacements.

On November 19 the Eighth Division left VIII Corps to give the Twenty-eighth Division a rest. The Twenty-eighth staggered out of fighting in the Huertgen Forest desperately needing rest and 3,400 replacements. They quickly settled into routine but had to be spread much thinner than the full-strength division they replaced. The Twenty-eighth was short almost a fourth of its fighting capability.

Thanksgiving Day, November 23, Middleton wrote Mrs. Middleton, noting, "This will be the third Thanksgiving day I have spent away from home during this war. I trust it will be the last."

On December 7, the Eighty-third pulled out to make room for the weary Fourth Division, Middleton's old outfit in World War I. The Fourth had taken a heavy pounding in the Huertgen Forest also and needed as many replacements as or more than the Twenty-eighth. Four days later, the Second pulled out to join the attack on the Roer River dams. The green 106th Division moved into the Second's place. A combat command of the Ninth Armored was sent north to the V Corps to provide it with a reserve.

Rain was sifting down through the evergreens when night fell on December 15. Stretched painfully thin over the eighty-eight-mile front were the 68,822 officers and men under Middleton's control in the VIII Corps.

Opposite were some 200,000 Germans, moved into position ever so artfully. They had traveled by night. They never got out from under the plentiful cover of the Eifel hills during the day. They maintained perfect quiet and all but perfect deception. The second-string troops which had faded back had been replaced by eighteen divisions making up the Sixth SS Panzer Army, the Fifth Panzer Army, and the Seventh Army.

Intelligence officers of more than one American division and all the way up to the top American command from time to time in November and December voiced their suspicions of the Germans opposite the VIII Corps. Middleton himself took up the question with Bradley, commanding the Twelfth Army Group, which included First Army under Courtney Hodges. It was, as Bradley said, a calculated risk. To apply strength in the north along the Roer River, weakness had to be created somewhere else—in the VIII Corps area. No one, at any level of command, made a great fuss about the risks being run, risks being routine in warfare.

Middleton's headquarters were in Bastogne, about twenty air miles from the West Wall positions held by the Germans. The Bastogne area, on a sketch map, looked like a daddy longlegs, with the town of some 5,000 as the body, and with three highways which passed through the town providing six spindling legs running north-south, northeast-southwest, and southeast-northwest. Bradley's headquarters were in Luxembourg City, about forty road miles southeast of Bastogne, reachable by the north-south highway running down to Arlon and by another running almost straight east from Arlon to Luxembourg.

To get to Bastogne the Germans would have to cross the Our River, almost precisely paralleling the front and in many places coinciding with the front, and pick up a principal highway running directly south from St. Vith to Luxembourg only two or three miles behind the Our River. A lateral road cutting off the St. Vith-Luxembourg highway led west to Bastogne. If the Germans could work their way sufficiently far to the west they could come down on Bastogne on the road from Liege, Belgium, through Werbomont and Baraque de Fraiture. The Clerf River cut a north-south course roughly paralleling the Our, but four or five miles west of the Our. Neither was a formidable stream but they carried runoff from the steady rains, through rough, sometimes precipitously hilly country. This was the High Ardennes plateau. The Germans had whipped through here in 1940 to surprise the French after knocking the Belgians aside. The Germans knew the terrain like the backs of their hands.

It would have been good if the American defenders under Middleton's command had known more about the terrain they were holding on December 15. The veteran outfits now off fighting along the Roer River had known the terrain. Little of their knowledge had rubbed off on their successors in the VIII Corps. The Twenty-eighth Division had come into the corps on November 19, the Fourth Division on December 7, and the novice 106th Division, on December 11. The 106th drew the most exposed positions in a small salient poking into the Schnee Eifel (Snow Plateau) across the German border. As the northernmost division in the VIII Corps, the 106th tied in with V Corps troops. To the south, the Twenty-eighth adjoined the 106th. A combat command of the Ninth Armored filled in between the Twenty-eighth and the Fourth, southernmost in Middleton's command. Corps Artillery was in the best shape of any group in the corps.

When the Germans struck at 5:30 A.M. on Saturday, December 16, they achieved almost perfect surprise. They hit hard at the 106th and the Twenty-eighth. The weather was with the attackers, with mist hugging the ground and clouds sitting almost on the treetops. After firing heavy artillery preparations along the line, the Germans switched on searchlights and sent tanks and infantry straight at the Americans. The Germans had moved nearly 2,000 artillery pieces up for the shoot, ranging from mortars to *nebelwerfers* (firing salvos of rockets weighing half a ton) to fourteen-inch heavy artillery. They laid explosives on the opposing American batteries, marked on their maps by special units which had maintained observation on the American positions for the past week. The German guns fired down a line from Monschau to Echternach, for as little as twenty minutes and for as long as an hour and a half.

Middleton was asleep in his van when the German artillery began firing. A guard awakened him. "I could hear the big guns there in Bastogne," Middleton recalled. Messengers began coming in soon after daybreak. "By 10 A.M. I had word that elements of sixteen different German divisions had been identified in the attacking force." This was no spoiling attack, intended to interfere with American plans for action further north. Middleton communicated his understanding of this fact to Bradley early in the day. Eight infantry and five armored divisions were leading the way for the Germans. Their weight crunched against the 106th and the Twenty-eighth Divisions and against the Fourteenth Cavalry Group, responsible for a sizable gap between the 106th and the V Corps sector. The Germans pushed the American cavalry back sharply by late afternoon.

Seven of the nine rifle battalions of the 106th were in position when the Germans attacked. German artillery fire had knocked out communications lines all along the northern forty-five miles of the corps front. Radio still worked but it served mainly to inform the adjacent units that there were Germans everywhere. Through the day the 106th lost relatively little ground, but the Germans pushed in more men all through the night. Major General Alan W. Jones threw in his reserves, except for an engineer battalion back at St. Vith.

By telephone, Middleton told Jones of his concern for the 106th's 422nd and 423rd Regiments on the Schnee Eifel, the night of December 16. A later call from Jones told of building pressures, with Jones suggesting that his two regiments be pulled back. Middleton approved and assumed that the pullback would be carried out. Earlier in the day, he had issued orders that units were to hold "at all costs" the positions they occupied behind the Our River. All of the 106th units were on the German side of the Our. Whatever the case, the two regiments of the 106th were not pulled back. On December 17 they were surrounded and cut off by Germans hitting them on both flanks. Broken into small groups, most of the men were captured. The last surrendered December 21.

The 106th had had but three full days in the line before the German attack. Men wiser in the ways of combat might have held out longer, but such was the exposure of their position, the task was the more difficult for the inexperienced defenders. Through all this action involving the 106th Middleton did not lose communication with the surviving units. Contact was broken only when the remnants of the 106th went under control of the V Corps when the boundary was changed the night of December 19, with General Bernard Montgomery taking command of all Allied forces on the north side of the area through which the Germans had broken.

The artillery fire which opened the Battle of the Bulge on December 16 did not awaken Middleton's senior aide, John Cribbet. He had attended an anniversary party the night before in observance of the VIII Corps headquarters arrival in England on December 16, 1943. They had had champagne. Cribbet wasn't too happy at his awakening. A junior aide also had to be awakened. He was Lieutenant Perrin Walker, whose father, Brigadier General Nelson M. Walker, had been killed shortly after entering combat in Normandy as an assistant division commander. Out of concern that Lieutenant Walker, much shaken by his father's death, might resolve to go out and kill Germans until he was himself killed in turn, Middleton asked the young lieutenant to join his staff as a junior aide. He had been with the VIII Corps since July. Shortly after the Battle of the Bulge began, when the 101st Airborne Division was ordered to hold Bastogne, Walker asked to be released from his aide's assignment to join the 101st as a platoon commander. Middleton gave his approval. Walker served out the war with the 101st.

To the south of the embattled 106th, the Twenty-eighth Division manned a front of some twenty-four miles. The Germans threw three divisions at the Twenty-eighth, concentrating an armored division and an infantry division totaling 31,000 men on seven miles of the ten-mile front held by the 110th Infantry Regiment. Colonel Hurley Fuller commanded the 110th. The irascible warrior who had talked himself out of a regimental command in the Second Division in Normandy and had taken his troubles to Middleton, who had been host at lunch to Middleton up on Skyline Drive a few days before, who was spoiling for a chance to kill Germans—now had his chance.

The Germans got a head start in Fuller's sector. Generalmajor Heinz Kokott, commander of the Twenty-sixth Volksgrenadier Division, had been reminded along with all the other German commanders that no troops were to cross the Our River line of departure until after the artillery had commenced firing the morning of December 16. Kokott reminded his higher commander, General der Panzertruppen Hasso von Manteuffel, that the Twenty-sixth Volksgrenadiers customarily put men across the Our nightly to hold a line of outposts until daybreak. The Americans would be suspicious, he said, if his division broke its behavior pattern. When Manteuffel agreed, Kokott pushed his advantage by moving two of his three regiments across the river and into line at the base of Skyline Drive. They were almost close enough to step into the breakfast mess line with the American defenders just over the ridge.

Opposing the attacking Germans were two battalions of Fuller's 110th Infantry, perhaps 2,000 men all told. A third battalion sat in reserve three or four miles back on the Clerf River. The reserve battalion could be thrown into action only by the division commander, Major General Norman D. Cota. As was the case all along the VIII Corps front, there was no continuous line of defense in front of the 110th Infantry. (Someone later asked Middleton why there had been no line of entrenchments along his front; the reply was, "Have you any idea how much manpower and effort would have been required to dig a trench eighty-eight miles long?") Fuller's battalions were split into company defenses set up around villages on or adjacent to Skyline Drive, a major north-south highway paralleling the Our River. During the day, soldiers manned outposts in the two miles or so of no man's land between the river and Skyline Drive. They spent the nights in the village strongpoints while American and German patrols operated in no man's land, each seeking prisoners from the other.

Middleton had talked over with Fuller the 110th's plans for dealing with any German attack. These involved holding the Germans at Skyline Drive until reinforcements could be brought up from the west. Fuller had strong defenses at Marnach, just off the Skyline Drive in the north; at Hosingen, on the drive in the center; and at Weiler, on a secondary road leading from the Our to the drive; as well as secondary positions between Skyline Drive and the Clerf River. Finally, he had must-hold positions at Clervaux on his northern boundary. Twenty-eighth Division headquarters were ten miles back at Wiltz. A bridge at Clervaux was essential to the German advance. Backing up the infantry strong points, General Cota had placed two batteries of artillery where they could fire on attackers either at Marnach or at Hosingen and could cover the approaches to bridges on the Clerf.

Six of Fuller's eight available companies were placed where they could deny German passage onto roads leading west. He put the other two companies on the north flank. His Second Battalion remained in divisional reserve with a battalion of tanks.

The Ninth Armored Division, under Middleton's command, had been split into three elements. One major combat command had been sent north to V Corps earlier; another major combat command sat in the gap between the Twenty-eighth and the Fourth Division. A smaller segment, Combat Command R (CCR), was at Trois Vierges, about eight miles northwest of Marnach. CCR could go to the defense of the 110th on short notice. Finally, Middleton had four engineer combat battalions, making up his formal corps reserve.

Bent on winning glory for their Fuehrer, the Germans were heading for the Meuse River, for Antwerp and its port facilities. They were told by their commanders that they could drive a wedge between the Americans on the south and the British and Canadians on the north and that all the advantages would then be theirs. Adolf Hitler had sold himself on such a proposition. Many of the Volksgrenadiers were young, seventeen and eighteen, going into their first battle confident that they would be instrumental in throwing the enemy out of the approaches to the fatherland.

As was the case all along the line, when the German artillery opened up at 5:30 A.M., telephone communications went out. The Germans were firing at map targets, carefully plotted to interfere with transportation and communications. In the predawn darkness they weren't hitting any highway traffic either on Skyline Drive or at main crossroads. Kokott's Volksgrenadiers, who had made a head start after a short hike, came up on Holzthum about 6 A.M. Americans on outpost duty spotted the approaching Germans but were unsure of their identity, so far forward were the first invaders; only when the Germans started shooting did the Americans respond. They beat off the attackers.

If they couldn't take Holzthum, the Volksgrenadiers decided, they would bypass it to the north. A radio message had gone from one of the nearby artillery positions to division headquarters, letting all the Twenty-eighth Division know what was beginning to develop. Artillerymen at Bockholz turned their guns toward the attackers and shook them up. A Volksgrenadier company was ordered to assault the artillery position. As it marched up a secondary road, the company's progress was blocked by a halftrack. Uncertain as to the identity of the halftrack, the Germans hesitated. Someone on the halftrack beckoned them onward. They resumed their approach. Before they could distinguish the markings on the vehicle, the quadruple-mounted .50-caliber machine guns aboard opened up, killing most of the marching company and dispersing the rest. The meat-chopper quad-50s were quite efficient.

The German attack plan called for speed, if the assault forces were to clear the Clerf and push on at least as far as Bastogne and Houffalize the first day. The attackers were to bypass positions they could not overrun. They were to capture Malmedy, St. Vith, Houffalize, and Bastogne, if not on December 16 then no later than December 17. The roads feeding through these towns were essential to the success of the attack.

Already trouble was brewing for the attackers. All day the Twenty-sixth Volksgrenadiers shuttled between Holzthum and Consthum, a mile apart—being denied in their efforts to take the villages and thwarted in their more important mission of getting through to a narrow but substantial bridge across the Clerf River two miles beyond the villages. The time the Volksgrenadiers had gained by crossing the Our during the night was lost against the stubborn Americans. When the artillery kept firing, a German commander ordered another attack. The Americans lowered their guns, set their fuses short, and cut down the German attackers, holding their position.

At Weiler, the company stood off two battalions of Germans with the help of mortars and antitank guns. Twice the Germans sought and were given permission to send out stretcher bearers to pick up their wounded. They reciprocated by offering the Americans an opportunity for an "honorable surrender" early in the afternoon. The Americans declined and kept up the fight until dark, when they ran out of ammunition and pulled out.

The Germans got across Skyline Drive between Hosingen and Marnach and tried for another bridge, at Drauffelt on another secondary road crossing the Clerf. The American artillery battery at Bockholz which had halted the attackers at Holzthum and Consthum, swung round and stopped the Germans in their tracks. The attackers at one point were moving from house to house in an attempt to take Hosingen, strictly against orders to bypass and move on.

During the day the Germans had managed to throw bridges across the Our at Gemund and at Dasburg. Now they were feeding tanks and assault guns across the Our. Though they put tanks and halftracks across at Dasburg, the Germans later ran into a roadblock of their own construction where they had felled trees across the road during their retreat in September.

By late afternoon, a Panzer Grenadier division worked its halftracks across the bridge and around the trees and took Marnach. The American commander was transmitting on his radio when the Germans broke in. No more was heard. The Second Panzer division, held up all day, now had to get by a battery of field artillery before it could cross the good bridge at Clervaux. Fuller had been busy all day, keeping up with the operations of his six companies along Skyline Drive. In Clervaux he had rounded up a scratch force of men in town on pass, sending them to protect the artillerymen. As night came on he asked General Cota for his Second Battalion, held all day in division reserve. Cota turned the battalion loose shortly before midnight, holding back a company to protect his headquarters. Fuller hoped to throw the reserve battalion into action at dawn on December 17 with tank support, but the German armor had moved in and it was too late.

The German Fifth Parachute Division had been scheduled to cross the Our on the Twenty-sixth Volksgrenadiers' left, with a dozen self-propelled 75-millimeter guns. The Fifth Parachute was responsible for four miles of front covered in the north by part of Fuller's 110th and in the south by the 109th Infantry Regiment. Then it was supposed to head for Wiltz and division headquarters of Cota. The parachute troops got across the Our without alerting the Americans but were held up all day by the 109th.

Nothing went as planned by the Germans the first day. It took two battalions to overcome an American company in one 110th area, a battalion to overcome a platoon in another. Fuller's cantankerousness had spilled over onto his men.

From his headquarters in Clervaux, Fuller planned counterattacks at first light on December 17. But the Germans, moving all night, had surrounded the 110th positions. All three German divisions were under orders to let nothing stop them. Their heavy tanks and self-propelled artillery smashed Fuller's light tanks.

Before daylight they were at the edges of Clervaux. By 9 A.M. they were at the top of the hill where the main road from Marnach led to the principal bridge of the two in town. Fuller's command post was in a hotel a few steps from the other bridge.

Middleton had ordered the Ninth Armored's Combat Command R to back up the beleaguered 110th. A company of nineteen medium tanks was dispatched to Clervaux. Fuller split the tanks, using a platoon to clear the Germans from the south end of Clervaux, sending a platoon north to ease the pressures on the northern approaches to the town, and sending another to his First Battalion, where the Germans had shot up American light tanks earlier.

By late afternoon German tanks and self-propelled tank destroyers were pressuring Clervaux again. They started moving in, with a tank-infantry team smashing the American 57-millimeter antitank gun defending the north bridge. A tank platoon came into Clervaux from the south. At 6:25 P.M. Fuller looked out the window of his hotel command post and sighted down the bore of a German tank gun. He telephoned Cota in Wiltz to say that his command post was under fire and that he would be leaving. As a German tank wheeled up and stuck its gun in a window, Fuller and some of his staff scurried out a back window. They hoped to make it out of town in darkness and to join Company G, supposed to be on its way to Clervaux from the west. Fuller was captured as he tried to get out of town.

His 110th was out of the picture, but it had delayed the Germans thirty-seven hours.

Middleton heard next from Fuller in April when Fuller was freed from a German prison camp. He wrote Fuller on April 19:

> I received your letter with much pleasure, it being the first information I have received on the fact that you are very much among the living. I made many inquiries concerning you, and also had a search made of the Clervaux area, but received nothing which would lead to your whereabouts.
>
> If General Cota prepares the citation for the 110th Infantry, I will certainly send it forward with a strong endorsement. I went over the ground where your unit fought it out with the Krauts, and left with sufficient data to leave no doubt in my mind that your outfit did a magnificent job. Had not your boys done the job they did, the 101st Airborne could not have reached Bastogne in time. As you know, with an eighty-eight-mile front, we were stretched very thin. However, the whole outfit gave a good account of itself and the Kraut took an awful beating. On the offensive which followed, we advanced straight through the northern half of our old front and on to Adenau, where we were in 1918–19. The area through which we advanced was a graveyard of destroyed German tanks, guns, and vehicles.

The other two regiments of the Twenty-eighth took much less punishment than Fuller's. To the north, the 112th was sideswiped by the panzers, falling back the second day to join in the defense of St. Vith. To the south, the 109th Infantry commanded by Earl Rudder was able to fold back on the Fourth Division and wasn't badly hurt. Rudder had led a Ranger battalion in scaling cliffs behind the invasion beaches of Normandy on D-day, later performing in outstanding fashion at Brest. Middleton had resolved to offer Rudder a regimental command as soon as a vacancy occurred.

Thus it was that two regimental commanders whom Troy Middleton had been instrumental in placing, were in the path of the Germans' hardest punches. The 110th was shattered. The 109th, after two days of fighting, sidestepped and went under control of the Ninth Armored.

When it was clear that Clervaux and its bridges were in German hands, Middleton ordered the Ninth Armored's CCR to block the distant approaches to Bastogne. The order went out at 11:40 P.M. on December 17, ten minutes after Middleton was informed that German tanks had crossed the Clerf and had good highway surface under their treads. From Clervaux out to the main highway coming in from Trois Vierges was a bare five miles. From the junction Middleton's headquarters in Bastogne was another nine miles.

CCR consisted of the Fifty-second Armored Infantry Battalion, the Second Tank Battalion and the Seventy-third Armored Field Artillery Battalion. Parts of the command had already been sent to back up the 110th Infantry. Colonel Joseph H. Gilbreth, commanding CCR, sent Captain L. K. Rose to the northern roadblock at the junction of the highway from Clervaux and the main highway from Trois Vierges. Task Force Rose comprised a company of Sherman tanks, an armored infantry company, and a platoon of armored engineers. Lieutenant Colonel Ralph S. Harper commanded the backup roadblock near Allerborn, nine miles northeast of Bastogne. Task Force Harper brought together most of the Second Tank Battalion and two companies of the Fifty-second Armored Infantry Battalion.

Task Forces Rose and Harper were in place soon after midnight. The infantry had dug into ground not quite beginning to freeze. The tanks had been placed to present a low silhouette, ready to fire on the German armor.

Before he ordered the CCR elements to their roadblock assignments, Middleton had committed all of his formal reserve forces, including four engineer combat battalions. With matters growing even more crucial, he asked First Army for use of three combat battalions of the 1128th Engineer Group already in the south half of the corps area doing road and bridge maintenance, wood-cutting, and helping keep communications open. First Army approved the request. The engineers, who had been working in relatively small groups wherever they were needed, shut down normal operations, moved their heavy equipment out of reach of the Germans, and drew weapons they ordinarily would not have been called on to carry, much less to use. They picked up ammunition, collected land mines and explosives, and went to defensive assignments. Experts in weapons and explosives ran familiarization courses for headquarters staff, cooks, bakers, clerks, drivers, showing them how to handle a bazooka, how to position and fire that elemental weapon, the mortar, and how to place a mine so cunningly that it would stop an enemy tank or halftrack. Everybody prepared to stand and fight if it became necessary, as it did for almost all of them.

Middleton put his engineers along a half circle running from Foy,

three and a half miles north of Bastogne on the main highway from Houffalize and Noville, around to Neffe, two and a half miles east of Bastogne
on the road from Clervaux. Task Forces Rose and Harper were further
out this highway, in position to meet the Germans on December 18.

Out at Wiltz, headquarters of the Twenty-eighth Division, fifteen
miles east of Bastogne, German infantry and armor with the highly efficient 88-millimeter gun pushed the defenders back. General Cota heard
that relief might be headed his way late that afternoon when he got reports
that a combat command of the Tenth Armored Division was headed up
the highway from Arlon toward Bastogne. Cota radioed Colonel William Roberts, leading the Tenth's CCB, to ask for his assistance at Wiltz.
Roberts couldn't oblige, earlier having received orders from Middleton
to report to corps headquarters in Bastogne. CCB arrived in Bastogne at
4 P.M., to find plenty of assignments awaiting.

When on December 19, the Fifth Parachute Division began attacking
Wiltz, Cota moved his headquarters to Sibret, fourteen miles west, on the
highway from Bastogne to Neufchateau. By nightfall the Germans were
pushing into Wiltz. Its defenders headed out through the woods. They had
held up the German advance four days. German tanks should by this date
have been at the Meuse, fifty miles west.

Task Force Rose troops, in position since midnight, saw their first
Germans at midmorning, slipping into a small wood. From the reconnaissance battalion of the Second Panzer Division, they preceded two battalions of tanks. The reconnaissance force started feeling out Task Force
Rose. The Americans responded with rifle fire and with direct artillery fire
from the Seventy-third Armored Field Artillery Battalion whose howitzers were close by. An hour after the first standoff, the Germans ran up
tanks. Under a well-laid smoke screen they closed within a half mile. The
first German tanks sat by for two hours until they were joined by a panzer
battalion. They moved in on the infantry protecting Rose's Sherman tanks.
The tank guns moved the infantry back, leaving Rose at the bottom of a
fast-closing pocket. Ordered by Middleton to hold, Task Force Rose was
doing its best.

When Colonel Gilbreth, CCR commander, heard of Rose's plight, at
2:05 P.M. he telephoned the corps command post to recommend that the
task force be permitted to fight its way back to Task Force Harper. Middleton had to say no. Any reinforcements moving to Rose's assistance al-

most certainly would have been taken by the superior German force, growing by the hour. The Germans pushed the American howitzers back, laid white phosphorus shells on the Sherman tank positions, driving them back from their hillcrest, and put a fastener on the pocket, surrounding Rose on the fourth side. At 2:30 P.M. the Germans overran the American positions, destroying seven Sherman tanks.

At dusk, with five tanks and an assault gun platoon, Rose took off cross country, hoping to make it to Houffalize. Traveling without lights, they ran into a German ambush. A handful of vehicles escaped. With the first roadblock cleared, most of the Third Panzer Regiment came onto the Bastogne highway, rolling freely down to the stronger roadblock, after losing five hours dislodging Rose.

At Allerborn, Task Force Harper was only nine miles from Bastogne. Past the first roadblock, German light elements came up to the Allerborn defenders in late afternoon December 18. They marked time, waiting for heavier tanks. Then the Germans swept the American positions with systematic machine gun fire. After dark, they destroyed two platoons of American tanks, set fire to lighter vehicles with tracers and picked off the infantry by the light of the fires. Colonel Harper was killed. The surviving Americans fell back to Longvilly, five and a half miles from Bastogne.

Longvilly was jammed with stragglers, who reported Germans on all sides. At 8 P.M. a courier reported to Gilbreth's CCR headquarters that a task force from the Tenth Armored Division was coming up from Bastogne. Lieutenant Colonel Henry T. Cherry commanded this force, under orders to stop at Longvilly.

As remnants of Task Forces Rose and Harper had come back on Longvilly, some directly and some circuitously, two armored field artillery battalions had kept up fire on the Allerborn road junction where Task Force Harper had been defeated. Riflemen from one company of the 110th Infantry and others who had been pulled into the defense, along with four tank destroyers, formed a line to protect the Fifty-eighth Armored Field Artillery Battalion south of Longvilly.

From Mageret, a little more than two miles down the road toward Bastogne, came the noise of firing shortly before dusk. German troops had come around and cut off the fire direction center of the Seventy-third Field Artillery Battalion. Both the Seventy-third and the Fifty-eighth, however, kept up their fire on the highway east of Longvilly. They shortened their fuses to accommodate targets only two hundred yards away at 11:15 P.M. Just before midnight, Gilbreth decided to pull out of Longvilly and head back to Bastogne through Mageret. A few vehicles started back and were promptly hit by the Germans who had taken Mageret. Traffic piled up on the outskirts of Longvilly, prompting Gilbreth to stop the movement until daylight.

Next, the Seventy-third Field Artillery Battalion was ordered to leave Longvilly, starting at 4 A.M., December 19. It began moving, with one battery covering the others until all three were out, still firing to the east, the south, and the north to cover CCR's withdrawal. The Fifty-eighth Field Artillery Battalion was hit by German mortar fire early in the morning. At 8 A.M. two German tanks materialized out of the fog. The artillerymen reacted first and knocked out the tanks. CCR's main column was nearing Mageret when German fire came from both sides of the highway at a roadblock. The fighting went on until midafternoon when CCR headquarters, the remaining self-propelled howitzers of the Fifty-eighth, and the stragglers picked up along the way left the highway tangle and worked their way back to Bastogne with the help of paratroopers from the 101st Airborne Division of whose presence the CCR force was unaware.

Middleton, under whose direction all the smaller group actions were unfolding east and north of Bastogne, had been in continuous contact with Bradley at Twelfth Army Group headquarters in Luxembourg. Characteristically, Middleton had been as much concerned about Bradley's safety in Luxembourg as Bradley had been about Middleton's welfare in Bastogne. The action, however, was closing in on Bastogne and not on Luxembourg. The Germans did not have the resources to attack on so wide a front. But they were almost at the point of moving into Bastogne. The Bastogne which formed the body of the sketch map "daddy longlegs" was being seized at the topmost joint of his southeastern and northeastern legs. Bradley and First Army commander Hodges decided that Middleton should take his headquarters to more hospitable surroundings seventeen miles southwest at Neufchateau on December 18. Accordingly, Hodges so instructed Middleton.

Middleton, aware that he could be of little use as a captive of the Germans, agreed that conditions could be better. He needed, however, to stay in Bastogne long enough to brief the commanders of his promised relief force, the 101st Airborne Division. He stayed overnight in Bastogne.

That afternoon and evening he entertained three welcome callers. First to show up was Colonel William Roberts, who had driven ahead of his outfit, CCB of the Tenth Armored Division, sent in from the south by Patton. Roberts and Middleton conferred, with consequences which will be detailed subsequently. Roberts had arrived at 4 P.M. Along about 5 o'clock, Brigadier General Anthony McAuliffe, acting commander of the 101st Airborne, checked in. He had taken a fortunate detour into Bastogne en route to Werbomont, where the 101st otherwise might have gone.

Middleton assured McAuliffe of the desirability of stopping his division off at Bastogne and proceeded to get a clearance from higher headquarters. Thus it was that the 101st drew the honor of becoming the "Battered Bastards of Bastogne." The same circumstance of fortune which sent McAuliffe into Bastogne for a quick—he thought—briefing on what his division might meet up the road at Werbomont, also turned Colonel Thomas L. Sherburne off the road to Werbomont. Sherburne, leading the 101st Division Artillery, was held up by the rear elements of the Eighty-second Airborne Division at a crossroads seven miles west of Bastogne at 8 P.M. He checked his map and decided that the long way through Bastogne was the quick way. He took it after being told by a military policeman at the crossroads that McAuliffe had made the same choice earlier. Sherburne instructed the MP to send the artillery column by way of Bastogne.

By accident, then, Bastogne received its defenders ahead of schedule. They were joined later in the evening by Major General Matthew B. Ridgway, on his way to his XVIII Airborne Corps headquarters in the north sector of the developing bulge area. Ridgway recalled his arrival at the VIII Corps headquarters in his book *Soldier*: "Just about dark we found the command post of General Troy Middleton's VIII Corps. The gloom inside that headquarters was thicker than the fog outside. This atmosphere of uncertainty was in no way the fault of General Middleton, a magnificent soldier with a wonderful combat record in two wars. But the most disquieting thing in any war is to be in a completely unknown situation. General Middleton knew that some of his units had been overrun. He knew the German attack had opened a great gap in his lines. But nearly all his communications with his forward elements were out, and he had no knowledge of where his forces were, nor where the Germans were, nor where they might strike next."

Things may have been bad but they weren't nearly that bad. After three days of fighting, the picture was far from promising, but Middleton had a pretty clear idea of what the Germans were after, how they proposed to go about getting it, and even where they were now heavily engaged by American defenders Middleton had sent to defensive positions. The Germans themselves had helped. Early in the first day's action, American troops had captured a young German officer carrying complete plans for the lightning stroke at the VIII Corps area.

"Why he had the complete plans—unless he was a messenger—I'll never know," Middleton said. "They called for taking Bastogne and moving through St. Vith on the afternoon of December 16, the first day. We wouldn't have needed any German plans to tell us how essential possession of the road net through Bastogne was, nor how useful St. Vith on the north side of the invaded area would be. Incidentally, St. Vith had been a German city until the realignment of national boundaries after World War I. Perhaps the Germans thought they would be welcomed and aided by the populace, many of whom were more cordial to the Germans than to their American liberators before and after the Battle of the Bulge."

Ridgway, whom Middleton held in high regard, was all for pushing on to his new command area on the night of December 18. Middleton dissuaded him, explaining that Ridgway's presence couldn't be that essential that night—especially if he had to chance capture by the Germans on his way out. "If he had persisted in going ahead that night, he almost certainly would have been captured by the Germans, everywhere north of us by that time."

Though the German timetable stipulated that they would have to take Malmedy, St. Vith, Houffalize, and Bastogne no later than the second day, at the end of the third day they had taken none of these objectives. Nor had they found rich stores of gasoline, food, and ammunition. "It was really a poor boys' front," Middleton recalled. "The Germans obviously thought they would be able to refuel and resupply their troops from what they captured on the way to the Meuse. We just didn't have big fuel and ammunition dumps because there was no need for them. We weren't building up for an attack when the Germans hit us. We were just in there minding our business."

While Middleton was entertaining his most welcome guests Monday evening, December 18, a potential party-crasher named Fritz Bayerlein, commander of the first-rank Panzer Lehr Division, pulled into Niederwampach, a village six miles east of Bastogne, about 6:30 P.M. He had crossed the Clerf River on the narrow Drauffelt bridge, with fifteen tanks and four companies of Panzer Grenadiers. Two miles to the north he could see muzzle blasts and exploding shells where the Second Panzer Division was tangling with the roadblock below Allerborn.

Bayerlein was under orders to capture Bastogne. He could go two ways. One would take him over a fairly good secondary road southeast for three and a half miles through Wardin and onto the paved main road leading seven and a half miles to Bastogne. Total: eleven miles. His other choice would send him up a narrow, rutted track three miles west to Mageret, from which it was only three miles to Bastogne. Bayerlein took the short cut.

For almost a mile he was on pavement. Then the road turned to dirt. The tanks made a loblolly of it. After little more than a half mile of this the road played out, becoming nothing more than a trail, running through the hamlet of Benonchamps and going the final mile to Mageret. It took the Bayerlein force more than five hours to traverse the six miles in darkness. At Mageret, some of Middleton's combat engineers fired on the German force, holding it up for another hour so that it was 1 A.M. on Tuesday, December 19, when the would-be party-crasher took control of Mageret. He had three miles to go to Bastogne and was fairly certain that the distance could be negotiated in the morning.

Then, an excitable sympathizer with the Germans—or a marvelously convincing admirer of the Americans—told him that a host of American tanks and infantry carriers had clattered through Mageret several hours earlier, led by an American major general. How many tanks were with the American general? Bayerlein asked the civilian. At least fifty, he was told. Since American major generals command divisions, this one might have as many as 263 tanks, Bayerlein recalled from his knowledge of the American order of battle books. With fifty-seven tanks in all the Panzer Lehr Division and with only a dozen of these on the ground at Mageret, Bayerlein considered his arithmetic. The odds were not in his favor. On the other hand, how could the Americans have moved in an armored division so incredibly fast? The same way they had thwarted the German armor through three days, holding it far short of its first-day objectives?

Second Panzer Division might be catching it from the mystery American force out at Longvilly right now. While his own force was halted at

Mageret he could hear tanks and other vehicles clearly on the night air.
The tank noise came from his own back at the rear of the column pulling
into Mageret. The other vehicles were those carrying the Americans who
were trying to get away from the areas where Task Forces Rose and
Harper had been smashed earlier. Should he take a chance and push on?
Bayerlein decided not to. It would be easy enough in the morning—when
he could see where the mystery American armored division had gone and
what his own panzers faced so close to Bastogne. He put out roadblocks
north and south of Mageret and opted for sleep.

No more than three miles away, Middleton and his overnight guests,
Ridgway, McAuliffe, and Roberts, were taking their rest in an old barracks
occupied earlier by the Germans. "The place was foul when we moved
into it in October," Middleton recalled. "Why the toilets wouldn't even
flush and the place reeked of sloppy housekeeping."

Middleton was to be up early in the morning as were his guests. Mc-
Auliffe would become the host for future gatherings. Roberts had put his
CCB to work wherever Middleton directed. Ridgway would go on to the
north shoulder of the bulge, by a safer route, to put the Eighty-second Airborne to work up there. The 101st, which he had contributed from his
command early because of McAuliffe's late afternoon detour, would continue coming into Bastogne all night and into the day.

When Roberts had come into Middleton's command post at 4 P.M. on
Monday, he knew he would be seeing an old friend. The two had served in
the first World War and had met again at Command and General Staff
School. Roberts was older than most men in his position. Furthermore
he knew how he intended to use his armor. Middleton quickly changed
Roberts' mind for him.

"How many teams can you make up, Robby?" Middleton asked.

"Three," Roberts replied without enthusiasm.

Middleton poked a finger at his map (marked, someone later said,
like an advanced case of measles) and told Roberts to send three teams
out at once, to Noville, five miles up the highway from Houffalize; to
Longvilly, five miles out the road toward Clervaux; and to Wardin, off the
road from Wiltz about three miles east. Roberts didn't like his orders but
he obeyed them promptly. Armor, he thought, should stick together. Instead, Middleton wanted him to scatter it all over the landscape. The scat-
tering couldn't have been more fortunate, as it turned out.

Before 5 P.M., CCB's leading team arrived. Roberts sent it off to what he thought would be the most crucial point, Longvilly, where the Germans had already made a big fuss. The team, commanded by Lieutenant Colonel Henry Cherry, included a tank battalion, an armored infantry company, a platoon of engineers, and a reconnaissance platoon. They were stopped west of Longvilly about 7 P.M. by a massive jam of vehicles full of men who wanted to go toward Bastogne. At Gilbreth's CCR headquarters, Cherry learned that the Longvilly defenders had fought about as long as they could, and that they hoped to make their way back to Bastogne by way of Mageret. Cherry took this word back to his force and sent his reconnaissance platoon under First Lieutenant Edward P. Hyduke out to screen west of Longvilly. The rest of Cherry's men would wait until CCR had decided what it would do next.

Cherry drove back to Bastogne to relate these developments to Roberts, indicating his misgivings about CCR. Roberts told Cherry to go back to Longvilly and hold on, authorizing him to add to his team any stray men, vehicles, or weapons coming his way.

The second team, entering Bastogne shortly after the first, was commanded by Lieutenant Colonel James O'Hara. Roberts quickly directed Team O'Hara to Wardin, where German tanks were expected soon. They would have come into head-on collision with Team O'Hara, if Bayerlein had not chosen to take the short cut to Bastogne by way of Mageret. O'Hara, with his armored infantry battalion, found Wardin quiet. The only troops he and his men saw were Americans, staggering in from the positions they had held in the Twenty-eighth Division area. They couldn't tell O'Hara much except that the Germans had a great many tanks.

Team number three from CCB arrived after dark. It was led by Major William Desobry, youngest of the three team commanders. Desobry was instructed by Roberts to take his fifteen Sherman tanks and a platoon of tank destroyers out to Noville and to hold tight. Roberts, noting Desobry's relative youth, said, "You're young, and by tomorrow morning you'll probably be nervous and you might think that it would be a good idea to withdraw from Noville. When you begin thinking that, remember that I told you it would be best not to withdraw until I order you to do so." Because he would have to creep along in darkness, Desobry sent a cavalry platoon ahead to pick positions for his tanks. Team Desobry arrived in Noville at 2:30 A.M. Tuesday, December 19.

Though Teams O'Hara and Desobry found no Germans, a special German paratroop force, dropped behind the V Corps front to the north, had caused some difficulties in the VIII Corps area. They had cut a buried cable linking First Army headquarters in Spa with Bradley's Twelfth Army Group headquarters in Luxembourg City. Middleton was thus thrown out of telephone contact with his army commander, Hodges, at Spa. The Germans had also sent English-speaking Germans in American uniforms driving American vehicles ahead of their attack forces to create confusion. The Germans in American uniforms were instructed to tear up communications, spread rumors, and misdirect American vehicle drivers. They did some physical damage, tore up some communications, and misdirected some drivers—but their greatest usefulness was psychological. For a few days Americans challenged Americans everywhere, all the way back to Eisenhower's headquarters deep in France. It was a good idea to know that the Brooklyn baseball team was the Dodgers and other bits of Americana every school kid should have known.

The Eighty-second Airborne, which had preceded the 101st through the road junction west of Bastogne, went on Werbomont to block the German SS Panzer Division which had shoved through a gap between the VIII and the V Corps. Originally it was planned that the Eighty-second, better rested, would precede the 101st to Bastogne on the 107-mile trip from Camp Mourmelon.

The 101st came into Bastogne under command of McAuliffe, its divisional artillery commander, with 805 officers and 11,035 men. Maxwell Taylor, division commander, was back in the States on a mission. Unlike conventional infantry divisions, the 101st was organized in four regiments rather than three.

For punch the 101st used three battalions of light artillery with the modified pack howitzer useful up to eight thousand yards. A battalion of 105-millimeter howitzers strengthened the artillery arm.

The 101st got its indispensable artillery support from the corps artillery Middleton already had under his command behind Bastogne and from three groups which arrived after the 101st. The 705th Tank Destroyer Battalion was ordered from Ninth Army, north of the bulge, to leave for Bastogne the night of December 18. German panzers moving west forced the 705th to take a wide detour, but the tank destroyers arrived in Bastogne the next night. They carried a relatively new weapon, the self-propelled 76-millimeter long-barreled gun. It was as good as anything German tanks carried, but not a match for the German 88-millimeter gun.

Group number two, the 755th Armored Field Artillery Battalion, was ordered from the north on the evening of December 18. It moved fast enough to arrive in Bastogne the next morning. Because its big 155-millimeter howitzers took up a lot of road space with their prime movers, Middleton kept it outside town until a traffic jam could be dispersed.

The third group of artillerymen comprised the 969th Field Artillery Battalion, with medium howitzers. They had been sent to back up the Twenty-eighth Division before the German breakthrough. When the 110th Infantry was knocked out, the 969th was told to go back west. They were on the way when orders came to join the party at Bastogne. McAuliffe put the 969th in with the 755th and the 420th Armored Field Artillery Battalion three miles southwest of Bastogne. From there they could fire on the Germans on all sides, though they did not yet have to contend with Germans in their rear.

Starting with the arrival of the 501st Parachute Infantry at midnight, the 101st men came in on their trucks and unloaded all night in the assembly area west of Bastogne. By 9 A.M. on December 19, all of the 101st was at Bastogne. It was up to McAuliffe to decide where his men should be placed to back up the teams sent east and north by Middleton and Roberts of CCB. Roberts worked with McAuliffe throughout the next week while the Germans were applying their heaviest pressure until a relief column broke through from Patton's command on December 26. As stragglers continued to come in from the east and northeast, Roberts put them into the line around the beleaguered town.

18 The View from Neufchateau

DAWN oozed through the overcast on December 19 as the last regiment of the 101st Airborne was rolling up. Hodges had ordered Middleton to leave Bastogne the night before but there had been too much to do before the VIII Corps commander could depart for his new headquarters seventeen miles southwest at Neufchateau.

Headquarters commandant Hornbeak had chosen a school building in Neufchateau as the new corps headquarters. Most of the corps staff had moved back there on December 18. Hornbeak had asked to stay in Bastogne with Middleton, as had the corps assistant chief of staff. Two enlisted men, drivers of a Packard and a Jeep, remained to take the officers to their new headquarters.

Having prevailed on Matt Ridgway to stay overnight rather than head for Houffalize in darkness, Middleton roused his guest early December 19, fed him, and saw him on his way, farther west instead of through Noville, where Team Desobry had settled into position a few hours earlier. Having conferred at length with McAuliffe the night before, when he had recommended areas for placement of the 101st's paratroopers, Middleton prepared to leave.

"Now Tony, you're going to be surrounded here before long. But don't worry; help is on the way from Patton. You've got fine men. There's a lot of artillery backing you up. It can put plenty of fire on any point around Bastogne. I'd prefer not to leave this place, but Hodges has told me I have to go. We'll be in contact with you all the time," Middleton said.

234

The two-vehicle convoy arrived in Neufchateau soon after full daylight. Middleton found his radio communications net working satisfactorily, linking him with the 101st in Bastogne, with Hodges in Spa, and with Bradley in Luxembourg City. Patton was on his way up to Arlon, having swung much of his armor around from east to north for the long run to Bastogne.

Middleton and Bayerlein had spent the night about three miles apart, each unaware of the other's presence nearby. Bayerlein was under orders to take Bastogne, but had given excess weight to a civilian's tale about an American major general and a great mass of tanks somewhere nearby. While Bayerlein had stopped within three miles, a considerably more powerful force from the Second Panzer Division had knocked out both American roadblocks on the highway from Clervaux and had come within five miles of Middleton's headquarters in Bastogne. All Colonel Meinrad von Lauchert's Second Panzer units had to do was to push with the same persistence they had used in reducing CCR's roadblocks, and they could have rolled close enough to take Middleton's command post under fire. But Second Panzer's orders did not include Bastogne. After knocking out the roadblocks and going halfway to Longvilly, the Second Panzer executed a sharp column right and headed off at a ninety-degree angle to keep to its assigned sector.

Team Cherry and Second Panzer's leading elements were on a collision course and only a mile apart when the Germans veered off. While Second Panzer's main weight took another direction, Lauchert let the Americans know he knew they were there, by sending a small force up to the American positions for some close-range shooting. Gilbreth's CCR defenders pulled out then, leaving it to Team Cherry to deal with whatever might come. Colonel Cherry found a substantial chateau for use as his command post three hundred yards south of Neffe and two miles west of Mageret. Cherry was heading back to his main force about 2 A.M. on December 19 when he learned that a panzer force had taken Mageret. This prevented Cherry, a little less than two miles from corps headquarters in Bastogne, from reaching his main force or advance guard by road, Mageret being squarely in the way. He radioed Captain William Ryerson to ask that he run the Germans out of Mageret. Ryerson, commanding Cherry's main force, sent a couple of squads of infantry to size up the situation. They found three tanks and a company of Panzer Grenadiers. Colonel Cherry reported this to Roberts and the two commanders decided to abandon Longvilly. Team Cherry's main force was ordered to fight its way back through Mageret to Neffe to join the headquarters force.

Lieutenant Hyduke, commanding the third group of Team Cherry, had tanks well positioned at Longvilly, commanding the highway approaches and protected against cross-country runs by German tanks because the ground was mushy on one side and too steep for tanks on the other. There was a hitch, however; Hyduke's tanks were also road bound, and they looked up to high ground south and southeast. The Germans threw in some shells from the high positions. Then they ran two tanks up to firing position. In the fog no one could say whether the tanks were German or American. The Germans settled the question by knocking out an American Sherman tank from CCR. The American response eliminated the two German tanks and little more was heard from that quarter the morning of December 19. Team Cherry's main force was trying to work its way back to Mageret, a little more than a mile, when a German anti-tank gun knocked out the lead tank and blocked the road. More American vehicles stacked up, and before long the two-mile stretch from Mageret to Longvilly was plugged tight with Americans.

The stage was unhappily set for a shoot. At the Longvilly end of the stretch, Hyduke's tanks and men were made targets at 2 P.M. Elements of three German divisions, each unaware of the others' intent, lashed out at Hyduke's small force. The Twenty-sixth Volksgrenadiers had marched all the way to Oberwampach and were one mile from Longvilly at dawn. General der Panzertruppen Heinrich von Luettwitz, commander of the German corps in the Bastogne sector, severely disappointed at the performance of the three divisions under his command, ordered the Volksgrenadiers to attack Longvilly, after they had rested through the morning and eaten under cover between Oberwampach and Longvilly.

While Luettwitz was pushing the Twenty-sixth Volksgrenadiers up to the line, Bayerlein was lining up Panzer Lehr to drive on the same objective. He put a regiment of Panzergrenadiers, an artillery battalion and twenty self-propelled antitank guns on the road at Benonchamps, two miles from Longvilly, at the same time the slower Twenty-sixth Volksgrenadiers were leaving Oberwampach. Although the Second Panzer Division had the night before turned away from Longvilly after dealing it a side-slap, the Second Panzer's commander, Lauchert, was angered when his force was shelled by a battery from the Ninth Armored Division. He sent six self-propelled 88-millimeter guns to deal with the American mischief makers.

Hyduke had fifteen Sherman tanks to contend with three converging German forces, none of which knew the others were aiming at the same objective. Since the Volksgrenadiers also brought along antitank guns, the Germans put into play more tank destroyers than there were American tanks, with the deadly eighty-eights overmatching any American weapon. Bayerlein's tank destroyers fired from the southwest. The Volksgrenadiers shot from the southeast. The Second Panzer's eighty-eights roared from the northeast. Their targets couldn't get off the two-mile stretch of highway. Hyduke and the survivors escaped on foot and joined Ryerson's main force outside Mageret.

Despite the loss of men and all the vehicles between Longvilly and Mageret, the northeast door to Bastogne did not swing wide. It might have been forced, late December 19, if the three German divisions had been disposed to make the effort. Second Panzer, of course, had turned away under its original orders and was not yet abreast of Bastogne. But Panzer Lehr had the strength to tackle the Bastogne defenders. Bayerlein elected not to do so, thinking he would have to contend with strong tank, infantry, and artillery contingents around his positions at Mageret. Kokott's Volksgrenadiers by now knew that the 101st Airborne was in Bastogne and chose not to hit head-on against the respected American paratroopers. Corps commander Luettwitz heard from the Second Panzer commander that Noville was exceptionally strongly held.

Luettwitz thus asked the Fifth Panzer Army's commander, Manteuffel, for permission to turn his three divisions to the task of taking Bastogne. No, said Manteuffel, the two panzer divisions were already too far behind schedule in their dash for the Meuse. They must go ahead, leaving the task to the Volksgrenadiers. Second Panzer, Manteuffel said, was already overdue at Dinant, more than forty miles west. Panzer Lehr was flubbing its assignment badly east of Bastogne after having come so close to taking its prime objective on the run the night before. Panzer Lehr did, eventually, get untracked and moved a mile west to Neffe, losing one tank to a mine along the way, halting at the Neffe railroad station at 7 A.M. While they were at the station, paratroopers from the American 101st Airborne started out from Bastogne to meet them.

The 501st Parachute Infantry, under Julian Ewell, had been first into Bastogne the evening before. Ewell sought a specific assignment from McAuliffe, who put the question to Middleton. Middleton said the German strength lay near the Longvilly road. Things had looked better the night before than they were to work out the morning and early afternoon of December 19. McAuliffe told Ewell to put his regiment on the Longvilly road at 6 A.M., to make contact, attack, and clear up the situation.

Knowing that the 101st would be alone in its defense for several days —aside from the artillery Middleton had had in position earlier—McAuliffe counseled conservatism rather than daring among the paratroop defenders. He accordingly did not send out a regiment; instead, Ewell took a combat team consisting of an infantry battalion, an antiaircraft battery, and a platoon of reconnaissance troops. In the predawn fog the reconnaissance platoon took the wrong fork at a split in the road not far out. Ewell detected the mistake quickly because he had walked over the same ground a month earlier while on leave in Bastogne. He stopped the movement and got word up to the point leaders to double back and get on the right road. The reconnaissance troops were back where they belonged when a German machine gun began firing on them half a mile west of Neffe. The paratroopers went to the ditches. When a German tank gun joined the serenade they left the ditches for higher ground.

Now came another impasse. The Germans interpreted the appearance of Ewell's force as part of a larger attack on the Panzer Lehr forces at Neffe. Ewell read the Panzer Lehr firing as evidence that it was in Neffe in strength. Leaving his First Battalion in place, Ewell asked for artillery support and brought up his other two battalions. The artillery came up on the double, taking positions so well chosen that they could lay fire on the enemy without drawing a return. Only a thousand yards behind the infantry, the artillerymen did not have to displace a single gun throughout the siege. Furthermore, the lightweight 105-millimeter gun made an authoritative noise. Bayerlein was sure the fire came from a tank, and that if one tank was firing it would be supported by others. The Panzer Lehr force took eighty casualties from this shelling. Besides the 101st's artillery, Bayerlein kept hearing rifle fire from his left, from Team Cherry's small headquarters force shut up in Chateau Neffe. Bayerlein's hearing must have become super acute: he was now imagining two battalions of infantry in the attack coming from Chateau Neffe and a squadron of tanks pushing out from Bastogne. Thus he went back to the comparative safety of Mageret.

Ewell's Second Battalion had to buck cross traffic in Bastogne and required nearly two hours to get to Bizory, where it strengthened the thin outpost lines of the combat engineers Middleton had sent out the day before. The Third Battalion couldn't work its way through Bastogne at all; it gave up this effort for a swing around the town, taking it into a supply column from Roberts' CCB, which was overstocked with infantry weapons and ammunition appropriated back along the line—as was the custom of veteran outfits. The armored troops were glad enough to share with paratroopers going into battle without rifles. By noon the Third Battalion was in Mont, where it was stopped by Panzer Lehr tanks sitting on higher ground a mile away in Neffe.

With his dispositions made by early afternoon, Ewell told the Second Battalion commander to take Mageret. The Germans reacted strongly and the result was a standoff. Cherry had held off German attacks all day at Chateau Neffe. By nightfall the chateau's wooden roof was ablaze and other fires had been caused by German shelling. Rather than oppose two kinds of fire, Cherry joined the Third Battalion in Mont.

The Third Battalion had had to sit tight in Mont rather than risk high casualties in a daylight assault over open ground. Its commander, Lieutenant Colonel George M. Griswold, remembered McAuliffe's injunction to use his force conservatively. Griswold did send Company I out to see whether there were any Germans between Neffe and Wardin, a mile and a half to the right.

In Wardin, Team O'Hara had spent a quiet night and a quiet early morning, greeting stragglers from the Twenty-eighth Division. When no stragglers showed up for half an hour, Team O'Hara prepared to greet other callers. The team's reconnaissance platoon eased down the road to await the Germans. First came a Volkswagen, unaccompanied. Its occupants died in a burst of fire. Then came two Mark IV tanks. Without anti-tank weapons, the American reconnaissance platoon gave ground. O'Hara asked his artillery backup to start shooting at Bras, a village two miles east where the highway was certain to be filled with Panzer Lehr vehicles.

Although no sun showed through the murk, their watches told the Americans it was noon. No sun had, in fact, relieved the overcast, the rain, and the snow since the German assault on the VIII Corps front began. An American artillery observer's tank came up and stood in silhouette near five other Sherman tanks as they waited for the German Mark IV's. The Germans pulled a dirty trick, having moved a self-propelled eighty-eight off the highway paralleling the route the Mark IVs were following. The eighty-eight wrecked the artillery observer's tank and knocked out a Sherman. The other Shermans backed off to safety. German artillery swung on Team O'Hara from the north. German infantrymen began moving toward Wardin. Edgy American tank crews, hearing that German infantry was coming, almost fired on the friendly paratroopers from Company I, wearing green that looked gray in the midday gloom. Company I had found no Germans between Neffe and Wardin and had pushed on to check on the roadblock, purportedly manned by friendly forces near Wardin.

Company I kept going to Wardin, ambushing a twenty-five man German patrol, killing or wounding them all. The ambushers were hit in turn by seven Panzer Lehr tanks followed by a battalion of Panzer Grenadiers. The Panzer Lehr tanks missed contact with Team O'Hara's tanks and pushed into Wardin.

With the abandonment of Wardin, Team O'Hara asked for a covering artillery barrage and pulled back to high ground north of Marvie. They were moving in tight on Bastogne, less than a mile and a half from the defenses behind Marvie. The First and Second Battalions were ordered to draw back to a defensive line behind Bizory and Neffe.

The 420th Armored Field Artillery had been busy throughout the day, once helping Team Cherry's main force stand off a Panzer Lehr attack on Mageret. At nightfall, Ryerson and what was left of Hyduke's force were still fighting off Germans. Rather than leave them there to face yet another panzer attack at dawn, Roberts at 3 A.M. instructed Ryerson to head cross country and bring his survivors through the Second Battalion's line at Bizory. They staggered in just before dawn, after most had been without sleep for forty-eight hours.

At daylight December 20, Bastogne's defenses had firmed down on an arc swinging from north of Bizory around beyond Marvie. On this line the 501st Parachute Infantry stood to the end of the siege, along with the engineers and motley forces which filtered into Bastogne and stayed to help. On the west side of Bastogne, directly opposite the Bizory-Marvie arc, the 705th Tank Destroyer Battalion arrived at 10:30 the night of December 19, after twenty-two hours on the road. That same night word came that the Fourth Armored Division was being sent by Patton, though it had quite a way to come. Somehow the defenders of Bastogne got the idea that the Fourth Armored might be expected within a day or two.

Out at Noville, Team Desobry was now the farthest from Bastogne of the armored groups sent out by Roberts. Second Panzer Division, which had turned away from Longvilly on its Meuse-bound mission, would go through Bourcy and would have to take Noville to get into the clear for its run westward. Team Desobry had placed a roadblock at Bourcy, a mile and a half east. At 4:30 A.M. on December 19 the roadblock defenders heard the clatter of a halftrack. Their challenge was answered in German. After a twenty-minute fight the Germans left.

Having been bluffed out of this attack, the Germans in the halftrack told their commanding officer the Americans were too strong to be pushed aside. When the report finally got to the Second Panzer commander, he was convinced Bourcy was too powerful to crack. Lauchert asked permission to swing north. Corps commander Luettwitz granted permission. Unfortunately for Team Desobry this put Second Panzer armor around to the north on high ground looking down on Noville and on another ridge southeast of Noville.

Desobry's roadblock crew up the Houffalize highway had an hour and a half to go on its night assignment before pulling back to Noville, when three German tanks crept within a hundred yards of them in a dense fog. The Americans got first crack but missed. The lead German tank knocked out both American tanks. After an exchange of small-arms fire the Americans pulled back to Noville. Desobry's third forward position, on his left on the road to Vaux, was not approached by the Germans and came back into Noville after daylight.

With the three roadblock teams back at their base, an eighty-eight opened up from the Houffalize highway, smashing six vehicles. Two Tiger tanks materialized out of the fog right at the American defense position. With bazookas, an antitank gun, and a Sherman tank's gun, the Tigers were put out of action.

Fog masked the Second Panzer movements another hour, although the American defenders could hear the German armor working its way into position. Then the fog faded. German tanks were everywhere except to the south. On the west they were within two hundred yards. In the north fourteen were lined up on high ground a thousand yards out. The tanks rolled closer, firing steadily at American vehicles and crumbling buildings in which American infantry was taking shelter.

As the morning wore on, the fog capriciously came and went. It lifted just as four American tank destroyers came up from the south and caught a long line of German tanks standing clear on the northern ridge. The tank destroyers knocked out nine German tanks before they could withdraw. The Germans kept pressuring with armor, but after an hour of futile attacks, the Germans dropped their tanks hull-down behind the northern ridge and set out to knock Noville down around the Americans' ears.

Desobry now gave some thought to Roberts' caution of the night before. He could look back down the road to Foy, a couple of miles south, where he would have the advantage of the high ground. So he called Roberts, suggesting that he be permitted to back out of the exposed position in Noville. Roberts was sympathetic, but he knew that the 101st's paratroopers needed time to get into position before having to take on a major armored attack. Roberts told Desobry to hold on and went to confer with McAuliffe. Before he found McAuliffe he encountered Brigadier General Gerald J. Higgins, assistant commander of the 101st. While they were conferring, up came the leading elements of the First Battalion of the 506th Parachute Infantry. Higgins put them on the road to Noville, with the battalion commander, Lieutenant Colonel James LaPrade, going ahead to Noville to talk things over with Desobry. Roberts went back to the telephone and told Desobry to use his own judgment about giving up Noville but that he had a battalion of paratroopers on the way to help.

Desobry decided to stick it out. The First Battalion arrived at 1:30 P.M. December 19. They attacked shortly afterward but soon stalled. With thirteen medium tanks, six tank destroyers, and a thousand men the American force, now under LaPrade's command, was taking on Second Panzer's seven thousand men, who had eighty of their starting eighty-eight tanks left, along with a full array of eighty-eights and supplemental guns.

The Germans stopped the American attack shortly after it began. They tried an assault of their own an hour later, with two columns of sixteen tanks backed by a battalion of Panzer Grenadiers. American paratroopers took on the grenadiers. The German tanks held back, out of respect for American bazookas, as smoke from Noville's burning buildings thickened the fog that had come in once more. The Americans dropped back to Noville in twilight.

Higgins came up to Noville after dark to promise that assault guns and tank destroyers would be sent up next day, December 20. Robert Sink, commander of the 506th Parachute Regiment, also came up and worked out plans with LaPrade and Desobry for the night defense. The executive officer of the First Battalion, Major Robert F. Harwick, unexpectedly joined the battalion at Noville at dusk. Heavy furniture had been placed against the walls to give added protection, with a massive wardrobe screening a window giving on the street. A high explosive shell from a German eighty-eight burst at the window, shredding the wardrobe, killing LaPrade, and dealing an excruciatingly painful shrapnel wound to Desobry's head.

Within hours after his arrival from Paris, Harwick was in charge of the defense. Major Charles Hustead took over for Desobry. The Germans fired all night and lost two tanks on the edge of Noville. But the Americans held out. They couldn't realistically expect to hold out all day December 20, however. Sink, the regimental commander, and Higgins conveyed their concern to McAuliffe, who concurred in their recommendation for a withdrawal. McAuliffe called Middleton at Neufchateau to ask his approval. "You can't do it," Middleton replied. "We can't hold Bastogne if we keep falling back." The Noville party was ordered to stay.

Overnight, two other battalions of the 506th Parachute Regiment had dug into positions, the Third at Foy, two miles south of Noville. The Second was another two and a half miles south at Luzery, half a mile from McAuliffe's command post in Bastogne. McAuliffe had wanted to bring the First back to Foy.

Now the Germans were ready to resume their attack. At 5:30 A.M. shells began raining in on the town. At 7:30 A.M. two German tanks came racing down the highway from the north and into the edge of Noville. Unaccountably, they stopped beside a house within ten yards of an American bazooka team. The bazookamen got the first tank. An American Sherman took the other. German artillery kept up a drumfire. With the Sherman tanks running out of ammunition, six panzers shoved forward. Tank destroyers stopped them. A Tiger tank banged into the heart of Noville, halting outside the armored infantry command post. A Sherman tank fired three rounds from sixty feet. The Tiger's tough skin held but the crew piled out and fled.

Back at Foy, the Third Battalion was attacked by tank and armored infantry teams from the northeast and northwest. The Americans backed out of Foy to positions on a ridge. Noville was cut off. The Germans were in strength on three sides and had possession of Foy. No help could go out from Bastogne. The two aid stations in Noville were overtaxed and most of the medics were wounded. Harwick passed the word to Bastogne: "All reserves committed. Situation critical."

McAuliffe thought of sending the Third Battalion from the 502nd Parachute Regiment, not yet committed, on a roundabout route to relieve Noville. The Third went part of the way and halted. Then McAuliffe took note of the inevitability of Noville's fall. He ordered strong attacks from both sides of Foy, telling Harwick to bring his Noville defenders back to Foy.

The defenders destroyed their remaining high explosive and heavy mortar shells, which couldn't be brought out, setting a delayed-action charge to do the trick. More than fifty American wounded were placed in vehicles along with the armored infantrymen and most of the paratroopers. The column was ready to move in unfortunately good visibility when the fog obligingly came down, shutting off the German view. Most of the column got through to Luzery soon after nightfall.

The Second Panzer Division was now hopelessly behind schedule. Twenty of their tanks had been destroyed and twenty-five more damaged. A battalion of Panzer Grenadiers had been lost. The Americans had swept up 142 prisoners. Lauchert again asked Manteuffel for permission to turn on his tormentors. Manteuffel told him to forget Bastogne and to go on to his prime objective, the Meuse River crossing.

Colonel Horace Rickey of Lafayette, Louisiana, had organized his engineers to defend Dinant's bridges over the Meuse. He had talked earlier with Middleton, before Middleton had left Bastogne for Neufchateau, and had been told that the Germans were striking for Dinant and downriver crossings. "Get your men ready, Horace," Middleton had instructed, "but I don't think the Krauts will make it that far. Put up your shovels and get some guns, in case they do." Rickey had done so. A few of the German panzers did come within five miles of Dinant before they ran out of gas and were smashed.

The Second Panzer commander headed west, where his forces captured a bridge across the Ourthe River at Ortheuville at midnight. Just beyond Ortheuville the Second Panzer had to wait for its fuel supply to catch up, losing another twenty-four hours. While Second Panzer was finally getting past Noville the night of December 20, equally powerful Panzer Lehr was not doing as well. Bayerlein put tanks and self-propelled guns from his Mageret position into a wood near the American defenses in Bizory, throwing in a battalion from the Twenty-sixth Volksgrenadiers for an attack just before dawn December 20 against the 501st Parachute Regiment's left battalion. Small arms fire backed by artillery, shooting from positions all around the Bastogne defense, turned back the Germans. Bayerlein let the 501st Parachute Regiment alone the rest of that day.

With the coming of night, Bayerlein decided to knock on other doors. He teamed Panzer Lehr and the Twenty-sixth Volksgrenadiers, banging at the east gate of Bastogne with an artillery bombardment and a tank charge from Neffe. The tank noise put Ewell of the 501st Parachute Regiment on notice. He asked for artillery and got so resounding a response that the Germans lost a Tiger and two Panther tanks. The rest backed off. Luckless infantry protecting the armor were all killed by paratrooper machine gun fire.

In an attempt to crash the eastern entrance again, Panzer Grenadiers and three self-propelled guns headed down the railroad tracks toward Bastogne. Their timing was bad, for a platoon of the 705th Tank Destroyer Battalion had just moved into place. All three self-propelled guns were destroyed by the 705th. The Panzer Grenadiers paid for their lack of opportunity to reconnoiter. They kept coming for four hours. Daylight on December 21 showed German dead draped over barbed wire fences into which they had blundered during the night. Held up by wire which divided the area into cattle-feeding and cattle-holding pens, the Germans were slaughtered by American machine gun fire.

Later that night, the Germans sent a column of tanks and infantry down the railroad track again. During the afternoon this much larger force of Germans coming down the railroad tracks had been spotted by an American patrol, which sent word back to the regimental command post. By that time, however, the Germans had pushed between the two American regiments, well past the open flank of the 506th, more than half a mile up the railroad beyond the 501st. This wouldn't do at all.

To cope with this new threat, from his headquarters less than two miles away, McAuliffe reached for his only reserves, the remainder of the First Battalion of the 506th withdrawn from Noville and resting in Luzery. They were called out at 5 A.M. and pushed through the fog and woods to head off the Germans. After having dropped back during the night, two companies from the 501st moved back up the railroad. The Germans coming down the tracks found reception committees waiting on both sides of the tracks, losing a hundred dead and two hundred prisoners in the day-long fight.

On December 20, Panzer Lehr's left-hand regiment, which had had trouble with the churned-up narrow roads approaching through the Wiltz River valley, had its shot at the Bastogne defenses. The Panzer Lehr group leader chose to leave the highway at a roadblock and head cross country for Marvie, three quarters of a mile west, where he could get back on the pavement. Marvie was defended by Team O'Hara, with a platoon of light tanks and with two Shermans well placed on high ground northeast of the village. The combat engineers sent out three days earlier by Middleton were all but exhausted. Now they were joined by the Second Battalion of the 327th Glider Infantry Regiment, whose timing could not have been more perfect. When the Panzer Lehr force attacked at 11:25 A.M. after a short bombardment, it appeared to them that Marvie was wide open. A self-propelled gun led four medium tanks and six halftracks carrying infantry. They knocked out a light tank and disabled another. The rest of the light tanks moved out as soon as permission was granted. The Germans drove on fast. They passed broadside to the unnoticed two American Shermans seven hundred yards away. The Shermans destroyed two German tanks and a halftrack. The remaining tank entered Marvie, only to be destroyed by the airborne troops, as the fourth tank fled back to the woods. The self-propelled gun shot up three empty vehicles but then fell victim to the American Shermans.

Of the Panzer Grenadiers in halftracks, four loads made it into Marvie. They fought hard, but by 1 P.M. thirty grenadiers were dead and thirty had surrendered. The sixth halftrack stuck in soft ground and was abandoned. The two Shermans took care of it. Bayerlein's misfortune multiplied.

At nightfall of December 20, Luettwitz's corps remained frustrated. The Second Panzer had finally passed by to the north, but was at the point of running out of fuel at Ortheuville. Panzer Lehr was getting far more headaches than it was giving. The Twenty-sixth Volksgrenadiers had proved good in cross-country movement but not so adept in battle. Part of Panzer Lehr was ordered to swing well to the south of Bastogne and to head on west. The Volksgrenadiers were to have the honor of attempting to break into Bastogne with help from part of Panzer Lehr.

As the Volksgrenadiers began their bypass move, biting cold moved into the Ardennes. Snow overlaid unburied bodies. Muck on the unsurfaced roads and trails quickly hardened. Roadbound tanks and other tracked vehicles could quit the narrow arteries choking down the German movement. Maneuver would be much easier. But there would be a mighty price to pay. With good weather, Allied air superiority would be felt. A German tank, gun, halftrack, or troop concentration in the open would catch it from the fighter bombers. Even in woods, where their telltale imprints in the snow would point, they couldn't hide from the bombers.

The German attack on the VIII Corps front had demanded a break from the weather. For five days, no one saw the sun around Bastogne. Fog played a capricious part in the fighting, sometimes favoring the Germans

Middleton as Commander of the VIII Corps, Battle of the Bulge (U.S. Army Photo)

and sometimes the Americans. "Talk about the fog of war," Middleton recalled. "Why, you couldn't get even a Cub plane up. The fog sat right on
the ground. We had to use lights on vehicles during the day. Though we
asked, for those first agonizing days we couldn't get supplies flown in for
air drops. We were running dangerously low on armor-piercing shells. We
were also in poor shape medically because the Germans had captured intact the hospital of the 101st Airborne the night they were moving into
Bastogne. The wounded kept coming in. And the cold! It was wicked. It's
hard to appreciate the difficulty weather can bring. At 1 A.M. one night the
temperature descended to sixteen below zero. The metal of a rifle would
stick to exposed skin at that temperature. You can't call off a fight because
of the cold, but the human body can stand only so much of it. From Neufchateau, I went out every day to visit some unit. I'd damned near freeze.
Of course, at night I had a reasonably comfortable place in which to sleep.
Our poor devils out on the defenses of Bastogne didn't have. That they
stayed and took it is a tribute to their marvelous staying powers."

In Neufchateau, seventeen miles southwest, Middleton could see on
his situation map much more than was visible on the ground around Bastogne. Eisenhower, back at Supreme Headquarters Allied Expeditionary
Force (SHAEF), had indicated on December 18 that he was contemplating
transfer of the VIII Corps from Hodges' First Army to Patton's Third
Army. The decision was made on December 19. It took effect at noon on
December 20. Eisenhower gave over command of the American forces on
the north side of the bulge to General Montgomery, taking First Army
from Bradley's Twelfth Army Group. The move was necessary, but it
didn't sit well with Bradley. It was not a matter of great moment to Middleton since tactical considerations seemed to demand such a change, but
he could not help recalling his own experience in Sicily with Montgomery,
when Montgomery had demanded exclusive use of a highway that he never
put to use, forcing Middleton to pull his Forty-fifth Division out of combat
and to move it ninety miles through another American division to keep on
fighting.

From Neufchateau, on a clear day, Middleton could have looked
seven miles up the road toward Bastogne, into Vaux-les-Rosieres. Sibret
would have been just off to the left of his line of sight, another five and a
half miles toward Bastogne. Villeroux would have been a mile closer to
Bastogne. Senonchamps would have been visible about two miles directly

west of the south end of Bastogne—given good weather and a liaison plane up a thousand feet or so.

Villeroux, Sibret, and Senonchamps were on the maps of the Twenty-sixth Volksgrenadier Division as next objectives. That division, with help from fifteen Panther tanks from Panzer Lehr, was to run around Bastogne, then curl back on the west and punch its way in. In Bastogne, more stragglers continued to accumulate. There wasn't any other place for them to go as they moved west out of the path of the Germans. Colonel Roberts had been authorized to sweep up all stragglers and put them into the town's defense. This motley group took the name Team Snafu (for situation normal, all fouled up). It numbered six hundred by December 20. Fortified by their first hot food in days and by a chance to get warm in a building, members of Team Snafu were sent wherever Roberts heard a call. He had worked out with McAuliffe a smooth arrangement holding the armor together for bold strokes and leaving most of the perimeter defenses to foot soldiers. The artillery, with its variety of guns, could fire in any direction.

The expected arrival of the Fourth Armored Division brought some embarrassing confusion. It was unrealistic of the defenders in Bastogne to expect the Fourth Armored so early. When Brigadier General Holmes E. Dager brought the advance party of CCB of the Fourth Armored as far north as Arlon, he asked Middleton for orders, requesting that his force be kept intact as a fighting unit. Middleton agreed. But someone at the VIII Corps headquarters called for a team from Fourth Armored to lend a hand to Ninth Armored at Bastogne. To Dager's objections, it was explained that the situation was growing desperate and that anything he could contribute would be important, perhaps crucial. Dager agreed to put together under Captain Bert Ezell a team of tanks, infantry, and self-propelled guns.

Dager's CCB moved up from Arlon and into position about halfway between Middleton's headquarters in Neufchateau and Sibret by midnight December 19. At 10:30 A.M., Ezell took his task force toward Bastogne. In Bastogne nobody was sure who wanted him for what. Colonel Roberts told him to take Task Force Ezell back about three and a half miles to Villeroux. Ezell went there at noon December 20. He was then between Sibret, where Cota's headquarters force was trying to organize a defense perimeter, and Bastogne.

Fourth Armored had just acquired a new commander, Major General

Hugh Gaffey, Patton's former chief of staff. The Fourth was his first divi-
sional command in combat. He bridled when Dager told him that someone
at VIII Corps was already asking him to break off a part of his division—
Task Force Ezell. Gaffey overreacted. He instructed Dager to call Task
Force Ezell back to the fold and to move his CCB to an area southeast of
Neufchateau. When Ezell obeyed Dager's orders, he didn't tell anyone in
Bastogne he was going, apparently assuming that Dager or Gaffey would
get the word to whoever needed it. As he pulled out late that afternoon,
Ezell saw no Germans. McAuliffe came along the same road from Neuf-
chateau after a conference with Middleton and saw no Germans at dusk.

When Kokott brought his Volksgrenadiers around later on the night
of December 20–21, he cut the road to Neufchateau. Dager's CCB, of
which Task Force Ezell was a part, could have held the road against the
Volksgrenadiers and the fifteen Panzer Lehr tanks. When Fourth Armored
finally did come back to the scene, it was only after hard fighting. The confusion involving Task Force Ezell, Dager, and Gaffey was understandable
but its results were painful. Liaison this time was a little less than perfect,
to the benefit of the Germans, for once on the perimeter of Bastogne.

Roberts had found out earlier that McAuliffe was ready with an answer when Roberts asked what he knew about the employment of armor,
with the implication that only a man at home in tanks could decide on their
uses. McAuliffe had asked with some warmth if Roberts thought that the
101st Airborne should be attached to Roberts' combat command. On
December 20, Cota, wearing one star more than McAuliffe, had called
Bastogne to ask McAuliffe to drive down to Twenty-eighth Division headquarters in Sibret for a conference. McAuliffe replied, "I'm too damned
busy for that."

Cota drove to Bastogne instead. He took in all that he saw in Bastogne: too much traffic, artillery units arriving and being dispatched to
their firing positions, Team Snafu's growing numbers, the independent
command posts of the Tenth Armored's CCB, and the 101st Airborne.
Back at his command post in Sibret, he called Middleton in Neufchateau.
"Troy," he said, "the way things are going in Bastogne, only one man
should be in command there." Cota recommended that the Fourth Armored's CCB task force should stay out of Bastogne's traffic tangles and
asked that his men who had been lumped into Team Snafu be sent on to
his command. This was all fine with Middleton, who called McAuliffe in

Bastogne to let him know that it was fully his show now. Roberts moved over from his own command post and spent most of his time alongside Mc-Auliffe thereafter.

Kokott's Volksgrenadiers came around south of Bastogne on December 20 at dusk, heading for Senonchamps. Sibret and Villeroux were in the way. German Fifth Parachute Division troops coming up south of Sibret encountered a roadblock placed by the 630th Tank Destroyer Battalion. American riflemen made so much noise that the Germans waited two hours for mortars to be brought up, then pushed the roadblock defenders back on Sibret. At daylight December 21, the Fifth Parachute Division company was joined by Panzer Lehr and the Twenty-sixth Volksgrenadier's reconnaissance battalions with tanks and self-propelled guns. They took out three American howitzers defending Sibret, leaving the town open to the Germans. The Americans headed for the new headquarters of the Twenty-eighth in Vaux-les-Rosieres, seven miles from Middleton's headquarters in Neufchateau.

Sibret wasn't supposed to have taken all night—it fell at 9 A.M. December 21. What about Senonchamps? Kokott began inquiring. His troops left Sibret for Villeroux, a mile away, expecting to swing out on a lateral road to approach Senonchamps, another two miles distant. The Germans chanced up on the American 771st Artillery Battalion headed the Germans' way. Before the Americans could swing around into firing position their drivers dived for the roadside and left the Germans twenty 155-millimeter howitzers.

When word came that Sibret was lost, Lieutenant Colonel Barry D. Browne of the 420th Armored Field Artillery at Senonchamps asked for help from the infantry. Two hundred infantrymen and fourteen Sherman tanks were dispatched from Bastogne and sent toward Villeroux. They encountered the Germans just south of Senonchamps. The Germans pulled off the road and the American 755th and 969th Field Artillery Battalions got out of the pocket and safely back to Senonchamps, losing a single gun. On the western approaches to Bastogne as dusk fell December 21, three hundred infantrymen, twenty tanks, three battalions of artillery, and a battery of antiaircraft guns were strung over a defensive line two and a half miles long.

The German force which had left the road outside Senonchamps decided to test the American defenses. Quad-fifty antiaircraft machine guns quickly changed the Germans' minds. The attackers backed off. The Germans had finally surrounded Bastogne, cutting every road, in places as close as two miles to the center of town and as far as six miles to the west.

Off to the south of Bastogne, another German force spread all the way across from Germany to the Bastogne-Neufchateau highway to screen the force besieging Bastogne from attack by the American armored column known to be moving up from Third Army. The German screening force knew as much about the progress and the whereabouts of the Fourth Armored as did Bastogne's defenders, perhaps moreso. They might even have puzzled over the reasons for Task Force Ezell's recall to CCB between Arlon and Neufchateau, but they moved willingly into the vacated spot.

As the day's last light faded, the German corps commander assessed his strength for the task he was sure could be accomplished next day, Friday, December 22. He had the Twenty-sixth Volksgrenadier Division, fifteen Panther tanks from Panzer Lehr Division, and strong artillery support from the field guns being worked into position near Bastogne. If they couldn't break through on the east and north side of Bastogne, surely, the Germans reasoned, they could breach the much more lightly manned western side. What did the Americans have to defend with? About eighteen thousand men. They stood to eleven battalions of artillery, manned self-propelled guns, and kept forty tanks at the heart of Bastogne's defense area, ready to go to any threatened point.

Luettwitz, the corps commander, thought his troops could do the job. Manteuffel, the Fifth Panzer Army commander, asked for additional help. It was promised him from the highest command in western Germany. At dawn on December 22, a German armored battalion, reinforced with self-propelled guns, launched an attack from woods north of Villeroux straight at the 420th Armored Field Artillery Battalion, whose guns had severely punished other German attacks for days.

Around the 420th were Team Browne's three battalions of howitzers, an antiaircraft battalion, seven medium tanks, a few light tanks, and three hundred infantrymen. Team Browne met the attack with fierce fire, quickly convincing the German leader, Major Kunkel, that he'd never get into Bastogne through Senonchamps. He backed off to contemplate other possibilities.

19   Care to
Surrender?

NO ONE is known to have run up a box score of surrender offers made and surrender offers accepted in the course of twentieth-century warfare. Middleton had made such an offer, indicating his willingness to accept the surrender of Fortress Brest from Hermann Ramcke, back in September. Ramcke's reply had been terse enough. At Bastogne, the Germans had captured the 101st Division hospital and numerous medics before the 101st got itself well situated in Bastogne. It now occurred to General Luettwitz that his corps might do the sporting thing by offering to accept the surrender of the American forces in Bastogne. Generalleutnant Fritz Bayerlein wasn't so sure the idea was a good one, but he went along with his superior. Generalmajor Heinz Kokott, whose troops would have to make good on the threat of annihilation in case the Americans chose not to surrender, entertained the strongest doubts.

When Middleton left Bastogne to move back to Neufchateau on December 19, he had left one overriding instruction with McAuliffe: "Hold Bastogne." When McAuliffe drove down to Neufchateau to confer with Middleton two days later, their conversation had ended with Middleton saying, "Now, Tony, don't get yourself surrounded." He had not, of course, meant this. For only by getting himself surrounded would McAuliffe shrink his defenses to the irreducible minimum in which the Germans could find no breach.

Luettwitz's notion had been converted into a formal written message not long after Kunkel made his futile attack on Team Browne at Senon-

253

champs. Shortly after 11:30 A.M., an emergency radio message came to
Major Alvin Jones, operations officer of the 327th Glider Infantry, from
its Second Battalion at Marvie. "Four Krauts have just come up the Arlon
road under a white flag to our Company F and they're calling themselves
'parlementaires.' What do we do with them?"

When Major Jones couldn't find Colonel Joseph H. Harper, the regimental commander, he called division headquarters and asked what to do.
With division's O.K., he drove on to Company F's command post. A German major and a captain waited there. Two German enlisted men who
had been with the officers were being detained at the Company F outpost
where they had first turned up under a white flag. The two officers had been
brought in blindfolded. They had accepted this necessary indignity. Now
they turned over to Jones the note they had brought. Someone wryly suggested that the Germans had come in to negotiate terms for their own surrender to the Americans, but this twist got little currency. The German
note read:

To the U.S.A. Commander of the encircled town of Bastogne

The fortune of war is changing. This time the U.S.A. forces in and near
Bastogne have been encircled by strong German armored units. . . .

There is only one possibility to save the encircled U.S.A. troops from
total annihilation: that is the honorable surrender of the encircled town. . . .

If this proposal should be rejected, one German Artillery Corps and six
heavy A.A. Battalions are ready to annihilate the U.S.A. troops in and near
Bastogne. . . .

All the serious civilian losses caused by this artillery fire would not cor-
respond with the well-known American humanity.

The German Commander

Jones delivered the note to McAuliffe, interrupting McAuliffe's departure for a spot on the defense perimeter where he was going to deliver
personal thanks for the work a roadblock defense team had done in beating off a German attack. McAuliffe took in the German demand and
dropped the paper on the floor as he departed. "Nuts," was his only
comment.

After his return, someone asked about a reply to the German ultimatum. The Germans had stipulated that the Americans would have two
hours to decide on a reply; that the message-carriers would have to be
turned loose in two and a half hours; and that the Germans would renew

their attack at 3 P.M. if the Americans chose not to surrender. McAuliffe, normally taciturn, turned over a few brief phrases of refusal, rejecting them all. He pulled up a chair and continued thinking. Coming up with nothing, he asked, "What should I say?"

The division G-3, Lieutenant Colonel Harry W. O. Kinnard, responded: "That first remark of yours would be hard to beat."

"What did I say?"

Kinnard reminded him.

In the basement of the 101st command post, a sergeant had just finished typing McAuliffe's reply to the Germans. In the presence of McAuliffe and the assistant division commander, Higgins, the sergeant whipped the sheet from his typewriter. McAuliffe nodded approvingly over the reply, certainly a record for brevity. McAuliffe handed Harper, who had by now reported to division headquarters, not his reply, but the original message from the German commander. He asked Harper for a suggestion. None came to him immediately. Then McAuliffe handed over his reply:

> To the German Commander:
>   Nuts!
>   The American Commander

He asked Harper to see that the message was delivered.

"I'll do it myself, General," Harper said. "It will be a lot of fun." Back at the Company F command post, Harper found the German major and captain standing blindfolded, under guard. Harper told the captain, who understood English: "I have the American commander's reply." The interpreter asked whether it was written or oral.

"It's written," said Harper, turning to the German major. "I will stick it in your hand."

Lest the German emissaries fail to understand good American English, Harper told them: "The reply is decidedly not affirmative, and if you continue this foolish attack, your losses will be tremendous." Then Harper drove the Germans back out to the Arlon road and delivered them to the American outpost where the two enlisted men were waiting and talking casually with the Americans. Harper had caught a lot of German attacks in his sector of the Bastogne defense the past few days; he didn't want the German emissaries to get away thinking that they were in control of the situation. Taking off the blindfolds, he told the German major, "If you don't understand what 'Nuts' means, it is the same as 'Go to hell.' " Then Harper threw in his own postscript: "I will tell you something else—if you continue to attack, we will kill every goddamned German that tries to break into this city." Ever correct, the two Germans saluted. One said, "We will kill many Americans. This is war."

Word of McAuliffe's reply whipped quickly around Bastogne, taking some of the edge off two disappointments: the unfulfilled promise of an air drop of supplies early that night and renewed word that the Fourth Armored Division was on its way (it arrived four days later).

By 3 P.M. Luettwitz's surrender message team was back where it could feed a clear translation to all the German commands. The Americans weren't surrendering. Bayerlein, whose Panzer Lehr had taken more guff from the Americans than it had dished out, was glad enough to push on beyond Bastogne. Kokott, commanding the Twenty-sixth Volksgrenadiers, was reminded again that his would be the honor of breaching the Bastogne defenses and making the Americans eat their impertinent nonsurrender note.

Though Field Marshal Gerd von Rundstedt, in charge of the whole German battle force in the bulge, had himself directed that Bastogne must be taken on December 22, the German surrender demand itself had set back any attack plans by four hours. Light snow had begun powdering the area while the Germans were awaiting the American response to the surrender demand. When the cease-fire period ended, Kunkel renewed his armored attack on Team Browne's sector. Combined tanks and artillery stopped the Germans. The Germans tried once more, unsuccessfully, before dusk. Kunkel's armored battalion lost half its manpower and half the attached self-propelled guns.

It appeared now that the fighting would taper off with the increasing density of the snowfall. But Team Browne began catching it from an invisible enemy: the German corps artillery had finally moved into range. It laid heavy concentrations on the areas marked on its maps. Without room to move around, Browne's team had to take it. Browne was seriously wounded. He was killed later when a bomb struck a building being used as a hospital.

At 5:30 A.M. on December 23, the German attack was a week old. It had taken seven full days to cut off the defenders of Bastogne in an irregular circle which looked like an inflating balloon with its stem poking straight west. The Third Battalion of the 327th Glider Infantry held the stem area sticking out to Flamierge. The First Battalion was off at Marvie to the southeast of Bastogne. The First Battalion was holding alongside Team Browne and the highway to Neufchateau. These three battalions caught the heaviest German blows struck on December 23.

Better news came with the rising of the sun. For the first time since the battle had started the sun beamed on Bastogne. A high pressure area had shoved away the rain, mist, and snow. Allied airplanes could get off the ground. In much smaller numbers, German planes also left their bases. Their bombers dumped some bombs on Bastogne before daylight. But in the glorious daylight the promised relief from the air came streaming in. The Ninth Air Force sent 240 cargo planes over open areas within the Bastogne perimeter, each of which dropped 1,200 pounds of supplies. Badly needed artillery shells dropped by the first planes were being fired at German armor before the day's last flight cleared Bastogne.

While the transports were dropping ammunition, medical supplies, and food inside the perimeter, German antiaircraft guns were sending up tons of projectiles against the planes. They knocked some down. American fighter-bombers, especially the P-47 Thunderbolts, in turn worked over the antiaircraft batteries and went for German tanks, tank destroyers, artillery, and troop concentrations. German tank commanders began heading for concealment in wooded areas, for they stood out as targets like beetles on a sand table. Off on the far northeast corner of the bulge, the Americans who had hung on to St. Vith and its road complex pulled out of their pocket and became part of the solid north shoulder. As the eighth day of fighting moved toward a close, the German attack had finally gained St. Vith, their prime target in the north, a mere four miles inside the German-Belgian border. They were badly snagged on Bastogne, although Second Panzer and most of Panzer Lehr Division had pushed on to the west.

On Christmas Eve, the 101st was reminding Middleton that Fourth Armored surely could bring in a welcome pre-Christmas present, and it got word that the rescue force was hoping to bring off a break-in later that day. The Germans took most of the day to shuffle their troops and to look for American weaknesses in preparation for a predawn attack on Christmas. Luettwitz was informed that he would be given the Fifteenth Panzer

Grenadier Division to help smash American defenses on the west side. Hitler himself had given the word to turn loose the Fifteenth and the Ninth Panzer Divisions, from reserve back in Germany. He had also demanded that Bastogne be taken to clear the way for a sweep to the Meuse.

Luettwitz was disappointed with the Fifteenth Panzer Grenadiers when they finally arrived. Instead of a division, he received an understrength combat team with one and a half rifle battalions, a reconnaissance battalion of about thirty armored personnel carriers, a mixture of twenty tanks and assault guns, an engineer company, and two artillery battalions. Not nearly what Luettwitz had hoped for. But he took it, assigning it a mission on the northwest, instructing the team commander to be ready to move long before daylight.

While the Germans were setting up for their attack next day, Colonel Kinnard of the 101st drew up a tighter defense plan which called for pulling in the neck of the balloon projecting to Flamierge. The Third Battalion of the 327th Glider Regiment would drop back nearly two miles. Flamierge, Flamizoulle, Mande-St. Etienne, and Senonchamps all would be left outside the perimeter, which would draw down tight on Champs and tiny Isle-la-Hesse. Each of the four regiments of the 101st covered its sector of the defense with added help from tanks, tank destroyers, and artillery. Roberts' CCB and what remained of Team Snafu stood by in reserve. Ground action remained light through Christmas Eve.

American planes came over in the clear, cold air, with C-47s dropping more bundles of supplies and P-47s flying cover for the slow transports. After the supply drop was complete, the P-47s went after German ground targets. They supplemented fragmentation bombs and machine gun fire with napalm, jellied gasoline which clung and burned fiercely on German armor and in troop areas.

While they did not venture out during the day, German planes came over Bastogne after dark, bombing indiscriminately. They smashed a building the Americans had converted into a hospital and burned numerous buildings in Bastogne. Team Cherry's command post went up in one explosion. Lieutenant Hyduke, who had held off the Germans five days earlier at Longvilly, was killed with three other officers in the night bombing.

McAuliffe took note of the nearness of Christmas with a message to all the Americans in Bastogne:

Merry Christmas!

What's merry about all this, you ask? We're fighting—it's cold—we aren't home. All true, but what has the proud Eagle Division accomplished with its worthy comrades of the Tenth Armored Division, the 705th Tank Destroyer Battalion and all the rest? Just this: We have stopped cold everything that has been thrown at us from the north, east, south, and west. . . .

Allied troops are counterattacking in force. We continue to hold Bastogne. By holding Bastogne we assure the success of the Allied Armies. We know that our Division Commander, General Taylor, will say: "Well done!"

We are giving our country and our loved ones at home a worthy Christmas present and being privileged to take part in the gallant feat of arms and are truly making for ourselves a merry Christmas.

McAuliffe, talking with Middleton that day, told him that the finest present the 101st could wish for would be a relief on Christmas Day. Middleton agreed: "I know, boy. I know."

Soon after midnight, Kokott nudged his Volksgrenadiers and their supplemental Fifteenth Panzer Grenadiers up to their line of departure. They were off and rolling before 3 A.M., with bombing support from German planes. Kokott applied a nutcracker squeeze to the American defenders of Champs, out on the northwest perimeter, and of Hemroulle, halfway between Champs and Bastogne. Kokott's upper jaw bit into the First Battalion area of the 502nd Parachute Infantry positions, with a Volksgrenadier regiment. Kokott's lower jaw was to snap hard at the First Battalion of the 327th Glider Regiment positions. The German upper jaw cut deep into Champs by 3 A.M., causing the American company commander there to ask for help from Colonel Steve Chappuis, the 502nd regimental commander. Chappuis sent Companies B and C hurrying out to Champs. Delaying movement of the lower jaw, Kokott sent his panzer regiment against the First Battalion of the 327th Glider Regiment at 5:30 A.M. The tanks overran battalion headquarters and swept on through the positions occupied by two companies. The Americans stayed in their foxholes until the tanks had moved on. Then they popped out and captured many Germans afoot behind the tanks. Kokott heard one jubilant tank commander radio that he was approaching the outskirts of Bastogne. Great! But the message wasn't followed up.

In the predawn darkness the Germans were swallowed up. The German upper jaw chomped down hard at Champs after the first penetrations. Tanks and infantrymen swung behind the American company in Champs to cut them off. As they reached the Champs-Bastogne road they bumped into Companies B and C of the 502nd, moving up. The two American companies swung off into the woods and with small arms fire stripped the seven tanks naked, killing, wounding, or capturing 110 German infantry. The tanks rumbled toward Champs, rolling into range of the 705th Tank Destroyer Battalion's Company C, which caught them from the side, smashing all the German tanks. With no upper jaw to chew against, the lower German mandible bit against Hemroulle. American tanks, tank destroyers, 57-millimeter antitank guns, and bazookas put away all ten of the German vehicles. Not a piece of German armor, not an infantryman escaped.

Two American battalions with their attached weapons smashed the Germans' last serious chance of getting into Bastogne. It was close, but as the maneuvers unfolded all the advantages came to the Americans. Having shaken two sizable German armored forces out of the foot of their Christmas stocking, the Americans on the west side of Bastogne had finished their job by 9 A.M.

Down at Florenville, behind the Senois River, another twelve miles south of Neufchateau, VIII Corps headquarters had been forced to drop back to avoid the risk of capture by the Germans. With a handful of troops to protect corps headquarters, Mack Hornbeak had a halftrack with one tread, a 37-millimeter antitank gun which couldn't have dented a German Mark IV tank, and a few machine guns. Corps headquarters was set up on the ground floor of a school for young girls. Middleton began his Christmas with a quick check on the situation at Bastogne, talking to McAuliffe by radio. Then he got a report on the dismayingly slow progress of the Fourth Armored.

Corps staff members off in the corner of the room huddled and came to a quick decision. "We'll do it," someone said. "We've been planning this for months now. No Germans are going to keep us from giving General Middleton his special Christmas present." What Christmas present was worth being presented in this tense atmosphere? The gift was brought out. It was an over-and-under 12-gauge shotgun with walnut stock, made by Browning of Belgium, beautifully inscribed "To Generalmajor Troy H. Middleton." There was some good-natured joshing. Somebody said it was an appropriate kind of gift under the circumstances. Middleton agreed.

To Middleton, the gift meant more than it said. And for his corps staff, it conveyed but little of the great esteem in which they held their corps commander. As Middleton's aide, John Cribbet, said: "Above all he understood the nature of war and the nature of men. His ability to work with people of diverse talents, to proceed without the necessity of raising his voice—or even issuing orders—to me was always a complete mystery. It seemed that he was able by quiet persuasion, by pointing out what needed to be done, to get people to carry out his exact orders."

Later on Christmas Day, "Nuns who ran the girls' school brought me Christmas dinner on a tray," Middleton recalled. "We were occupying quarters downstairs while the girls were going to school upstairs." Looking over the finely crafted shotgun after lunch, Middleton recalled peacetime hunts on which he'd gone with friends.

Help from Fourth Armored, having been promised almost daily for a week, did not materialize on Christmas Day. The Germans who were in the way fought stubbornly at every control point along the highways approaching Bastogne from the south. The sun went down on disheartened Germans all around the Bastogne perimeter. They tried one more time next day, when Kokott's Twenty-sixth Volksgrenadiers sent ten self-propelled guns and grenadiers in halftracks around from the west to north of Bastogne. As they bore down on the American line, American artillery and antitank guns destroyed the entire force. At Assenois, two and a half miles south of Bastogne on one of the roads leading toward Neufchateau, a dozen American tanks returned the Volksgrenadiers' visit by smashing the command post of one of Kokott's regiments.

What in the world had been holding up the Fourth Armored Division all this time? First, recall that the division had a new commander in Hugh Gaffey. Recall too that Gaffey had taken sharp exception to what he thought was a misuse of his armor when "someone"—unidentified—at VIII Corps headquarters was said to have requested that the division assistant commander, Dager, put together a combat team to go at once to Bastogne, back on December 20. Recall, finally, that Gaffey, former chief of staff in Patton's Third Army, probably overreacted as his former army commander had been known to do, in pulling back Task Force Ezell from a strong position on the Neufchateau road that day.

Patton was on his way to Arlon on December 20, while Gaffey was reacting to what might have been interpreted as a slight to Ezell. Patton had arrived in Luxembourg City that morning and had been told there that

Dager's CCB had been attached to VIII Corps and might be sent on alone to Bastogne. The road from Neufchateau to Bastogne was open, though the Germans were closing in on it. The Fourth Armored had long been one of Patton's favorite outfits; it had done well in Normandy and in the run across France in Patton's Third Army. Patton now checked with Bradley, in overall command of American forces south of the bulge, and proceeded to rescind Middleton's order concerning CCB. It was after this that Ezell pulled his force out of a good position and went back to CCB, without letting anyone know he was leaving.

From Luxembourg City, Patton had called VIII Corps to have Middleton drive over from Neufchateau for a meeting at Arlon. When Middleton arrived at Patton's headquarters in Arlon, he was received with what an outsider would almost certainly have interpreted as an outrageous outburst. "Troy," said Patton, "of all the goddamn crazy things I ever heard of, leaving the 101st Airborne to be surrounded in Bastogne is the worst!"

Middleton discounted Patton's flamboyance. Patton had given Middleton in Brittany what Middleton candidly recalled as "damnfool orders" concerning the bypassing of St. Malo and the quite impossible business of a hurried run out and a surprise attack on Brest. In brief, Middleton paid no attention to Patton's expostulations. He respected Patton as an extremely capable, highly inspirational armored commander. He was under no illusions about Patton's shortcomings. Middleton's soft answer turned away Patton's feigned wrath. He told Patton that anyone would have to agree on the importance of holding Bastogne, sitting as it did astride all the important highways in that part of Belgium. Patton said no more. (Later, he formally commended Middleton for the "stroke of genius" which led him to put the 101st in Bastogne to be surrounded—and to thwart every German effort to dislodge it.)

As quickly as he had snapped at his old friend, Patton now sought his counsel. "All right, Troy, if you were in my position, where would you launch the attack? From Arlon, where we are, or from where you are in Neufchateau?" Take the shortest way, Middleton said. Put the main effort of Fourth Armored on the Neufchateau road, on the far left. With the rest of III Corps, including the Twenty-sixth and the Eightieth Infantry Divisions, hit far to the right to cut off the Krauts instead of pushing straight against them.

But Patton, wearing three stars, assigned the main weight to the Arlon road. That's the way it went.

It took six days of hard fighting for the Fourth Armored to cover less than thirty miles. On iced highways, tanks and other vehicles kept sliding into the ditches. The Germans fought hard and smart.

So it was that the Fourth Armored's lead tanks reached within six miles of Bastogne on Christmas Day, after a hard-won gain of only two miles on Christmas Eve. As late as 4 P.M. December 26, it looked as if Bastogne was still a day away. At 3:30 P.M., Lieutenant Colonel Creighton W. Abrams, commanding the Thirty-seventh Tank Battalion, and Lieutenant Colonel George Jaques, commanding the Fifty-third Armored Infantry Battalion, stood on the high ground at Clochimont, more than three miles south of Bastogne, assessing their chances of making it all the way in. After a Christmas thaw, returning cold had hardened the ground again. P-47s, unasked for but welcome, had turned up in the morning and bombed German armor up the road. The P-47s, in fact, had given the Germans so much trouble that Clochimont was open and waiting. Abrams had twenty Sherman tanks left. Jaques' battalion was at three-quarters strength.

Earlier in the day, it had been decided by a higher command that CCR, of which Abrams and Jaques were a part, would take Sibret (full of Germans) and go into town on the Neufchateau road, the path Middleton had originally recommended. Looking three miles toward Bastogne, where slow C-47s were dropping more supplies to the defenders and catching hell from German antiaircraft, Abrams decided to make a straight run for Bastogne. The followup force could take care of Sibret.

Captain William Dwight, operations officer of Abrams' battalion, was given the assignment of leading Task Force C to Bastogne. It comprised a tank company and an armored infantry company, each chosen because it had the largest machine gun ammunition supply. From Clochimont to Assenois was a little more than a mile. As they neared Assenois, Dwight called for artillery fire on the town and the woods to its north. The artillery was delivered on call and 155-millimeter shells were still dropping when the force arrived. Two halftracks were disabled by this friendly artillery, so close was the timing. Five tanks and a halftrack continued toward Bastogne. Jaques' men dropped off in Assenois to deal with the German infantry. The Americans took 500 prisoners in the Assenois fighting deep into the night. Three American tanks pulled well ahead of the other three vehicles. So wide was the gap that Germans came out of the woods and hastily placed Teller mines on the road. A mine stopped the halftrack. Dwight left his tank and with the help of his men cleared away the mines. The three lead tanks hurried on.

Tony McAuliffe of the 101st had got word that Fourth Armored elements could be seen approaching Bastogne. He went out to watch from high ground on the south perimeter.

First Lieutenant Charles P. Boggess, commander of Company C, Thirty-seventh Tank Battalion, rolled inside the American line south of Bastogne at 4:50 P.M. December 26. Dwight's tank came up next. Clean-shaven paratroopers waved a greeting to the grimy tankers. Dwight climbed the hill to McAuliffe's observation point. He saluted and inquired, "How are you, General?"

McAuliffe responded, "Gee, I am mighty glad to see you."

The siege was broken. The battle was not over but it was won.

20 Shrinking the Bulge

THE BATTLE of the Bulge did not end with the relief of Bastogne. It took another week to peel the Germans back from the southern and western approaches to the half-destroyed town. Adolf Hitler screamed that Bastogne must be taken. It was, he said, a bone in his throat. Nine German divisions were brought to the fight, with two corps headquarters. They couldn't break in. Larger forces from the Fourth Armored came into Bastogne about 1 A.M. December 27, after the German defenders of Assenois had been killed or captured.

Middleton had stipulated that the first men to be taken care of after the relief of Bastogne would be the wounded. Seventy ambulances followed the forces of Fourth Armored's CCR. For a day and a half, ambulances streamed back out of Bastogne taking 964 wounded to hospitals. Men too seriously wounded to be transported were tended by surgeons who came in December 27 in a flight of gliders that escaped an antiaircraft curtain thrown up by the Germans west of Bastogne. German antiaircraft took down nine of thirteen C-47s that flew in the last cargoes of supplies required.

But now Manteuffel, in command of the full army which had moved against the southern sector of the bulge, had to think of defense while he was trying to carry out Hitler's renewed demands for the capture of Bastogne. He tugged at the coattails of his Second Panzer and Panzer Lehr Divisions, both well west of Bastogne, pulling them back to screen a new set of German attackers. The two armored divisions had been roughly

265

treated; they lost 2,500 killed, more than 1,000 prisoners, 81 tanks, 81 guns, and 674 vehicles.

Early in January Middleton moved back to Bastogne. His VIII Corps acquired new divisions after the relief of Bastogne. The Eighty-seventh Infantry, under Brigadier General Frank L. Culin, Jr., came in December 29. It had arrived on the Continent early in December and had been down in the Saar with Third Army. It was sent to SHAEF reserve at Reims the day before Christmas and was at full strength when its troops climbed onto trucks for the 100-mile ride to VIII Corps. The Eighty-seventh was assembled north of Neufchateau for an attack on the German flank to the north.

On the Eighty-seventh's right was the Eleventh Armored, under Brigadier General Charles S. Kilburn, a green division just brought over from England to help defend the Meuse River line if the German attack carried that far. The division was turned over to VIII Corps on December 28. Middleton told Kilburn to bring his armored force to Neufchateau, eighty-five miles. Heavy snow and ice slowed the move through the night of December 28–29, but the leading elements arrived about 4 P.M., two hours before Middleton issued the corps attack order. Combat Command A was first to arrive. CCB and the rest of the division came on into the night. With the attack set for 7:30 A.M. December 30, there was no time for reconnaissance; Kilburn's assault plan was worked out on the map.

From the west, the lineup was Eighty-seventh, Eleventh Armored, the remainder of CCA of the Ninth Armored, and the 101st Airborne. The 101st was to hold its position at Bastogne, and the other three were to swing north with the Eighty-seventh and the Eleventh carrying the main load. Ten battalions of corps artillery were backing up the attack.

While Middleton was preparing for the 7:30 A.M. attack, his opposite number, Manteuffel, had set precisely the same hour for his corps' stroke against the reconstituted VIII Corps line. Manteuffel told his division commanders that the original aims of their Ardennes offensive had been scrapped. Now they were to concentrate on Bastogne. They were first to throw a collar around it, then to shove the Americans back toward Neufchateau and Arlon, and finally to overrun Bastogne. The Third Panzer Grenadier Division's commander, Generalmajor Walter Denkert, had noted that the Americans usually did not move earlier than 8 A.M. and sometimes started at late as 9 A.M. He figured to be on the way first. Starting from a position four miles from Bastogne, on the western doorstep of the town, the Germans tried to slam straight south to Sibret. They didn't get far against the Eleventh Armored Division.

On the VIII Corps' far left, CCA of the Eleventh Armored moved ahead without substantial opposition for several hours. Then, as CCA's Sixty-third Armored Infantry Battalion worked to the top of a ridge, it was hit hard by German heavy guns. Two American tanks were lost and a hundred infantrymen became casualties as they tried to force their entrenching tools into the frozen earth. At midafternoon the Germans had stopped Eleventh Armored's CCA.

Kilburn asked Middleton for permission to drop his CCA back and swing it to the right, around a wooded area, to line up beside his CCB. This would leave CCA's vacated area to the infantrymen of the Eighty-seventh. Middleton agreed, and CCA began pulling away at 11 P.M. December 30. All three combat commands of the Eleventh were directed to push straight north on December 31.

While the Eleventh's armor had stalled, the infantrymen of the Eighty-seventh were more successful on the corps' left. They, too, covered their first five miles without bumping into the Germans. Then they took heavy losses in pushing attacks on Moircy and Jenneville, but the Eighty-seventh carried its objectives.

Southeast of Bastogne, strong armored attacks were broken up by the Fourth Armored and the Thirty-fifth Infantry Division. American artillery used the new proximity fuse (each shell carried a little radar set in its nose, setting off its explosion at a predetermined distance from the ground or any obstacle). Many Germans were killed or wounded by these shells. Captured German officers marveled at the killing efficiency of what they took to be fuse settings perfectly calculated by American gunners. Fourth Armored was supposed to move left to join Middleton's corps, but a decision on December 30 left it with the Thirty-fifth Infantry. On December 31, January 1, and January 2, the Eighty-seventh's infantrymen fought well in snow, sleet, and deepening cold. They accomplished their mission of cutting the highway linking the Germans at St. Hubert with supply sources back in Germany.

The Eleventh Armored, on the other hand, continued to have more difficulties than the strength of the enemy explained. The Eleventh did not work its way up on line with the Eighty-seventh, but achieved some limited success. The night of January 1, Middleton visited Kilburn at his command post at Morhet. Earlier, he had found the division commander directing traffic at a crossroads. "I told him a PFC could do that," Middleton recalled. "I told him to move on. He was very nervous and kept most of those around him nervous. He wanted to do too much himself."

Middleton instructed Kilburn to have his troops consolidate their positions on January 2 and to turn over the job to the Seventeenth Airborne Division on January 3. In four days, the Eleventh Armored gained six miles against strong opposition, losing 220 dead and missing and 441 wounded, plus 42 medium and 12 light tanks. Middleton found the division seriously lacking aggressiveness in its leadership.

The VIII Corps stood on an irregular line stretching fifteen miles directly west from its anchor force in Bastogne, the 101st Airborne, at the close of day on January 2. On January 3, the corps was to join in a smashing blow against the Germans all along the northern and southern lines of the bulge. For eighteen days the momentum had rested with the Germans. Now it was to go over to the Americans and their British allies.

Looking back at the fighting which had swirled around Bastogne, numerous authors interviewed Middleton, beginning in 1945 and continuing for more than twenty years. For his admirable book, *The Bitter Woods*, John S. D. Eisenhower spent some time in Baton Rouge talking with Middleton about the Battle of the Bulge, command decisions, and troop performances. John Eisenhower made an effort to see every major commander who had figured in the battle, coming to Baton Rouge in 1967. Middleton told him then, "At this late date, I'd say that you'll get more misinformation than correct information. Those fellows have had plenty of time to justify their actions or inactions."

Later, Middleton said, "It sometimes gives me the creeps when some of our latter-day tacticians ask why Middleton didn't hold the Germans at the Our River. If the Germans had launched their attack against the divisions originally on that line, they'd never have broken through.

"The Second Division was fit, but it had gone back to the Roer River line when the Germans made their move. Fate played into the German hands at first. Some say the Germans knew of the deficiencies of the American forces opposite them. They did know who was in the line against them. But they were committed by plans. In November I had the Eighty-third, the Eighth, and the Second Divisions. All three had been with me out at Brest. All were well led. Then all three were moved out. The Second put some steel in the northern shoulder after the Germans broke through December 16. The Germans never did make any headway against the northern shoulder. It held tight and cramped their style badly; the Germans had hoped to widen a much bigger base for their attack than they got—forty-seven miles instead of sixty or so.

"We expected something in the way of an attack from the Germans before December 16. Our patrols were sent across the Our River every night. Some stayed out as long as five days. I had a standing order that we were to take one or more prisoners each night. Only once did we fail to bag a prisoner. Though we usually got little information from prisoners, on the night of December 14–15, we captured two Germans in front of the cavalry group north of our 106th Division. The prisoners, from a Volksgrenadier division, said an attack was coming in that area. On the afternoon of December 14, a German woman came across the Our and reported that a great deal of bridging material was being moved in at night near her home. She also told us that other residents talked of seeing troop concentrations coming into the area every night.

"I sent this information out immediately to Bradley's Twelfth Army Group down at Luxembourg City. But it was not taken seriously. All I could do was to alert all my troops. I had no reserves. The Germans regularly used smoke, even at night, to try to confuse us. They put artillery fire on crossing points on the Our. But we weren't sitting on our hands. Hurley Fuller's 110th Infantry Regiment in the middle of the Twenty-eighth Division sector had a good plan for dealing with the Germans. He couldn't begin to cover his sector in a linear defense, but his islands of defense made the Germans pay a disproportionate price for their moves against Skyline Drive, which Hurley's troops defended the first two days.

"The Battle of the Bulge was the Battle of Small Units. People from different units pulled together and fought. Stragglers joined them. Roadblocks were held by small units. People like Steve Chappuis, who won the Distinguished Service Cross for holding the Bastogne perimeter and knocking out the last serious German threat against Bastogne after two armored forces had cracked into the 502nd's territory, knew how to rally men to fight against any odds. William Desobry, with a relatively small armored force at Noville, blocked the whole Second Panzer Division for two days. The Germans eventually got around Noville, but they lost valuable time deploying to attack and treating the defenders as the major part of a division rather than a small team. Some commanders might have left in the face of so overwhelming a German force, but Desobry didn't," Middleton said.

"I went against the book and broke up our armor into task forces. When Bill Roberts came up to Bastogne on December 18 with his combat command, I asked him how much strength he had. Then I told him to break up his fine outfit into three task forces. Bill didn't like it at all. He told me, 'Troy, that's no way to use armor.' And I told him that I knew it as well as he did. But we weren't fighting any textbook war there. Without some armor to back up our roadblocks, we couldn't have stopped anything. As it was, our task forces, sometimes fleshed out with clerks, cooks, and mechanics, greatly puzzled the Germans. They figured us to have far stronger forces at these points than we were able to put out there.

"I noted again in this battle what I had known right along: the average man is an imitator. Put someone like Steve Chappuis, Earl Rudder, or Bill Desobry in the lead, and others will do as their leaders do. We didn't have a great many leaders, but we did have lots of good followers. They hung in there and stopped the Germans.

"Concerning those efforts at deception we tried against the Germans in October, November, and December, I'm glad I held out on the elaborate scheme in December, using special troops to try to con the Germans into thinking the Seventy-fifth Division was going into position with VIII Corps. Bradley asked me to move sizable contingents of corps artillery down that way from the positions I'd assigned them on the far north end of the corps line. I told Brad I couldn't afford to move so many of my big guns for this purpose. It was a good thing I didn't. Those 155-millimeter guns helped hold the Germans off Elsenborn Ridge and really cramped their style on the northern shoulder of their attack.

"I simply didn't believe the Germans could run the 101st out of Bastogne. I'd had those fellows with me on the Cotentin Peninsula. I knew they wouldn't run away. Besides, I had Roberts' combat command with tanks and guns, plus two corps artillery battalions, each with thirty-six 155-millimeter guns that would reach anywhere around the defense perimeter. I also had one and a half battalions of tank destroyers. We had a lot of power and it was used well, as the Germans kept finding out, no matter where they hit us. I'm not saying all these things with the aid of hindsight. I say them for the same reason I told Georgie Patton, down at Arlon, that we weren't running any risks when I left the 101st in Bastogne. We made the Germans take the risks. They had to have all the roads that ran through Bastogne. They had to try to take them away from us. That 'stroke of genius' George later attributed to me for deciding to hold Bastogne was just common-sense soldiering," Middleton said.

"My Jeep driver crossed words with George the night of December 30 while I was up at the Eleventh Armored command post and George came up for a conference. My driver was outside under a little lean-to with his back drawn up against the side of the structure and with his feet sticking out. George came tramping up in the snow in the dark and stumbled over my driver's feet. My driver snarled, 'You son of a bitch, why don't you look where you're going? Can't you see I'm trying to sleep?' He'd chosen George's favorite salutation. Maybe that's what threw George off guard, for he replied somewhat lamely, 'You're the first son of a bitch around here who knows what he's trying to do.'

"When the American command was split and my corps passed from Hodges' First to Patton's Third Army, with Montgomery taking command on the north side, St. Vith was no longer in my command area. I never would have withdrawn our troops from St. Vith (as was done on December 23). That was a key point. Its being surrounded by the Germans didn't mean all that much. It wasn't long before we had to fight our way back to retake St. Vith (the Seventh Armored, which had held out against the Germans, retook the town the afternoon of January 23, a month after leaving it through a corridor to the west) when we went over to the attack. When you hold onto key points, you deny the enemy freedom of movement. They have to eat and be supplied. We held out at St. Vith for a week, denying the Germans the roads.

"After Montgomery took command on the north shoulder, I kept waiting for more positive action against the Germans there. Lightning Joe (J. Lawton) Collins was ready to go with a counterattack days before Montgomery turned him loose. Collins could have dug deep into the German flank. We heard that Montgomery was straightening up his lines and tidying up the front before taking offensive action. With an attack from the north, the Allies could have caught a great many Germans who eventually succeeded in getting back all the way to Germany.

"On the Fourth Armored Division's approach to Bastogne from Arlon, I recommended, when George asked my advice, that he tell Gaffey to take the road from Neufchateau in. The Arlon road bridges had been blown to keep the Germans from going south. The Germans were in that area in some strength. They held up the Fourth Armored far beyond the time they said they could have relieved Bastogne. As Fourth Armored moved north it gradually moved to the west as I'd originally suggested.

"When Patton gave me his first reserves after the relief of Bastogne, I put the Eighty-Seventh Infantry, the Eleventh Armored, and the Seventeenth Airborne into action before there was ever a hint of action from the north side where Montgomery was in command. My men here ran into the Germans coming back from the west to join in the last effort to break into Bastogne. If I'd sat back and waited at the end of the year, instead of attacking on December 30, the Germans most likely would have got into Bastogne. Patton called me up and said my men must be tired since they weren't making much progress. We didn't know it at the time but my new divisions in the VIII Corps were running into the Germans on their way back. I talked to William M. Miley, who commanded the Seventeenth Airborne, new to action. Miley said, 'I don't know what's the matter with my men. We're just not getting anywhere.' Of course, the deep snow made travel hard. But we didn't find out until later how many Germans were coming back from the west and punching at us from the north," Middleton said.

How did Middleton assess the Battle of the Bulge, years after the many, many actions which determined the outcome of the fight? "Eventually," he said, "it will go down in history as one of the great battles of all time. To my way of thinking, two major mistakes were made in the battle. The first was made by the German army in launching the attack. They didn't have sufficient resources to pursue the operation to completion. With what they had, they couldn't possibly have advanced to Antwerp. Merely to take more ground in that barren area of hilly country could not help the overall cause of the German army. It could not even build their morale. If the German high command had not wasted so much in the battle, they could have given a better account of themselves later. If they had not committed strategic and tactical suicide and had used the Rhine River as a defensive line, they would have made it very difficult for the American army. If they had not made the mistake, they could have prolonged the war—probably through 1945.

"The other mistake, as I saw it, was the failure of some American and British troops north of the bulge to attack as soon as preparations could be made. If some of those troops had attacked in the direction of St. Vith, they would have cut off and destroyed a lot of German troops that escaped. I don't think there would have been any risk involved. Some may say that such a statement is hindsight, but I said the same thing on several occasions while we were involved in the battle. As you will recall, the VIII Corps, with what it had, never stopped attacking. Patton came in shortly with Third Army troops and went right into the line fighting. We fought on the south side all the time. I doubt that the Germans would have gotten many men out of the salient if that attack had been launched from the north along with the one that came from the south.

"What if the VIII Corps had been sitting around, tidying up, instead of attacking toward Houffalize on December 30? The Germans might have run right across our front and broken into Bastogne after all. You could call the coincidental launching of attacks by both armies just west of Bastogne, one of the fortunes of war. After the Germans saw they simply could not take Bastogne, they executed a general withdrawal. The American forces, including VIII Corps, continued the advance past the Siegfried Line this time and on toward the Rhine," Middleton recalled.

What was the matchup of attacking Germans and defending Americans as the battle began on December 16? It pitted 200,000 Germans against 68,822 Americans. The attacking infantry outnumbered the defenders three to one along the front and six to one where the heaviest concentrations were gathered. The Germans advantage in medium tanks was about two to one. Counting self-propelled guns used as tanks, the German advantage was four to one. The American proximity fuse, kept secret until this battle, proved exceedingly effective but was in limited use. In the air the American advantage cost the Germans dearly. Though the Germans were able to carry out night bombings, their planes were never able to venture forth in substantial numbers during daylight. When the skies over the Ardennes finally cleared on December 23, American transports were able to resupply the Bastogne forces, and American fighter bombers were able to deal great misery to German armor and troop concentrations.

When the battle was over, the German gamble looked like a bad one. Middleton thought the Germans would have lost the fight even if their main effort had carried well beyond the Meuse River. "There was much more back there than they could possibly have coped with," he said.

Just about the last mail going out of APO 308, the VIII Corps postal designation, before the Germans attacked on December 16, was a letter from Middleton to James E. Smitherman, a member of the LSU Board of Supervisors in Baton Rouge. Dated December 15, it read in part:

> Colonel E. Monnot Lanier came to my headquarters today and left me a file of correspondence and his reply regarding the Louisiana State University-William Helis oil lease. Colonel Lanier has requested me to express my views.
>
> Not having the lease before me, I cannot recall its exact provisions. I can state, however, that at no time did the Finance Committee of the Board of Supervisors signify a willingness to alter the terms of the lease. The committee took the stand that, without further ado, the contracting parties abide by the terms of the lease. It appears to me, therefore, that the lease should speak for itself. It was my understanding that if Helis did not continue development of the property, he should (on or about August, 1941) declare the productive area of the lease and release the balance of the property to the University. When the dry hole was drilled in 1941, I am of the opinion that Helis had no further intention of continuing development. I do not believe that the then producing wells constituted continued development under the provisions of the lease. Only the continuation of a drilling program would constitute continued development according to my understanding.
>
> The passing of General Hodges is a shock to all his good friends in the service. I shall miss his splendid fellowship when I return to Louisiana.

Having taken care of that piece of university business brought his way by Lanier, Middleton was busy with other matters for the next few weeks. Campbell Hodges, retired from the army for ill health in the summer of 1941, had lasted a little longer than three years in the exacting presidency of LSU. Though Middleton did not get the word for awhile, Hodges was succeeded by William B. Hatcher, a former parish superintendent of education, professor of history, and dean of the LSU Junior Division.

So highly did the Board of Supervisors regard Middleton's opinion, they had forwarded to Europe a file dealing with the university's oil lease agreement with the principal operator in the university field. Middleton had developed considerable knowledge of the oil picture on university property, and adjacent to it, since the day in 1938 when he asked Henry Howe whether the Middletons' proposed new home site on Highland Road might be surrounded by oil wells some day. Howe had told him he could count on it.

21 The Rhineland Revisited, Then Victory

AFTER relieving the Eleventh Armored, the Seventeenth Airborne had to fight desperately to avoid being overrun by the Germans. At Flamierge, west of Bastogne, the 513th Parachute Infantry had to fight around the clock to take and hold the town against German counterattacks. Middleton sent his congratulations when Flamierge was finally secure. Germans in American uniforms took part in this fight, with some being captured.

In six days of steady fighting, the VIII Corps line moved slowly northward against the German flank. On January 9, Middleton had four divisions: the Fourth Armored, the Eighty-seventh Infantry, the Seventeenth and the 101st Airborne. On his right the III Corps had three infantry and one armored division. The eight divisions attacked January 9. The Fourth Armored and the 101st Airborne led off against Noville, where Desobry's force had held up a German armored division earlier. The Noville position was no pushover this time, either. It took the 101st Airborne until January 15 to reclaim Noville.

Not until the morning of January 16 did American forces closing from south and north come together at Houffalize. With this meeting, the Americans swung east and pushed the Germans steadily back to where they had started from on December 16. It took twelve more days to shove the Germans back across the Our River into Germany.

Commanding an army corps involves more than coordinating the fighting of its divisions. On January 3, after sending his corps off in the

275

attack, Middleton turned to his official mail. It included a letter from Colonel Carlton D. Goodiel, commander of the 102nd Evacuation Hospital. The hospital had been criticized, and Goodiel needed a response from Middleton immediately. Middleton had visited the hospital several times, and Goodiel wanted his appraisal of it. Middleton's reply to Goodiel read:

> The 102nd Evacuation Hospital has served the VIII Corps on the Cherbourg Peninsula, at Brest, and in Luxembourg. I had occasion to visit the hospital while located at Ettelbruck, Luxembourg. My opinion is as follows:
>   a. Appearance of the hospital—Excellent.
>   b. Military courtesy displayed—Excellent.
>   c. Professional attention given patients—Appeared to be excellent.
>   d. I saw no evidence of confusion in the hospital.
>   e. The limited personnel I observed appeared to be cooperative.
>   f. I have heard no unfavorable comments concerning the unit, nor its commanding officer. Insofar as I was able to observe, the unit performed its function in a satisfactory manner.

Another noncombat chore for Middleton involved the Eleventh Armored Division which had come back into the VIII Corps by January 10. Kilburn, the division commander, had evidently been having some difficulties with subordinate commanders. He asked Middleton's advice and assistance. Middleton answered Kilburn in writing, telling him that the responsibility for action on charges against two officers under his command rested with Kilburn. Middleton also stated that the "charges referred to are, in my opinion, quite serious, and merit a thorough investigation and proper trial by courts martial. I further feel that any attempt to cover up, or any tendency to view the matter other than as a serious one, would fail to take proper cognizance of the violation of the conventions to which we subscribe and of which we are a part. From the information you gave me concerning the subject, it seems to me that the matter is a proper charge under AW 92 or AW 96." (Article of War 92 deals with failure to obey a lawful general order. Article of War 96 deals with the release of a prisoner without authority.)

As divisions in the VIII Corps continued their offensive against the slowly withdrawing Germans, Middleton began hearing officially that his decision to hold Bastogne had been a good one, after all. Patton wrote him January 20:

> 1. The magnificent tactical skill and hardihood which you and your com-

mand displayed in slowing up the German offensive, and the determined valor and tactical prescience which caused you to retain possession of Bastogne, together with your subsequent resumption of a victorious offensive, constitute a truly superb feat of arms.

2. You and the officers and men of your command are hereby highly commended for a superior performance.

3. You will apprise all units concerned of the contents of this letter.

Middleton saw to it that every soldier under his command shared in Patton's praise.

With the restoration of the front as it had stood on December 16, the American advance halted temporarily. The VIII Corps continued with the Eighty-seventh Infantry and the Eleventh Armored, and acquired the Ninetieth Division from the III Corps, which had fought alongside the VIII all the way from Bastogne. Bradley summoned corps and army commanders to Twelfth Army Group headquarters. First Army had come back into the fold from its temporary position under Montgomery. Bradley told his commanders that Hodges' First Army would advance to the Rhine and that all supplies and reinforcements would be furnished to First Army. Third Army, under Patton, would remain in position until the First Army reached the Rhine. The Rhine was more than a hop and a skip distant, up to fifty miles from First Army positions and seventy-five miles from Third Army.

While the VIII Corps was fighting its way back across Belgium late in January and early in February, Middleton acquired another aide. His G-1 came in, grinning, at the corps command post near Trois Vierges. The corps personnel officer had driven back to the rear area replacement depot to pick up the corps' share of replacements. "He told me he was looking over the list of officers and came across the name of a second lieutenant freshly arrived from the States, Troy H. Middleton, Jr. He went to the officer in charge and told him, 'I want that boy. His old man will probably give me hell for this, but I want him just the same.' He brought Troy back with him. Thus I acquired a junior aide. He stayed with me through the rest of the war," Middleton recalled. Troy, Jr., was billeted in a Trois Vierges schoolhouse along with John Cribbet, Middleton's senior aide, and Gillis Long, commander of the headquarters company which guarded corps headquarters.

Patton had orders to hold his Third Army in place while Hodges'

First Army shoved to the Rhine. Bradley's words had been plain enough. Nevertheless, Patton questioned the advisability of keeping his command in place. In addition to the VIII Corps, he had the XII and the XX Corps under Major Generals Manton Eddy and Walton H. Walker. The VIII Corps stood on the left as Third Army faced toward the Rhine. When Patton renewed his request to go on the offensive, Bradley again reminded him that he would not be able to get replacements needed in an attack and that no extra ammunition or supplies would be forthcoming while First Army was on the move. Two armies could not, in the circumstances, be supplied properly. "George very reluctantly accepted Bradley's explanation," Middleton recalled.

Then Patton was seized by inspiration. He called Eddy, Middleton, and Walker together and asked the three corps commanders for their concurrence in a bit of semantic maneuvering. "Can't you, Walton, with all the strength you have, sort of sidle ahead about ten kilometers and capture Trier? And, Manton, what's to keep you from edging forward and capturing Bitburg?" Then he turned to Middleton. "Troy, don't you think you could maneuver about eight kilometers and take Gerolstein?"

The three corps commanders agreed to sidle, edge, and maneuver— straight ahead. "I told George that, with what I had, I thought I could take Gerolstein, but that when I did so, I would have no artillery ammunition left. And, knowing George as I did, I reminded him how emphatic Bradley was when he told Patton to remain in place. "If you should fail in this endeavor, there might be serious consequences as far as you're concerned." Patton replied, "I'll take that risk."

"We sidled, edged, and maneuvered—as George called it—and in a couple of days were on our objectives. I don't know what George told Walker and Eddy thereafter but he told me, 'I would appreciate it if you would continue to advance toward Koblenz.' I did, and the VIII Corps was on the Rhine when First Army reached it. I never learned what Bradley's attitude was when he discovered what George had done, nor did I ever know at what point he made the discovery.

"When the VIII Corps reached the Rhine, George came to me and told me he would have to take all of my divisions but one. He said he was starting an operation up the Rhine with the XII Corps, that it would require more troops, and that the ultimate objective would be crossing the river near Mainz. I don't recall what mission he gave the XX Corps, but

I'm inclined to believe it was rather inactive. George left me with only my corps troops, consisting of considerable artillery, and the Eighty-seventh Division. Taking a leaf from George's book, I asked him to let me capture Koblenz with the Eighty-seventh," Middleton recalled. "George laughed and said, 'Only a fool would attempt such an operation with so few troops.' I said, 'Let me try; if I find it too well organized I can suspend the operation.' We captured Koblenz with the Eighty-seventh, finding only about five hundred German troops in the city. The remainder had crossed the Rhine rather than be penned up in Koblenz, between the Moselle River and the Rhine.

"After we took Koblenz, the XII Corps came up to the river near Mainz and some of its troops crossed. Then Patton gave the VIII Corps a front of about twenty-five miles which included Koblenz on the left and extended on up the river beyond Boppard and the famous rock, the Lorelei. George then sent me the Eighty-ninth and the Seventy-sixth Divisions, giving me a total of three for the Rhine crossing. George designated the day for the crossing, several days after he issued the order."

Reconnoitering the west bank of the Rhine and checking for exits from the east bank, Middleton found that Ehrenbreitstein, on high ground across from Koblenz, was well organized and quite strongly held. He elected to look farther upriver, near the storied Lorelei rock, where the Rhine passed through a gorge. Heavy vineyards folded down on either side, and narrow, winding roads led to the river's edge on both sides. There were no bridges on this front. As a matter of fact, all bridges on the Rhine had been destroyed, after, through a marvelous stroke of luck, the Americans had captured the old Ludendorff railroad bridge at Remagen and held it long enough to put five divisions across. German demolition charges placed on the bridge failed to go up when the Germans tried to set them off on March 7. For ten days the Germans, well back from the Rhine, frantically fired artillery at the Ludendorff bridge. It finally collapsed into the Rhine on March 17.

"Two days after Patton told me to get ready to cross the Rhine, he came to my headquarters and asked, 'Where are you going to cross?' Between Boppard and the Lorelei, I replied. Patton looked surprised. 'Why, man, haven't you read your history?' he asked. Yes, I have, I answered. 'Then, you must know that no one has ever crossed the Rhine in that area,' Patton persisted."

Middleton's answer disposed of Patton's doubts. "George," he said, "I know the Germans have read their history also. They know nobody has ever crossed there. Therefore, they don't expect me to try to cross there. Besides, I don't believe they're holding the river in any strength along there." Patton said no more. Middleton proceeded to issue orders for a crossing at that point.

Shortly after dark on the night the crossing was to be made, troops of the Eighty-ninth Division began inflating their big assault boats. Because the hairpin turns in the road down to the river bank were so tight, the boats had to be muscled down the slope half-inflated and the job finished at water's edge. The Eighty-ninth put all its infantry across the Rhine before daylight, against practically no resistance.

The Germans had, indeed, read their history. They knew nobody could cross the Rhine in such obviously difficult terrain. "They didn't expect us and therefore had very few troops watching the crossing," Middleton recalled. "We started crossing on both sides of the Lorelei rock about 1 A.M. By daylight we were putting heavy stuff across. Our artillery remained on the west side to give supporting fire in case the Germans tried to interfere. We had a pontoon bridge strung by 6 A.M., and tanks immediately began rolling across it. Snipers harassed us a bit that night, firing from the Lorelei, but they pulled out before dawn.

"Colonel Montgomery, the VIII Corps chemical warfare officer who was in the G-3 section and kept the corps situation map, was killed before we got our pontoon bridge in that night. A shell fragment hit him. I went down to the bridge shortly after daylight while the Germans were harassing us with their 20-millimeter guns. I saw Troy, Jr., there and said, 'Why don't you get in that ditch over there. One of those bullets may have your number on it.' He said, 'None of them has hit me yet.' He went on to his Jeep.

"We poured enough stuff over the river through the first afternoon so that we could deal with any German threat. While we were crossing that day and using our pontoon bridge on succeeding days, the Germans tried to float mines down to blow up our bridge. We took care of that by stringing chicken wire nets across the river above the bridge and posting riflemen on the bridge with instructions to shoot at any floating object. The net result was that we caught a lot of fish with our chicken wire. My headquarters remained on the west bank. As I crossed back over the Rhine one afternoon a soldier held up a four-foot string of fish and said, 'Look what I got, General.' "

If the Germans weren't ready for the VIII Corps and the Eighty-ninth Division crossing at Boppard, they were waiting for the Eighty-seventh at Koblenz. Although the terrain was favorable for a crossing there, the Germans put up so much resistance that it was decided that the Eighty-seventh should move another ten miles up to Boppard for its crossing, which went smoothly. Within two days, the three divisions in the VIII Corps were across the Rhine ready to advance east.

On the way up to the Rhine earlier, the VIII Corps headquarters had approached within a few miles of Adenau, Germany. Noting his calendar showing the date as March 9, Troy Middleton turned to Mack Hornbeak and told him to prepare to set up headquarters in Adenau.

"Mack asked me if the war was getting to me. I told him it wasn't but that I had departed Adenau just twenty-six years earlier, March 9, 1919. That wasn't enough for Mack. He said, 'The Germans are still in there.' And I told him we would run them out. We did. I found Adenau unchanged except that they had added a third story to the little hotel (with thirty to forty accommodations). I stayed there only one night. The action was fast. The Germans were heading across the Rhine and we had to get along after them. When I got up to Remagen the familiar old Ludendorff bridge had already fallen in. I reminded Mack that my old regiment had guarded that bridge in 1919 and that the same Forty-seventh Infantry Regiment, in the Ninth Division now instead of the Fourth, had secured the bridge. What I saw of the little towns around Remagen where I'd been on occupation duty a war earlier, indicated that they had changed but little in a quarter-century. Some joker started a yarn to the effect that there was a noncommissioned officer in the Forty-seventh Infantry Regiment, March 7, 1945, who had been with the Forty-seventh back in 1919 at the same Remagen bridge, but he never stepped forward," Middleton recalled.

Official mail kept coming in. General Charles de Gaulle sent word up to notify the VIII Corps headquarters staff that it was to receive the French Legion of Honor award. Middleton was to pick up the officer degree, his second earned in helping France throw off the German yoke. The chevalier degree was prescribed for Brigadier General John E. McMahon, Jr., of VIII Corps Artillery and ten colonels.

The recurring difficulties of the Eleventh Armored Division came up

once more on March 8. Middleton wrote, but let sit overnight, a letter to
Patton saying that he was relieving Kilburn as commander of the Eleventh
Armored and sending him to Third Army headquarters with the recommendation that he be reassigned as a combat commander of another armored division. Next day, having given the matter further thought, Middleton wrote a two-page, instead of a one-page, letter recommending the
relief of the Eleventh Armored's commander:

1. At the present time, the Eleventh Armored Division is commanded by
Brigadier General Charles S. Kilburn. This situation has existed prior to the
assignment of the division to the VIII Corps in December, 1944.

2. During this period I have made almost daily visits to the division and
have observed it in action at Bastogne, Belgium; in the breach of the Siegfried
Line near Lutzkampen, Germany; and in recent operations of the division
from Prum, Germany, to the Rhine River. Based upon my observation, I have
reached the following conclusions:

a. The division is timid and over-cautious.

b. The division is not a well coordinated unit.

c. The division does not employ all means of reconnaissance to best
advantage.

d. The commanding officer of the division engineers does not appreciate
his proper function, as exemplified by his acting as a traffic control man when
there was vital engineering work to be done.

e. The division lacks confidence in its own ability to do a job, there being
a tendency to call for help when in fact help is not required.

f. There is an attitude in the division that when fired upon by the enemy,
the unit is stopped. Specific cases were in the division's first operation at Bastogne, Belgium, and more recently in the crossing of the Kyll River in
Germany.

g. Proper reconnaissance by unit commanders is not made. A specific
case was the crossing of two medium tank companies and some light tanks over
the Kyll River and into a pocket from which it was reported that the tanks
could not advance due to nearby physical features. It was necessary to recross
the tanks.

h. Some of the planning in the division is not good and is done without an
appreciation of what is necessary in the larger picture. A specific case was the
movement of non-essential elements of the division on March 8, 1945, on critical roads when such elements could have been parked for several days without
jeopardizing the operations. Another case was placing too much traffic on a
single road during a given period, which resulted in a column approximately
twelve kilometers in length with many vehicles bumper to bumper. Due to the
congestion, the column spent much of the time standing on the road and thereby blocking other traffic.

i. I believe the infantry in the division is not aggressive and it is my opinion that the tanks and infantry do not work as a team.

j. I feel that the division has had sufficient combat experience to enable it to be an aggressive and bold organization and thoroughly capable of using its tremendous fire power and ability to maneuver.

3. Based upon my reaction to the division, I recommend as follows:

a. That Brigadier General Charles S. Kilburn be given a combat command in another armored division appropriate to his grade.

b. That an experienced General Officer, who has proved himself in this war, be assigned to command the Eleventh Armored Division. In the selection of the officer, if he be a Brigadier General, he should be one whose early promotion is contemplated.

A week later, March 16, Middleton sent the Adjutant General in Washington the required periodic efficiency report on general officers under his command. The summary paragraph rounded up his impressions of Kilburn's work. And finally, on March 18, Middleton wrote a comprehensive memorandum to Patton wrapping up the case of the Eleventh Armored Division and its change of command. Middleton, as in every case involving the relief of a commander, leaned strongly backward to avoid any unfairness, in one passage noting that he had perhaps leaned too far backwards at the outset. Thus Middleton closed his file on the command structure of the Eleventh Armored.

On a far more pleasant note, next day, March 19, he addressed a commendation to Frank L. Culin, Jr., commander of the Eighty-seventh Infantry Division, whose outfit had joined the VIII Corps the same day the Eleventh Armored came to it on the outskirts of Bastogne.

1. On the completion of the advance of the Eighty-seventh Infantry Division from the vicinity of St. Vith, Belgium, through the Siegfried Line defenses and on to the Rhine River, which culminated in the capture of the historic city of Koblenz, I desire to take this means of expressing my appreciation for the excellent performance of the officers and men of your command during the advance in question.

2. It has been my duty to assign the Eighty-seventh Division difficult tasks while it has been in the VIII Corps. I am pleased to say that the division has always accepted its assignments with the spirit of "Can Do." Furthermore, the division has accomplished all missions given it in a most satisfactory manner. The most recent mission of forcing a crossing of the Moselle River, capturing Koblenz, and clearing the enemy from the area from Koblenz to Boppard was a difficult one made easy by the hard work and superior cooperation by all members of the division and attached units.

At the Rhine, while waiting to take the VIII Corps across, Middleton forwarded to General Patton an accounting of what the Germans had lost in the VIII Corps area between Bastogne and the Prum River. "In view of the difficulty in searching an area thoroughly, I doubt that all destroyed equipment was reported. Furthermore, in view of the fact that divisions reported nothing outside of their own zone of action, I doubt that duplicate counts have been made. As for American equipment, there was very little lost, except in the immediate vicinity of Bastogne. These figures are of interest in the light of press reports that the United States Army lost much equipment in the Bulge. The press has said nothing about what the Krauts lost—we are a modest people," Middleton wrote. The total German loss was impressive: 2,422 vehicles, weapons, and major pieces of equipment. In addition, the VIII Corps count on captured German ammunition ran to 123 tons, plus major and minor ammunition dumps not inventoried because they were mined and booby-trapped by the departing Germans, as well as twenty tons of assorted ammunition not identified sufficiently to be broken down into classifications.

The VIII Corps counted, between Bastogne and the Prum River: 20 ambulances; 42 armored cars; 210 passenger cars; 35 Volkswagens; 16 passenger buses; 19 staff cars; 274 halftracks; 6 halftracks, with 20-millimeter antiaircraft guns; 96 halftrack and fulltrack prime movers; 250 tanks; 768 trucks; 148 motorcycles, tractors, and specialized trailers; 89 self-propelled 76, 88, 105, and 155-millimeter guns; 169 towed 37, 57, 75, 76, 88, 105, and 155-millimeter guns; 77 horse-drawn wagons; and a wealth of individual weapons.

Manton Eddy, commanding the XII Corps, after the Rhine crossing was on Middleton's right. The two were old friends. "Manton called me up and asked excitedly, 'Do you have a battalion not engaged?' I told him yes, and asked what was the matter. Eddy said, 'I've got a German outfit behind me.' And so he had. It was a reinforced infantry battalion of about eight hundred Germans with mortars, machine guns, lots of automatic weapons—but no artillery and, even more important, no transportation. Eddy didn't know this."

Middleton told him that he was sending the requested assistance, a battalion, and that it would be along as soon as the ammunition and rations aboard the trucks needed could be unloaded. "Manton's headquarters was about five miles beyond the Rhine then. The Germans turned up about halfway between the Rhine and XII Corps headquarters. That was the only time I ever knew Manton to get excited—and we had been in both world wars together. I thought I'd kid him a little, after I assured him help was on the way. I told him. 'The Krauts won't get much if they do capture your headquarters.' He responded, 'It isn't funny; they're after us.'

"If the Germans had intended to, they could have taken the XII Corps headquarters. But they weren't looking for a fight; they were just looking for some outfit to surrender to after they'd gone without food a couple of days. They kept looking and found an obliging outfit in Eddy's corps, which accepted their surrender."

Not long after this, Eddy suffered a heart attack and was sent back to the States to recover. Major General LeRoy (Red) Irwin took over XII Corps. "I thought I'd do the neighborly thing and go over to say hello," Middleton recalled. He asked his sergeant pilot, who flew an L-5 light plane provided to corps headquarters, if the pilot could find Irwin's headquarters. The sergeant assured Middleton they'd have no problem. They took off and went skimming down the valley. The pilot set the plane down in what looked to Middleton like a mighty tight piece of terrain. "The pilot wiped his brow after the plane stopped rolling and told me we were going to have a hell of a time getting out of the place. We went down to headquarters and I found Red. We had a pleasant visit. As the sun sank lower, the pilot got fidgety. He asked if we shouldn't be leaving. I told Red we'd have to be pushing on. As we lifted off after a mighty short run, I could feel the pilot pulling hard to clear the chimney pots of houses in the German town. We made it back all right, but that may have been my tightest squeeze in all the time I was on the Continent."

As the VIII Corps headquarters moved up to the Main River late in March, not far from Aschaffenburg, George Patton came to Middleton's headquarters, greatly agitated.

"Troy," he burst out, "I'm in trouble again. This time I've really done it; I've sent Alex Stiller off to his death. He kept nagging me until I told him to go ahead on a special mission to this prisoner of war camp at Hammelburg with this outfit I was sending."

"Wait a minute, George. Let's have that again," said Middleton.

Patton told him he had heard that a German prisoner of war camp was not too far away at Hammelburg and that he had sent an outfit through the American lines to hasten the release of the Americans the Germans were holding there. Then he had heard that the special outfit had run into a sizable party of Germans on the way and had been badly shot up.

"I loved that boy (his aide, Major Alex Stiller) like a son. Why did I let him talk me into letting him go along?" Patton said.

Middleton was sympathetic. He asked Patton, "What sort of outfit did you send?"

Patton replied, "Oh, something like a reinforced company."

"A reinforced company!" Middleton exclaimed. "You surely have played it. You needed at least a combat command for a mission like that."

Patton continued his lamentation, saying Stiller "had looked so sick" when he was told he couldn't go along with the rescue outfit, that he—Patton—had relented and told him to go ahead.

The undersized American task force encountered trouble, all right. A number of Americans were killed. The rest dispersed and most of them made their way back to friendly forces, who were continuing their eastward move. Stiller was taken prisoner. He was released in mid-April when Third Army troops reached the prison camp which held more than twelve hundred Americans among some thirty thousand Allied captives.

Patton's son-in-law, Colonel John K. Waters, who had been captured by the Germans in North Africa and was painfully wounded during the Hammelburg raid, was also released from the camp with the others.

"Some people said later that the raid on the prison camp had been made to free Colonel Waters, but I don't believe that this was so," Middleton recalled. "But it did reflect bad judgment on George's part to have tried to bring off the rescue with so small a task force. That was his impetuous nature at work. I doubt that he knew his son-in-law was in that camp."

Patton may have been dissimulating when he blurted his story to Middleton. John Toland, in his 1966 book, *The Last Hundred Days*, wrote a different version. Toland said that Patton had sent a 307-man force, led by Captain Abe Baum of the Fourth Armored Division, to fight its way from near Aschaffenburg sixty miles to the prison camp outside Hammelburg, starting March 26. The force got there and opened the camp gates, but did not have enough vehicles to transport the freed prisoners back to the American lines. The Germans closed in and smashed the small task force, taking Baum prisoner, as well as Stiller.

News reporters persisted in inquiring about the raid until Patton called a press conference at which he said he had ordered the raid to mislead the Germans as to his military intentions after he crossed the Main River. A reporter asked if it was only a coincidence that Patton's son-in-law was a prisoner in the camp. Patton replied that he did not know of Waters' presence there until nine days after the raid.

Toland wrote that Patton, seeking to prove his disavowal, showed his official and private diaries and said, "We attempted to liberate the prison camp because we were afraid that the American prisoners might be murdered by the retreating Germans." But, Toland wrote, Brigadier General William Hoge, Colonel (later General) Creighton Abrams, and Major Alex Stiller knew otherwise, yet "as good soldiers kept silent. Stiller died without revealing the truth and the other two waited for almost twenty years."

Contemplating Toland's account of the motivation behind the Hammelburg raid and recalling his own conversation with Patton at the time of the raid, Middleton said again, "I don't really think George knew his son-in-law was in the prison camp. My opinion then and now (in 1973) is that the raid was a damn fool stunt attempted with a pitifully under-strength force."

As the VIII Corps advanced eastward, its route led the headquarters through Eisenach, sixty miles north of the Hammelburg prison camp. In Eisenach, "I was met by the mayor, who spoke English," Middleton recalled. "He asked that I set up my headquarters in a hotel he owned. This was the town in which Martin Luther had been imprisoned. The mayor took me to the building where Luther was supposed to have thrown an inkwell at the devil. The ink spot was right there on the wall, and the room had been preserved for the edification of tourists. I've often wondered how many quarts of ink have been used in renewing that ink spot."

From Eisenach corps headquarters moved eastward. "Some of my infantrymen made a horrifying discovery after we had moved across the Fulda River. The infantrymen were mopping up behind the armor, cleaning out Krauts in one of the villages, when they came up on a concentration camp at Ohrdruf, near Erfurt. The sights there were enough to sicken anyone.

"I called Patton and told him to come up. I had something he would have to see to show the nature of some of the Nazis. He got Bradley and

Eisenhower and brought them up for a look. Later, I had leaders in that German town brought in for a look at the bodies of those who had been tortured and had died in the concentration camp. Almost to a man, they maintained that they had had no idea of what was going on there. The mayor stoutly insisted that he knew nothing of all that. But that night he and his wife chose to commit suicide, so they must have figured that they would be called to an accounting.

"At the concentration camp they had dug a wide, deep trench several hundred yards long, into which they threw the bodies of the dead. Most of the living we rescued were nothing more than bones and skin."

On April 19, Middleton sat down to write a letter of condolence to the wife of John McKee, assistant commander of the Eighty-seventh Division, after the death of their son. Captain McKee had served a tour of duty with the ROTC staff at LSU under Middleton, in 1932–1934. Commandant and Mrs. Middleton had known Captain and Mrs. McKee and their

Generals Patton, Bradley, and Middleton Inspect a Nazi Concentration Camp, 1945 (U.S. Army Photo)

young son John in Baton Rouge. Now Middleton wrote to Mrs. McKee back in Arlington, Virginia:

My dear Grace:

It is difficult to write one who has experienced the tragic loss of a son. I do, however, wish to convey to you my sincere sympathy on the loss of John, Jr. You and John have lost a splendid boy and soldier, and John, Jr.'s young wife has lost a devoted husband.

I have spent some time with John, and am happy to say that he is taking the loss of his boy in a manner befitting the fine man and officer he is. He feels the passing of John, Jr., deeply and keenly; yet, he apparently realizes that war is full of tragedies, and one must be prepared to meet them. John, of course, is much concerned about the shock you have received. I have, however, tried to impress upon John that, even though it is your greatest loss, you will accept your loss in the spirit of a true soldier and in a manner which we know that John, Jr., would have you accept it.

May I again express my deepest sympathy, in which Jerusha would join me if she were here.

Not long after the VIII Corps crossed the Rhine, the Fourth Armored Division was assigned to it. "With the Fourth Armored leading the way, it was an easy matter to move on down the road," Middleton recalled. "The infantry divisions would pick up what hostile force the armor had by-passed. The corps continued east until its leading elements came to Chemnitz, population 345,000. We got orders to stop here and to hold the terrain we were occupying. I had the Fourth Armored as the leading element in Chemnitz, the Eighty-seventh between Chemnitz and the Czechoslovakian border, and the Eighty-ninth in the general area. Since our advance had not met much resistance, officers and men could not understand why we were halted.

"I was informed that it was the desire of the High Command that the Russians meet us at that point, which they did, shortly after hostilities ceased. About a week before the German surrender, I received an order that the corps would discontinue taking prisoners. We were getting so many that it was a supply problem in the rear area. We finally worked out an arrangement for handling the Germans who wanted to surrender: when they appeared in front of our outpost line, we would have them form into organizations, placed under command of a German officer if one was available, and we would give him instructions to march the prisoners to the rear, pointing out the roads he would follow. After we received the order not to accept any more surrendering Germans, thousands of them found their way through the VIII Corps front during the night. We had to collect them after daylight and send them on their way. The Germans did not want to surrender to the Russians."

At this juncture it was apparent that the war in Europe was almost over. General Eisenhower distributed to higher commanders a letter dealing with redeployment of American soldiers with long combat service. "Failure to return all those eligible for discharge to the United States at the earliest possible date," he wrote, "will not only result in a loss of confidence by the soldier in the army, but will also develop an unfavorable public opinion which could well result in a loss of good will built up by the army in its successful campaigns. You will have no more difficult command task than you will face in the redeployment of your command. I expect you to give it the same zealous personal attention which you have given to your combat assignments."

Since Middleton's corps troops represented a relatively small number, there were no complications here. He reminded his division commanders of the necessity for rigorous fairness in their decisions about who would go back to the States, who would stay on in Europe, and who might be ticketed for the Pacific, since it appeared on April 19, the date of Eisenhower's secret memorandum, that the war might go on indefinitely as American forces moved closer to Japan.

On April 21, Middleton sent a memorandum to commanders within his corps, preparing them for the eventual meeting with the Russians. The message went to the Seventy-sixth Infantry, the Eighty-seventh Infantry, the Eighty-ninth Infantry, the Fourth Armored, and the Sixth Cavalry Group:

1. To avoid confusion and prevent expansion to areas to be occupied by Soviet forces, troops of the VIII Corps will not advance beyond the present limiting line nor patrol beyond the present patrol line.

2. It is to be expected that Soviet forces will contact elements of the corps at an early date. When such contact is made, our troops will remain in present positions, except that patrols will not operate beyond the present limiting line.

3. It is assumed that Soviet forces, other than liaison parties, will not enter the area occupied by our troops. If, however, these forces desire to enter the area in large numbers, the commander of our troops will request that such not be done until after a conference with the Commanding General, VIII Corps.

4. When contact is made with Soviet forces, the senior American officer

on the spot will contact the appropriate Soviet commander, offer cordial greetings, explain our situation on the immediate front, and obtain the situation and plans of the Soviet commander. The result of such conference will be reported so as to reach division commanders without delay. Division commanders will, in turn, notify this headquarters of the situation.

5. In all cases, report of first contact of Soviet forces will be reported to corps headquarters.

6. When contact on a division front is made, division commanders should arrange for a meeting with an appropriate senior officer of the Soviet forces and arrange for positions and mutual conduct of troops on the front. There is no objection to local adjustment of troops in order to simplify a situation. Requests for major adjustments will be submitted to corps headquarters.

7. Every effort will be made to avoid any accidental clashes with Soviet forces.

8. Dissemination of reports of incidents, or of rumors which may lead to unfortunate incidents, is prohibited.

9. Troops will be impressed with the necessity for caution in order that Soviet troops are not fired upon when contact is made. After contact is made, the disposition of forces should be known to both sides, in order that proper contact and proper relations may be observed.

10. Recognition signal to be used by Soviet forces and American forces is being furnished all concerned under separate cover.

A Russian cavalry corps came up the last week in April and made contact. From South Russia, the cavalrymen stood in sharp contrast to the Americans. Much of their transport was animal-drawn. Many of their trucks carried familiar American manufacturers' emblems. The Russians were not as well armed or as well clothed as the Americans. The Russians did not encourage movement of Americans through and into their area, held to await their arrival under the agreement laid down by higher command.

"Soon after the Russians came, my corps headquarters invited the commanding general of the Russian corps and his staff to have lunch. They arrived in good order. I thought we gave them a reasonably good luncheon, considering that we were troops drawing field rations. Four or five days later, my staff and I received a luncheon invitation from the Russian commander. When we arrived at the Russian outpost line, we were met by guards and escorted to a German club, not in the city but out in the country. We were escorted by an indirect route off the main highway. When we arrived, there were several hundred Russian officers, among them several interpreters. I have never attended a more elaborate banquet.

They drank a lot of vodka and cognac. Entertainment began at 11 A.M., along with the serving of drinks. We finally sat down to lunch at 1 P.M. You seldom see as much food as was on the table. In front of my plate was a whole roast pig. I could see that the luncheon was going to last a while; when no one made an effort to carve this pig, I asked the interpreter, 'What about carving the pig?' The Russian interpreter replied, 'That is your pig, and you are the only one who can issue instructions to have it carved.' I did so, but there was so much other food on the table that very few ate any of the pig.

"We finally got up from the luncheon table at 4 P.M. and were returned to the American lines by the same circuitous route. At no time while in contact with the Russians around Chemnitz were any of our forces permitted to go into the Russian lines. We had no such restrictions on the Russians but very few visited within the American lines. At this luncheon, in mid-May, after the Germans had surrendered, the Russian commander presented me with a cavalryman's saber. It was no ceremonial piece, but a real working saber with grinding marks at the base of the blade, sharp as could be, and capable of cutting a man in half."

On May 9, two days after the German surrender in the American sector, Patton issued his General Order Number 98 to "soldiers of the Third Army, past and present," thanking them for their accomplishments. "During the 281 days of incessant and victorious combat, your penetrations have advanced farther in less time than any other army in history. You have fought your way across twenty-four major rivers and innumerable lesser streams. You have liberated or conquered more than 82,000 square miles of territory, including 1,500 cities and towns, and some 12,000 inhabited places. Prior to the termination of active hostilities, you had captured in battle 956,000 enemy soldiers and killed or wounded at least 500,000 others. France, Belgium, Luxembourg, Germany, Austria, and Czechoslovakia bear witness to your exploits."

Earlier, on April 25, after quiet had descended on the Third Army sector, Patton had written another commendation of Middleton:

From December 21, 1944, to April 22, 1945, the VIII Corps formed part of the Third Army.
During this period General Middleton demonstrated outstanding tactical skill and determination. His magnificent resistance against the extension of Von Rundstedt's attack to the west was only equaled by the tireless energy and

unfaltering aggressiveness with which he subsequently attacked, breaking the Siegfried Line, crossing the Prum and Kyll Rivers, capturing Koblenz, crossing the Rhine in its most difficult section, and finally terminating his successful offensive on the Mulde River.

He is hereby highly commended for his superior performance of duty.

Along with this formal commendation, Patton sent a personal note to Middleton.

Again the exigencies of war have separated the VIII Corps and the Third Army. We are all most regretful.

None of us will ever forget the stark valor with which you and your Corps contested every foot of ground during Von Rundstedt's attack. Your decision to hold Bastogne was a stroke of genius.

Subsequently, the relentless advance of the VIII Corps to the Kyll River, thence to the Rhine, your capture of Koblenz, and subsequent assault crossings of the Rhine at its most difficult sector, resulting in your victorious and rapid advance to the Mulde River, are events which will live in history and quicken the pulse of every soldier.

Please accept for yourself and transmit to the officers and men of your command my sincere thanks and admiration for the outstanding successes achieved.

May all good fortune attend you.

With hostilities officially over for a week, Middleton's thoughts turned to his family, to LSU, and to Baton Rouge. There was nothing more for him to do in Germany. He wrote to Bradley, commander of the Twelfth Army Group, on May 13:

Apropos of my letter to you with reference to release from active duty, and your reply thereto which came yesterday, I desire to state that, situation permitting, it would be to my advantage if I could return to my post at the Louisiana State University on or before August 1, 1945. This would give me time to become properly oriented as the financial and business manager of the institution prior to the opening of the school year in September.

I can assure you that my departure from the VIII Corps will be with much regret, not having been absent from the Corps for a single day since March, 1944. I have formed ties which cannot be forgotten. However, if I am to continue in my position at LSU, I feel that I should return when my services in the Army are no longer reasonably required. With my increasing age, I feel that if I should remain longer on active duty, when my services are not needed, I might well forget my civilian activity and remain in the service until the 60-year law automatically places me on the retired list.

To have served under your direction from Sicily to the heart of Germany has indeed been a privilege. That men such as you, Ike, Joe Collins, Courtney Hodges, and others have accomplished so much in this war, are available to guide the future of our Army, we cannot but feel that the future is in safe hands.

The same day, Middleton also sent a letter to President Hatcher at LSU, telling him that he was ready to pick up his civilian pursuits again.

There remained one more official goodbye to be said by Middleton. He addressed himself on May 18 to the officers and enlisted men of the VIII Corps:

> On taking leave of the VIII Corps, I do so with a mixed feeling of pleasure and regret.
> I am pleased because, after an absence of more than three years, I am returning to my home and family. I am also pleased because, in departing the army, I can look back on my service with the VIII Corps as the high water mark in my army career. I am further pleased because of the fine spirit of comradeship which exists in the corps.
> I regret leaving the corps because this will probably terminate my active service in the army. It separates me from the men of the Corps, whom I have learned to admire, to respect, and with whom I have formed a bond of friendship which is difficult to leave.
> We have come a long way together since March, 1944. At times, the road to success has not been an easy one. I am indebted to you for your loyalty and for your professional efforts which made the travel less difficult. We have accomplished much. We have cause to be proud of our efforts. Had we not been a group of men who could work as a team, we could not have accomplished our tasks in the quiet, businesslike manner in which it has been accomplished. I am grateful to each of you for the part you have played on the team.
> . . . .
> To each of you I leave my thanks and my gratitude for your devotion to duty and for your accomplishments, which will appear in history with the great accomplishments of all time.

Middleton was the only commander the VIII Corps had in combat. "From the time I took the corps into combat in June, 1944, until we finished the job in May, 1945, I had twenty-seven different divisions under my command. Never in that time did I have a division without an LSU man in it who had been a student during my time at LSU (1930–1936 and 1937–1941) or who had been a member of the faculty or staff. I played a kind of game, seeing who would turn up. It took me awhile, but I finally found a man in the Eighty-third. Usually, of course, they came to look me up. The grapevine works in the military just as it does everywhere else."

About May 25, Middleton received information that chosen groups of officers were to be returned to the United States for short visits, after which they would rejoin their commands, wherever they might be. He was also told that in all probability the VIII Corps would be sent sometime during the year to the Pacific and that it was likely that there would be an attack on the islands of Japan late in 1945.

"They sent the officers, I assume for propaganda purposes, back to a large city in the States near where they had been born. I same home with a group headed by Courtney Hodges, who was commanding First Army. Walton Walker, who had had the XX Corps, was in the group, along with a number of other generals, a number of colonels, and a few in the lower grades. Troy, Jr., came back with me. I had left John Cribbet, my senior aide, behind, after urging him to go on to Command and General Staff School if he was interested in an army career. But he told me he was ready to go back to law school at the University of Illinois, to pick up where he had left off. Cribbet went on to join the faculty and to become dean of the University of Illinois Law School."

Middleton's party was flown to New York by way of Iceland. They stayed overnight in New York, at the Waldorf-Astoria. The Middletons, father and son, ordered the best steaks in the house and had just cut into them when others in the group came along and told them they'd have to leave or be late for the opening curtain of a performance of "The Bloomer Girls." They left their steaks sizzling on the platters. From New York the group flew to Atlanta for a reception by the mayor and other dignitaries and for a parade. Mrs. Middleton and Bernice were there to greet General and Lieutenant Middleton. Their picture appeared in the May 25 issue of the Atlanta *Journal* with the four Middletons each clutching a bottle of Coca-Cola, the beverage born in Atlanta. (Incidentally, when General Eisenhower and Russian Marshal Zhukov met at Potsdam, Germany, a few days before the Middleton homecoming, the high commanders had exchanged gifts. When Eisenhower inquired as to Zhukov's deepest desire, he was told it was for a case of Coca-Cola. An American representative of the company was already in Germany and triumphantly produced the cola for the general to present the marshal.)

From Atlanta the group dispersed to their homes. The Middletons were flown to Baton Rouge for 15 days leave. General Middleton had been away from home 1,223 days since his departure in January, 1942. He had been overseas twenty-four months. He had been in combat 480 days—logging more combat time than any other American general officer in World War II.

When the home leave expired, Middleton returned to Washington. General Marshall told him, "You can return to the VIII Corps in Germany if you wish, but it is being prepared for return to the States, preparatory to movement later to the Pacific. It will be staged at Brownwood, Texas. Unless there's some particular reason why you want to return to Germany, you may remain in the States until the corps reaches Texas. If you want to, you may return to Baton Rouge and spend your time there. I'm going to tell you something in confidence; I don't think you'll ever need to go to Japan." Middleton elected to go to Baton Rouge.

"I was in Baton Rouge when the atomic bomb was dropped on Hiroshima. I went back to Washington and saw Marshall. He told me, 'I can't be sure about this, but in my opinion, the VIII Corps will not go to the Pacific and it's my feeling that no other troops will go to the Pacific,' indicating that he thought the Japanese would soon surrender. Marshall asked, 'Would you like to stay in the army?' I had been advanced from major general to lieutenant general, the appropriate rank for a corps commander. I suppose the fact that we had no corps commanders with lieutenant general's rank was because Eisenhower had not yet been made a

General Middleton After Two World Wars (Photo by Fonville Winans)

five-star general and we had army commanders who were still lieutena
generals. When Ike was promoted he could give his army commanders
four stars and his corps commanders, three," Middleton recalled.

"I told Marshall I had no desire to remain in the service once the war
ended, that I had made my decision to retire in 1937, and that it was my
desire that when I was no longer needed as a combat soldier, I should return to my position at LSU. This I did about the middle of August. Orders
were issued by the War Department returning me to retired status."

A Railway Express Agency man rang the Middleton doorbell on a
morning late in August. "Got some stuff on the truck for you, General,"
he said. It was his gear, shipped from Chemnitz in footlockers. Unpacking
later, he dug out a wrinkled barracks bag which had been folded into a
compact rectangle. Curious, he went into it and found, cushioned in paper,
a vaguely familiar looking whisky bottle. It was the bottle of Johnnie Walker Black Label Scotch that Mack Hornbeak had brought back to the VIII
Corps enclosure on the eve of the corps' dispatch across the English Channel in June, 1944.

Where had the bottle been all this time? Middleton recalled handing
it to his orderly before they embarked for the channel crossing. His orderly
had snuggled it into a briefcase and lashed the briefcase underneath the
general's Jeep. That bottle of Johnnie Walker, its contents vigorously agitated from time to time, but still full, went from the Cotentin Peninsula,
through the breakout at Avranches, to the siege of Brest, across France, to
Bastogne, through the Battle of the Bulge, through the Rhine crossing and
all the way to Chemnitz.

"When I was ordered home in May, 1945, I suppose my driver, Sergeant James F. Saffer, giving the Jeep a good overhaul, must have found
the briefcase lashed underneath. He put it in a barracks bag and had it prepared for shipping. I called Hornbeak, the original purchaser of the bottle,
and invited him out on a day when my first aide, Alfred Glassell, came to
town. We had a drink, after duty hours, amusing ourselves recalling how
many combat miles that bottle of whisky had traveled. My Jeep had a
one-inch steel plate welded underneath to absorb some of the shock if we
happened to run over a German land mine in combat. We drove in a lot
of out-of-the-way places and on some first class roads in that old buggy."

22   The Bulge
After the Bulge

W HEN MIDDLETON reported to President Hatcher that he was ready to resume work as comptroller of LSU late in August, 1945, he took up a position at the receiving end of the redeployment pipeline. Two months before, he had been on the feeding end of the redeployment process, sending home as expeditiously as possible millions of Americans who had served in overseas theaters. Now, at LSU, he was faced with the principal share of the task of providing physical accommodations for the thousands who would be returning and for thousands more who would be beginning their deferred entrance into the university.

The GI Bill of Rights, as it was popularly termed, paid registration fees, bought books, and provided money for lodging and food. The first of the swelling number of returning GI's registered in September, 1945. A crush was to follow in February, 1946. An avalanche was to come in June and September, 1946. Enrollments bulged. Dormitories were overrun. Many students were married and had, or were beginning, families. The university couldn't let them down, Middleton reasoned.

Before he could get down to the business of providing housing for returning GI's, Middleton studied the business affairs of the university with the detachment his long leave of absence gave. He found that changes had been made. As comptroller, he was assuming responsibility again for the direction of business affairs. Hatcher seemed to be seeking more centralized control of certain business affairs in his own office, perhaps recalling

298

how he had managed the affairs of the East Baton Rouge Parish school system.

"I had a conference with President Hatcher and in no uncertain terms expressed my concern over these changes," Middleton said. "The president very graciously said, 'General, if there's anything that you dislike, then you restore the organization to the same structure you had when you left.' I thought this was a very fair approach. So, the following day, the organization was returned to the status it had when I departed in January, 1942."

The tempo of university life quickened greatly with the return of thousands of veterans. They were matured by their war experiences and serious about the education they wanted. "Many of these men were married. They didn't want to be separated from their families while they attended school. It was up to the university to make some provision for them," Middleton said. "When I returned to the comptroller's office I found plans and specifications ready for advertising for bids for the first really large dormitory unit for men on the campus, consisting of Hodges, Hatcher, and Johnston Halls (the names came later)—commonly referred to then as the Tiger Arms.

"I was not in accord with the location of these buildings adjacent to Tiger Stadium, but our arrangement had gone too far to change. These buildings offered no solution to the plight of married students. I started looking around and found help at the Higgins Company in New Orleans. Andrew Higgins had done a great job of shipbuilding and had provided a basic form of housing for his employees and for some overseas use. From the Higgins Company we procured small one-room plywood buildings which we got for practically nothing. We added a kitchen and a bath and put these buildings over in the area later occupied by most of the new dormitories for women. GI families leaped at the chance to move into these quarters, which they called hutments.

"Later, my continuing search around ports of embarkation turned up a supply of buildings that were crated and ready for shipment to the South Pacific. No longer needed overseas, these were procured by the university and placed alongside Nicholson Drive. They made homes for two families to each building. Built of plywood, these quarters were intended for a life expectation of not more than three years. The War Department told me they'd last no longer. We brought the first of these buildings to the campus and put them together in 1946. The last one was torn down in 1964. The apartments, with utilities furnished by the university, rented for a pittance."

Middleton's knowledge of military planning and procurement procedures gave LSU a great advantage in the hunt for surplus materials usable on a campus. His next coup involved the finding of a group of navy steel buildings, knocked down, which were shipped to the campus in the summer of 1946. These were to provide apartments for younger faculty members who were having difficulty finding housing in Baton Rouge. Seven of these, called the Naval Barracks, containing a total of eighty-four two-bedroom apartments, were erected on massive concrete slabs poured on the east side of the campus, across the street from the hutment area set up in 1945. Eighty-four families jumped at the opportunity to move into the Naval Barracks and a long waiting list soon formed. Occupancy was restricted to junior faculty. A limit of two years occupancy was suggested.

The author of this book, returning from service as a newspaper publisher in Berlin, and more recently from an assignment at Fort McClellan at Anniston, Alabama, at the Infantry Replacement Training Center there, was one of the first tenants to move into the Naval Barracks, with his wife and their children, Virginia and James Patrick, aged four and one. Before entering the army, the author had been an instructor in the School of Journalism and adviser to the *Daily Reveille*, LSU's student newspaper. The director of the School of Journalism, Marvin G. Osborn, short-handed, heard that the army would give early releases to faculty needed to teach the returning throngs. He asked for the author's early release and said that he would arrange for an apartment in the Naval Barracks, then under construction. The army did its part and four Prices arrived in Baton Rouge the first week of September, 1946. The author went straight to the campus next morning, only to be told that there must have been some misunderstanding; his family was on the reservation list but down at number 105— and there were only 84 apartments.

From the housing office, he was referred to the comptroller's office, where he told of the mixup about an apartment reservation. He was ushered in to see Middleton.

"You're Jimmy Price and you're just out of the army, aren't you,"

Middleton said. "You don't have any housing problem. Take Mrs. Price and your children and go on over to the east side where they're hurrying to finish those buildings. Pick yourselves an apartment. Then come back and get the key."

The grateful Prices hiked across the campus. They chose Apartment P-47, downstairs, facing west, in the center building of seven. They went back to Alumni Hall, acquired the key, and moved in at once. After a tourist court in Anniston, the Naval Barracks apartment offered pure luxury in two sizable bedrooms, a gigantic living and dining room, a kitchen, a bathroom, and a giant walk-in closet. What if the floors were bare concrete, the gypsum board walls separating living room and dining room from the hallway and two bedrooms rose but seven feet from the floor, the bathtub was cast concrete, and the principal bathroom fixture had been roughed in but not installed? The kitchen had a serviceable cooking stove and a genuine icebox.

The faculty tenants were told that decoration schemes could be of their own choosing. They painted the interiors and congratulated themselves on having the opportunity to do so. Plumbers came in and hooked up the commode. This apartment was to be the Prices' home for the next twenty-one months. The other eighty-three apartments were soon filled with other veterans' families. When workmen ran out of corrugated iron which formed the sides and roofs of the steel and concrete buildings, on the seventh building they daubed stucco. The buildings were sturdy enough, riding out a hurricane the first year they stood. They were later stripped down to their I-beam skeletons and rebuilt into seven dormitories for women, then renamed Nora Neill Power Dormitories in the 1960s.

Comptroller Middleton saw to it that other young faculty families found a home when they returned from military service, too. "The Naval Barracks presented a special challenge. Plumbing fixtures came from all over the country. We got the commodes from Little Rock. Lumber came from other states. The only expense incurred in getting the steel barracks was the cost of freight. But when we started asking for bids on erecting the barracks we hit trouble. Bids for pouring concrete for the floors were far out of line. I asked the Board of Supervisors to approve our pouring the concrete ourselves. We saved $25,000 a building that way. I stayed over there much of the summer with Richard Mornhinveg, university superin-

tendent of operations and maintenance, with Frederick von Osthoff, the
university architect, and with the contractor on the project. We saved
$175,000 on the contract figure."

Though he was retired from the army, Middleton was soon called
upon by the army for another chore—this one not requiring his re-entry
upon active duty. In April, 1946, he was appointed to the Doolittle Board,
officially named the Board to Investigate Officer-Enlisted Men Relationships, headed by former Air Corps General James H. Doolittle and consisting of former officers and enlisted men. Don Robinson, who had edited
the *Forty-fifth Division News*, wrote an article for *Army Times* which said
in its April 6 issue:

> This is my vote of confidence in the "Board to Investigate Officer-Enlisted
> Men Relationships."
>
> "Just another whitewash," I told myself when I first read of the appoint-
> ment of the board. Then I found on the list of those named to the board: "Lt.
> Gen. Troy H. Middleton."
>
> My whole opinion changed then and there. This board was on the level.
> If it weren't, Middleton wouldn't be there.
>
> Bill Mauldin called from New York. He said the same thing: It must be
> on the level if Middleton's on it. Fred Sheehan, once with me on the *45th Di-
> vision News*, now American Broadcasting Company's Chicago news editor,
> wrote precisely the same opinion. All of us had known Middleton well in our
> 45th Division days in the States, in Sicily, and in Italy.
>
> Soon after the board began its meetings, the former 45th Division com-
> mander and I were lunching in a Washington hotel.
>
> "I didn't want to come up here for this," Middleton told me. "I have a lot
> of work to do at home. None of the others can spare the time, either. We're
> not going to drag this thing out indefinitely. We'll hear the witnesses, decide
> upon our recommendations, and go home."
>
> The board members, he told me, had requested that the witnesses be heard
> in secret session. They had nothing against the press, he said, and the witnesses
> were free to tell the reporters what they had told the board if they chose. But
> this was to be an investigation, not a show.
>
> And General Middleton said he thought the men selected for the board
> were a well-balanced group. Both officers and enlisted are represented, and all
> are level-headed. The officers are ex-EM.
>
> Now, the purpose of the investigation is not to recommend revenge upon
> the officer class in behalf of the millions of aggravated EM who had to put up
> with the so-called caste system during the war. The board is neither pro-officer,
> nor pro-enlisted man. It's pro-army, the general told me. The object is to find

a way to make the army more compatible with a democratic nation without in any way weakening the effectiveness of the army.

General Middleton is a soldier. He was a soldier in the last war, and he enhanced his reputation in this one. He can swing the axe on an enlisted man, but he can swing it on a brother officer, too.

"I had to relieve one of my best friends from a regimental command," he recalled during our bull session. "He just wasn't a combat man. He never has forgiven me."

And that's the way it went. I remembered the incident, and that spread-eagle had been relieved damned promptly. I recalled to his mind some other cases.

During his service with the 45th, I had noticed that Troy H., as we had called him among ourselves, had always demanded more of the officers than of the men. They were supposed to set the example, weren't they? They were paid more, weren't they?

Middleton, too, is the man responsible for the full blossoming of Bill Mauldin's fame, in a way. Before Bill had become famous he was already making light of the foibles of the brass. The brass had not much sense of humor, and higher echelons demanded that this brat be squelched. It was Middleton who stood between Bill and the wrath from on high. If those upper-class generals had booted Bill into a line company and taken his drawing board away there would have been no howl from the general public then.

In addition to saving Bill, the general saved the *45th Division News* many times. Once an order came down to stop publication. The general kept kicking it back with endorsements until the division had moved out of the command originating the order.

The Doolittle board made a number of recommendations for improving relationships between enlisted men and officers, one of the more significant being that noncommissioned officers be permitted to establish their own clubs. Mauldin came in and spoke in support of this recommendation.

The Department of Defense called upon retired Lieutenant General Middleton again in March, 1949, while he remained busy at LSU. This time he was asked to serve on the Military Education Panel of the Service Academy Board, to study the curricula and other programs of the United States Military and Naval Academies and to recommend a program for the proposed Air Force Academy. With two other retired officers from the navy and the air force and three active generals, Middleton worked part-time for nine months in arriving at recommendations for the service academies.

"I strongly urged more liberal education for the academies," he recalled. "I got some scorching letters from service people who disagreed with me. Nevertheless, much of what I held out for was worked into the academic program at the academies."

Middleton was invited back to Fort Benning on September 28, 1951, where he spoke to the third 1951 class of seventy-five second lieutenants at commissioning exercises, during the war in Korea. The United States Military Academy called on Middleton in December, 1958, to come to the academy for three days and to return in January, 1959, for two days, to review the curriculum offered at West Point. Middleton, with other committee members, took another look at the academy's courses of study.

President Hatcher, who had been appointed to the LSU presidency after the death of Campbell B. Hodges in 1944, resigned because of ill health on February 8, 1947. He had been in the hospital since November, 1946. Dean of the University Fred C. Frey was appointed acting president. President Emeritus Hatcher died April 3 and the Board of Supervisors began a search for a president for the third time in six years.

"It may be of some interest that I was called before the Board of Supervisors at this time and asked if I would be interested in the presidency. I told the board and Acting President Frey that I was not interested, that I was happy in the position I was then holding. A committee of the board was appointed to carry out the search for a president. It was agreed that the university should seek a professional educator. Charles Sherrouse, representing the board, went to Boston to interview a highly recommended prospect named Harold W. Stoke, then president of the University of New Hampshire. Sherrouse came back, enthusiastic about Stoke. The board set a date for a decision on the presidency. The day before the selection was made, I was again called before the board and asked if I would not reconsider and permit my name to be placed in nomination. Again I refused. I understand—this may not be accurate, but I heard the report—that when the vote was taken, four members of the board voted for me.

"I regretted this, because if it was true, the incoming president might have felt that I was seeking the position. In my belief, the presidency of a university with the standing of LSU is so important that no man should ever seek the position. The university should seek the man," Middleton said. President Stoke took office in September, 1947.

Enrollment in the university had shot up from 3,678 in September,

1945, to 8,705 in February, 1947, when the full weight of GI's began to be felt. Middleton remained busy, supervising the building program and stretching the university's physical resources to meet the great demands for housing and additional classroom space. Through 1948 and 1949, large enrollments taxed the physical facilities of the university.

During these years, as the university's chief financial officer, Middleton was involved in the preparation and the presentation of the university budget. More than once he was surprised by President Stoke's attitude about money. "General," Stoke once told Middleton, "our business is to spend money, not to save it." Middleton understood that the president was but giving voice to an exasperation of the moment, but he told himself, "Good lord, this man doesn't understand business." Middleton believed in devising a budget fully and fairly representing the university's needs, and then impressing upon the Louisiana legislature the fact that the university presented its budget without an ounce of fat in it.

Stoke was sometimes doctrinaire. In his workings with the Board of Supervisors he adopted a formality which first puzzled and then began to annoy a minority, and later a substantial number of the fourteen-member governing body. His relationships with Middleton remained cordial. He retained the respect and the admiration of almost all the faculty. "He had a habit of writing out everything," Middleton recalled. "He would read his communications to the Board of Supervisors." Finally, Tom Dutton, a board member, spoke out. "Anybody can read a message to us, Mr. President; just tell it to us."

"Bucking up against a tough character like board member Monnot Lanier must have been a shocking experience to Dr. Stoke," Middleton recalled. "Lanier understood finances; he asked a lot of searching questions and he expected a fully informed answer. I learned that about him when I was asked to take over the university's financial affairs after the 1939 scandals."

23 "We Have Elected You President"

PRESIDENT Stoke's differences with the Board of Supervisors came to a head at the end of 1950, though it is likely that most members of the board were unaware of the depth of Stoke's growing concern. He decided to offer his resignation and asked the board to hold a special meeting December 28, 1950, to act on his resignation.

"The first I heard of Dr. Stoke's intended resignation was when he called me the morning the board was to meet in special session," Middleton recalled. "He had always had me present in board meetings. That morning he called me and said, 'The board is meeting this morning; I am submitting my resignation. If you care to attend the meeting, you may do so.' I was shocked. I replied, 'Dr. Stoke, whom have you discussed this with?' He said, 'Very few people, because I don't want to involve people. But the situation has become so incompatible that I feel it's best that I submit my resignation.'

"Of course, I did not attend the meeting, but about an hour and a half or two hours after this telephone conversation, three members of the board walked into my office and told me, 'The board has elected you president of the university and we are here to notify you. It is the board's desire that you accept,' " Middleton recalled.

"I had been with the university, except for a year when I was in the Philippines and when I was in World War II, since 1930. I had served in several capacities. My service had been such that I had had an opportunity to get to know the university and to know the people of Louisiana. The

306

university had been good to me; its people had been good to me; the city of Baton Rouge had been good to me. I discussed this matter with the three members of the board. They didn't want to wait because they said they felt a certain danger in delaying too long in replacing the departing president.

"In a very short time I had to make my decision. I made it out of respect for the people with whom I had worked and who had been so good to me. I did not profess to be an educator even though, except for fighting two wars, I had spent most of my time in the classroom. I had found very little difference between teaching in the service schools and teaching in a university. If I had had any misgivings about my ability to carry on as head of the university, I would not have accepted," he said. When he went home to lunch that day, he told Mrs. Middleton he had been elected president of LSU and that he had accepted the position. Mrs. Middleton called their daughter Bernice, now Mrs. Ashton Stewart, the wife of a Baton Rouge attorney to whom she was married December 11, 1947. She also called Troy, Jr., who had been married in August, 1950, to Martha Caruthers of

E. Monnot Lanier and Tom Dutton Tell Middleton: "We Have Elected You President," 1950

Columbus, Mississippi, while he was serving on the faculty of Mississippi State University's ROTC department at nearby Starkville.

Of his predecessor in the presidency, Harold Stoke, Middleton said, "He had so many good qualities—everything but judgment. He simply could not work with the Board of Supervisors. He would fly off the handle when he lost patience with a member. You can't afford the luxury of a temper. You have to learn to ignore the criticism and to go ahead and do the job. Dr. Stoke was magnificently equipped to be a graduate dean. He was a fine scholar. If he'd only had patience and exercised calmer judg-

Three Generations Family Photograph. Standing: Jerusha (Judy) Stewart, Martha Caruthers Middleton, Troy H. Middleton, Jr., Bernice Middleton Stewart, Ashton Stewart. Seated: Jerusha Collins Middleton, Troy H. Middleton, Troy H. Middleton III, Bingham Middleton Stewart, and Martha Emily Middleton

ment. He was always thoughtful of me. Knowing of my friendship with Ike, he asked me to represent LSU when Dwight Eisenhower became president of Columbia University."

Students were away from the university for the Christmas holidays when Stoke presented his resignation to the board, to take effect February 1, 1951. When the students returned, they read in the *Daily Reveille* about the resignation and the board's appointment of a new president. In addition, the January 5 issue of the *Reveille* carried a scathing condemnation of the board's acceptance of Stoke's resignation, written by the editor, J. Dafydd Hawkins, a mature and scholarly young man. The editorial read in part:

BETRAYAL OF STOKE—DEED OF SHAME

When Dr. Stoke came to LSU there was general rejoicing that so eminent an educator should administer a university too long dogged by the specter of instability and politics.

When he resigned there was general shock that his services were lost. And there was indignation and puzzlement.

Just a hugger mugger session of the Board of Supervisors, barred to the public, then the president's announcement that a "fundamental incompatibility" between his views and those of the board existed, and LSU had lost the services of a man so renowned among his peers that some did not scruple at the praise of "best in the country."

The crux of the president's resignation message was that he was not only prevented from carrying out effectually an administration of his own, but that the board itself had no plan with which to replace it.

In the place of a board plan of administration—better than nothing at all —there was a furtive disunity, smacking of spoils and favors and words in the right place. Faculty members who opposed the president's aims had the ear of individual board members. The board itself would direct one thing and disregard it once it was done.

Why bring in an honorable, able man, concerned only with his profession and excelling in it, and then relentlessly trip and snare his every effort?

And when his views are defeated and his policy mocked—why go behind closed doors to take his resignation? If his resignation was indicated or desired, why was it not asked for openly, with reasons stated, that the people who have a right to know should understand? All we have for answer is the secrecy, the hole-in-wall atmosphere—these are the only tokens of the transaction.

Well, we have lost him, and those responsible for the loss can take what comfort they may from their actions. Most of us will mourn—mourn the loss of an educator, of an earnest friend of the university, and most of all, the loss of an honest man.

The *Reveille* issue of January 11 carried a letter by Joseph Dermody, Jr., saying in part: "Even considering your admirable editorial on President Stoke, there is still considerable that can be said:

"The selection of General Middleton cannot be attacked. He carries the well wishes and confidence of everyone who has the interests of LSU at heart. No one need expect that his appointment will mean a lowering of standards.

"But the selection of an able successor is not the point of this affair. . . . No, it wasn't the acceptance of Stoke's resignation that was evil, it was the blow at LSU's future. Surely, no capable men, such as Stoke, will consider offers from LSU. The insecurity evident here when one dares suggest reforms in the educational system, demotes a dean or two, prefers an educational building to an addition to the football stadium, or tries to force the students to study—this will keep them away."

The Stoke resignation remained strong in the news. The board of managers of the Louisiana Parent-Teachers Association, meeting in Alexandria, adopted a report demanding the resignation of all members of the Board of Supervisors, charging the board with "unwarranted interference" in the administrative affairs of the university. Board Chairman Tom Dutton responded with a denial that Stoke's resignation was forced. "The board," Dutton said, "is composed of fourteen leading citizens of this state, lawyers, doctors, businessmen, farmers, and bankers, all of them LSU alumni, working loyally for LSU and the state without one cent of remuneration. I am sure that the people of this state and the real friends of LSU must know that the action of the board in the Stoke matter was actuated by the highest sense of duty and that there must be two sides to this situation."

The PTA report charged that "when an attempt was made by Stoke to change the word-in-the-right-place (playing politics) policy to an across-the-board administration, friction resulted." To this assertion, Dutton replied: "These statements are based largely on misinformation. The board cooperated with Stoke 100 percent. The time came, however, when there was a lack of confidence on both sides. His was not a forced resignation in any sense. Stoke resigned of his own accord and we were surprised. Maybe he didn't expect us to accept his resignation. I don't know."

The PTA report, referring to the reasons given by Stoke for resigning, said that the board had "permitted groups within the university to apply public pressure (naming the Agricultural Extension Division, the Athletic

Department, and 'old guard thinkers' on the LSU faculty). Failure of the board to cooperate with this outstanding educator has lost Louisiana many years of immediate progress in education and deprived the youth of the state of fine leadership."

On January 15, Stoke made his last appearance before the Faculty Council in a special session. For once, attendance was remarkable. Those late in arriving stood across the back of the room. Stoke read his temperately phrased 4,000-word "Explanation to the Faculty." When it was over the faculty stood and applauded long. Some wept openly.

Of his "fundamental incompatibility with the Board of Supervisors," Stoke said, toward the end of his address:

The important thing, it seems to me, is to recognize that it is not a struggle, as so many appear to believe, which can be compromised or ignored. Life is full of situations on which bargains and compromises can be struck and it is also full of relationships in which bargains and compromises cannot be struck. It is no small part of the difficulty of living to determine which belong to which. A jury may bargain all day as to whether to punish the prisoner at the bar with one year or ten years in prison, but if the issue before them is whether he is to be allowed to live or whether he is to die for his crime, no compromise is possible. One side or the other must win absolutely. And the basic issues here are not subject to compromise. Either you have a university which is devoted to the purposes a university is created to serve or you don't really have a university at all.

My best wishes go, of course, to General Middleton as he assumes new responsibilities for the university. He knows the institution and its environment as I could never know it. You know him, and his strength is your hope. Two other things, among many, will be greatly to your advantage. These are that General Middleton will be able to command the degree of support from the board which I am now unable to do. This is indispensable. The second is the withdrawal from a complicated situation of an irritant, namely, me. People who are associated with irksome ideas after awhile themselves become irksome. I must admit that I have become a source of irritation to a substantial number of board members, rubbing them the wrong way, exasperating them sometimes beyond words, sometimes to words. And I must also say that I can understand their exasperation. There is no one so obnoxious as the person who is incessantly calling to our attention things we had just as soon not hear. I am afraid I am to a number of people an illustration of Pope's couplet: 'No wild enthusiast ever yet could rest, till half mankind were like himself possessed.' To create an irritation has been no part of my intention and I should have been glad to avoid it if I had known any way to do so except by the abandonment of the ideas which give rise to the irritation. I realize there is a narrow line between tenacity and contentiousness, between conviction and stubbornness and I am probably too much of a party at interest to draw the line accurately. Nevertheless, for the things I have advocated, I should have to confess even now that if I have been wrong, I am still unrepentant.

The *Reveille* of January 16 devoted a full page and half another to the Stoke address, as well as an expression of regret at his departure. The same issue carried a news story on two resolutions of the Faculty Council. The faculty's resolutions bespoke a grave concern with the manner in which the Board of Supervisors had chosen Stoke's successor, Middleton. The faculty was not of one mind in the matter. Some were frankly happy to see Stoke go, principally those who has managed to line up support among board members for their own projects and concerns. But it is almost certainly correct to say that most members of the faculty were much more disturbed by the manner of choice rather than the choice of the new president. This, Middleton clearly understood. He had had no notice of Stoke's decision to offer his resignation at the special meeting of the Board of Supervisors on December 28. He had been elected to replace Stoke and had been asked to decide at once whether he would accept the presidency. Having done so, he was under no illusions about faculty feeling concerning the manner in which the board had hurried to replace Stoke.

Compounding the difficulties of that period, Paul Hebert, dean of the university, submitted his resignation on January 13, saying that he intended to enter the active practice of law in Baton Rouge on February 1. Hebert had received an invitation to join a leading law firm. "I regret," he wrote to President-elect Middleton, "that my decision to leave the university must be reached at this particular time, as I would naturally wish to support and assist your administration in any manner within my power. Our close official and personal relationship at the university has been one of the aspects of my work which I valued highly."

To Middleton, the imminent departure of Hebert was a blow. Back in 1939, when he had been asked to take over the university's business management, he worked with Acting President Hebert. The two developed great mutual respect.

"I couldn't help but think, when Mac Hebert's resignation came to me, of all that he had contributed to the university. If he had been appointed president rather than acting president back in 1939, he almost certainly would still be president (in 1973). But Tom Dutton of the Board of Supervisors probably would have dropped dead if Mac Hebert, a Catholic, had been chosen then," Middleton said later. "You know, the university owes Mac Hebert a tremendous debt. His eloquence and his frankness were superb. Thanks to the work that Mac started, the university recovered $280,000 after the 1939 troubles."

"I worked openly for Mac's appointment as president both before the Board of Supervisors chose Campbell Hodges and before it picked Harold Stoke. I am convinced that religious prejudice alone prevented Hebert's selection as James Monroe Smith's successor," Middleton said, "and again in 1941 and 1947."

Middleton recalled how he had gone to his office in David F. Boyd Hall back in 1939, on a Sunday afternoon, to find Acting President Hebert in an adjacent office, "wallowing deep in work."

"I told Mac that we ought to get someone to handle all of this law work. He told me, 'I'm a lawyer.' And I replied, 'I know that, but you've got too much to do. Let's get Ben (Benjamin B.) Taylor.' Mac said 'O.K.' I drove out to Charles Manship's camp on the Amite River, where we all liked to go on Sunday afternoons, and found that Ben Taylor was in North Carolina. I drew his law partner, Vernon Porter, aside and told him what we had in mind. I'm sure some of our friends must have thought I was in some kind of trouble, talking with Vernon that way over on the sidelines.

"Vernon heard me out and said that their law firm would take on the assignment. They'd do the university's law work for $10,000. When Ben Taylor got back to town from North Carolina, he gave me unshirted hell. Ben told me, 'Why, I give more than that to charity.' I told him I knew that. He fussed at me some more, but he finally agreed to take the job. Their firm has represented the university ever since."

So Paul Hebert was going into the private practice of law after twenty years of association with the university.

The *Reveille* reported on January 17 that the Boyd-Ewing Post of the American Legion, made up of faculty, staff, and student members, had voted to extend its congratulations and assure its support to "the first of its members to attain the office of president of our university. More than one member of the faculty was heard to say, "That's just like those military people for you, speaking up for one of their kind."

The campus settled down to examinations and the midyear break. When the next *Reveille* appeared on February 1, a photograph of President Middleton and former President Stoke appeared on the front page, with the two shaking hands. A new editor, Eric Smith, took over for the second semester. Smith added his editorial opinion on the changes in the presidency:

MIDDLETON TAKES COMMAND ON READY–MADE BATTLEFIELD

Resulting from the swift-moving events which transpired between Christmas and final examinations—resignation of Dr. Stoke as LSU's president, subsequent appointment of General Middleton to that post, Dean Hebert's resignation and the predictions in some newspapers of a "general exodus" of faculty members from the university—there has developed around the campus an apathetic attitude based on the assumption that, "Well, a degree from LSU won't mean a thing anymore, just as it was back in the 'country club' era of the school."

Into this hasty appraisal of LSU's future we must interject an optimistic "tsk, tsk," and wait to see what the consequences of the changes will actually be. The eyes of the entire university will be focused mainly on the new president, General Troy Houston Middleton; and his actions and decisions will be subjected to a very searching scrutiny by students, by faculty, and most important of all, by parents of potential students.

It is regrettable that General Midleton has to assume the responsibilities of university leadership on such inauspicious terms. Policy matters, like the question of dual pensions for Agricultural Extension Service workers, will be dumped in his lap secondhand and after the lines of demarcation have already solidified. He has been put in the peculiar position of judicial review, when he is in effect the executive branch of our university setup.

What, then, are we to expect from General Middleton? Is this to be a laissez-faire period of LSU's administration? Will the Board of Supervisors be the dominating force in all decisions governing the university, large or small?

General Middleton's experience as an administrator would indicate a negative answer to these questions. The very fact that his capabilities lie more in administration and less in education than those of our former president points to a firm handling of university policy, tempered by a judgment which acknowledges and placates the whims of the critical.

Preliminary enrollment figures for the second semester dropped 16 percent from the September figures, from 6,341 down to 5,327. Some reduction from first to second semester was usual, but the war in Korea was also affecting enrollment. From 8,705 students registered in February, 1947, the comedown to 5,327 was steep.

24   LSU's President
Is the "Saving" Kind

PRESIDENT Middleton made his first talk after taking office, at the annual football banquet on February 12. He declared, "I feel a young man who participates in a sport for which we sell tickets and from which we derive revenue is entitled to financial support." He said that he didn't believe in tramp athletes, who never intend to be graduated, but added that "so long as an athlete remains a student—does reasonably well in his academic work—I'll back him 100 percent. When he fails, though, he and I are going to part company; I'm taking one road and he's taking another, and you can imagine which way he's going."

Middleton was formally introduced to the student body at a convocation opening Religious Emphasis Week on February 19. As chief executive of the university, he took up a rigorous work schedule. A prime objective in his first year was to increase faculty salaries. At a May 3 meeting of the Board of Supervisors, he reported that $525,000 in proposed faculty salary increases would be sought for the next year. "The number one need is personnel," he said.

LSU alumni leaders early in May invited the student body to take part in a Middleton Day program, May 15. The day went off well with an afternoon parade by the Cadet Corps; a fifteen-gun salute; a barbecue; a presentation of an honorary lifetime membership certificate in the Alumni Federation, a three-star general's flag, and a bouquet of gladioli to Mrs. Middleton. A Board of Supervisors member, Theo F. Cangelosi, spoke, calling upon the Louisiana legislature and public officials to stop the move

315

toward placing a college in every part of Louisiana, saying that the state could afford only one first-class university, LSU.

At its May 1 meeting, the Student Council decided to seek more information on university building priorities, with a view to advancing an auditorium ahead of an enlargement to Tiger Stadium. In October, 1950, the Board of Supervisors had authorized issuance of $5,700,000 in bonds to be used for enlarging the stadium by from 28,000 to 30,000 seats by adding seven rows to the top of the stadium and twenty-one rows in a second deck above the original stands. Expansion of the Medical School in New Orleans and construction of a new library on the Baton Rouge campus were also to be financed at least in part by the bond issue, advertised for sale on November 28.

When the bond sale was authorized by the board, the members voted to increase the stadium seating capacity by 26,000—not by the original plan of raising a second tier of seats, but by enclosing the south end to complete a bowl. Government controls, imposed after the outbreak of war involving the United States in Korea, however, prevented the board from proceeding with its announced intent to enlarge the stadium before taking up any other university building need. Stadium expansion, it was announced, would have to await government lifting of controls on nonessential building, in which classification the stadium project fell.

At its May 15 meeting, the Student Council renewed its effort to get information on the proposed stadium enlargement, authorizing Charles Farrell, student body president, to write to Monnot Lanier, secretary of the Board of Supervisors, regarding whether an auditorium might be built instead. The council asked for *Reveille* help in determining student opinion on whether a larger stadium or an auditorium was preferred. The *Reveille* obliged by publishing in its next issue a ballot inviting all students to express a preference for an auditorium, a new library, or an enlarged stadium. When the ballots were finally counted, 290 students called for the auditorium, 39 for the library, and 11 for the stadium. The Student Council held a quick meeting May 22 and voted to ask that the legislature put an auditorium before stadium enlargement. There the matter rested as the semester ended.

LSU entered a compact with the United States Army to begin offering extension instruction to Americans in military service in the Panama Canal Zone, starting July 16, and dispatched two history instructors by plane to open the program in the Canal Zone. On August 2, after six months in office, President and Mrs. Middleton invited the summer graduating class, their families, and the LSU faculty and staff to a reception at the President's Home.

One of the conditions attaching to the presidency of the university was the requirement that the president live in a home at the heart of the campus, on Highland Road at Semmes Drive. The Middletons had moved there from their home down Highland Road, where they had lived since 1938. Mrs. Middleton, used to her home and spacious grounds at 4782 Highland Road, continued to be a good soldier after years of having a husband in the army, but she was less than happy with the official presidential residence on the campus.

"I felt like a housekeeper, bottled up in the president's home on the campus. It needed repairs. The roof leaked over the living room. It was a wonderful place to entertain, with the big solarium. But it just wasn't my idea of a home," Mrs. Middleton recalled. "I suppose our happiest days on the campus were when Troy was commandant of cadets and we lived in the commandant's house. I enjoyed talking with cadets. The children played on the lot where Pleasant Hall is now."

Mrs. Middleton's mention of life in the commandant's house reminded President Middleton of a complaint his wife had made to him about the picturesque language used by workmen on a project near their former residence. "I took it up with George Caldwell, the building contractor, telling him our son was coming home using some pretty strong cusswords and that Mrs. Middleton was upset, thinking the workmen were too crude in their language. Caldwell told me he'd take care of it. The cursing must have stopped; we heard no more of it from Troy, Jr., who was not yet in his teens. Later, Caldwell told me it was he who was doing the cussing rather than his laborers," Middleton recalled.

With the summer commencement of 1951, at which six hundred received undergraduate and advanced degrees, came a breathing spell for Middleton. He could go back through the letters of congratulation he had received and meticulously replied to, back in January.

One had come from his old company commander at Galveston, Captain Alexander T. Ovenshine, now a retired general living in San Antonio. Another came from retired Major General William Durward Connor, the Army War College commandant who had praised Middleton's thesis in

1929. Another World War I associate, A. L. Crawford, wrote his congratulations on the letterhead of the Cornelia, Georgia, Coca-Cola Bottling Company. Crawford reminded Middleton of an incident at Leon Springs, Texas, in 1918. "I am the student officer whom you called up and told that he was to be sent back to his company because Captain Simpson reported that I was unable to work out problems of drill on the field. I pleaded with you for a chance on the field, you to give me the problems and I to work them out. You came on the drill field later that morning, gave the problems, and our company went through all of these formations without an error. I am sure you suspected what had happened before the drill was over. The whole company knew that Captain Simpson was out to 'get' me that morning and they worked as never before. Of course I was happy to graduate, later receive my commission, and go to France with my division, the 31st."

From George M. Gloss, a former member of the LSU faculty, came a letter on the stationery of the Advanced School of Education of Teachers College, Columbia University: "I never will forget when I was called up by the secretary of a legislator in Louisiana, and my position threatened if I did not pass a student. I went from one administrative office to another and got no help until I reached you, at which point you called the representative, and gave them what I would call, in simple language—'hell.' It took guts." There was another letter from school principal Glynn H. Brock, president of the St. Tammany Parish Chapter of the LSU Alumni Federation. "As an alumnus and as a school principal, my ties with the university are still many and I hope that you will do all within your power to make the school attractive to our students rather than restrictive. Many of our students in this section are going to other colleges because of two paramount reasons: 1) cost; 2) they feel that the standards have been raised too rapidly and too high for them to successfully stay in the university."

It was soon enough made apparent that Middleton was not one for lowering standards to accommodate any student who might wish to spend some time at LSU.

Much to Middleton's liking were letters from his comrades in arms in World War II. Anthony C. (Tony) McAuliffe, then Chief Chemical Officer of the Department of the Army, who told the Germans "Nuts" at Bastogne, wrote congratulations and recalled "with pleasure my enjoyable visit to Baton Rouge, and particularly the delightful luncheon with Mrs. Middleton and yourself and your many friends, the visit to your beautiful campus, and the fine football game." From Tony McAuliffe, the man of few words, that was a mouthful.

Raymond S. McLain, a lieutenant general in the office of the Chief of Staff, had served as assistant division commander of the Forty-fifth Division under Middleton in Sicily and Italy, wrote congratulations and his best wishes.

Ike Eisenhower wrote, too, as did scores of Middleton's army associates and hundreds of others who had cause to be grateful for Middleton's sense of rigorous fairness.

Away from the LSU campus, Middleton faced one of the sternest tests of his life, from peer group members at the annual meeting of the Southern University Conference (SUC) at Edgewater Park, Mississippi, April 11 and 12, 1951. He had been in office a little more than two months. He had attended a 1939 meeting of the SUC in Atlanta, at Acting President Hebert's request, to deal with questions about the university's finances, but had not been to such a meeting since.

Middleton drove to Edgewater Park fully aware that he would face a cool reception. Cool? Frosty, if not frigid! He had not met most of the presidents. All of them had known Harold Stoke, whom they held in high esteem. They had read in their newspapers that Stoke had resigned under pressure and that Middleton had been named his successor the same day. Perhaps the other presidents had notions, too, about the adequacy of any military man in the presidency of a major university. Stoke himself, as secretary of the SUC, attended the meeting although he was no longer at LSU.

Dr. Doak S. Campbell, president of Florida State University, Tallahassee, recalled the circumstances of the meeting at Edgewater Park:

"There was considerable tension in the atmosphere. Some of the members of the conference felt that official notice should be taken of political interference and had prepared a resolution of censure. The resolution covered two points that involved ethical considerations. First, a president of a member institution had been removed under direct political pressure. Second, a member of the institution's administrative staff had accepted appointment to fill the vacancy thus created.

"It was assumed, therefore, by several members of the conference that censure was due the board of the university for improper political interference with the orderly administration of the university. Furthermore, the newly designated president deserved censure because his action could only be interpreted as condoning the action of the board.

"The resolution was presented with due deliberation and gravity. It was apparent that most of those present were sympathetic with the spirit of the resolution and that affirmative action would be taken after little or no debate. It was under these circumstances that the new president of Louisiana State University first attended a meeting of the Southern University Conference.

"I had never seen General Middleton before this occasion except once, while visiting the campus, I had met him casually. I knew nothing of the man—his antecedents, his character, his abilities. When he modestly requested the privilege of making an explanatory statement he did so knowing that sentiment was against him.

"No one who was present at that meeting could forget the manner in which Troy Middleton faced the situation. His approach was calm. He entered no denial of alleged facts. He expressed understanding of the spirit and intent of the proposed resolution. He stated that not all of the essential facts had appeared in the press reports. He made but one simple request, namely, that no action be taken until a full examination of all relevant facts had been made by a committee of the conference. His forthrightness and his candor commanded the respect of all who were present.

"No official action was taken. No word concerning the matter appears in the *Proceedings of the Conference* for that year. It is possible that most of those present that day have forgotten many of the details of the episode. It is doubtful, however, that any who were there could forget that on that day Troy Middleton demonstrated his great ability to handle a most difficult problem in a statesmanlike manner. From that day forward he 'belonged.' During subsequent years it was my privilege to work with General Middleton on regional committees and boards where I came to know him well and to regard him highly. His calm judgment and administrative skill gained for him a secure place in the confidence and esteem of the educators of the South."

Campbell's recollections of the conference were borne out by Middleton's. The new LSU president recalled that Chancellor Harvey Branscomb of Vanderbilt University "really took them apart" after the proposed object of censure had further acquainted conference members with the circumstances of Stoke's resignation and his acceptance of the LSU presidency. "President Rufus Harris of Tulane also spoke up in my support," Middleton recalled. "In 1956, when I was elected president of the Southern University Conference, Rufus got up and reminded the group, 'Five years ago you were trying to throw this man out and now you've made him president.'

"I never met a man who did more for high standards of education than did Rufus Harris. He not only had high ideals, he lived up to them," Middleton recalled.

In the February issue of the *LSU Alumni News* he wrote to alumni, characteristically:

"I greet you as a green and humble chief executive of your University. When, as commandant of cadets, I worked with many of you in your cadet and coed days and held the reins of discipline over you, it did not occur to me that some day the tables would be turned and you, the alumni, would be not unwilling to tell me how to conduct the affairs of the university. This is not meant to imply that I will not welcome your guidance and counsel because such is the prerogative of an alumnus and a sport in which I have engaged from time to time.

"I assume the office of president of your university with a full realization that the duties carry many important responsibilities. Not unmindful of the fact that no individual has the ability to solve all of the many problems which will arise, I approach my duties with a knowledge that the university has loyal and capable people on its faculty, its staff, and among its graduates and former students. I have had no honor which equals that of being privileged to serve as your president and to be listed among those splendid men who have preceded me. I regard the office to which I have been promoted as a symbol, and I am aware that the man who serves there must do so with a high sense of duty, loyalty, and honor. To this I dedicate my future. I seek no personal gain. The greatest reward that I could have when my days are done is to have served so that the alumni might say, 'He was one of us.' "

With the opening of the fall semester in September, 1951, enrollment on all the university campuses totaled 6,608, exceeding earlier estimates by 1,000. For this first full academic year under Middleton's presidency, 5,664 students were gathered on the Baton Rouge campus. At the Medical School in New Orleans were 438, along with 307 in the School of Nursing Education. At F. T. Nicholls Junior College in Thibodaux were 181. Only

18 were enrolled in the School of Vocational Agriculture at Chambers, a figure which had consistently run far below original expectations for the highly specialized school in farm management. The center became the nucleus for LSU at Alexandria, which opened its doors as a two-year branch of the university in 1960. Total enrollment, pinched by the Korean war, was off 666 from the 1950 figure of 7,272, a drop exceeding 9 percent.

Coincident with the start of the new school year, Middleton looked back to the beginnings of the debate over whether LSU most needed a library, a stadium, an auditorium, or an addition to the Medical School in New Orleans. His own priorities were a new library and an auditorium, then the Medical School addition.

Middleton had heard while he was comptroller under President Stoke that the state might soon be having some surplus funds. He was told by the state treasurer, A. P. Tugwell, that the Department of Education would within the year complete paying off a bond issue with money dedicated to that purpose by the legislature. Tugwell said, "The last payment on that bond issue is coming up. If you can get Governor Earl Long to go along with you, you can get the dedication changed to give the university the money." Comptroller Middleton told President Stoke of this chance at a windfall. Stoke urged him to do what he could to get the state to give the money to LSU to help with its acute building needs.

"I made an appointment with Earl Long and took Dean J. G. Lee of the College of Agriculture along with me. I told him, 'Governor, we need a library and an auditorium and an addition to the Medical School. I understand that $300,000 a year dedicated to retiring a Department of Education bond issue will no longer be needed. Can we have that money each year for the LSU building needs?' The governor asked me, 'How big an auditorium will you want?' I told him we'd need to seat at least 3,500. He replied, 'That's too small. How about me getting you $50,000 a year more to give you a total of $350,000 a year? I'll get the legislature to go along.'

"I came back to the campus and told Dr. Stoke. He was overjoyed. We gave the word to the Board of Supervisors. The board agreed that this was a real stroke of luck. But within a few days, T. P. (Red) Heard, director of athletics, heard about it. He began working on the board members. Some of the very board members who'd approved seeking the money for a library and auditorium turned right around and switched their votes to put the money into an addition to the stadium. And that's the way the matter went to the legislature. The stadium had no business being given first priority, but that's the way things worked out," Middleton recalled.

"After I became president, I took up the matter again with the Board of Supervisors, asking them to separate the stadium from the other building needs. Eventually we got approval for completion of the stadium—the board always came back to that—and for an addition to the Medical School, and, finally, for a new library building. I stayed with my quest until we got an appropriation to build the library. Though it took several years to win this battle, I ran into some rear guard actions from within the board over location of the library.

"I held out for the spot on which the library was eventually built. Some people objected strenuously, saying that to build it there would do great esthetic damage; it would destroy the view of the inner campus quadrangle, they said. Well, there just weren't any great, sweeping vistas to destroy. My idea about a library was that it should be conveniently located. Board member Theo Cangelosi told me how wrong I was: the library should be built several blocks south of there, well away from the classroom buildings. I continued to hold out for the central location. When someone told me that some of the faculty might object, I said somewhat mischievously that I was going to insist on this location so that the faculty could have no excuse for avoiding using the library; it would be across their paths no matter what direction they took on campus. That was one battle that I won. The library went up right at the heart of the campus, where it should have gone. After all, a library—and a good one—is the essential heart of any worthwhile university.

"I insisted that the library foundation be constructed strong enough to support two more floors in addition to the original three, knowing that it would be necessary in another decade or so to add more stack capacity. And in 1973, it was obvious that the library's holdings required additional space," he said.

Aside from his university responsibilities, during his first year in the presidency Middleton was asked by an old army friend to help with a grave situation. In the spring of 1951, General J. Lawton (Lightning Joe) Collins, who had just been made Chief of Staff of the army, called Middleton from Washington. "Joe said, 'I've got a job for you. You can't say no. I can't tell you about it on the telephone. I'm sending a courier. He'll be at your office in the morning.'

"What do you do in a case like that? I told Joe to send his courier. We were old friends. If Joe needed my help, I was prepared to do what I could, though I had no idea what he was talking about. When General Collins' courier arrived next day he told me as much as he knew. The matter involved alleged wholesale violations of the honor code of the Cadet Corps at the United States Military Academy at West Point. I was to serve on a special committee with retired General R. M. Danford and Judge Learned Hand, a distinguished jurist, to look into the cadets' handling of the inquiry. We were not to take over the investigation but to oversee what the cadets themselves did in the case," Middleton recalled.

"What had happened was this: The honor representative of a cadet company at the academy had developed suspicions that cheating on examinations was going on at the academy—not among a few but among a considerable number. The honor code at the academy is clear cut. It provides for dismissal of anyone who cheats. It further provides for dismissal of anyone who observes cheating and does not report it. When the honor representative of a company was convinced by his own observation that cheating was going on he did the honorable thing; he went to see the superintendent of the academy. When he asked the adjutant for an appointment, he indicated that the matter was serious and quickly got the appointment. The honor representative told the superintendent that it was unlikely that a solid case could be made unless the superintendent authorized the representative to join the cheating group. He was given the go ahead.

"When he had all the evidence he needed, the cadet honor board took over. A preliminary report by a faculty committee at the academy was not a whitewash but it went quite light on punishment. General Danford, Judge Hand, and I were there as involved observers. We met at West Point in two sessions. The first lasted ten days. We drove back nightly to New York City rather than stay in Highland Falls, the nearby village, in an effort to keep our deliberations out of the press until they were complete. Our presence in Highland Falls would have been all too obvious; in New York we were swallowed up. We went back to West Point for another session after the final report on the matter was written. It was our recommendation, painful as it was to me, that all the cheaters should be dismissed from the academy. There can be no winking at the honor system—else there can be no honor system—we decided. With our concurrence, eighty-two cadets were dismissed for cheating, including most of the members of the army football squad. Army football suffered, no doubt, but there was never any question as to whether the cheaters should go. They went," Middleton recalled. A headline in the New Orleans *Times-Picayune* wryly summarized the case when it was announced to the press: "Army Football Team Severely Penalized for Illegal Passing."

"As a result of our participation in the investigation," Middleton recalled, "the Military Academy made some changes. I told the superintendent and others on the faculty, as well as the cadets we worked with, that it was unrealistic to continue giving an exam one day to one regiment and repeating the exam the next day with another regiment. It brought temptation on the scene. Now temptation is to be resisted—we all know that, I said. Then I told a story about how I had trained a bird dog with a stuffed sock representing a downed quail. As long as I was around the dog would retrieve the sock and bring it to me. He wouldn't touch it thereafter. But one day I had to go in the house on some errand. When I returned, my dog had torn that sock into tiny bits. He couldn't resist the temptation. Don't, I said, leave a stuffed sock lying around. At our suggestion, the practice of giving identical examinations on successive days was halted."

The assignment at West Point was anything but a pleasant one. Middleton was tapped for it by Chief of Staff Collins because Collins knew of Middleton's reputation for rigorous fairness. Middleton was not a graduate of the Military Academy, yet no army officer, retired or on active duty, commanded more respect. When an opening came on the Board of Visitors of the Military Academy in 1952, Middleton was asked to accept appointment to a three-year term. He served from 1952 to 1955.

"You know," he recalled, "I got some awfully nasty letters after the cheaters were dismissed from the Military Academy; some of the letters came from Regular Army people. I suppose they were thinking of the old days, when a man's rank in his class was determined by his grades. You stayed in that position in the Regular Army. This was important to an old timer. It was not so important at this time, but the old test-giving practice at the Military Academy had persisted."

With enrollment down and income from student fees sharply reduced, the university went out to prospective students by setting up extension courses at Camp Polk near Leesville in September, 1951. Pleasant Hall, which was no longer needed as a women's dormitory when enrollment dwindled, was converted to a conference center in the fall as the university sought to reach greater numbers of adults. Middleton turned the first spade of earth at ground-breaking ceremonies for the new LSU Laboratory School and construction went on through 1952.

Charles E. Smith, professor of history, was named head of the university's new evening college, which offered a degree program to those whose schooling had been interrupted and who could no longer attend regular daytime classes. A degree of Bachelor of General Studies was authorized. Middleton, who had pushed for creation of the evening program, told of one woman who came to him later to say that she had earned a degree at last after having been out of college more than thirty years.

In a January, 1952, report in the *Alumni News*, Middleton wrote: "For several months now your university has been reevaluating its entire program of instruction, research and public service. It is a penetrating analysis which will lead to considerable redirection and might very well set a course for LSU to follow for many years to come." Penetrating, it was. Faculty members were asked to evaluate their own grading standards. They did so, with considerable grumbling. At Middleton's request, department heads were asked to study their course listings in the General Catalogue and to dispense with any course that had not been taught within the past three years. To the person outside the academic world, this may have seemed to be about as routine a request as could be made. Not so with every department head and faculty member, however; some saw threats to their academic integrity. When it was all over, more than four hundred listings were pruned from the catalogue. The likelihood is strong that none of them were missed.

When the Board of Supervisors met on February 2, 1952, at the start of Middleton's second year in office, the members agreed to ask the legislature for an additional $5,000,000 to offset declining sums coming from student fees and to help bring faculty salary levels up from the "genteel poverty" in which Middleton found them when he took office. The board also voted to seek additional funds from the legislature to permit construction of a new library—Hill Memorial Library having long been overwhelmed by the books and students it could not accommodate—and an auditorium that students were clamoring for.

The simmering controversy was pointed up again when the Board of Supervisors met April 5 and decided, the *Alumni News* reported, that

"LSU needs a library in the immediate future more than an enclosed stadium in some nebulous era when construction bans are lifted. In an informal agreement, the board authorized President Middleton to place before the legislature a request for $3,500,000 for the badly needed library. A portion of the sum would be made up by allotting $2,350,000 originally set aside for the south end of the stadium, to the library fund. President Middleton told the board members he 'would lay his cards on the table' with the legislature and tell them, 'The university needs $3,500,000 to build a new library. It has $2,350,000 set aside by legislative act for a stadium project. It cannot build a stadium now. It will be all right with the university if the legislature wants LSU to use the $2,350,000 to apply on the library, with the possible provision of funds later for enlarging the stadium.' "

Middleton went further: "I do not believe the people of this state will understand why we would let money lie around unused when we need a new library so badly. I believe they would say go ahead and use it now for what we need."

Why did the board majority turn bashful and insist upon an informal agreement rather than a formal vote on the library and stadium matter? It was the least painful way out; in the absence of a recorded vote, no member need defend himself against a charge that he favored football over a library. The board agreed to pay $63,000 in architects fees for the drawing of plans to enclose the south end of the stadium, increasing seating capacity from 45,000 to more than 65,000, at this meeting. This clearly indicated the majority's intent.

Theo Cangelosi asked, "Have we ever filled the stadium except for games with Tulane?" Middleton said no. Margaret Dixon, another board member from Baton Rouge, who was also managing editor of the Baton Rouge *Morning Advocate*, sought to persuade fellow board members to go on record in favor of a library instead of a stadium addition. Middleton reminded the group that since the legislature had already allotted the money for the stadium addition, a legislative amendment would be required to change the dedication. "Then," said Cangelosi, "it seems to me that LSU would be much better off if we made such a recommendation."

J. Stewart Slack, a member from Shreveport, disagreed. He said, "The whole bond issue was predicated upon LSU getting money for the Medical School. It was approved by the legislature with the provision that a portion of the money be used to complete the stadium. We need money for other things—no question about that—but we would never have received the money for the Medical School if the stadium project had not been included. I know; I talked to a lot of people. A majority of the legislature wanted the stadium completed. We would not be carrying out our part of the bargain. We should go ahead with the stadium plans, whether we complete it next year, or in two years, or later." He was joined by C. J. Dugas, a member from Donaldsonville.

Thomas Leigh of Monroe spoke up for the library. "Circumstances flatly prevent us from completing the stadium project now," he said, and went on to urge that the board would be keeping faith with the legislature in seeking rededication of the funds from the stadium to the library.

When Leigh suggested that the board exert some leadership and say what it thought were the best ways to spend LSU funds, he ran into objections from another board member from Shreveport, James Smitherman, who said it would be unwise to ask the legislature to undo something it had already done. The discussion ran on awhile, but it was obvious what the majority sentiment was. Mrs. Dixon withdrew her motion calling for a formal vote. The stadium had triumphed.

At that same meeting on April 5, in its open session, the board voted to increase Middleton's salary from $16,000 to $18,000. Then it went into executive session, as had been its custom. Mrs. Dixon, only recently appointed to the board, was a veteran newspaper reporter. She knew when there were genuine reasons for conducting an executive session and when there were not. For the next day's *Morning Advocate*, she wrote an account of the actions taken in the executive session (knowing that Louisiana law requires that any actions binding on the public purse must be taken in open session). Mrs. Dixon reported that the board had approved a request for capital outlay totaling $4,542,000 and including a library building. She also reported that the board had voted 6–5 to seek $500,000 for a men's dormitory at the School of Vocational Agriculture at Alexandria, and noted that the minority's objections were based on the extremely small enrollment at the school.

On the back cover of the May–June, 1952, issue of the *Alumni News*, Middleton again recorded his view that LSU's prime need was a library. But none appeared to be coming soon.

The legislature met for sixty days, beginning shortly before the second

semester of the 1951–1952 session ended. It rejected the university proposal to release the tied-up stadium enlargement funds for construction of
a library.

When the board met in the fall, it authorized a study of distinguished
professorships which might be helpful in drawing to the university ranking
scholars in all fields, an idea with great appeal for Middleton. The board
session hadn't exactly started out to create these professorships, later authorized as the Boyd Professorships, after David F. and Thomas D. Boyd,
former presidents of the university. The members earlier had heard Dean
Hebert of the Law School (he had returned from private practice to the
deanship) explain his difficulties in holding onto law faculty members who
could earn considerably more money in private practice. To help hold the
law faculty, the board authorized substantial increases in pay to them. This
action led several board members to suggest that word of this action would
almost certainly lead to serious repercussions from other faculty areas.
"Why not," someone suggested, "reward faculty excellence in other departments by creating distinguished professorships. We have some excellent men around, worthy of such designation now."

To ease the pains of the full faculty, the board authorized payment
of a 5 percent increase to cover additional costs of living. The board also
heard Middleton report that, in accordance with its wish, the university
had made application to the National Production Authority (NPA) for
permission to proceed with the stadium enclosure, though he doubted that
the NPA would approve.

Students were pressing again for their favorite building project—an
auditorium. Middleton told the board that such a project would probably
have to wait until 1960. (It waited longer, being completed as the LSU
Assembly Center in 1971, with full financing from the state rather than
through the university budget, thanks in part to the repopularization of
basketball during the Pete Maravich era.) Meanwhile, he said, something
would have to be done with the John M. Parker Agricultural Center arena
acoustics. Offices ringed the outer concourse and research went forward in
the adjacent laboratories. Students and the public, however, usually saw
only the arena portion. Commencements were held here in the spring and
summer, and no amount of airing could fully dispel the lingering reminders
of hard use of the arena by cattle and horses during the spring rodeo.
Squadrons of sparrows nested in the high reaches of the great vaulted roof,

adding their shrill accompaniment to the vocalist's version of "The Star Spangled Banner" or the "LSU Alma Mater." Basketball was enjoying a revival after almost twenty lean years, with tall Bob Pettit leading the Tigers to a rare Southeastern Conference championship.

All the complaints about the arena's acoustics fed upward to Middleton. "The time has come," he told the board, "when we should either do something about the sound in the place or stop talking about it. I get cussed out every time we have a convocation there. People say they can't even hear in the front row. We have plans under way to spend about $100,000 to improve the acoustics."

At the fall board meeting, Middleton reminded the body that the university was heading into "patterns of consolidation" which would merge the language departments into one modern language department and would place the Social Science Department under the Sociology Department. Charles E. Smith, who had launched the night college program, was appointed dean of the university in the fall of 1952. He pushed the work of consolidation and tightening of grading standards.

In September, the largest freshman class registered, running the total in the Junior Division to 2,359. Unused dormitory rooms found tenants again. The academic pulse quickened. Veterans came back from the Korean War. Some of the complications attending low enrollments were eased.

The Board of Supervisors, at its December 6, 1952, meeting, proceeded with the earlier proposal to create distinguished professorships to recognize outstanding faculty members. Boyd Professorships would go to faculty members who had attained regional or national distinction. Administrators with the rank of director or higher were not to be eligible. An addition of at least $1,000 in salary would be made, and a floor of $9,600 was established.

"The idea for the Boyd Professorships originated with me," Middleton recalled. "One of the first things I set out to do was to reward excellence among faculty members. I proposed to the Faculty and Studies Committee of the Board of Supervisors that we work out a plan. I talked it over with deans, suggesting a minimum salary increase of $1,000 a year and no maximum. I thought that an outstanding Boyd Professor could be paid more than the president. Recommendations for these professorships could be made to a faculty committee. I went around to offices of faculty members to talk up the idea, instead of asking them to come to me. Among those suggested for the faculty committee which would choose the Boyd Professors was Dr. C. W. Edgerton, professor of botany."

"Dr. Edgerton said, 'You don't want me on this selection committee; I'd be too tough.' I told him, 'That's exactly why I want you.' When I unfolded the criteria for a Boyd Professorship before the Board of Supervisors, several board members said that the requirements were too rigid. I told them rigidity in this instance was exactly what we intended. Our first three Boyd Professors, Dr. Eric Voegelin, Dr. Philip West, and Dr. T. Harry Williams, were splendid choices. Their selection started the Boyd Professorships on just the right note."

With the start of the second semester, the University Laboratory School moved into its new building, under construction since August, 1951. Alumni kept alive the warm debate over stadium and library priorities, calling upon the Alumni Council to hear both sides. The council president, T. C. Glaze, brought the council together February 21. From former Alumni Federation president Carlos Spaht, the council heard a review of the two-and-a-half-year-old controversy. Spaht noted that the legislature in its 1952 session had eliminated the library and substituted a School of Veterinary Medicine, despite Middleton's argument that a library was preferable to a larger stadium. The Alumni Council finally voted, 11–4, in favor of a resolution expressing confidence in the legislature and in the Board of Supervisors. Three days later, the New Orleans Metropolitan Division alumni chapter voted to ask the board to cancel stadium enlargment plans because they were an "unjustified present expenditure of a large amount of university funds." If the board declined to cancel, the New Orleans alumni asked that a one-year delay of the stadium enclosure be ordered.

Middleton went to Monroe in February to talk to alumni from northeast Louisiana. He reported that faculty salaries had been increased an average of 15 percent in two years and that though, "This does not place the top salary people at the university with other top salary people, nor the lower ones on scale with some high school teachers, nevertheless some progress has been made, and nothing is better than for a man to be able to buy a new suit every three years and a new dress for his wife every five years." He also told of the success of University College, the evening program, in drawing 268 students the first year and 337 in its second year, with 700 day students also taking advantage of the night class offerings.

LSU athletics was booming too. The Tiger basketball team won the Southeastern Conference championship with a record of 22–1 overall and 13–0 in the conference, and went to the National Collegiate Athletic Association regional tournament. Middleton, who had been introduced to basketball in his last year at Mississippi A & M and had played some at Fort Leavenworth, rarely missed a home game. Four of football coach Gaynell Tinsley's assistants had resigned after an unsuccessful 1952 season. Their replacements included Charles McClendon, who arrived in time for spring practice.

After a last-ditch fight by opponents of the measure, the Board of Supervisors finally ended debate on enlargement of the stadium, February 27, 1953. It voted 8–5 to accept the bid of $1,242,342 by Farnsworth and Chambers, Inc., of Houston, for enclosing the south end of the stadium. The board deliberated six hours that day. To advocates of a library, member Lewis Gottlieb said, "You had every opportunity to have the state law changed. You say the state is aroused. If it's aroused why doesn't the legislature express itself? If you reject these bids you're insulting the intelligence of the legislature. You'll be telling them they voted $2,000,000 without knowing what they were doing."

James Smitherman of Shreveport, moving to award the contract to the low bidder, said, "I believe we should carry out the mandate of the legislature. I do not believe it is wise for us to fly in the face of those from whom we get money."

Ella V. Aldrich Schwing, a recent appointee, suggested that the board go on record in favor of a library over the stadium enclosure and that Governor Robert Kennon be asked to inform the legislature of the board's stand; additionally, the legislature would be polled for its views. Mrs. Schwing's motion failed, 6–7. She was joined by Margaret Dixon, Thomas W. Leigh, Homer L. Brinkley, J. M. McLemore, and C. J. Dugas. Dugas in an earlier meeting had voted with stadium advocates. When the final vote on the stadium contract was taken, Dugas joined the prevailing side, which included Tom W. Dutton, Stewart Slack, Lewis Gottlieb, J. E. Smitherman, Horace Wilkinson, Jr., John J. Doles, and Theo Cangelosi. Cangelosi in earlier discussions had been a strong advocate of the library in preference to the stadium enclosure.

Mrs. Dixon, after hearing from spectators at the board meeting that private lobbying by members of the Athletic Department staff had gone on at legislative sessions, made a motion to investigate the department. She was ruled out of order by Chairman Slack, whose ruling was sustained, 9–3. Mrs. Schwing, an LSU librarian for nineteen years, declared it "outright treason" to vote for the stadium over the library. Leigh said he would continue opposing the stadium enclosure. Mrs. Dixon said that the legislature's earlier actions did not have to be accepted as final. "I have enough confidence in the legislature that education will sell itself. We should vote our convictions, not our fears," she said.

The stadium prevailed despite strong faculty and student opposition. With the final vote taken, the board appointed a committee to deal with library plans. It would recommend a site, a general design, and a means of financing, as well as prepare an estimated cost.

In April, 1953, the Alumni Federation decided to honor Middleton for his long service to the university, by seeking alumni contributions to a Troy H. Middleton Portrait Fund, with the expected surplus funds to be placed in the Troy H. Middleton Scholarship. The early response was extraordinary. Within three months, 1,000 individuals had mailed in contributions. The portrait commission, after a year's search, was awarded to an LSU alumnus, Burny Myrick, who had earned his bachelor's and master's degrees in art and who, during three years of service in the army in World War II, had painted numerous portraits of military men.

In his September, 1953, report to alumni, Middleton noted that the upturn in enrollments recorded in 1952–1953 was expected to continue, and that 8,450 students were expected where 7,800 had enrolled the preceding September. The enrollment increase made women's dormitory space inadequate, the president said. Either Pleasant Hall must go back to its original use as a women's dormitory or additional dormitories must be built to accommodate women. Pleasant Hall, Middleton reported, had been used by 37,238 persons during the 1952–1953 school year, for continuing education. He also said that work on the enclosure of the south end of the stadium had been moving so fast that part of it was expected to be ready for the first game in September and that the job would be finished by the time of the Tulane game late in November.

With the library-stadium controversy behind it by six months, the Board of Supervisors met September 19 and agreed to give priority to a new library, to cost $3,600,000 and to be built in front of and connected with the existing Hill Memorial Library. Departmental libraries would go back to the new library, except in the case of the Law School and perhaps a few others, Dean of the University Charles Smith explained. The new library would seat 2,500 and accommodate a million volumes. No sooner had circulation been given to the announcement that branch libraries would be recalled, than Dean Smith began receiving reasons why departments could not possibly surrender their holdings to the main library.

Other building needs listed by the board for the next five years, in an $18,000,000 program, included an engineering building, an addition to the chemical engineering building, an agricultural extension building, an addition to the physics building, a building for F. T. Nicholls Junior College at Thibodaux, a dormitory and general purpose building at the School of Vocational Agriculture near Alexandria, additional housing for men, plant pathology and sugar cane breeding facilities, a home economics building, a dairy department building, a forestry building, a music school addition, a poultry laboratory, a laboratory school addition, a physical education building, an additional vocational education building, and an auditorium.

Looking to the May, 1954, session of the legislature, Middleton began early to lay in ammunition to support the university's growing financial needs. Louisianians were told that the university had, in eight years, 1946–1953, awarded 13,535 degrees, whereas in the eighty years preceding World War II, 1860–1939, it had conferred 11,534 degrees. Louisianians heard that while undergraduate enrollments in the university were up 38 percent over ten years before, graduate and professional enrollments were up by 184 percent; and that cost of educating graduates and professionals was more than double that of educating undergraduates.

Louisianians were told also that state appropriations for education since 1940–1941 had increased 352 percent while LSU's appropriations had gone up only 101 percent. They read that LSU received 7.6 percent of state receipts in 1940–1941 and 4.1 percent of state receipts in 1952–1953. They were told also that each citizen's average tax contribution to LSU amounted to only $4.52 a year.

The university's information campaign, headed by Middleton, must have been effective. For Middleton, in his September, 1954, message to alumni, reported that the legislature had given the university every cent that it asked for, including funds for a new library and other buildings urgently needed. "Confidence in Louisiana State University as the state's major institution of higher learning has never been more fully expressed than it was at the recent biennial session of the legislature," he wrote. The university asked for and received $25,357,771.12 from tax-supported sources, an increase of $4,636,960. Most of the increase was for higher faculty and staff salaries.

The university's success with the legislature was in large measure a reflection of the legislature's confidence in Middleton. At his insistence, $800,000 had been trimmed from departmental requests before the budget was submitted. He believed, in 1954 as he had when he was comptroller under Stoke in 1947–1950, that the university budget request should reflect the absolute needs and not a penny more. Stoke had reproved him gently on more than one occasion for his "saving attitude."

Dan Borth, who was comptroller of the university during Middleton's eleven-year administration, said of him:

Basically the General was conservative and liberal at the same time. He wanted a happy faculty, one which could bring credit to LSU and the state, but he was also mindful of the economics of the state. He always instructed that the budget be prepared for the amount he thought was reasonable. Once prepared on that basis, he would rarely back down but would fight for what he thought was right. Budget presentations were serious business with him.

In budget meetings with the legislature he was a master at getting the committee on his side—that is, the university's. In private conversations with me, the General used to characterize me as his 'hatchet man,' the individual who would state cases bluntly and frankly and let the chips fall where they may. Of course, the General ameliorated my recommendations in some instances. In making personnel recommendations for the deans, academic directors, and other chief administrative officers, it was understood between us that I would make recommendations by position without attention to the personality in the position. The General, in turn, would raise or lower my figure, depending upon his reactions to the individual in the position.

Although freshman English had long been a major hurdle for excessive numbers of LSU students, as was true in almost all universities, until 1949 the faculty and administration had done little more than lament the continuing incompetence of students taking the basic freshman course. That year, an advisory committee on Junior Division achievement was set up to study problems relating to freshmen. Freshman English led all. Dean Cecil G. Taylor of the College of Arts and Sciences, Dean Stephen A.

Caldwell of the Junior Division, and members of the English faculty quickly established what just about everybody already knew about the existing
teaching of freshman English: (1) too many students who completed the
course continued to write poorly; (2) too many students didn't pass the
course.

Rejecting on all grounds any thought of lowering standards simply
to assure that more students would pass the course, the investigators decided to test incoming freshmen to determine their ability and their preparation in English. They found that 14 percent—one student in seven—
performed no better than an average sixth grade pupil. A few did no better
than a fourth grader. Happily, a few scored as well as a college graduate.
These findings gave the English faculty something to go on. They had been
directing their instruction at about 60 percent of their students, overshoot-
ing about 30 percent, and undershooting the remaining 10 percent.

The Cooperative English Test showed that LSU freshmen were equal
in aptitude to the national average, but that they came to LSU with seriously deficient backgrounds. Acknowledging this fact, the committee set out
to devise courses of instruction that would serve the needs of freshmen on
three levels. English courses 1A, 1B, and 1C were planned. The Faculty
Council gave its approval. The freshman would be required to complete
one, two, or three semesters of English, depending upon his aptitude and
his industry. He would receive credit for all.

In 1A the student would be taught principles he had missed in high
school, including the basics of grammar and punctuation and the mechanics of sentence construction, receiving a great deal of individual attention.
In 1B he learned to organize material, to meet conventional standards of
usage, and to strive for clarity and exactness. In 1C he would be encouraged to seek smoothness, variety, and individuality in expression.

The new system of teaching freshman English went into effect in
1951–1952, Middleton's first full academic year as head of the university.
He examined with keen interest the test findings which showed that LSU
freshmen, under the new system, pulled themselves up from a substantial
deficit to a standing equal with the national average at the end of their
freshman year, with a mean score of 55.76 upon entering and a mean score
of 60.72 upon completing the year. The national average for the year was
59 at entrance and 60.5 at completion. The new system quickly proved it-

self. Bleak unhappiness with freshman English was not dispelled among all freshmen, but it remained a problem for only a relative few.

Middleton recalled another kind of problem—this one an instance of fatherly indulgence. There had been considerable talk on campus about the desirability of reducing the number of cars brought to the campus by students. One father in a high elective office engaged Middleton in earnest conversation. Finally he got around to what he'd come to talk about: "Why don't you ban student ownership of cars on campus?" he asked.

"I replied, 'What's the matter? Is your trouble that you don't have the courage to tell your boy that he can't have a car here?' Middleton recalled. "The father turned bright red. That was it, all right. He wanted me to say no when he couldn't bring himself to do so. From time to time, members of the Board of Supervisors brought up comparable questions. When I would tell them to have at it—that they had the authority to deal with car ownership on campus—they backed away every time."

Enrollment on the Baton Rouge campus in September, 1954, reached 8,202. Registrar John A. Hunter, after studying figures from a State Department of Education report on elementary school enrollment, forecast an enrollment of 10,000 on the Baton Rouge campus by 1960, 12,000 by 1965, and 14,000 by 1970.

To meet the needs of the day and to cope with the steady growth of the student body, the university in 1955 entered its most ambitious building program, involving $9,000,000 in new buildings, expansion, remodeling, and repairs. Plans for the new library were delayed by the complexity of the project, but were ready by midyear. A $200,000 gymnasium for the Laboratory School was begun. A $300,000 building for the Forestry School, involving the new lift-slab technique of construction, was started. A $750,000 building for Agricultural Extension Division offices was authorized, with extensive parking space being provided at Highland and South Stadium Roads. A new creamery and dairy plant, costing $350,000, was on the planning boards. Two new wings were planned for Laville Hall, to accommodate 324 more women students, with the money coming from a recently floated bond issue. The cafeteria on the ground floor of Highland Hall was converted to dormitory rooms. A new Highland Cafeteria, costing $325,000, was completed, to serve 350 diners at the time. An $850,000 state-funded feed and fertilizer laboratory was authorized, replacing a facility which had outgrown its space in the state capitol. Veterinary research facilities were authorized to be built with the remaining money from the 1950 bond issue. At the underused School of Vocational Agriculture near Alexandria, a $300,000 administration building including classrooms, a cafeteria, and a dormitory, was authorized. A $750,000 gymnasium and classroom building at Nicholls Junior College at Thibodaux was authorized. The original Pentagon Barracks, constructed in 1925, were thoroughly renovated, with new electrical and plumbing facilities and asphalt tile going down to replace badly worn wooden floors. The university bought land adjacent to the North Louisiana Hill Farm Experiment Station at Homer and expanded sweet potato research facilities at Chase. Another $100,000 went for alterations and additions to the chemical engineering building, for renovations in Coates Laboratories. Finally, efforts were begun to waterproof the stucco finish on Peabody Hall; if these were successful, the same technique would be applied on other buildings, all of which had a tendency to soak up much of the rain falling in Baton Rouge's humid climate.

The LSU football team, in its seventh season under Gaynell Tinsley, had done poorly in 1954, winning five and losing six games, defeating minor opponents and losing to major foes, with the single exception that the Tigers defeated Tulane, 14–13. Tulane had won but one game that season and led LSU 13–0 before the Tigers finally came alive. The year before, Tulane had been heavily favored, but LSU had triumphed 16–0, and Tinsley had been rewarded with a pay raise. In his seven years as head coach, Tinsley had won thirty-five games, lost thirty-four and tied six.

Soon after the season ended there was talk that a number of members of the Board of Supervisors wanted to buy up Tinsley's contract and dismiss him, but this number was less than a majority in December. By February, 1955, a majority of the board came round to the December minority's way of thinking.

Middleton requested a special meeting of the board on February 5. The board dismissed Tinsley, agreeing to pay out the two remaining years of his contract at $12,500 a year. The board also retired T. P. Heard from the athletic directorship after his service of twenty-three years. The special board meeting was called after the Athletic Council, made up of faculty, alumni, and students, had several days earlier recommended that Tinsley be discharged for cause, which would have permitted the university to cancel his contract without paying out the last two years of the obligation. Heard, knowing of the Athletic Council recommendation, sent his resignation to the Board of Supervisors. The board accepted Heard's resignation but found no substance to allegations that Tinsley had recruited an athlete whose scholastic record was below acceptable standards. Heard, who had lobbied hard against the university's larger interests in seeking a stadium enclosure when other needs were greater, was let go without any great regrets. In Tinsley's case, the regrets were principally financial— $25,000 for two years of coaching he did not have to deliver.

"Coach Tinsley's trouble," Middleton recalled, "was that he was not a strong disciplinarian or a good recruiter. To get a quality player he would accept several second-raters pushed by high school coaches. I told Gus that he was going at this business wrong. When he asked how he should go about it, I said, 'Go to the high school principal first for information on the prospective recruit. Then go to the corner druggist to find out his estimate of the boy's reputation in town. Then go to a faculty member who has taught the boy. If all three didn't recommend the athlete, scratch him from the list. He'll bring nothing but trouble.'

"Just such a case came along," Middleton said. "He was a real troublemaker. I told Gus he'd signed himself a problem. Gus said that the coach had said that the boy would be a great ball player. I asked him if he had checked with the druggist and the teacher. He hadn't, of course.

"The gang most critical of Gus Tinsley was the gambling bunch who liked to put some money on games. They stood around on corners and frequented the bars, talking football as if it were the most important thing in town. The same bunch started out after Gus Tinsley's successor when he didn't do so well in his first couple of years." Middleton said. "Gus Tinsley, at bottom, was just too nice a guy for his own good."

The selection of a successor to Tinsley excited more discussion than any campus personnel matter since Middleton had replaced Stoke December 28, 1950. When the board's decision had been reached, board member Oliver (Ike) Carriere went straight to the assistant coaches' office in the stadium to report what had happened. The assistant coaches, hoping that one of their number might be chosen to succeed Tinsley, were at the point of writing their choices on slips of paper when Carriere arrived. He advised against this move since the board had already decided to go outside the LSU coaching ranks for a replacement. Carriere also advised the assistants that he would recommend to the board that the assistants be retained when a new coach was chosen.

Peter Finney, in his LSU Press book, *The Fighting Tigers*, a history of the school's football, wrote that Carriere telephoned Middleton, who agreed that it was reasonable that the assistant coaches be retained and asked that the assistants be informed that defensive coach Charles Mc-Clendon would be acting coach and Harry Rabenhorst acting athletic director until both jobs were filled.

A board-faculty committee of five was appointed to begin the search for a new coach. They were under instructions not to seek: (1) a high school coach, (2) a current assistant at LSU, (3) anyone who had coached or played as a professional in 1954, (4) a head coach under contract, (5) a head coach who had been discharged, (6) an assistant coach in the Southeastern Conference. Six interviews were soon set up, with coaches not on the proscribed list: Stanley Galloway of Southeastern Louisiana College; Ben Martin, an assistant at the United States Naval Academy; and Paul Dietzel, an assistant at the United States Military Academy, would come in one day and be followed the next by Ed McKeever, who had been an assistant at LSU and had entered private business in Baton Rouge; Chuck Purvis, an assistant coach at the University of Illinois; and Perry Moss, an assistant at the University of Miami.

Dietzel was the eventual choice of the screening committee and of the Board of Supervisors. The personable twenty-nine-year-old Dietzel took over a staff of assistants all of whom were his seniors. In his sports column in the New Orleans *Times-Picayune*, sports editor Bill Keefe wrote on February 15, "Because of the Army angle I'd venture the prediction that Dietzel will be the next Tiger coach. General Middleton's opinion is so highly regarded by all connected with LSU and his army contacts so strong I don't think it out of order to call the shot on the new Tiger coach."

Keefe was right about Dietzel but wrong about Middleton's feelings in the matter. "Dietzel would not have been my choice at the time. I'd have picked Ben Martin of the Naval Academy. He had graduated number five in his class at Annapolis. He was the senior midshipman. He had lettered in four or five sports at the academy. He was an assistant at the Naval Academy. When a member of the Board of Supervisors asked me to choose between Martin and Dietzel I indicated my preference for Martin but said that I had nothing against Dietzel. I place great value on a person who stands at the top of things, as Martin did. He was obviously a good athlete, a good student, president of his class. You just had to give him a high score. He went soon to become coach at the United States Air Force Academy."

When Dietzel came to his new job, to which he was appointed February 15, he asked Middleton, "Have you any advice for me?" Middleton responded, "Yes. Recruit in Louisiana. Alabama and Notre Dame have been taking away good Louisiana boys. Go after our share of them."

"Paul Dietzel had it rough his first two years at LSU," Middleton recalled. "He had to start with less than top quality players. The wolves were not long in setting up a howl." Dietzel in 1955 won three games, lost five, and tied two. LSU tied Tulane, 13–13. In 1956 the Tigers won three games and lost seven, defeating Tulane 7–6. In 1957 the Tigers won five and lost five, defeating Tulane 25–6. In 1958 Dietzel's team won ten games and lost none (humiliating Tulane 62–0), defeated Clemson 7–0 in the Sugar Bowl, and was proclaimed national champion. After a highly successful seven-year tenure at LSU, Dietzel elected to go back to West Point as head coach at the Military Academy.

In an interview with Baton Rouge *Morning Advocate* sports writer John Musemeche at Houston, Texas, March 17, 1973, Dietzel recalled his early years as coach at LSU. "We had three straight losing seasons and a lot of the Third Street quarterbacks and Cajuns wanted to fire me because I was the stupid, greenhorn, idiot coach. If it hadn't been for Middleton (then LSU president) they might have succeeded. Then we got some good athletes and overnight I became a genius. I was the boy genius of Louisiana, the smartest, most intelligent, best football coach in America." Troy Middleton and Paul Dietzel remained on the best of terms.

In the March–April, 1955, issue of the *Alumni News*, alumni were again offered an opportunity to contribute to a Middleton Scholarship Fund, more than enough money having been contributed by alumni for the painting of a Middleton portrait by alumnus Burny Myrick. The portrait was pronounced ready for an unveiling ceremony in the Greek Theater on May 11. "Plans for both the portrait and the scholarship were made without President Middleton's knowledge," the magazine reported. "However, when the plans were revealed to him, he made no secret of the fact that the scholarship was closer to his heart, since it was a plan that would bring the means of higher education to many students." A long list of guarantors made known their intentions to contribute to the scholarship fund, which totaled $11,242.32 by late summer. This money was invested, with the interest to be paid to Middleton Scholarship winners.

The portrait showed Middleton in a dark suit, standing, with his right hand in his jacket pocket. Mrs. Middleton unveiled the portrait. Lewis Gottlieb, chairman of the Board of Supervisors, accepted it for the university along with Frank Foil, president of the student body. Governor Kennon presented the scholarship fund. Another old friend, General Graves B. Erskine, director of Special Operations in the Department of Defense, came from Washington to speak.

Mrs. Middleton, Lewis Gottlieb, and President Middleton, at Portrait Unveiling, 1955

From the White House, President Eisenhower wrote: "I am glad to know of the forthcoming ceremonies in honor of General Troy H. Middleton and of the establishment of a scholarship fund bearing his name." Arthur S. Adams, president of the American Council on Education, wrote from Washington: "Among Troy H. Middleton's many admirable qualities is a keen awareness that every institution of higher learning is part of a nationwide educational system which, though extraordinarily complex, has a common dedication to the public welfare. We have reason to know how readily and how well President Middleton answers the call to assist in solving educational problems national in scope." Lewis Webster Jones, president of the Association of Land-Grant Colleges and Universities, wrote from Washington praising Middleton's "great services to the Land-Grant College movement."

Words of praise indeed were these from Washington, directed to a man who, until he was given a chance to speak, was supposed to be up for censure at his first meeting of the Southern Universities Conference at Edgewater Park, Mississippi, a mere four years before.

His pastor, the Reverend Philip P. Werlein, of Saint James Episcopal Church in Baton Rouge, in the dedication program, wrote: "It is a privilege to be able to speak of General Troy Middleton's membership in St. James Church. He has been a regular attendant for many years and has served a number of times on the vestry, the governing body of the church."

Frank S. Craig, president of the Rotary Club of Baton Rouge, whose meetings Troy Middleton attended faithfully, wrote: "The ideals of Rotary are expressed in its slogan 'Service Above Self,' and the Rotary life of Troy Middleton has been a perfect expression of those ideals. In the twenty-five years he has been a member of the Rotary Club of Baton Rouge his service has been completely unselfish and untiring." Middleton was Rotary president in 1940–1941.

Though LSU had acquired a new head football coach quickly in February, 1955, it was not until April that the Board of Supervisors decided on a successor to T. P. Heard. James J. Corbett, who had been sports publicity and public relations director from 1945 to 1949 and from 1950 to 1953, came back to LSU as athletic director, from a sports liaison job with the National Broadcasting Company. He and Dietzel teamed with extraordinary effectiveness in telling Louisiana about LSU football.

In his 1955 report to alumni, Middleton told of the outstanding accomplishments of faculty members and graduates who had won international and national honors. He noted that the Board of Supervisors had approved a budget exceeding $18,500,000 and that $1,200,000 was earmarked for faculty and staff salary increases. "We have closed a salary gap in the cost-of-living that had existed for fifteen years," he reported.

He also revealed that the President's Home, from which he and his wife had only recently moved, back to their beloved home at 4782 Highland Road, was to become Alumni House.

In his spring, 1956, report to alumni, Middleton put alumni and the legislature on notice that the university would be needing substantially more money, saying that a sizable portion of the 1956–1957 budget had been earmarked for salary increases and for additional faculty needed to keep up with growing enrollments. He raised his sights to an estimated 25,000 students to be enrolled by 1970.

Six years after the entry into LSU of its first Negro student, who matriculated in the Law School, Middleton on April 7, 1956, presented a formal report to the Board of Supervisors, entitled "LSU and Segregation" and published in the May–June, 1956, issue of *Alumni News*. It read in part:

When a situation has existed for many years, there is a tendency for the facts surrounding it, particularly those concerned with its origins, to become somewhat obscured by time. Apparently this is what has happened in connection with the Negro situation at Louisiana State University if one is to judge by the comments and criticism directed at LSU recently.

With your permission I should like to review the Negro situation at LSU in an effort to bring the whole picture into sharp focus once again. These are the essential facts:

1. The university has been admitting Negro students since 1950. It has done so reluctantly, under court order.
2. All Negro students admitted were scholastically qualified for admission despite recent statements by misinformed sources to the contrary. Many have been denied admission because they did not possess the prescribed qualifications.
3. While there are some 117 Negroes enrolled at LSU, the historic policy of the university is not to admit Negroes. It is unlikely that there will be any change in this policy.
4. LSU has been in the courts almost continuously since 1946 defending this policy, for the most part unsuccessfully, in spite of the fact that it

has associated itself with the state's best legal minds and has employed reputable consultants in the preparation of its defenses.

5. All Negroes attending LSU are here as a result of decisions based on the separate-but-equal doctrine which was nullified by the Supreme Court in its decision of May 17, 1954.
6. Federal court decisions have opened to Negroes the Graduate School, the School of Social Welfare, the Law School, the School of Medicine, and the combined curriculum in Arts and Sciences and Law.
7. Negroes attending LSU today are all graduate or professional students.
8. One undergraduate was admitted to LSU to pursue the Arts and Sciences-Law Curriculum. His registration was later canceled when the university successfully appealed a lower court decision. This student and others similarly situated are today legally entitled to enter the university, but there are no undergraduates at LSU at this time.
9. Practically all Negroes attending LSU are school teachers or education majors seeking advanced degrees.
10. In the admission and handling of Negro students the university has acted responsibly and has been guided by the Supreme Court's McLaurin Decision which said that Negro students must be accorded treatment equal to that accorded white students. Further it has refused to resort to any kind of subterfuge in its admission policy.

To understand more fully the Negro situation as it applies to LSU it is necessary to go back to 1938, the year of the Gaines decision. This decision stated in effect that a state was bound to furnish within its borders educational facilities for Negroes *substantially equal* to those for whites, and that in the *absence* of such facilities Negroes were entitled to use white educational facilities.

There was an *absence* of Negro graduate and professional educational facilities in Louisiana *in 1938* and there is still an *absence* of these facilities *today*. In spite of the Supreme Court's clear warning and the fact that Negro leaders have long since made their intentions exceedingly clear, only one positive step—the establishment of a law school at Southern University—has been taken by the state of Louisiana in eighteen years to provide equal graduate and professional facilities for Negroes.

LSU has been far from silent during this long period. It is a matter of written record that the university repeatedly urged that steps be taken to provide advanced higher education for Negroes on a separate-but-equal basis. One university document in 1945 issued this warning:

"There is no dodging the fact that so long as the state of Louisiana makes no provision whatever for Negro education beyond the bachelor's degree Negro students who wish to pursue their studies further are *legally entitled* as American citizens to utilize the facilities of Louisiana State University. . . ."

Again in 1946 LSU demonstrated its concern over the impending breakdown of segregation by initiating the action which was to result in the establishment of a law school at Southern University. Meetings of a joint committee of the LSU Board of Supervisors and the State Board of Education were called at LSU's behest, and when the projected law school for Negroes was finally approved and some funds provided for its operation, LSU personnel played major roles in the planning and organization stages, and once classes began LSU professors taught in the new school for several semesters.

Aside from this one exception, Louisiana has kept its head buried in the sand. More and more frequently one hears that if Louisiana is to maintain segregation it must provide equal school facilities for Negroes. But the record speaks for itself. Only once in eighteen years has any affirmative action been taken in the realm of advanced higher education. . . .

This statement would be incomplete without some mention of two recent actions of the Board of Supervisors related to the Negro question. On February 18, 1956, the board declined to alter the university's admission and athletic policies.

The admissions policy was reaffirmed after a study of various proposals, one of which would have required of each applicant a written examination, a health certificate signed by his parish coroner, character references signed by his probate judge and sheriff, and recommendations signed by alumni of LSU from his parish. Of the proposals received from outside the university, there was no suggestion of standard admission requirements for all state colleges but LSU was singled out to provide the solution for the state.

Clarification of the athletic policy had been requested in connection with a football contract between LSU and the University of Wisconsin signed in 1955 calling for contests in Madison in 1957 and in Baton Rouge in 1958. The possibility of the Wisconsin squad having Negro athletes in those years had been noted recently.

The action of the board in declining to alter its admissions policy does *not* constitute an open invitation to Negroes to apply for admission to the university. It does not mean that the board has abandoned the conviction, shared by a majority of the people of Louisiana, that segregation in education is desirable. Nor does it mean that the university will no longer contest the admission of Negroes to those divisions not already opened to them by court order.

It *does* mean that, like most of our citizens, the board believes in law and order and that it respects the decisions of our courts. It also means the board believes that in the conduct of the university's affairs it should set an example as a responsible, law-abiding body. And further, it means that the board does not propose to delegate to persons outside the university the responsibility for screening applicants who desire to obtain their education at LSU. This responsibility belongs to the university, and *only* to the university.

The board's decision to maintain its long-standing athletic policy was based on the conviction that a major university should carry on a program of intercollegiate athletics against major competition, including intersectional contests. The board believes that such a policy is important to the university's total program and is in accord with the public interest. Changing conditions elsewhere have made it inevitable that Negro students representing other institutions will compete infrequently in athletic contests with LSU students if a strong athletic program is to be maintained. The board saw in this fact no compelling reason for taking restrictive action that would seriously jeopardize, and perhaps destroy, this worthwhile program.

In summary let me emphasize the following points:

1. Louisiana State University has repeatedly made it clear it does not want Negro students. Like several other of the state's institutions of higher learning, it admits them under court order. They attend LSU through no fault on the part of the university which to date has done more than any institution, organization, or individual to try to preserve segregation in Louisiana. During one law suit after another it was left strictly to its own devices. Few outside the university expressed concern, and fewer came forward with suggestions or offers to help.
2. LSU has also made it clear it will continue to admit Negroes only on the basis of court decisions or legislation. But the university has likewise indicated that in all matters related to the problem it will act as a responsible public body; it will abide by the law and respect constituted authority no matter how strongly it may disagree; and at the risk of criticism and reprisal, LSU will at no time resort to subterfuge in the application of its policies.
3. Irresponsible statements and purely negative actions will never solve the problems raised in Louisiana by the Supreme Court's segregation decisions. The situation calls for clear thinking, a united front, and positive steps. LSU welcomes all the support it can get from those sincerely interested in preserving segregation. A major step can be taken by making certain that Negroes are given equal facilities at all levels, beginning with the graduate and professional areas where desegregation is not an imminent problem but an accomplished fact.

An accompanying table showed that 633 Negroes had enrolled in LSU beginning in 1950–1951 and including the first semester of 1955–1956. Of that number, 39 has earned graduate degrees, 2 earned law degrees, and 1 earned a social welfare degree. All Negro students at the time of the report were in graduate school, with most of them seeking advanced degrees in education and 8 seeking degrees in social welfare.

The report to the Board of Supervisors was a sobering document. It acquainted newcomers to the university with the background of the university's resistance to Negro enrollments. It gave the university community solid food for serious thought about the ethical questions involved. It did not still the strident voices of those who cried "Never!" But some began to see the futility and dreadful expense of having to supply duplicate facilities in every area of advanced education.

One fairly quick consequence of the statement about athletic policy was that the two football games between LSU and the University of Wisconsin were postponed for more than a decade. The games were finally played, first at Wisconsin in 1971 and then at LSU in 1972. Only white players represented LSU at Wisconsin, where the Tigers won. There were black players on both sides when Wisconsin returned the visit and LSU won again.

In September, 1956, Middleton told alumni, "I am happy to report that for the second successive biennium the legislature appropriated to the university the full amount of its request for operating funds." A new capital improvements program failed when the legislature declined to provide new taxes to support a bond issue of $26,500,000 for the next seven years. The legislature did come through with a 10 percent increase in operating funds, totaling $15,701,963 for 1956–1957.

With some of its other requests the university was not quite so fortunate. Although the legislature passed the bills, Governor Long vetoed an appropriation of $750,000 to the School of Vocational Agriculture near Alexandria—renamed the Dean Lee Agricultural Center—for capital outlay and operating expenses. The governor also vetoed a $1,500,000 appropriation for a home economics building on the campus at Baton Rouge. Finally, he vetoed a $3,000,000 appropriation for capital outlay for the New Orleans Metropolitan Commuter College, leaving the newly authorized branch of LSU forlorn prospects for its start in 1958, which would have to be accomplished with $599,000 for all expenses through June 30, 1958.

The university, on its own authority, announced plans to issue revenue bonds totaling $12,700,000 to build a Student Union on the Baton Rouge campus (the name was changed to LSU Union before its construction) and to provide dormitories and apartments for married students in Baton Rouge and at the Medical School. For a start, the board authorized $2,650,000 in bonds to build two new men's dormitories and more housing for married students in Baton Rouge.

The governor having scratched $5,250,000 of capital funds with his veto pen, Middleton served warning that the university could not continue its services and absorb the growing obligation to more students on more campuses. "We may have to hold enrollment to 10,000, a figure we are now approaching," Middleton said. On the Baton Rouge campus, the figure came to 9,601. Among that number was the 100,000th student to enter LSU, Miss Diane Taylor, a freshman from New Iberia. She was appropriately greeted by Middleton and other university officials.

25   Grow, Grow, Grow

LOUISIANA State University in New Orleans, which the New Orleans Metropolitan Commuter College soon became (its name changed to University of New Orleans in 1974), grew out of a meeting between four men and one woman legislator from Orleans and Jefferson Parishes with President Middleton.

"One of them called me and invited me to have breakfast with them at the Heidelberg Hotel in Baton Rouge. I asked why they were inviting me down there," Middleton recalled. 'We'd like to talk about the prospects of a commuter college for the New Orleans area,' the spokesman said. 'We don't want dormitories or anything like that—just a college for commuters.' I said all right, let's have breakfast together and look the situation over. We did, and I told the delegation they would be hearing from me. I appointed a faculty committee of six in January, 1957. The committee spent a week gathering information and came back to report to me that we could count on a minimum of 1,500 students there the first year."

Where could 1,500 students be gathered in New Orleans? "That was the stumbling block. We had no place in New Orleans to put a branch of the university. I went down with two business staff members to call on Mayor deLesseps (Chep) Morrison, an LSU alumnus. Chep said the city administration was just then preparing to move to splendid new quarters and that we could have the old City Hall. It was much too small for our purposes. Well then, how about the old Charity Hospital? It was too tum-

350

bledown. Then we heard that the Naval Air Station property out on Lake Pontchartrain was going to be vacated by the navy.

"I went to Louis Roussel, president of the Orleans Levee District Board of Commissioners, to talk about the use of that property and its still serviceable buildings," Middleton recalled. "Roussel said, 'No, we couldn't give you that property.' I asked why not, and Roussel said, 'Oh, we need that acreage for development.'

"I went back to Chep Morrison. He said he could give us fourteen acres. I told him that wasn't nearly enough. We'd be growing fast. When Chep came to Baton Rouge to a football game in the fall of 1957, he told me he hated to have to turn us down but that he couldn't offer anything more of the lakefront property.

"I went to Earl Long, who was getting well into his last term as governor. I told him our troubles. He said we could quit worrying about it; he would get the property for us. He did, by firing the whole Orleans Levee District board and appointing a more obliging board, one interested in educational opportunities for New Orleans youth. That's how we got the Naval Air Station property," Middleton recalled.

Getting the lakefront property was one thing. Finding the right man to head the institution became the next chore. The university acquired a ninety-nine-year lease on the 178 acres for one dollar a year. With the Naval Air Station's move off the property early in 1958 the university would acquire a barracks, a cafeteria, eight classrooms, and a power plant, mainly temporary structures put up during World War II.

To become dean of LSU in New Orleans, Middleton looked nextdoor in David F. Boyd Hall, where Dr. Homer L. Hitt was associate dean of the Graduate School and chairman of the Departments of Sociology and Rural Sociology. Hitt was a hard-working associate dean who often was in full charge of the graduate dean's office in the absence of Graduate Dean Richard J. Russell, a distinguished geographer whose travel schedule kept him out of town for weeks at the time. Hitt, a native Texan, had earned bachelor's and master's degrees at LSU, master's and doctor of philosophy degrees at Harvard, and had joined the faculty in 1941 as an assistant professor. He had been associate dean of the Graduate School since 1954.

When Middleton told Hitt that he was just the man LSU needed to head the new school in New Orleans, Hitt said no. "I could see that he didn't make it a flat-footed no, so I told him to take a couple of days to think it over. After two days he still protested against the move, but he took the job. He's been there fifteen years, done fine work," Middleton recalled in 1973.

Hitt said of the new school, "It will be a modified liberal arts school. There will be no attempt to duplicate the program on the main campus in its entirety. The objective is to establish a college of which Louisiana State University and the people of New Orleans will be proud. There is a tremendous advantage in the new college being affiliated with the state university, sharing in its accomplishments and its prestige. The growth and development of New Orleans will benefit from the new college, since trained manpower is a problem there, as elsewhere, and individuals trained in this college will be a definite asset to the area."

When LSUNO opened its doors in September, 1958, it drew 1,459 students. Hitt had assembled an exceptionally strong faculty for an institution in its first year. He attributed this largely to the fact that he had a strong group of chairmen and the new faculty members would be joining a going concern as part of LSU. Middleton attended a convocation of LSUNO students in a large hangar on the former navy air station and told them: "I believe we have done as well thus far as circumstances, time and finances will permit . . . we want no part of a watered-down academic program. We are conscious of the fact that we come into an area in which there are two well-established and distinguished universities—Loyola and Tulane—and that unless we maintain here an extension of the University with high standards we will certainly suffer by comparison."

The year 1958 was in many ways the most satisfactory one of Middleton's presidency at LSU. A magnificent new library opened. LSU in New Orleans began its first session. The LSU football team went undefeated for the first time in fifty years and won the national championship. Middleton told the Board of Supervisors that his seventieth birthday would come on October 12, 1959, and that he would like to retire June 30, 1959. Instead, the board asked him to continue indefinitely as president.

Two years after Middleton had made clear the university's official position on segregation in higher education, in a long and detailed statement, April 7, 1956, segregationist members of the Louisiana legislature continued to fight blindly and to strike out blindly at anyone who dared criticize their tactics. During the 1958 session, legislation was introduced which would have closed public schools if the courts ordered public school integration. In retrospect, the legislation was insane; in the heat of the fevered times, some responsible criticism of the proposed legislation was clearly called for. That criticism came in the form of a Louisiana Civil Liberties Union petition signed by fifty-nine LSU faculty members.

In a paroxysm of rage, segregationist legislators demanded that Middleton and university deans come down to the capitol and explain. Political columnist Ed Clinton of the Baton Rouge *State-Times* wrote on June 11, 1958: "At least once in every legislative session the legislature, or some part of it, displays the mark of immaturity—acting on the basis of emotion rather than reason. They've had their turn for this session. The House, which Monday summarily ordered General Troy Middleton and the deans of the colleges at LSU to appear before it and explain why some faculty members at the university had signed a petition opposing the legislative package being pushed by the Joint Committee on Segregation, acted hastily. It tacitly conceded that yesterday when it softened the order and directed a special committee to hold public hearings on the hassle."

Middleton went to the capitol that day to appear before a ten-man legislative committee to explain, as an Associated Press account said, "why approximately 10 percent of his faculty signed a Louisiana Civil Liberties Union petition against segregation bills to close public schools."

"I'm a Deep Southern boy," Middleton said. "I believe in segregation. On the other hand, whatever the law is, I'm going to comply with it." He defended the right of faculty members to have opinions and to speak out on them, for here in the legislative summons to the university president was a perfect example of what Middleton had warned against in his long "LSU and Segregation" statement of 1956. A lesser man than Middleton might have heard more from the dissident legislators. He was firm and he was affirmative. The tempest at the capitol quickly abated.

The library for which Middleton fought so hard opened its doors to students and faculty in September, 1958. Under construction since April 5, 1956, the building was ready to receive books in August, 1958. Student workers, including a number from the LSU Laboratory School, helped pack and move enough books to fill eleven miles of shelves in the new library. More than 2,000,000 items were moved into the new archives area, from the Law Building. Books poured in from the branch libraries, the first group coming from the School of Journalism library in Alumni Hall. Dr.

Sidney Smith, director of libraries, invited Middleton to place the first book in the new library.

Since it was known that Middleton would be required to retire at age seventy under university regulations, the Alumni Council in its September 6 meeting in Alexandria, adopted a resolution asking the Board of Supervisors to waive the age requirement: "Whereas, General Troy Middleton has served as president for the past seven and a half years, and has been closely associated with the university throughout most of his career, and by his characteristic energy, understanding, and dedication, has demonstrated his qualifications for the task before him; and he has won the respect and admiration of his faculty and administrative staff, and of citizens of all parts of Louisiana, and whereas the university has entered upon a period of critical growth and financial crisis, and has never faced a greater need for experienced leadership . . . be it resolved that the LSU Alumni Council does hereby request of the Board of Supervisors that the board continue the appointment of President Middleton beyond his scheduled date of retirement, and the board urge President Middleton to accept such appointment and continue his services as president of Louisiana State University."

Middleton Places First Book in LSU's New Library, 1958

The board did so, unanimously calling upon Middleton to stay on. "General Middleton's personal stature has directly and immeasurably contributed to the increasingly high standing of our university, not only among the people of Louisiana, but throughout the United States, and in the opinion of this board, his tenure as president has seen LSU make its greatest strides forward in every area of usefulness. General Middleton's experience in administration, his appreciation of the needs of higher education in this state, his intimate familiarity with the specific problems which confront LSU, and the respect and esteem with which he is everywhere regarded, all combine to insure that his value to the university and to the board will be even greater in the future than it has been in the past."

Faced with so sincere an invitation to stay on, Middleton replied briefly: "The university I serve has been good to me. I don't want to appear ungrateful or inconsiderate. I will continue as president."

The LSU football team in 1958 won its first eight games and was the only undefeated team in the nation when it went to Jackson, Mississippi, to play Mississippi State University on November 15. In the rain, LSU fumbled on its own twenty-two-yard line in the second quarter. Mississippi State scored but missed its extra point try. LSU scored a touchdown in the third quarter and kicked the extra point to win 7–6. Middleton, one of Mississippi State's most distinguished alumni, visited the LSU practice field the following Monday afternoon. The Tiger team, rejoicing after its tightest squeeze of the season, gave Middleton the game ball. He accepted with pleasure, later recalling that he was one of the few hundreds who could say that they had seen the all-conquering LSU teams of 1908 and 1958 both defeat his alma mater.

In April, 1959, the Board of Supervisors made three key appointments. It named Dr. John A. Hunter, former registrar and current dean of the Junior Division, to a newly created position, dean of Student Services. Dr. George H. Mickey, chairman of the Department of Zoology since his return from Northwestern University in 1956, was appointed dean of the Graduate School, succeeding Dean Russell, who wanted to give more time to activities of the Coastal Studies Institute. Dr. Martin D. Woodin, head of the Department of Agricultural Economics since 1957, was named director of resident instruction in the College of Agriculture, succeeding the late Dr. Roy L. Davenport.

Another group of appointments and title changes came early in the

summer of 1959. Daniel Borth, whose title had been changed from comptroller to dean of administration in 1956, was named executive vice president. Dean Milton M. Harrison, who was assistant to President Middleton
from 1951 to 1958 and had then been dean of the Law School, was named
vice president for academic affairs, succeeding Dean Charles E. Smith,
who had died in May. Dr. James W. Reddoch replaced Harrison as Middleton's assistant. Dean Hitt became vice president in charge of LSUNO.
Dr. Paul M. Hebert returned to the university from private law practice for
his third term as dean of the Law School, succeeding Harrison.

In the summer of 1959 the university was invited to join the highly
select Council of Southern Universities. An *Alumni News* account said:

> Louisiana State University has been unanimously elected to the Council of
> Southern Universities—the first addition to the original membership of the
> council and the first land-grant institution to be so honored.
>
> The Council of Southern Universities is a nonprofit, general welfare cor-
> poration created to strengthen and improve higher education in the South
> through consultation, scholarship, research and other desirable means.
>
> The eight charter institutions are Duke University, Emory University, the
> University of North Carolina, Rice Institute, the University of Texas, Tulane
> University, Vanderbilt University and the University of Virginia.
>
> "LSU accepts membership in this select group of distinguished institutions
> of higher learning with grateful thanks and appreciation," said President Mid-
> dleton. "It is no small honor to be recognized by our colleagues as one of the
> leading universities in our section of the country."
>
> The Board of Supervisors commended President Middleton and his ad-
> ministrative staff for exercising the exemplary leadership which led to LSU's
> election to the council.

This Council of Southern Universities should not be confused with
the Southern University Conference, which had started out to give Troy
Middleton a hard time at its convention in 1951 and had elected him its
president five years later. The Council of Southern Universities was then
and has remained an extraordinarily exclusive organization. Election to its
number spoke eloquently of the stature LSU had attained among an elite
which included five private institutions and only three state universities in
fourteen states.

Enrollment on the Baton Rouge campus passed 10,000 for the first
time in September, 1959. Registration at the School of Medicine was 519.
LSUNO drew 2,144. The three-campus total was well above that of the

previous year. Middleton welcomed a special group of 35 freshmen who were awarded Centennial Honor scholarships from a $40,000 fund supporting superior high school graduates. "These are students whose brain power will make possible the continued supremacy of American democracy. It is these students above all that should be urged to go to college and we should render financial assistance wherever necessary," Middleton said.

In the spring of 1959 a delegation from Alexandria had asked the Board of Supervisors to consider converting the Dean Lee Agricultural Center at Chambers into a two-year branch of the university. The board was willing, provided that studies showed a need and enough prospective students, that the legislature would provide the money, that the State Board of Education be consulted (Northwestern State College at Natchitoches was but fifty-five miles away), and that Congress would release the land for college use.

The legislature obliged by appropriating $1,000,000 to expand existing facilities into a two-year college. Then Congress cleared the rededication of the 3,113-acre site originally given by the federal government for "an agricultural and vocational school." Middleton appointed a committee of six faculty members to make recommendations on faculty, curricula, and space needs in the fall. At its September, 1959, meeting the Board of Supervisors decided to name the branch LSU at Alexandria. A year later, on September 8, 1960, LSU at Alexandria opened its doors to 329 students. Martin D. Woodin, who had been director of resident instruction in the College of Agriculture since April, 1959, was named dean.

With 1959 came a drastic reduction in state income from bonus bids for leases on state-owned lands, especially in offshore areas. In February, the state received $60,000,000 in bonus bids for leases. The legislature in its spring session, apparently counting on a continuation of the high lease bonus income, voted to distribute $40,000,000 to state agencies. LSU was to get $8,000,000 for building needs, mainly on the LSUNO campus where a general purpose classroom building, a library, a science building, and a utilities plant were on the planning boards. Expansion of air conditioning to more buildings on the Baton Rouge campus was also scheduled. The blow fell in September when bonus bids dropped to $12,000,000. Only the state college building needs, first in the legislature's program, were funded from the sharply reduced lease bonuses.

The university marked its one hundredth birthday on January 2, 1960. Having dedicated the new library earlier, Middleton led the faculty, staff, student body, and alumni into a semester-long series of symposiums, open houses, and other observances. Alumni launched a campaign to provide some supplemental financing to the university. A Spring Alumni Day was established to bring alumni back to the campus for workshops and other gatherings in the second semester.

Construction on the Baton Rouge campus early in 1960 went on in every direction. Major building projects completed in 1959 were the Industrial Education Building; additions to the Music and Dramatic Arts Building; air conditioning of Nicholson Hall; renovation of Hill Memorial, the old library; renovation of Peabody Hall. An eighteen-hole golf course and clubhouse were built with money from the sale by the Athletic Department of Westdale Golf Course to the city for $700,000. The Athletic Department had acquired Westdale during the depths of the depression in the 1930s, for $25,000, as providential an investment as could be found for earnings from early football bowl games. The Dairy Department, in compensation for the agricultural lands going into the golf course, received a $300,000 Dairy Production Teaching and Research Center. Other Athletic Department spending went into a new lighting system in Tiger Stadium and improvements at Alex Box (baseball) Stadium.

Projects begun earlier and continuing included a new Electrical Engineering Building; an addition to the Dairy Science Building; an addition to Nicholson Hall for the Physics Department; a three-story administration building linked to the one-story and two-story units of Thomas D. Boyd Hall, making three in all; the feed and fertilizer building bearing the name of Harry D. Wilson, late state commissioner of agriculture; the Home Economics and Nursery Building; and Pleasant Hall, closed down for air conditioning and for conversion into 150 bedrooms with 50 private baths and accommodations for 300 persons in its Adult Education Center facilities.

Most noticeable to returning alumni and to visitors to LSU in 1960 was the stark look of the Memorial Tower. It had suffered over the years from water intrusion and cracking of its masonry sides. It was cut down to its steel framework and rebuilt. At its base, an information center and an Anglo-American Art Center were constructed to house furnishings from old English and American homes, the gift of an anonymous donor.

No more distasteful duty came Middleton's way than one which began unfolding on Sunday morning, January 10, 1960. The body of Dr. Margaret Rosamond McMillan, an assistant professor at LSU in New Orleans, was found on a lane off the River Road south of the LSU campus. She had been savagely beaten. No weapon was found. Her car was a few feet away.

The East Baton Rouge Parish sheriff, Bryan Clemmons, and his deputies began an investigation immediately. In Miss McMillan's purse they found a wallet containing a picture of Dr. George H. Mickey, who had been appointed dean of the LSU Graduate School in April, 1959, and a card which asked that he be notified in case of accident. Dr. Mickey had been Dr. McMillan's teacher at Northwestern University, had directed her doctoral dissertation, and had helped her find a teaching position at LSUNO.

Dr. Mickey was informed that Dr. McMillan's body had been found. He did not go to identify her body. The identification was made after 1 P.M. by an LSU science professor who knew Dr. McMillan by sight.

Five days later, January 14, sheriff's deputies took Mickey into custody and booked him into the parish jail in connection with the murder. Mickey employed legal counsel at this point.

As the investigation proceeded, Mickey said that on the night of the murder he had had dinner at a Baton Rouge hotel with a federal education official from Dallas. Asked about what he had eaten, he said, "fried chicken." That Saturday night, investigators found, for the first Saturday in thirteen years, the hotel dining room had *not* served chicken. Mickey could not recall the name of the federal official and further inquiries, investigators said, established that no such person existed. District Attorney J. St. Clair Favrot said that Mickey's alibi for the night of the murder was "unfounded."

Police announced that they had found blood spots inside the grillwork at the front of Mickey's car, which had been washed on the morning after the crime. The blood matched the victim's type, police said.

The East Baton Rouge Parish grand jury began its hearing in the McMillan murder case on Monday, February 15. Thirty witnesses, many of them university faculty friends and associates of Mickey, were heard as the grand jury deliberations ran on and on. Finally, on March 3, the grand jury voted to pretermit the case, leaving it open. The grand jury might have voted a true bill, formally accusing Mickey of the crime; it might have voted a no true bill, freeing Mickey of any charge; it chose instead to leave the case in a state of suspended animation. A murder indictment could be voted at any time that convincing evidence could be presented to any subsequent grand jury.

Mickey was bonded out of jail the night after the grand jury decision to pretermit. The next day he was told by Middleton that he would remain on the university payroll but that he would not resume his duties as graduate dean or as chairman of the Department of Zoology "as long as the charge remains." Board of Supervisors chairman Theo Cangelosi told newspaper reporters the case "is not in the board's hands; it is in the hands of President Middleton. I have confidence in his ability to handle the matter."

On April 2 the board met and voted unanimously to reduce Mickey to the rank of inactive professor of zoology. The Baton Rouge *State-Times* noted that the board acted in open session without debate after a long closed meeting. After the board decision was announced, Middleton said, "I hope this action will not be misinterpreted. It need not be. No judgment of the charge against Dr. Mickey is implied."

Middleton explained further that a graduate program must be marked by conditions of stability and continuity, "conditions which obviously could not continue to exist under present circumstances. This action taken today simply makes it possible for the university to proceed openly with the business of selecting a permanent graduate dean." He noted that Mickey would continue on his salary of $10,000 as a professor of zoology.

Mickey, after his release from jail, went back to his zoology laboratory on the campus. Growing uneasiness over his presence on the campus finally brought action. Middleton had thought that Mickey would "do the decent thing and submit his resignation." Finally, it became obvious that he did not intend to. Middleton called him in, reviewed the circumstances of the case, and suggested that Mickey "do the right thing" without delay.

A *State-Times* front page story said on April 28, 1960:

"Dr. George H. Mickey—no longer a dean, no longer a professor— only a man once accused of murder, will now try to escape into oblivion after scorching under the public spotlight for more than three months. Theoretically a free man now, Mickey is a teacher without a school, a scientist without a laboratory. In a surprising move yesterday, unknown even to East Baton Rouge Sheriff Bryan Clemmons, District Attorney J. St.

Clair Favrot recalled a murder warrant that charged Mickey with the slaying of Dr. Margaret R. McMillan."

With the recall of the warrant, Mickey was free to go. He resigned from LSU that day and left Baton Rouge shortly thereafter. Middleton received an inquiry from a research institute in a New England state, saying, "If you were in our place, would you employ Dr. Mickey?" Middleton replied, "I can't put myself in your place to make a decision. I can tell you that technically the man about whom you inquire is an accomplished scientific researcher."

Thus ended nearly four months of tension on the LSU campus.

The East Baton Rouge Parish alumni chapter met in the Gymnasium-Armory on March 22, 1960, and paid special tribute to President and Mrs. Middleton. Alumni presented Mrs. Middleton with a radio tuner for her stereophonic sound system at home. To Middleton they gave a desk pen set. Called upon for remarks, Middleton told the alumni, "We have difficult times ahead. You can rest assured that we're going to need everything we ask the legislature for this year, and if we don't get it, we're in trouble."

University Executive Vice President Borth earlier in the year had detailed university budget needs and raised serious questions about whether Louisiana could continue to diffuse its educational spending over state colleges with proliferating programs and do justice to the university.

After his retirement from the presidency, Middleton recalled his policy on university budget matters. "I believed in asking only for what was needed—without padding. I thought the best people in the university should be on its budget committee. The greatest difficulty the university had with the legislature during my administration came when Robert Kennon was governor. Percy Roberts, Charles Duchein and I went to see the governor at the mansion. Governor Kennon and Allison Kolb of his staff offered to restore some of the funds that had been trimmed from the budget the university sent the legislature. They asked if what they restored would cover the university's needs. I said, 'No.' They asked what we needed. I said we needed every cent that we asked for—and that I would never let a padded budget get past me. We got what we asked for as a result of that conference at the mansion.

"You know," Middleton said, "it's unfair to the department head and the dean who have assembled a budget, reviewed it, and confined themselves strictly to needs—real needs—if others draw up a budget reflecting requests not tied to real need.

"Sometimes funds for research were requested when they were by no means essential. When you have a qualified researcher, I believe in supporting him to the hilt. But on the other hand, not every faculty member is automatically a good research man. The College of Commerce under Dean Trant at one time had every faculty member on a research project. It's impossible to find that much research talent, so I told Trant he should try again with that fact reflected in his budget."

Of all the duties of the university president, the budget was topmost for Middleton. "As head of the University budget committee, the president had to go to the legislature informed, else he'd run into trouble," he said. "I always reviewed the university's budget request with the state Division of Administration. Unless I could sell the head of the division I was in trouble. The best man up there in my time as president was J. H. Rester. He knew people. You couldn't fool him, and I would never have thought of trying. He'd pick up any flaw in a minute. When we had his approval we knew we had a good chance of getting what we needed."

"As president of LSU, it was my belief that no student should ever be dismissed from the university except on the signature of the president. I talked to every student dismissed under my administration, and sometimes to parents. When several coeds were dismissed for spending the night with a group of boys in a motel, I talked with their parents. Some wanted their daughters kept here and professed not to understand why they were being dismissed. Some of the mothers tried to pressure me, but it didn't work. They didn't think it was wrong or else they thought it wasn't much of an offense. Yes, it was rather unpleasant to hear protests and see tears. But that's one of the things a president is paid for. "I always appeared before each entering freshman class and told them they would be dismissed for cheating, stealing, or lying. When a youngster was brought to face discipline, he'd almost always recall what I had said. Very few students who were dismissed would I have declined to readmit. Most of those who did come back did make good," he recalled.

"I have no patience with the instructor who gives an *F* in the course to a cheater but otherwise makes no case against him. It's so important to know why a student has been dismissed."

During Middleton's presidency, a strike by telephone company employees was called. Some university students chose to work for Southern Bell Telephone Company in place of the striking workers. "While I was at my desk one day, my office filled and there was some spilling into the hall of protesting Southern Bell employees on strike. They were protesting against students taking their places while they were on strike. I told the union members protesting that I had no right to restrain anyone from working who was twenty-one or older. And I told them further, 'I won't tell any student he can't work in your place since there's no illegality or immorality involved, and I've told those under twenty-one that with written permission from their parents that they can't be stopped either. I'm sure you have other things to do today. I do. Thank you for coming. Good morning.'"

Middleton was in court only once, he recalled, in his university capacity, when a head of the carpenters union entered suit against the Board of Supervisors after the university rejected a $20,000 bid for construction of a carpenter shop on campus and elected to do the job for about half that sum. The suit went to Judge Charles Holcombe's division of district court in Baton Rouge. Holcombe threw it out. When efforts were made to organize university carpenters, plumbers, and other operation and maintenance employees, they rejected the idea of a closed shop.

Before the United States became involved in World War II, Middleton recalled, "One of our former carpenters came in from Camp Livingston to see me, saying he wanted his old job back. He said he'd held his construction job there until union dues were collected and then he was cut off. I told him to go over to Keesler Field at Biloxi and get a job. He said he'd rather come back to LSU and work for less money. 'All right,' I told him, 'you've got your job back.' We serve all the people; we have no right spending taxpayers' money, to say to a nonunion man that he can't work here because he isn't a union man."

As the 1959–1960 academic year neared its close, Middleton once more offered his resignation. He was approaching seventy-one. The board declared his services essential. Middleton smiled and reminded the board that no man was indispensable, but said he'd stay on one more year—just one more.

After hearing from Middleton and out-of-state alumni, the legislature rejected a proposal which would have raised out-of-state fees at LSU and all state colleges, thus "fencing off Louisiana education from the rest of the world."

When Douglas Manship, president of Baton Rouge television station WBRZ, approached the university in 1960 with an idea for a television series to be called "The Pursuit of Learning," Middleton reacted favorably. He asked the Bureau of Public Relations to work with WBRZ in drawing faculty members into the program, which went on for several years. The programs were placed on film for use by Louisianians.

As the 1960–1961 academic year ended, Middleton wrote in the *LSU Outlook*: "It is a startling fact, but is nonetheless a fact, that in order to house those who will be demanding higher education, this nation will have to spend more money for construction between now and 1970 than has been spent for this purpose since the Revolutionary War. For LSU alone the construction bill may run as high as $100,000,000 during the remainder of this decade." Edsel E. (Tad) Thrash, director of Alumni Affairs, urged alumni to help the university to have restored almost a million dollars that the state was withholding across the board from all state-supported agencies.

Middleton, now seventy-one and closing in on his seventy-second birthday, for the fourth time informed the Board of Supervisors of his intent to seek retirement. He had, he said, yielded more than once to the board's importuning to stay on. This time, though, he was ready to step out, as of February 1, 1962. The board reluctantly accepted his request for retirement.

In his last semester as president of LSU, Middleton made numerous talks. He was, as always, accessible to all who telephoned or came to see him at his office. As he reminisced later, he said: "You know, nothing irritated me so much as having someone call me and when I came on the phone for his secretary to tell me, 'Mr. Soandso will be with you in just a minute.' If Mr. Soandso wanted to talk to me, he could jolly well stay on the phone and do so. I never was one to have my secretary call anyone and then ask the other fellow to wait, because I thought it was bad manners to do so."

In the January, 1962, issue of the *Alumni News*, editor Dan Bivins wrote: "Elsewhere in this issue is an account of the ceremonies honoring Troy H. Middleton prior to his retirement from the presidency of LSU.

Although it may be considered journalistic heresy, your editor must confess that the printed word in the printed magazine somehow seems inadequate for the occasion. Can adjectives, verbs, and adverbs—no matter how carefully selected—fully express the feeling in thousands of hearts toward this man whose service to the university has earned such respect and admiration?

"If the alumni body's collective memory is functioning properly, it will recall much about Troy Middleton. These memories, if collected, would make a formidable storehouse; after all, members of thirty years of LSU classes would be contributing. This works both ways. Troy Middleton has many memories of LSU alumni. In fact, he has been doing some first-class reminiscing in several recent talks. He has a twinkling eye as he retells tall-but-true tales about campus pranks he witnessed in his years at LSU. Lest any good alumni readers blush too quickly, the General hasn't been calling any pranksters by name in public."

Bivins, who had been editor of the *Daily Reveille* a decade earlier, might have recalled how sturdy a friend and defender of student journalists Middleton had been through the eleven years of his presidency. One recurring question asked of Middleton was, "Why don't you do something about that damned *Reveille*?" It was disrespectful toward authority, it was too demanding, it was too critical, complainants said. Board of Supervisors members were among this number. Yet, in those eleven years, Middleton refused to call an editor on the carpet, as earlier presidents had done.

As adviser to the *Reveille* for sixteen years before becoming director of the School of Journalism for thirteen years, the author of this book worked under four presidents of LSU. All but Middleton had summoned editors, adviser, and Marvin G. Osborn, longtime director of the School of Journalism, to confer on complaints. Each president passed along complaints, spoke sternly of what might happen if the *Reveille* did not, as he phrased it, act more responsibly. Osborn, just as regularly, asked each president to put in writing exactly what it was that he wanted of the *Reveille*, "so that, Mr. President, there can be no misunderstanding about what is desired." Just as regularly, no written instructions were forthcoming from the earlier presidents.

When Middleton retired, among the scores of plaques, scrolls, citations and certificates presented him was a sheet of parchment in a bronze frame, saying: "In Appreciation from Student Journalists of Louisiana State University to Troy H. Middleton, for Three Decades Good Friend of Free and Responsible Journalism, December 15, 1961."

When the author was gathering hundreds of items from President Emeritus and Mrs. Middleton at their home for inclusion in the Middleton Collection, the last item Middleton surrendered was the expression of thanks from LSU journalists. "It has stood," he said, "on my chest of drawers ever since you gave it to me eleven years ago."

Darrell Eiland, editor of the 1958 *Summer Reveille*, recalled his experience with Middleton during a particularly trying time in the University's life:

"Dr. Price, director of the School of Journalism at that time, looked over each of my editorials before they were printed. But in no sense was he my censor. My editorials tended toward the liberal side, but to this day, I do not know what Price's politics are or were. At my request he checked my work for lucidity, coherence, and other editorial bugaboos. He would sometimes advise me as to what results I could expect from various things I wrote and did, but he never attempted to get me to go against my conscience in anything I wrote, not even when a state senator [Senator Willie Rainach of Summerfield] began reading my editorials on the floor of the Senate and calling for an investigation of the School of Journalism and my expulsion. (The legislature that summer, in a panicky effort to forestall desegregation, called at least five special sessions, and I chided them for the stupid laws they were passing. To show the quality of the laws, they would pass them in the morning and a federal judge in New Orleans would declare them unconstitutional in the afternoon.)

"I received no indication at this time from LSU faculty or staff that my editorials were improper. But I was aware that the university would have to go before the legislature to seek its next appropriation. Harking back to my view of my responsibilities as an editor and my interpretation of the role of a newspaper, I became afraid that I might be injuring the community I was trying to serve.

"Accordingly, I asked for and received an audience with the president of the university, General Troy Middleton. I opened our talk by saying that I realized that my editorials had drawn attention to LSU, attention that was perhaps unwanted at this time. I assured the General that I had not deliberately undertaken a campaign to embarrass the university and that I was quite prepared to take any steps (short of a recantation) that the General might feel necessary to protect the university.

"The General looked at me silently for a few moments, then asked, 'Mr. Eiland, the views you have expressed in your editorials, they are your own?'

"I replied emphatically that they were.

" 'Well, Mr. Eiland, I have read your editorials carefully. I do not agree with all you have said, but you have advocated nothing immoral, indecent, or illegal. You have done what you are supposed to do: express an opinion. Some people have suggested that you should be expelled from this university. Let me assure you, here and now, before I allow that to happen, I will resign this post.'

"The rest of the conversation I do not recall, except that it was friendly and light. Eventually, I was politely eased out of the General's office by his secretary, and I walked across the campus, dazed by this unexpected offer of protection from a man whom I admired and who, I knew, was being unreasonably attacked because of my writings. His noble defense of my rights accomplished something which no amount of threats or punishment could have done. I decided to hold off on further criticism and see what happened in the legislature," former editor Eiland wrote.

After reading Eiland's letter in 1972, Middleton recalled the session. He also told one of the author's classes, to which he was invited at the students' request, "You know, if I was starting out again as a student, I think I'd choose journalism. You people can have such a great impact on affairs and exert so much constructive influence."

January 11, 1962, was proclaimed "Troy H. Middleton Day in Louisiana" by Governor Jimmie H. Davis. Classes were suspended, an honor guard from the Cadet Corps formed, Secretary of the Army Elvis J. Stahr, Jr., came to address the convocation in the Agricultural Center, and LSU conferred upon its most distinguished president, the honorary degree of Doctor of Laws. In its first 102 years, the university had been most sparing in awarding honorary degrees. But if ever such a degree was deserved it was this one. The Law School, headed by Middleton's friend and associate Paul Hebert, had been the recommending faculty (all recommendations, under university protocol, must originate with the faculty of a college or autonomous school and be approved by the board). The citation accompanying award of the degree read:

For his distinguished and innumerable contributions to the case of higher education in the state, in the region, and in the nation;

For his truly outstanding services to Louisiana State University and to the state of Louisiana throughout a career of thirty-two years of affiliation with the university as Commandant of Cadets, as Dean of Men, as Dean of Administration, as Comptroller, as Vice President, and as President;

For the clear stamp of integrity and for the tremendous respect he has provided for the university and its administration as its president through eleven years of growth and change;

For the friendly and practical encouragement of faculty and students toward increased scholarship and higher academic achievements;

For his invaluable and timely efforts as a soldier in the defense of his country at highly critical periods in its history;

The Graduate Faculty of Louisiana State University representing the university in its entirety, recommends the conferring of the Honorary Degree of Doctor of Laws upon Troy Houston Middleton.

So it was that Middleton acquired his third honorary degree of Doctor of Laws. The University of the South at Sewanee, Tennessee, and Tulane University earlier had seen fit so to honor him.

From Ike Eisenhower came this message:

Troy Middleton—soldier, educator, citizen—my friend of many years and my erstwhile instructor in the military arts—through a half century of adult life has exemplified high courage, patriotism and dedication to duty.

In World War I, as a young officer, he commanded a regiment in battle. Twenty-five years later, when he was a division commander in the liberation of Sicily and Italy, a corps commander from Brittany to the Danube, his decision to hold Bastogne against Hitler's Panzer forces added to American history a new chronicle of heroism.

But his chief contribution to the Republic and its future stems from his return, after war, to Louisiana State University, where his leadership has assured that its many thousand graduates through years to come will reflect in their lives Troy Middleton's own ideals and code of free, responsible, informed, patriotic citizenship.

The author later interviewed Eisenhower at Gettysburg, August 19, 1965, where the conversation for forty-five minutes dealt with Middleton.

The conversation turned to Eisenhower's view of why Middleton earned the confidence of so many persons.

"First of all," Eisenhower said, "he had moral courage, and he had common sense, and he took full advantage of all the experiences he'd had. You know, I like that saying attributed to Napoleon, that the genius in war

Middleton Receives Honorary Doctor of Laws Degree on Troy H. Middleton Day, January 11, 1962

is the man who can do the sensible thing or an average thing, when every-body else around him was crazy. Well now, that was Troy Middleton. Troy Middleton never got stampeded. He did what was necessary, and that's the kind of fellow you want in war.

"I was impressed always by his complete command of himself and of the situation. He was not one of these swashbuckling types. He was always calm and quiet, and I like that in soldiers—it incites my confidence in them. The swashbuckler sometimes gets away with what he shouts around, but it comes more often in reputation than in performance. But not with Troy. Troy performed all the time.

"Troy typified what you think of as the best in the Regular Army. He was intelligent, dedicated, and loyal. He always acted according to the old aphorism: Always take your job seriously and never yourself. If the war had gone on, he would certainly have led an army because we were still bringing in people."

LSU's thirteenth president, its third general heading the university, kept to his regular schedule through January 31 on the campus. He had a citation from the Board of Supervisors framed for safekeeping. Essentially, it said, "Words cannot express the love and devotion of the board, the faculty and staff, alumni and students of LSU and the people of the state of Louisiana for President Middleton, who has brought LSU to its deserved recognition as a great institution of higher learning in the region, the nation, and the world."

In the eleven years of his presidency, Middleton was instrumental in the creation of the Boyd Professorships for outstanding faculty and of these agencies: University College, the Adult Education Center, the Curriculum in Community and Family Living, the In-Service Law Enforcement Program, the Computer Research Center, the Veterinary Research Center, the Nuclear Science Center, the Department of Architecture, the International Center for Medical Research and Training, the Anglo-American Art Museum, the Coastal Studies Institute, the In-Service Training Program for Firemen, and the Gulf States Law Enforcement Institute. LSU in New Orleans and LSU at Alexandria were started and given strong support by Middleton.

When Middleton left office and became president emeritus of LSU, he stipulated that he wanted no farewell dinner and no sendoff gifts. With the new president occupying a suite in Thomas D. Boyd Hall, across the

Memorial Tower plaza, Middleton chose a room in David F. Boyd with a desk, bookshelves, and four armchairs. On the walls of his office hung pictures of former LSU President Thomas Duckett Boyd, General John J. Pershing, Jefferson Davis (another former Mississippian), and General Robert E. Lee. The picture of General Lee was a gift from a former Board of Supervisors member, Colonel John Tucker of Shreveport. Tucker's eye for detail had detected an unfastened button on Lee's tunic. That wouldn't do, he said; he supplied a new picture in which the general's tunic was perfectly buttoned. An autographed picture of General of the Army George C. Marshall ("the greatest man I have known") hung on a wall at home.

As president emeritus, Middleton resolved not to offer unsolicited advice to anyone, on or off campus. He chose Wednesday mornings to go to the office, where he was provided with the services of a Graduate School staff secretary who handled the typing of a considerable volume of letters going out in response to the General's mail.

When he was asked for comment, he gave it forthrightly. On March 11, 1964, he wrote Dean Jack Carlton of the College of Sciences at LSU in New Orleans, commenting on a paper Dean Carlton had sent Middleton, dealing with the changing scene in higher education. "On teacher training," Middleton wrote, "if I had my way I would abolish all Teachers Colleges. I would charge the Arts College with the programs. I fear that until we break the 'union' found in our Teachers Colleges we will never bring order out of the present mess."

At age eighty-four, he was still regularly receiving mail from men he had known in the army, from men still active in higher education—often seeking his advice, twelve years after his retirement.

26 "Retirement Means You Work Without Pay"

IN A TALK he made to retired staff members of the LSU Cooperative Extension Service, November 9, 1967, nearly six years after his own retirement, Middleton said:

"When a person approaches retirement several decisions are presented. The two most important for me were: (1) Where to live? and (2) How shall I occupy my time? When service people retire, many congregate in a few areas; San Antonio, San Diego, and St. Petersburg are favorite spots. Some years past I saw a picture showing sixty-five retired generals sitting around the swimming pool at Fort Sam Houston. A friend who saw this picture asked me why I did not live in San Antonio. The sixty-five generals were sitting there fighting a war. It may have been the French and Indian War. When you get that many old soldiers together a war always breaks out. No! I have no desire to fight another war.

[At age seventy-eight, Middleton had other things to do. At age sixty, however, shortly after the United States entered the Korean conflict, he had written Army Chief of Staff Collins offering his services. Collins had thanked him warmly and said that the army had no plans to recall retired officers, but that he would be called if the situation warranted.]

"As for occupying my time, I realized that on retirement unless I divorced myself from the university I would be accused of meddling in its affairs. I am happy to say that neither have I meddled in the affairs of the university nor has the university asked for my advice or counsel.

"I did not realize, however, that even though I could turn my back on

372

university affairs, I could not in good conscience turn my back on demands that would be made upon me as a citizen of the community, the state, and the nation. Nor do I think any retired person can afford to do so. If you are a good churchgoer, you will serve on committees and on the vestry. The Red Cross can use your services. The United Givers Fund may even elect you president and ask you to raise a million dollars.

"Time has not hung heavily over my head. For example, in the October just past, out of the thirty-one days I was called upon to meet commitments on twenty-two days. None were at LSU. The only difference between being on the active list and the retired list was that the work is free.

"Being retired, seeing others retired, and those about to be retired has caused me to give some thought to the matter. Science and improved medical care are stretching the life span. With automatic retirement age getting lower and lower, a lot of useful manpower is being wasted without consideration of physical and mental capabilities. Pension incomes are low, and pensioners' economic position in society is steadily deteriorating. In general, a person must get along on from one-third to one-half of his working-time income. But, inflation eats into the buying power of his reduced income. Few organizations increase pensions for people already retired to compensate for the rising cost of living. While many retired persons seek employment to supplement their retired income, only a small percentage are successful.

"To relieve this situation I have these suggestions. Give more thought to the standard retirement age. I think it wasteful to retire some people at sixty-five or below (many are in their fifties) when the individual is both mentally and physically able to do a good job. At LSU a man was retired at sixty-five and then joined the faculty of another university, doing a good job of teaching for more than ten years. A few years ago LSU retired a man for age, who joined the Mississippi State University faculty for a time and is now on the faculty of an Arkansas college. During these years, the college he left at LSU has been short of faculty. All this does not make sense to me. I maintain that to set a retirement age below seventy-five and require retirement without regard to one's mental and physical ability to carry on is a lazy way to administer personnel."

Then he took note of the plight of wives with retired husbands on their hands, recalling something he had read: " 'I did not look forward to my husband's retirement mainly because he had no special interest or hobbies. However, I accepted the fact that I was going to have a man around the house most of the time and made up my mind to make a success of his retirement business. The biggest thing I lost was my independence. My friends do not call as they used to. When they do call I can feel my husband getting tense, if the conversation goes on for very long.' My advice," said Middleton, "would be for the woman of the house not to make an adjustment but carry on as though the old man was still at work."

Having dwelt on the pleasures and the shortcomings of retirement, the General (by which title he was addressed by everyone after his retirement) proceeded to acquaint his audience with a major project which at that time required his energies almost daily. Soon after Governor John J. McKeithen had come into office in May, 1964, he had sought to ease the state's growing racial tensions, fanned principally by whites both in and out of political office. Finally he hit upon the creation of a biracial commission to be composed of twenty-one blacks and twenty-one whites, with a white director and a black associate director. Who, the governor asked himself, would command the sort of respect essential to the successful working of such a commission?

Who but Troy Middleton? "When Governor McKeithen called me up and asked me about serving on a biracial commission, I suggested we talk it over at greater length. After we had, the governor asked if I would serve as chairman. I said I would—for a year." It turned out to be a long year, running from August 27, 1965, through May 28, 1970, when McKeithen disbanded the commission after being told that "the commission had fulfilled its original purposes." McKeithen chose a white attorney, John Martzell, and a black attorney, Jesse Stone, as director and associate director to head the staff of the Commission on Human Relations, Rights, and Responsibilities. Equal numbers of blacks and whites made up the commission.

Middleton, telling these retired extension workers about the commission, said:

"I know that from at least some of the letters and telephone calls I have received some of you wonder how or why a former country boy from Mississippi who had contact with Negroes on a cotton plantation could become involved in such a hazardous venture. It might be worthwhile to explain why I went out on the proverbial limb.

"With interracial trouble in many parts of the country, and with the passage by Congress of the Civil Rights Act and the trouble between the races at Jonesboro and at Bogalusa, the Council for a Better Louisiana (CABL) suggested to the governor that it would be wise to have such a commission advise him. CABL suggested that salaries be limited to the director, associate director, and a clerk, and that office and travel expenses should include the forty-two commission members.

"When Governor McKeithen called me and asked that I serve as a member of the commission I thought an easy way out was to tell him that among his appointments would be several cheap politicians and that I had no desire to become involved with people who would make the commission into a political football. His reply was: 'Here is the list I am inviting to serve; if you think any of the people are the kind you fear, please let me know.' On scanning the list I knew most of the whites but only a few of the Negroes. Of those I knew, some did not vote for the governor. I could not take issue with any I knew. This being the case, I accepted the appointment. I accepted for another reason: It was apparent that we might have serious trouble between the races. Congress had passed the Civil Rights Act. It was and is the law. The act is of course unpopular with some people. Its unpopularity would suggest that many of its provisions would be violated by some people and that such violation would probably lead to trouble. I asked myself this question: What right have I to refuse to help a governor when it is apparent that he will need help? Refusal would lead to some other person doing an unpleasant job, because it was apparent that someone must do it.

"The day after I accepted a place on the commission, the governor asked me to be the chairman. I declined. McKeithen is a persuasive individual, so the end result was that I became chairman and am still the chairman. The commission serves without pay and only in an advisory capacity. We have no authority to tell any person to comply with anything. This being the case, we are misunderstood by many people. Some believe that we serve no good purpose and that we are merely forty-two troublemakers. I noted recently in the press that Congressman John Rarick, if elected governor, would dissolve the commission because he felt that it served no useful purpose.

"I have had nasty letters and uncomplimentary telephone calls. I took an oath in 1910 to defend my country, obey the laws, support the president, and in short to try to be a law-abiding citizen. The Civil Rights Act is a law; to violate it would be to violate my oath. I shall never do that.

"We have had, during the tenure of Governor McKeithen, several instances where interracial trouble was brewing. The director and associate director and some members of the commission spent much time on these cases. Except for Bogalusa, which began before the commission was appointed, we have not had serious trouble. Do not gather from this that we could not have serious trouble. However, the longer we live with the situation, the less likely we are to have trouble. Time cures a lot of ills. No member of the commission has resigned. Two members, both white, have died. I have not been paid, nor have I submitted an expense account. None of the members has been paid and I cannot name one who has submitted an expense account. Some may have been reimbursed for travel; this I do not know.

"For my part, I have met once a week with the director and the associate director; the commission has had quite a few meetings. I can't say that I have enjoyed the work; it is not the kind of work one would especially enjoy. If I felt that the commission had not performed a useful service I would ask to be relieved. Had Congressman Rarick been elected governor the commission would have passed from the scene. I seriously doubt, however, that the problem between the races would pass with the passing of the commission.

"Much of our trouble stems from a disregard for our laws. If our laws are not what we should have, then we should work for repeal and not spend our time disregarding them. I fear that disregard for law and order in this country is on the increase. We are certainly not helping the situation by burning draft cards, cursing the government, and refusing to be good citizens," Middleton said.

In other comments to the extension workers, Middleton spoke of two problems confronting Louisianians in even more pressing fashion in 1973. "I do not want any of you to conclude that my lack of contact with LSU has caused me to lose contact with education. I am still keenly interested in our educational system from kindergarten through work for the Ph.D. I am so much interested that I am critical of some of the things we are doing. I have not been nor shall I ever be in agreement with the so-called double administrative systems for higher education in Louisiana. To have LSU and all its appendages administered by one independent board and the other state-supported colleges and universities plus the elementary and secondary schools administered by a different board, neither coordinating its work with the other, is certainly not good business. To me this is not unlike a big business trying to operate under two separate boards of directors, neither coordinating its work with the other.

"Too much emphasis is now being placed on a college degree and not enough on preparing a boy or a girl for the job to be done in life. What I refer to is better vocational and technical schools. We do not have the schools to prepare our young men and young women to fill the jobs in the industry now doing business in Louisiana and those industries which will be looking to Louisiana for a place to operate. Our educational system is not tooled for boys and girls whose high school record is evidence that they can not do college-level work. To put it bluntly, we are putting too much of our energies and our money into giving some people a college degree who are not capable of receiving it. Such young people, however, have a place in society, and we fail in our duty unless we help them find their place. No doubt this is realized by some who are unwilling to break with tradition. I prefer those who make mistakes by advanced thinking and planning to those who make mistakes by observing the status quo," Middleton said.

When McKeithen was seeking members for the biracial commission in 1965, at the time he asked Middleton to serve he also asked Dr. Albert Dent, Negro president of Dillard University in New Orleans, to serve. After Middleton looked over the list of prospective members, he changed his mind and agreed to an appointment. After the governor let it be known that Middleton was on the commission, Dent said he too would serve. Middleton then told McKeithen that he was pleased to be serving with Dent and would be even more pleased if Dent would accept the assistant chairmanship of the commission. The two worked together as long as the commission was in operation.

While the commission was in its early stages, a state senator in northwest Louisiana came out violently against the appointment of black attorney Jesse Stone as assistant director of the commission. Middleton inquired of an old friend and highly respected attorney in Shreveport as to the attorney's opinion of the senator and his objections. In short order, the Shreveport attorney said that Stone would be an excellent choice for the assistant directorship and that no attention should be paid to the segregationist senator's loud talk.

How did the commission work during its five years? "We organized area committees. I always felt it was most important when questions came up, or serious situations threatened to develop, that people from the area move in to deal with them. For instance, if a problem developed in the Shreveport area, Martzell and Stone would go there to confer with the area members of the commission. First thing you'd know the problem would have been settled.

"These commission members were people of the highest caliber—able, highly successful—and they had to be public spirited, considering the work the commission was called on to do. I saw McKeithen to fill him in as often as was necessary, as frequently as three times a week or as infrequently as once every three weeks, depending on how much was going on," Middleton recalled.

People learned to call the commission with all kinds of requests. Students and faculty at Southern University in Baton Rouge had long been unhappy with having to wait for trains on their drives to the campus. They were regularly promised an overpass, and just as regularly disappointed. Finally a grade crossing accident at the edge of the campus led to the threat of a march by Southern students. The student complaint was referred to Middleton. He noted that the commission was not empowered to act in such a case but made it a point to confer with McKeithen's executive assistant, William Redmann, to suggest that the governor act at once if he had promised help. McKeithen went to the Southern campus, saw the situation for himself. Quickly, work began to provide the rail overpass.

In 1966 and 1967, the Alexandria area committee worked long hours in Ferriday, where there was general laxity in law enforcement and Negroes were discriminated against and regularly subjected to abuse. (The sheriff of Concordia Parish in 1973 was sentenced to prison for perjury over his role in nonenforcement of the law in Ferriday and the area.) A Negro-owned service station was burned, Negro churches were set ablaze. "The situation was about to explode. A Negro Catholic priest worked hard to bring peace. Attorneys Martzell and Stone went there many times. Finally peace was restored," Middleton recalled.

Early in 1967 Negroes picketed at a shopping center in Opelousas, seeking more job opportunities. "It was touch and go there for a while. Our area team was busy there, with the result that more jobs began opening to Negroes," Middleton recalled. "In New Roads a movie theater was opened to Negroes early in 1968 after word was quietly passed from the governor to the theater owner that he was required to abide by the Civil Rights Act.

"The Commission on Human Relations, Rights, and Responsibilities was definitely responsible for opening the ranks of the Louisiana State Police to qualified Negro applicants. I told Tom Burbank, the director, that he would have to use eligible blacks. I told him not to put Negro troopers in desk assignments but to send them out on the highway where they could be seen. I thought it was better to do it this way rather than, as Negro attorney A. P. Tureaud suggested, to give wide publicity to the selection of the first few Negro state troopers. Middleton told commission members— speaking mainly to the black members, as he recalled it—that it wasn't enough to talk about getting Negroes into the state police; it would be necessary to go out and find competent men. As a result, three Negroes with high qualifications applied. When someone suggested to McKeithen that Burbank appoint a Negro probationer to the state police force, Middleton said he couldn't agree. "Let the applicant be qualified and go through the same academy training program as all the rest. It is important to have the same standards for all."

In his second year as chairman of the biracial commission, Middleton received a telephone call at his home at 10 o'clock one night. The caller identified herself as a Mrs. Grant (Middleton thought the name was phony). She wanted to ask some questions about the work of the commission. "Go right ahead," Middleton told her.

"Is it true that federal money supports the commission?" the caller asked.

"No, it is not true," Middleton replied.

"What is your salary?" she asked.

"I receive none. Most members of the commission don't turn in expense accounts to seek reimbursement," Middleton said.

"I understand that the director gets the same pay as the governor," the caller said.

"No," she was told; "the director gets $15,000 while the governor receives $20,000."

"She told me," Middleton recalled, "that she was a strong segregationist. She had tried to get the information she wanted from the governor's office but wasn't successful there. So, she said, she decided to call me.

"While I was chairman of the commission, one of the state's more

dedicated segregationists called me and invited me to sit at the head table
at a dinner at which the consul from the Republic of South Africa was
to speak. What, I asked, was the consul to talk about? I didn't need to ask,
of course. He was coming to address the hate group on the virtues of apar-
theid in South Africa. I wasn't foolish enough to fall into that trap," Middleton recalled.

"I received a number of invitations to attend comparable meetings
during the years the biracial commission operated. The callers must have
known me well enough to realize that I wouldn't violate any law, and that
I'd take a sensible position. What they wanted to be able to say was that
the chairman of the Commission on Human Relations, Rights, and Responsibilities had come to their meetings and sat at the head table. Well,
I didn't fall for any of their pitches."

While he was busy with the affairs of the biracial commission in late
May, 1967, he received a long distance telephone call from Washington.
What could Washington want? Middleton thought; the commission oper-
ates on state funds only. On the telephone came a brisk, accented voice.
On being assured that he was indeed speaking to retired Lieutenant General Troy H. Middleton, the caller identified himself as the Polish orderly
who had served Brigadier General Cyrus Searcy, chief of staff of the VIII
Corps during World War II. He asked if Middleton remembered General
Searcy's orderly. Yes, Middleton did remember. The caller talked on for
twenty minutes. Ten minutes later, he called again. "If you go back on
active duty, General Middleton, I want to be your orderly," he said. "I
assured him that he would be my orderly if I were recalled to active duty,"
Middleton said. At age seventy-seven, he wasn't expecting further combat
service.

In its third year of operation, Middleton said he "got to thinking that
the commission had about run out of advice for people in the problem
areas around the state. The word was getting around pretty well. At Tallulah, for instance, Negro school children were not being transported, as the
law required, in desegregated buses. We sent Martzell up there to explain
the requirements of the Civil Rights Act. It wasn't long before the responsible people in Tallulah decided to obey the law. Our most serious concerns
when the commission went into operation involved working to see that
Civil Rights Act provisions on voting and equal opportunity in employ-

ment were carried out. Many hundreds of hours of quiet, earnest talk helped bring about the desired results."

Almost all of the actions of biracial commission members were carried out quietly. Though newspaper, radio, and television reporters may have known of the conversations going on, almost nothing was published or broadcast, to prevent offering opportunities to rabble-rousers to come in and preach their hate doctrines.

"Finally, as the gubernatorial campaign of 1967–1968 began taking shape, I told Governor McKeithen that the state no longer needed me in the chairmanship of the biracial commission. I thought we could go on using the area task forces in different sections of the state, though there were fewer occasions demanding their presence. The director and associate director at the capitol should be able to handle anything that came up. And since the appointment of this commission was originally recommended by the Council for a Better Louisiana, I thought it would be the courteous thing to inform CABL of the current situation. The commission members agreed with me, but they wouldn't buy my stepping out of the chairmanship. I agreed, finally, to continue on as chairman but not from an office in the capitol building. With an election campaign coming on, I didn't want the biracial commission involved in any way. It was, on the other hand, all right for individuals to involve themselves on their own. I had gone on television earlier to speak in support of the constitutional amendment which permitted McKeithen to succeed himself as governor. I did so because I didn't think it made good sense to deny the state the services of a good man in the governorship, whether it be McKeithen or any other man who might choose to seek two successive terms," Middleton recalled.

"You know," he said on May 31, 1967, "I've been in hundreds of sessions with the governor and in weekly meetings with the Commission on Human Relations, Rights, and Responsibilities. A few nights ago I attended my granddaughter Judy Stewart's graduation from high school. A Negro girl sat in the front row among the honor graduates. Seventeen Negroes were in the graduating class. At the commencement ceremonies my son-in-law, Ashton Stewart, told me that among the graduates was the daughter of Negro lawyer Johnny Jones, an attorney who had earned Ashton's admiration and respect over the years. As a college student, Jones had foregone meals to save his money to date the girl who later became Mrs. Jones. The world is changing; the commission helped make the necessary change a bit smoother."

Early in February, 1968, Martzell told Middleton that he felt he was no longer earning his pay as director of the biracial commission. Stone said that he felt likewise. Middleton suggested a conference with McKeithen. The governor said that the salaries of Martzell and Stone were the finest of investments if paying them meant that there would be no difficulty forthcoming between the races. "The money is being well spent," McKeithen said as he prepared to enter his second term as governor, the first in this century to succeed himself in Louisiana.

At this time, retail stores in Baton Rouge were beginning to employ numbers of Negro clerks. "I make a point of going to the Negro clerks when I go shopping," Middleton said. "They are courteous and helpful. I went to the Tic-Toc Shoe repair shop to have a suitcase stitched, expecting to have to leave it and come back. A Negro woman clerk asked if I had five minutes. I said I did and took a seat. She was back with the repaired suitcase in five minutes. When Baton Rouge stores began hiring Negroes, I visited stores to observe. I've seen nothing to indicate any inferiority to white clerks."

Commission members followed a policy of not using their personal influence to help a person get a job. But it was Middleton who told McKeithen, "You have a number of Negro employees up here, but they're all handling mops and brooms. When a good Negro typist's name appears at the top of a Civil Service list, hire her to work in your office."

Deep into his second term as governor, McKeithen "shifted gears on civil rights," Middleton observed in October, 1970. "Maybe he has been a segregationist at heart and it has finally come out now. Dr. Dent, president of Dillard University, was going to resign from the biracial commission. I told him, 'You can't do that,' and he agreed to stay on." McKeithen continued, however, to seek Middleton's counsel.

"I told him to get rid of the State Sovereignty Commission and the UnAmerican Activities Commission, neither of which was doing anything useful," Middleton recalled. "The Sovereignty Commission was knocked out but the UnAmerican Activities Commission somehow was slipped back in."

Eventually, Middleton decided that McKeithen was beginning to make political use of the biracial commission's director and associate director. He went to the governor with the suggestion that the time had come to phase out the work of the commission. The governor agreed, Middleton said. "He sent letters of thanks to all the members in May, 1970. We asked the legislature the next year to close the book on the biracial commission."

In the five years the Commission on Human Relations, Rights, and Responsibilities was in business, "We never moved to take over in any community; we always waited for the governor to send our members or until we were invited," Middleton said. "I never went to a community on biracial commission business in those five years. I felt that it was much more important that the people of a troubled area work out their own problems with the help of Martzell and Stone."

James Winfree, chairman of a group representing three major oil refining companies, came to see Middleton in November, 1967, seeking his views on a federally financed job training program which would draw Negroes off the streets and into classrooms. The oil companies would lend teachers for courses in drafting and other job skills. The cost would be about $4,500,000. Middleton's first thought was that the program should have originated with the state and should have been funded by the state. This observation brought up a subject in which he was finally to take the lead: Louisiana's desperate need for coordination in education.

"I looked around at the state's support of vocational-technical schools, at their substandard facilities, at their haphazard direction in many instances. We have put entirely too much emphasis on the worth of a college degree," he said. As he sat at his desk in his office on the LSU campus, he turned and looked through the venetian blind behind him. The Memorial Tower clock had struck the half hour and students were hurrying across the Tower plaza. "You know, six or seven hundred of this student body of eighteen thousand will flunk out of LSU at the end of the semester. Most of them would have been better off if they had gone to vocational school—if we had the space to accommodate them. With proper counseling, many of them would never have tried LSU or any other college.

"I don't agree with some of my good friends who think we should continue the old open door policy on the Baton Rouge campus, admitting every freshman who shows up with a high school diploma. Chancellor Taylor tells me that if we set admission standards we would eliminate the late bloomers. I don't think we'd eliminate many. They should be ready when they come to the campus. When their placement scores show they aren't prepared, it's a terrible waste to let them pour into our classrooms, only to have them leave frustrated, sometimes embittered," Middleton said.

"I've just heard," Middleton said in January, 1968, "that the Phi Beta Kappa visitation group has turned the university down again. The problem, I am told, lies on the fringes and not in our College of Arts and Sciences, which is much better than those on a number of campuses which have long had Phi Beta Kappa chapters. I think Governor McKeithen is improving the membership of the Board of Supervisors with most of his appointments. You know what the Phi Beta Kappa visitors must think of a board, eight of whose fourteen members were old athletes known more for athletic feats than for any interest in the problems of higher education. With an improvement in the quality of the board, I feel that a change in our admissions policy alone might persuade the Phi Beta Kappa people that LSU deserves a chapter of the highest scholarship society," Middleton said.

"Our open door admissions policy is not only silly; it's sad. We flunk out the unqualified and forget them. What would happen if our high schools had better counseling systems to which academically unqualified seniors could be referred—even if only half or a third could be given good vocational advice? After I retired, I had a secretary for awhile whose husband wasn't making the grade in LSU. She told me about his problems. I told her to have him come in and see me. We had two or three sessions. I told him to go to Delgado Trade Institute in New Orleans, where he could apply his considerable mechanical aptitudes. He wasn't fitted for the academic world; he was a good mechanic. He did well at Delgado and soon gained confidence in himself. He's doing quite well with a large drug company now."

Long an outspoken advocate of coordination among the state's institutions of higher education, Middleton in January, 1968, commented on a proposal by state Senator Frederick L. Eagan of New Orleans, calling for creation of a coordinating council to be composed of the chairman of Louisiana's Board of Education; three members of the state board; the president of LSU; three members of the LSU board; and two or three faculty members. "I'd invite representation from the private colleges and universities to sit with the coordinating board. Coordination is inescapable. We're wasting millions now because we haven't had it. The dollar finally will force us to coordinate," Middleton said.

"I'd put the Board of Education in charge of public elementary and secondary schools. The board dealing with higher education would strictly coordinate. We would need a man of the highest competence at the head of the coordinating staff. He would be empowered to straighten out business practices at all institutions of higher education and to cut sharply the size of administrative staffs on campuses."

A New Orleans *States-Item* editorial on September 22, 1966, quoting Middleton, summarized the case for coordination long before the legislature came to grips with it. Under the headline, "Taming an Uncoordinated Giant," the *States-Item* editorial said in part:

> Higher education in Louisiana has become a hydraheaded monster, the ill-conceived creature of lack of vision, petty politics, and timorous leadership.
>
> Louisiana higher education, in the words of General Troy H. Middleton, president emeritus of Louisiana State University, "is a hodgepodge. There is no real connection between LSU and any other system. Our board is jealous of its prerogatives and never coordinates with either the State Board of Education or the private colleges."
>
> New impetus has been given the drive for coordination by a Public Affairs Research Council study published this week. PAR points out that in the last few years, the legislature has authorized seven institutions of higher learning, although no recognized study established their need. The inevitable outgrowth of this approach is empire-building. An almost inexorable expansion of plant and curriculum, quite apart from need, follows authorization of a new college. There is more than enough evidence to establish a prima facie case for coordination of higher education in Louisiana.

On March 28, 1968, Middleton bent one of his self-imposed rules about meddling in university affairs. His old friend, General Maxwell Taylor, former commander of the 101st Airborne Division, former superintendent of the United States Military Academy, former chief of staff of the army, former chairman of the joint chiefs of staff, was coming to the campus to speak. At the previous day's Rotary Club meeting in downtown Baton Rouge, Colonel Thomas Blakeney, commandant of the ROTC, had told Middleton that he could find out nothing about plans for meeting Taylor at the airport. When Middleton's discreet inquiries turned up no information, he decided to drive his own car to the airport to meet General

Taylor. Middleton took three students and met Taylor at the airport. "I didn't see anyone from the LSU faculty or staff out there, but there were thirty or forty hippie types carrying signs protesting American involvement in the war in Vietnam. That was our greeting to Max Taylor, one of America's great soldiers. And you know, if I hadn't pushed I wouldn't even have been invited to hear Max speak," Middleton said.

Governor McKeithen had by this time appointed a Committee on Coordination of Higher Education, which invited Middleton to air his views on April 5, 1968. He did so, with the summary remarks that, "The ultimate solution will be one board for all higher education. The membership will not be educators. There will be a small staff with the best educational brains you can get. We need better management even more than coordination of higher education."

When the creation of the Coordinating Council for Higher Education was authorized, in January, 1969, McKeithen asked Middleton if he would serve on the council. Since he had been its most outspoken advocate in the state for several years, Middleton felt that he couldn't refuse. "All right; if you'll serve," said McKeithen, "how about being chairman?"

"No, sir," Middleton responded. "You remember what happened to me on the biracial commission. You appointed me chairman for one year and every time I came to you at the expiration of a year, you said the commission just wouldn't work without me. This is one commission that's going to work without me being its chairman. I was the only chairman the biracial commission had in its five-year existence."

After the coordinating council had been at work for two years, Middleton said, "We never cut out anything in education. The Southern Regional Education Board was once a good thing. Its concept was sound. But the plan wasn't used too well. The only way Louisiana profited was in veterinary medicine. We paid $1,500 a student a year to Texas A & M, which had a good program. Everything in education should have a built-in cutoff date. Let it run a maximum of ten years, then require a justification for it to continue.

"The coordinating council has more than justified itself in just two years. We recently denied an application from the University of Southwestern Louisiana for permission to start a law school that simply isn't needed. We turned down a legislative authorization for a two-year division of LSU at Ferriday. The LSU Board of Supervisors referred it to us; the coordinating council made a study and then rejected the proposal as educationally unwise. Politicians may try to reinstate it, but they'll be wrong if they do.

"Northwestern State University wanted to put in a flight program, saying that it wouldn't cost anything—which was not true. We turned them down at the last coordinating council meeting. You see, Northwestern had been slipping in enrollment and was looking for something to jack up attendance. When the two-year program at LSU in Shreveport was started in 1967, they said they didn't want a four-year program. Now (in 1971) they're asking for four years. They have Centenary College in Shreveport and three state colleges within sixty to seventy miles: Northwestern, Louisiana Tech, and Grambling. They don't need a four-year LSU in Shreveport. I don't think the LSU Board of Supervisors would vote now for a four-year LSUS. Of course, before long, they might play politics with the legislature and succeed. (In 1972, the legislature authorized creation of a four-year LSUS.)

"At our April (1971) meeting of the coordinating council, my old friend Albert Dent, former president of Dillard University, and I were talking about the possibility of a merger of Southern University in New Orleans with LSU in New Orleans. He said he thought a merger was a possibility. I had to disagree—not that a merger wasn't desirable, but because I couldn't see anyone at either school in New Orleans favoring a merger that might cost some administrators their jobs. The state could save much more than a million dollars annually by merging the two universities in New Orleans. More could be saved by merging Southern and LSU in Shreveport. I'd make vocational-technical schools of the buildings now occupied by Southern in New Orleans and in Shreveport. That way the state would be serving far greater numbers of blacks and whites who don't qualify for or don't want college education but could benefit from good vocational training," Middleton said.

"Another thing that has cropped up is the proposal for thirteen- and fourteen-year high schools, which I think the coordinating council will reject. I have received a number of phone calls recently, asking my support of the idea, to add vocational training at night at high schools with regular programs during the day. One East Baton Rouge Parish school board member declared this would be a good thing, 'to keep youngsters off the streets at night.' I told the board member I couldn't agree. We need vocational-technical schools, but we don't need them as appurtenances to high schools. We should bring industry into the consultations to find out what industry thinks is needed to qualify young people to go into industrial jobs.

"There ought to be more leadership forthcoming at LSU in advising on coordination with the people in vocational-technical education. LSU is off on other continents with programs that might bring international prestige when we'd be better off concentrating on Louisiana's needs. Lord knows we have our quota of problems, with the lowest literacy rate in the United States and with industries having difficulties finding the semiskilled and skilled workers we might be providing through more intelligent use of greater vocational-technical teaching facilities.

As recently as the spring of 1971, there was considerable sentiment in the black community of Louisiana for mergers in higher education, but feeling was beginning to change. In October, 1971, at his LSU office, Middleton had three visitors from the black community—a leading clergyman, a prominent businessman, and a ranking member of the Cooperative Extension Service. They asked Middleton to oppose and to use his influence on the coordinating council to help block any move to merge Southern University and LSU in Shreveport and in New Orleans. "I listened but I made no promises," Middleton said. "My friends' vested interests were showing mighty plainly."

Throughout his retirement years, beginning in February, 1962, Middleton went to his campus office before going to the weekly Rotary Club luncheon at the Capitol House Hotel downtown. October 7, 1970, was a fairly typical Wednesday at Middleton's office. Chancellor Taylor stopped in for a thirty-minute chat. At eleven o'clock in trooped a party of seven bearing coffee pot, cups, and cookies. They formed a semicircle in front of Middleton's desk and delivered premature birthday greetings, five days before his eighty-first birthday. The greeters were Richard Mornhinveg, superintendent of operations and maintenance; retired Marine Brigadier General Louie Reinberg, director of the LSU Foundation; Quinn Coco, comptroller; Walter B. Calhoun, university system vice president for finance; George Schwab, purchasing agent; Dr. Joseph Reynolds, system vice president for instruction and research; and Ray Nolen, manager of the LSU Bookstore. Half the group had been cadets in the ROTC under Middleton.

A "Do you fellows remember the time?" was good enough to launch a flotilla of recollections. Schwab recalled having been offered the bookstore managership by President Smith back in the 1930s. "I went to you, General, for advice on whether I should take the job. You were cagey; you wouldn't advise me, saying 'I'm not your boss.' I persisted. You still wouldn't advise me. Years later I found out why. You were suspicious of the university's business management—and were you ever right!"

To Mornhinveg, a longtime fishing companion, Middleton said, "Do you remember, Dick, how hard I had to work on you to get you to take the job of running the operations and maintenance department back in 1939 when your boss, George Caldwell, got swept up in the scandals investigation? Did I finally have to threaten you with a suggestion that if you didn't take that job someone might think you'd been in cahoots with old George?" Mornhinveg grinned his recollection.

To Coco, Middleton said, "Do you remember, Quinn, right after I took over the presidency from Harold Stoke, my telling you, 'You know, the university sure was a hell of a lot easier to run from the other side.' ?"

They laughed over Sam Montague's (he was one of those dismissed in 1934 at Huey Long's instance, then reinstated in 1941) misadventures with his little Austin car, which was forever materializing in a classroom or on top of the Indian mounds.

And Middleton reminded them of the outbreak of panty raids which came along with the emergence of the Ole Miss-LSU football game as the season's high point, of his eventual loss of patience and announcement that raid participants would be dismissed from the University. "There was this graduate student—plenty old enough to know better—who asked, 'Are you going to dismiss me? All I was doing was pushing a fellow through a window in the girls' dorm.' I told him, 'All I'm doing is dismissing you from LSU.' I did so. He came back the next year and received his degree—and I imagine he learned something from the incident.

A year later, October 6, 1971, Mornhinveg, Nolen, Schwab, Reinberg, and Coco gathered again in Middleton's office on the Wednesday preceding his eighty-second birthday. The recollections flowed again, in the course of which Schwab recalled having heard a professor of business administration say that Middleton once declared, "The best committee is a committee of three, with two of them in the hospital."

Middleton, having made a phone call earlier, was reminded of an occasion during his presidency of the university when he called someone on the campus (he placed his own calls, usually, and waited for them to go through) and was told by a secretary that the person was busy. "I'd heard this once too often, so I responded to the young lady, 'He'd better be busy. That's what we're all here for. Now, I'd like to talk to him, please.' Believe me, that got results."

Reinberg said he'd noticed that the Army and Navy Club in Washington was observing its fiftieth anniversary. "Well, I'm a charter member," Middleton said. "This piece of choice property became available in Washington. We all went into our cookie jars and bought the property. Somebody in the group thought to bring in Henry Ford and John Philip Sousa at $1,000 a head. We built an eighteen-hole golf course and expanded it later to twenty-seven holes. That's how the club got its start," Middleton recalled.

Someone else asked what the General heard from Dan Borth, living now in retirement in Arizona. Both the General and his former executive vice president were having circulatory problems with their legs. "You know," the General said, "Dan wanted to resign when my successor came into the presidency. I told him to stick it out till he was sixty and then check out. He did, earning his one-third pay at retirement. Then he went to Washington and into the highest paying Civil Service job in the federal government, at $28,000. They had the highest regard for Dan in Washington, where he'd served two tours, helping them straighten some things out in the Pentagon. All Dan wanted to do was to work. He was the most efficient man I ever saw. I told Dotty (his wife) I'd quit a fellow who worked till eight o'clock every night."

At the 1970 pre-birthday gathering, Middleton had just been to Lake Charles for a preview showing of the movie, *Patton*, on invitation of the producers. It was, he thought, "about what you'd expect of a movie—some parts representative, some not." He gave his visitors the correct version of the incident in which Patton stumbled over the feet of Middleton's driver, who was sleeping under a lean-to outside the command post of the Eleventh Armored Division just after Christmas during the Battle of the Bulge. "That was George, all right."

That led to another question. What about the real Patton, if it didn't come through in the movie? Middleton replied: "From the standpoint of the high commander who had to do something besides just fight, Bradley was much Patton's superior. Brad considered all the angles. He got along better with people. Patton's principal worth was that he kept things moving. He kept everybody else moving—not only his juniors but his seniors. Otherwise, during the Battle of the Bulge, there would have been a tendency to play Montgomery—to dress up the lines instead of getting in there and hitting the Germans hard. I think the German High Command had a high regard for George, but even they erred in underestimating George's ability to move from Metz to Bastogne so fast. For that matter, Ike himself didn't believe George could move that fast. I must say I shared in George's view of Montgomery, the British commander on the north side of the Battle of the Bulge area. The leadership up there was poor. Montgomery should have moved in and launched a counterattack long before he turned his troops loose. Joe Collins would have attacked the Germans long before he was allowed to, if he had had his way."

The movie *Patton* reminded Middleton again of the Battle of the Bulge. "I had to draw a line our troops couldn't drop behind in that battle," he recalled. "There are times when you have to stay and fight, no matter what the odds. Little groups of Americans threw the Germans so far behind schedule at the start of the Ardennes fight that they were never able to get far along with their drive to the Meuse River."

Again, in May, 1971, Middleton came back to the question of education for careers. "We're not doing this right. We're doing a terrible job of providing vocational-technical education. With only 11 percent of Louisiana high school graduates being graduated from college, how can we say we're providing educationally for even a major fraction of our young people? I think vocational-technical education should be given autonomous status between high school and college," he said.

When the Public Affairs Research Council of Louisiana published a report on educational leadership in Louisiana, with a recommendation that the state superintendent of education be made appointive, that strict qualifications be set up, and that the State Board of Education be given all of the superintendent's powers except administrative ones, Middleton spoke in agreement. He noted also that Louisiana is the only state electing both its superintendent and its board of education. "You can elect too many," he said. "By the way, Representative Lillian Walker lost my vote by writing a letter to the coordinating council director expressing disappointment over the council's rejection of the proposal to put in thirteenth and fourteenth grades at Glen Oaks High School here for vocational education. She said she would try to push it through the legislature. Maybe they'd put it in; that's our trouble." (As things turned out, Representative Walker herself failed to win reelection, being unseated by a Republican who won a rare victory in East Baton Rouge Parish.) No more was heard officially from the proposal to add two years to high schools.

At that time, Middleton said, "I want to get off the coordinating council. It's not that I've lost interest in education, but I'll be eighty-two in October and I think it's time." He continued beyond his eighty-third birthday and, late in 1973, was well along toward completion of the term which was to run through 1974.

At the end of his second term, John McKeithen was succeeded as governor by former Congressman Edwin W. Edwards. Middleton, wanting to end his service on the coordinating council, told the chairman, Joe D. Smith, he was ready to step down even though his appointment was to run through 1974. "The chairman agreed that he thought I'd done my part, but he said I'd have to stay on and see a single board created to head all higher education in the state. What could I do but agree to continue serving?" The 1972 legislature authorized creation of such a single board, to take effect in two years, setting off a great many efforts to block the so-called "superboard"—efforts energetically pushed through 1973.

Middleton liked to fish and hunt. Fishing he found to be a great age leveler. With his grandsons, Troy H. Middleton III and Bingham Stewart, he, in his late seventies, found the two fifteen-year-olds companionable on a stream bank or out in the Gulf of Mexico. He cut down on his duck hunting as he approached eighty. Mrs. Middleton, herself a good shot, had hunted quail and duck with the General before and after World War II, but now elected to enjoy her retirement mainly indoors. General and Mrs. Middleton spent much of their leisure time on the covered patio at the back of their home and enjoyed a swimming pool which was even more attractive to their grandchildren. The Stewarts, with their children Judy and Bingham, lived in Baton Rouge. Troy, Jr., his wife, and their children Troy III and Emily, last stationed at Fort Polk, made their retirement home in DeRidder after 1972, held there by the attraction of nearby Toledo Bend Lake.

Having leisure time was fine with Middleton, but he claimed less than the share of a man in his seventies and then in his eighties. "When I retired from the presidency of LSU," Middleton said, "I had no intention of going into inactivity. You don't do that and stay meaningfully alive. I told the Board of Supervisors I didn't want any farewell party; I wasn't going anywhere. I didn't want people being hit up for a contribution for a banquet and a gift. This may have puzzled some board members, but not the ones who really knew me.

"The board authorized me $1,800 a year for travel. I cut that back to $600. At the end of my first year in retirement I had spent nothing, so I cut the travel item from the modest budget of the president emeritus. Somebody—maybe Quinn Coco—restored the travel item at $300. I knocked it out again, and this time it stayed out," Middleton said.

In 1962, his first year of retirement, Mississippi State University proclaimed Troy Middleton its alumnus of the year. He joined the company of a select group headed by United States Senator John C. Stennis, the 1958 designate, among the first chosen by Mississippi State alumni.

Through the 1960s, the General and Mrs. Middleton drove in their Thunderbird car to many out-of-town LSU football games. Their picture appeared in the September 20, 1964, Baton Rouge *Sunday Advocate* with the notation that they "seldom miss a home game and travel in their sports car to many of the out-of-town games." Middleton continued doing his own driving to his campus office, to Rotary Club on Wednesday, and to the grocery, the laundry, the post office, in 1973. On advice of his physician he gave up long out-of-town drives at the start of the 1970s.

After the retiring United Givers Fund president, Harry A. Cassady of Southern Bell Telephone Company, presented his report and thanked his fellow officers for their work in a record-breaking campaign in the fall of 1963, at the UGF spring meeting in 1964, Middleton found himself facing a new challenge as 1964–1965 president of the United Givers. He went right to work. When the fund campaign began in October, 1964, the planning that went into it was soon apparent. In the March 29, 1965, *Torch Bearer,* Baton Rouge's UGF newsletter, Middleton wrote: "A total of $946,302 was raised during the drive—the largest single amount ever raised by any organization in the history of Baton Rouge. Not only were you a part of this great effort, but another outstanding feature is that you were the best campaign group in the state."

When the East Baton Rouge Chapter of the American Red Cross moved into handsome new quarters at 1165 South Foster Drive on Feb-

ruary 11, 1965, it took up its headquarters in a building on a site thereafter to be known as Middleton Place. The $90,000 building was erected
with funds collected and invested during World War II. Middleton was a
member of the chapter board of directors and headed the building committee. Manager Frank McGurk of the East Baton Rouge Red Cross
Chapter noted that it was a consensus decision to name the center and its
site for Middleton, leader in war and in peace.

The postman was forever bringing Middleton letters from men who
had known him in his earlier capacities. In mid-May, 1965, came a letter
bearing a clipping from the Montgomery, Alabama, *Advertiser-Journal* of
Sunday, May 16. It was a copy of a column written by Burns Bennett, Alabama director of Selective Service. Bennett had been a drum major with
the LSU Band during the last years of Middleton's first tour at LSU, when
he was both commandant of cadets and dean of men. Bennett's column
read in part:

> At a recent Reserve Officers Association luncheon here, Major General
> John E. Kelly, Birmingham, U.S. Army IV Corps commander, talked about
> the Reserve Officers Training Corps in colleges and universities. And in my
> Selective Service job I'm asked often by prospective collegians about taking
> military in schools.
>
> I can't speak for other colleges, but at Louisiana State University the
> Cadet Corps was the pride of the campus, and I wouldn't take a million dollars
> for my ROTC days there.
>
> They say that in many schools military training isn't exactly popular. Well,
> I wouldn't know about that, because in the mid-'30s I think half the kids in
> Louisiana lived only for the time when they could climb into one of those gray
> and black LSU uniforms. In those days, and I hope it's still true, "Old Lou's"
> Cadet Corps was recognized and respected from Shreveport to New Orleans,
> and from Bogalusa to Lake Charles, in the other corner.
>
> I was a bandsman, and traditionally bandsmen are the world's worst
> soldiers. I can't honestly say that I did much to destroy this tradition. ROTC
> at LSU gave me the association of two of the finest men I've ever known—
> Colonel Troy H. Middleton, the commandant of cadets, and Regular Army
> Sergeant William B. Smith, who really ran the school. That sergeants always
> run the army is pretty well known. LSU's soldiers were no exception. Colonel
> Middleton was probably the most popular man ever to hit the Tiger campus.
> But if the problem was really important, we'd "go over Colonel Middleton's
> head," and take it up direct with Sergeant Smith.
>
> That Colonel Middleton later became Lieutenant General Middleton, CG
> of the World War II VIII Corps, attests to his military ability. Afterwards he

returned as one of LSU's great presidents, which witnesses to his popularity and executive skill.

On March 30, 1966, the LSU ROTC Company of the Association of the United States Army chose to name itself the General Troy H. Middleton Company, and made a presentation to Middleton in the ballroom of the LSU Union. Middleton had turned the first spade of earth for construction of the Union a few years earlier.

The Baton Rouge chapter of the National Conference of Christians and Jews chose Middleton to receive its annual brotherhood award at a dinner on January 20, 1966. Governor McKeithen led the praise, added to by the Right Reverend Iveson Noland, Episcopal bishop coadjutor of the Diocese of Louisiana, and by Paul Hebert, dean of the Law School. Lewis Gottlieb handed Middleton the organization's plaque in token of appreciation for his work in achieving racial harmony in Louisiana through the Commission on Human Relations, Rights, and Responsibilities.

Middleton responded to the presentation, saying, "You are not here to honor Troy Middleton . . . you are here because down in your hearts you believe in the rights and brotherhood of man. . . . I have seen great changes in religion and in the approach of human beings to each other. When I was a boy in Mississippi, I don't recall seeing a Catholic in that part of the state. When I was a youngster I was told that there were two political parties, but I was at least ten years old before I found out they were not Democrats and the Methodist Church. But times have changed. When the governor asked me to head the biracial commission, I was reluctant to take the responsibility. But I realized that I had no right to turn down a man who was trying to do a good job for Louisiana. I took the job because I believed in the things we are talking about here tonight," Middleton said.

For his accomplishment in racial peace-keeping, the Louisiana Association of Broadcasters, meeting in New Orleans, September 10, 1966, chose Middleton as their Louisianian of the Year, awarding him a bronze plaque.

Middleton's deep interest in his old cadets surfaced many times during his retirement years. He read in the Baton Rouge *Morning Advocate* on July 2, 1970, that one of his cadets from the graduating class of 1936, Major General George S. Bowman, Jr., had just returned from Vietnam and had become commanding general of the United States Marine Corps base at Camp Pendleton, California. "You know," Middleton began, "General Bowman—he was Junior Bowman as a backfield star on the football teams of 1933–1935—was one of our best graduates in the ROTC. I gave him his appointment as a second lieutenant in the marines in 1936. In those days, we issued commissions to a select few in other services than the army.

"Junior came to me one day in September, 1935, his senior year, saying 'I've got to give up football. I'm the cadet colonel of the ROTC, an engineering student, and a football player. I don't have the time for all three; something's got to give.'

"I told him not to be too quick to make a decision, suggesting that he write down what he had to do each day, and how much time he was devoting to each task. If, after doing this, he found that he really would not have the time for all three of his major assignments, then he should give up the least important, football. He gave it some thought and came back to tell me that he was going to manage all three."

Not only his former cadets but others in the university during Middleton's presidency sought his counsel and advice when they were considering job changes. Edsel (Tad) Thrash, LSU director of Alumni Affairs, came to Middleton to ask his advice on seeking an appointment as executive secretary of the Mississippi Board of Higher Education. Thrash, a former national intercollegiate boxing champion, explained why he was interested in the challenge. Middleton listened, then said, "I think you're a good man, Tad, and I'll recommend you in exchange for a promise: Don't ever blame me when you come up against the problems I know you're heading into. I'm a former Mississippian like you and I know things there won't be always to your liking." Thrash took the job.

When Middleton's successor in the LSU presidency, John Hunter, announced early in the year that he would retire June 30, 1972, after ten and a half years at the head of the expanded university system, speculation began at once on who would take Hunter's place. Among the names heard in conversations around the campus were those of retiring Governor McKeithen, at least half a dozen others, and that of Martin Woodin, university system executive vice president who was the eventual choice of the Board of Supervisors.

Though Middleton had repeatedly said he would not play any role in the matter, friends of a number of the prospective choices for the presidency asked for his "thoughts" about a choice. Reminding them all that he had made no recommendations and had scrupulously refrained from expressing an opinion when his own successor was being chosen in 1961, he declined to put in a word for anyone. His telephone rang at home and at his LSU office on Wednesday.

Governor McKeithen, saying that some of his friends had suggested that he might entertain the idea, was heard to wonder what Middleton thought of the friends' suggestion. A friend of World War I days brought overtures in behalf of the governor; Middleton smiled over them but said he would not enter the picture. A few days later McKeithen himself telephoned and said he'd like to meet Middleton at the General's campus office to explore his friends' suggestion that he might be presidential material.

"It wouldn't look right, Governor," Middleton responded, "for you to come out here. Why don't I come down to your office and we can talk things over."

Middleton drove down to the capitol. He and the governor conferred. "I told him of the advantages and the disadvantages he might have. I told him it would be essential that any prospective president have the respect of the faculty," Middleton said. There matters rested, with the clear understanding that Middleton would speak to no one in the governor's behalf and with no suggestion from the governor that he do so, in mid-February, 1972.

Through March and into April, others called or came to see Middleton. A member of the Board of Supervisors came to the General's office on a Wednesday morning. "I'm in trouble," the board member said. "I've jumped the gun on this, speaking out for one man."

Middleton replied, "I can't help you on this presidency matter. I didn't speak out last time and I won't this time. But I agree that you are in trouble. You make a big mistake in ignoring faculty wishes in this selection."

A week later, Middleton's phone rang. It was Washington calling. An old friend from Middleton's days in the LSU presidency, John Hannah, retired president of Michigan State University, renewed acquaintance, asked whether the LSU presidency had been decided, was told that the job was still open, and asked Middleton if he would put in a good word for a younger associate of Hannah who was currently president of a California college. Middleton told his caller that he should write a letter to the Board of Supervisors in behalf of the Californian, but that he—Middleton—would remain strictly neutral.

After the call, Middleton said, "You know, Hannah was one of the land-grant college presidents who impressed me most at our national meetings. I remember attending my first such meeting in Houston in 1952. When I go to a meeting I look around to see who's running it. I sort out the leaders and the stuffed shirts. At Houston, I was struck by the leadership of three men, the presidents of Clemson, of the University of Minnesota, and of Hannah, who was in Ike's cabinet later."

Other callers came, to renew speculation on the presidency. The name of Dr. Otis Singletary, an alumnus who was president of the University of Kentucky, was injected. "Yes, I know Otis well. When he had a chance at the Kentucky presidency, he came to see me and asked my advice. I told him, 'If you want to go into a presidency, take it. The University of Kentucky is not a strong university. You might build its strength.' Maybe his mind was already made up, but anyhow he took the Kentucky job and has done well at it. Any man who comes here to take the presidency in July will find a lot to do."

When the Board of Supervisors finally made its choice for the presidency, it named Martin Woodin, whom Middleton had sent to Alexandria in 1960 to be the first dean of LSU at Alexandria.

In his fourth year after retiring as LSU president, General Middleton was invited to donate his memorabilia to the university. The Board of Supervisors, meeting as a committee of the whole on August 6, 1965, heard Sterling Gladden's motion that the president emeritus be asked to consider donating his memorabilia to the university. The board unanimously adopted such a resolution. Following adoption of this resolution, the board's minutes reported, Gladden suggested that Middleton be invited to the next regular board meeting where all members of the board could join in requesting him to make the donation.

At its meeting the next day, the board formally heard from member Joseph LeSage that "Mr. Gladden had informed him that the expense of remodeling and preparing an appropriate room for the memorabilia of General Middleton, in the event he donated them, would be borne by individuals and would not be at the expense of the university."

The matter of the memorabilia might have moved relatively routinely

along and an "appropriate room" might have been constructed fairly soon
but for a mistake of commission and a subsequent omission. The Baton
Rouge *Sunday Advocate* on August 8 and the *State-Times* on August 9,
reporting the board meeting, erroneously said that Middleton, rather than
the board, had made the request that a room be prepared to house his
memorabilia. This, board member Lewis Gottlieb told the author in 1973,
had the effect that might have been expected. The two newspaper accounts
saying that Middleton had come forth with the suggestion about the memorabilia left him greatly annoyed.

Nothing further came from the Board of Supervisors concerning the
memorabilia. The author became involved in the matter of the memorabilia in 1968, when in the course of gathering information from Middleton,
the author was told, "Those folks up at Mississippi State University are
after me to turn over to them my medals and awards and things like that."
The author's response was, "Why, General, you can't do anything like that.
You're an LSU man."

"Well," he said, "let me tell you about those things. Several years ago
the Board of Supervisors adopted a resolution saying they'd like to have
my memorabilia to go in a room in the LSU Library. The idea was all right
with me, but I haven't heard a thing from the board since—except that
Buck Gladden came by to tell me about the resolution."

The author, who had been interviewing Middleton on Wednesday
mornings for three years, said: "General, we can't let your memorabilia go
off to Starkville. Before anything like that happens you ought to give them
to me. I'll see to it that they find a home here at LSU." He extracted such
a promise on the spot.

Immediately after leaving General Middleton that morning the author went to the office of Chancellor Taylor, who said he would make the
appropriate inquiries. The inquiries were eventually made. Mrs. Kitty
Strain, secretary of the Board of Supervisors, supplied a transcript of the
1965 board meeting at which a room for the memorabilia had been mentioned first. Board member Carlos G. Spaht recalled the board's original
action. "Maybe some of us have been derelict," he said; "I'll get right on
this." He spoke to Lewis Gottlieb, who years before had said that he would
be pleased to provide the funds for a room. Gottlieb was still willing, "although," he said, "if I find the cost too steep I may invite some others in."
Spaht was authorized to take up the question again with Middleton. The

General was willing. Spaht so informed the Board of Supervisors. Six years after the subject was originally broached and the word conveyed to Middleton by Gladden, planning for a room to house the Middleton memorabilia began.

Chancellor Taylor on March 30, 1971, appointed a committee made up of T. N. McMullan, director of the LSU Library; Milton M. Harrison, professor of law who had been assistant to President Middleton from the time he took office in 1952 until Harrison was appointed dean of the Law School; and F. J. Price, the author. They set to work immediately.

After preliminary conversations with Ralph Bodman of the architectural firm which had designed the LSU Library, it was clear that a first-class room to house the Middleton Collection would cost as much as $50,000. This information was conveyed to Gottlieb, who did not flinch.

"Remember," Middleton had said at the outset, "this room shouldn't cost the taxpayers of Louisiana a cent. I wouldn't want the room if it did." The planning committee decided to place the room next to the Lincoln Room on the ground floor of the Library. Middleton said he'd be in a good neighborhood there.

Into the twenty-four by fifty-four-foot room were to go pictures, letters, citations, awards, and plaques; Middleton's uniform from World War II with ribbons representing decorations presented in two wars by the grateful nations of Europe, in addition to two Distinguished Service Medals, the Legion of Merit, the Silver Star, and the Bronze Star of the United States Army; the riding boots and saber Major Middleton wore when he was first assigned to LSU as commandant of cadets in 1930; the prized shotgun his VIII Corps staff had given him for Christmas during the Battle of the Bulge; his corps commander's three-star flag that was a special present to Mrs. Middleton. A collection of eight hundred books dealing with the two World Wars was contributed through a gift from Charles P. Manship, Jr., and Douglas Manship, whose father, like Middleton, was a transplanted Mississippian who had stayed in Baton Rouge.

After two postponements caused by delays in construction, the dedication of the Middleton Collection came on Saturday, March 24, 1973. At the speaker's stand in the lobby of the Library he had worked so hard to expedite, Middleton looked at a lobby full of friends from all over the United States and noted that the day had brought "typical infantry weather," a downpour which persisted for twenty-four hours. He thanked his friend Lewis Gottlieb for his gift making possible construction of the room. He listened as his biographer recounted the story of how the room came to be and to his summary comment:

"Thus we come to this good hour, to the dedication of these graphic representations drawn from the eighty-three years of Mississippi's finest gift to Louisiana. In the eleven years Troy Middleton served as president of LSU, the university made more gains than in any other two decades of its history. In the six years he served as commandant of cadets, the ROTC tripled in size, becoming a prized activity instead of an onerous chore within one year after Major Middleton assumed command.

"Here is the Middleton Collection of Memorabilia. In Baton Rouge off South Foster Drive at Red Cross headquarters, is a street named Middleton Place. But the most lasting Middleton place is in the minds and in

Troy H. Middleton Collection of Memorabilia in LSU Library (Photo by Ken Armstrong)

the hearts of tens of thousands who have been inspired by Troy Middle-ton's example, in war and in peace, with 'his rare gift of understanding, his unending patience and his ability to inspire others.' "

With five hundred others, General and Mrs. Middleton splashed over to the LSU Union Royal Cotillion Ballroom for a luncheon. Roman Cath-olic Bishop Robert Tracy, an old friend, and Bishop Maurice Schexnayder, an older friend, jointly presented the Papal Benemerenti Award to good Episcopalian Troy Middleton for his great works. Major General Charles E. Spragins, representing the Department of Army, spoke for Chief of Staff Creighton W. Abrams, who, as commander of a relief column of tanks, broke the German siege ring at Bastogne.

Middleton recounted events and memories of his two careers in the army and at LSU, delighting his audience with sharply specific recollec-tions. He sent them home while they were asking for more.

The following Monday, Middleton and the author talked by tele-phone. "You know," said the General, "I was a little tired so we went to bed about eight Saturday night. Then a little while after midnight I came as wide awake as a man can—and then I thought of all the good stories I could have told my captive audience at the luncheon earlier."

On Wednesday he was back at his office on the LSU campus, where the phone rang and the late-arriving good wishes came in to join the stack from one-, two-, three-, and four-star generals and from the one living five-star general who had fought alongside Middleton.

"I've got to go over to that room we dedicated Saturday and do some catching up," he told himself. An old cadet dropped in and said, "I saw your light on and wondered if you have a moment. . . ."

A moment Troy Middleton always had.

Bibliography

BOOKS

Ambrose, Stephen E. *The Supreme Commander: The War Years of General Dwight D. Eisenhower*. Garden City, N.Y.: Doubleday & Company, Inc., 1970.

Bach, Christian A., and Henry Noble Hall. *The Fourth Division, Steadfast and Loyal*. Issued by the Division, Garden City, N.Y., 1920.

Baldwin, Hanson W., ed. *Command Decisions*. New York: Harcourt, Brace and Company, 1959.

Blumenson, Martin. *The Duel for France, 1944*. Boston: Houghton Mifflin Company, 1963.

————. *U.S. Army in World War II, European Theater of Operations, Breakout and Pursuit*. Washington, D.C.: Office of the Chief of Military History, Department of the Army, 1961.

————. *U.S. Army in World War II, The Mediterranean Theater of Operations, Salerno to Cassino*. Washington, D.C.: Office of the Chief of Military History, United States Army, 1969.

————. *Sicily: Whose Victory?* New York: Ballantine Books, Inc., 1968.

Bradley, Omar N. *A Soldier's Story*. New York: Henry Holt & Company, 1951.

Bryant, Arthur. *Triumph in the West, 1943–1946, Based on the Diaries and Autobiographical Notes of Field Marshal the Viscount Alanbrooke*. London: Collins, 1959.

Bykofsky, Joseph, and Harold Larson. *U.S. Army in World War II, The Technical Services, The Transportation Corps: Operations Overseas*. Washington, D.C.: Office of the Chief of Military History, Department of the Army, 1957.

Chandler, Alfred D., Jr., ed. *The Papers of Dwight David Eisenhower*. 5 vol.; Baltimore: The Johns Hopkins Press, 1970.

403

Clark, Mark W. *Calculated Risk.* New York: Harper and Brothers, 1950.

Cline, Isaac M. *Tropical Cyclones.* New York: Macmillan Company, 1926.

Cole, Hugh M. *U.S. Army in World War II, European Theater of Operations, The Ardennes: The Battle of the Bulge.* Washington, D.C.: Office of the Chief of Military History, Department of the Army, 1965.

Eisenhower, John S. D. *The Bitter Woods.* New York: G. P. Putnam's Sons, 1969.

Ellis, Lionel Frederic. *History of the Second World War: Victory in the West.* Volume II, *The Defeat of Germany.* London: Her Majesty's Stationery Office, 1968.

Elstob, Peter. *Bastogne: The Road Block.* New York: Ballantine Books, Inc., 1968.

Essame, Major General H. *Normandy Bridgehead.* New York: Ballantine Books, Inc., 1970.

Farago, Ladislas. *Patton: Ordeal and Triumph.* New York: Ivan Obolensky, Inc., 1964.

Fifth Army History (Part I, From Activation to the Fall of Naples; Part II, Across the Volturno to the Winter Line; Part III, The Winter Line). Registered Copy No. 98. Florence, Italy, 1944.

Finney, Peter. *The Fighting Tigers: Seventy-Five Years of LSU Football.* Baton Rouge: Louisiana State University Press, 1968.

Garland, Albert M., and Howard McGraw Smyth. *U.S. Army in World War II, The Mediterranean Theater of Operations, Sicily and the Surrender of Italy.* Washington, D.C.: Office of the Chief of Military History, Department of the Army, 1965.

Hart, B. H. Liddell. *The German Generals Talk.* New York: William Morrow & Company, 1948.

Kirk, John, and Robert Young, Jr. *Great Weapons of World War II.* New York: Bonanza Books, 1971.

Kleber, Brooks E., and Dale Birdsell. *U.S. Army in World War II, The Technical Services, The Chemical Warfare Service: Chemicals in Combat.* Washington, D.C.: Office of the Chief of Military History, United States Army, 1966.

MacDonald, Charles B. *Airborne.* New York: Ballantine Books, Inc., 1970.

MacDonald, Charles B. *The Mighty Endeavor, American Armed Forces in the European Theater of Operations in World War II.* New York: Oxford University Press, 1969.

MacDonald, Charles B. *U.S. Army in World War II, European Theater of Operations, The Siegfried Line.* Washington, D.C.: Office of the Chief of Military History, Department of the Army, 1963.

MacKenzie, Fred. *The Men of Bastogne.* New York: David McKay Company, Inc., 1968.

Macksey, Major K. J. *Panzer Division: The Mailed Fist*. New York: Ballantine Books, Inc., 1968.

Marshall, Samuel Lyman Atwood. *Bastogne: The First Eight Days*. Washington, D.C.: The Infantry Journal Press, 1946.

Mason, David. *Breakout: Drive to the Seine*. New York: Ballantine Books, Inc., 1968.

Mason, David. *Salerno: Foothold in Europe*. New York: Ballantine Books, Inc., 1972.

Mauldin, Bill. *The Brass Ring*. New York: W. W. Norton & Company, Inc., 1971.

Mayo, Lida. *U.S. Army in World War II, The Technical Services, The Ordnance Department: On Beachhead and Battlefront*. Washington, D.C.: Office of the Chief of Military History, United States Army, 1968.

Merriam, Robert E. *Dark December*. Chicago: Ziff-Davis Publishing Company, 1947.

Montgomery, Bernard L. *Normandy to the Baltic*. London: Hutchinson, 1947.

Nobécourt, Jacques. *Hitler's Last Gamble: The Battle of the Bulge*. New York: Schocken Books, 1967. (First published in France under the title of *Le Dernier Coup de Dés de Hitler*.)

Palmer, Frederick. *Our Greatest Battle (The Meuse-Argonne)*. New York: Dodd, Mead and Company, 1919.

Pictorial History of the Second World War. Vol. III and IV; New York: William H. Wise and Company, Inc., 1946 and 1948.

Pictorial Record, U.S. Army in World War II, The War Against Germany: Europe and Adjacent Areas. Washington, D.C.: Office of the Chief of Military History, Department of the Army, 1951.

Pitt, Barrie. *1918—The Last Act*. New York: W. W. Norton & Company, Inc., 1962.

Pogue, Forrest C. *U.S. Army in World War II, European Theater of Operations, The Supreme Command*. Washington, D.C.: Office of the Chief of Military History, Department of the Army, 1954.

Ridgway, Matthew B. *Soldier: The Memoirs of Matthew B. Ridgway (As Told to Harold H. Martin)*. New York: Harper and Brothers, 1956.

Ruppenthal, Roland G. *U.S. Army in World War II, European Theater of Operations, Logistical Support of Armies*. 2 vol.; Washington, D.C.: Office of the Chief of Military History, United States Army, 1966.

Sears, Stephen W. *The Battle of the Bulge*. New York: American Heritage Publishing Company, Inc., 1969.

Toland, John. *Battle: The Story of the Bulge*. New York: Random House, 1959.

————. *The Last 100 Days.* New York: Random House, 1966.

Whiting, Charles. *Bradley.* New York: Ballantine Books, Inc., 1971.

————. *Patton.* New York: Ballantine Books, Inc., 1970.

————. *Battle of the Ruhr Pocket.* New York: Ballantine Books, Inc., 1970.

Williams, T. Harry. *Huey Long.* New York: Alfred A. Knopf, 1969.

PRINCIPAL INTERVIEWS WITH THE AUTHOR

Ralph Bodman, Daniel F. Borth,* John E. Cribbet,* Paul Arthur Cundiff, General of the Army Dwight D. Eisenhower,* Milton M. Harrison, Paul M. Hebert, Mack H. Hornbeak, T. N. McMullan, Lieutenant General Troy H. Middleton,* Mrs. Troy H. Middleton, and B. B. Taylor, Jr.

AUTHOR'S CORRESPONDENCE

Dr. Stephen Ambrose, General of the Army Omar N. Bradley, Dr. Doak S. Campbell, Darrell Eiland, Alfred C. Glassell, Bill Mauldin.

TROY MIDDLETON CORRESPONDENCE

Letters to Middleton from:

General Creighton Abrams, Dr. Arthur S. Adams, Mahlon T. (Red) Birch, the Reverend William D. Borders, W. M. Brabham, General of the Army Omar N. Bradley, Major General E. M. Brannon, Glynn H. Brock, Lieutenant Colonel William H. Boyd, Jr., Colonel C. M. Chamberlain, Jr., Brigadier General Bruce C. Clarke, General J. Lawton Collins, Comrades of the Twenty-ninth Infantry, Major General William Durward Connor, Frank Craig, Lieutenant General Willis D. Crittenberger, General Malin Craig, A. L. Crawford, Paul F. Dietzel, Brigadier General R. L. Dulaney, General of the Army Dwight D. Eisenhower, John S. D. Eisenhower, Enlisted Men of the Forty-seventh Infantry, Colonel John D. Forsythe, Colonel Hurley E. Fuller, Captain Hurley E. Fuller, Jr., Dr. William L. Giles, Dr. George M. Gloss, Dr. Rufus C. Harris, Major General Stephen G. Henry, Major General Mark L. Hersey, Lieutenant General Fred Irving, Senator J. Bennett Johnston, Gainer Jones, Colonel Lawrence M. (Biff) Jones, Brigadier General Harris Jones, Dr. Lewis Webster Jones, Charles P. Knost, Senator Russell B. Long, Lieutenant General LeRoy Lutes, General of the Army George C. Marshall, General Anthony C. McAuliffe, Major General John L. McKee, Lieutenant General Raymond S. McLain, Lieutenant General Lesley J. McNair, the Reverend John Melton, Hermann Moyse, Major General Alexander T. Ovenshine, Major General F. L. Parks, General George S. Patton, Brigadier General B. A. Poore, Generalleutnant Hermann Ramcke, General Matthew B. Ridgway, Brigadier General Cyrus H. Searcy, I. D. Sessums, Major General Robert Bruce Smith, Major General James C. Styron, Brigadier General G. A. Taylor, the Reverend Philip P. Werlein, Colonel Wil-

* Tape recordings are available in the Troy H. Middleton Collection of Memorabilia in the LSU Library.

liam L. Wharton, Colonel Maybin H. Wilson, Major General Shirley Wood, General Melvin Zais.

Letters from Middleton to:

Baton Rouge Rotary Club, July 27, 1943; General Omar N. Bradley, May 13, 1945; General of the Army Dwight D. Eisenhower, on election to presidency of Columbia University and to presidency of the United States; Colonel Hurley E. Fuller, April 19, 1945; Colonel Carlton D. Goodiel, January 3, 1945; LSU President William B. Hatcher, May 13, 1945; *Hazlehurst Courier*, September 10, 1908; General George C. Marshall, July 5, 1940; Mrs. John McKee, April 19, 1945; Mrs. Troy H. Middleton, November 11 and 23, 1944; General George S. Patton, April 29, 1945; Major General Matthew B. Ridgway, July 7, 1944; George Shurman, December 12, 1912; James E. Smitherman, December 15, 1944; Lieutenant General Brehon B. Somervell, March 13, 1944; Officers and Enlisted Men of the VIII Corps, May 18, 1945.

MAGAZINES

Garland, Albert N. "From the Papers of Lt. Gen. Raymond S. McLain: They Had Charisma—Marshall, Bradley, Patton, Eisenhower." *Army* (May, 1971).

"Heart & Head." *Time* (March 2, 1959).

"La Bataille de Normandie." *Paris Match* (June 13, 1964).

Larsen, Carl W. "20 Years Ago with the Stars and Stripes." *The Quill* (December, 1964).

Louisiana Leader, Louisiana State University monthly (June, 1930–December, 1934).

LSU Alumni News (1950–1963).

MISCELLANEOUS

Broadcast editorial, WDSU Radio, New Orleans, August 14, 1961. Typescript in possession of the author.

Combat Tips (for Fifth Army Infantry Replacements) with cartoons by Bill Mauldin. Italy, 1945 (56–page pamphlet).

Fifth Army at the Winter Line (November 15, 1943–January 15, 1944). American Forces in Action Series, Historical Division, U.S. War Department, 1944.

From the Volturno to the Winter Line (October 6–November 15, 1943). American Forces in Action Series, Military Intelligence Division, U.S. War Department, 1944.

The Invasion of Western Europe (June 6–December 31, 1944). Department of Military Art and Engineering, United States Military Academy, West Point, New York, 1945.

Louisiana State University *Gumbo* (yearbook), 1931–1973.

Middleton, Major General Troy H. Correspondence, personal file of Middleton as commanding general, VIII Corps, March, 1944–June, 1945.

_____. Lecture at Army War College, March 7, 1923, "Infantry and Its Weapons."

_____. Memorandum to Commanders Fighting in Hedge Row Country, July 9, 1944.

_____. Memorandum to Corps Staff, Division and Separate Unit Commanders, April 1, 1944. "Observations and Suggestions as a Result of Participating in the Campaign in Sicily in 1943 and the Campaign in Italy from the Landing at Salerno in September, 1943, to January, 1944." (A distillation of General Middleton's lessons learned from combat.)

_____. Staff memorandum (equivalent of thesis), "Proposed Reduction of Equipment and Transportation in the Infantry Division." U.S. Army War College, 1929.

Official Army Register. Washington, D.C.: War Department, Adjutant General's office, 1914–1945.

Operations in Sicily and Italy (July, 1943–December, 1944). Department of Military Art and Engineering, United States Military Academy, West Point, New York, 1945.

Pollard, James E. "Forty-Seventh Infantry: A History, 1917–1919." Manuscript in possession of the author.

A Report and Recommendation to the Secretary of Defense by the Service Academy Board. U.S. Department of Defense, January, 1950.

NEWSPAPERS

Abilene (Texas) *Reporter-News,* October 28, 1950.

Alexandria (La.) *Daily Town Talk,* December 5, 1960.

Army Times, April 6, 1951.

Atlanta Journal, May 25, 1945; May 23, 1958.

Baton Rouge *Morning Advocate,* July, 1930–March, 1973.

Baton Rouge *State-Times,* July, 1930–March, 1973.

Columbus (Ga.) *Enquirer-Ledger,* September 28, 1951.

The Doughboy, Weekly Publication of the Seventh Infantry Brigade, Fourth Division, May 24, 1919, Adenau, Germany.

Forty-fifth Division News, July 13–November 20, 1943, Sicily and Italy.

Galveston Daily News, April 20, 1914; January 7, 1915.

Haynesville (La.) *News,* September 9, 1965.

Hazlehurst (Miss.) *Courier,* September 10, 1908.

Houston Post, February 22, 1959.

Jackson (Miss.) *Clarion-Ledger,* June 2, 1908; August 22, 1961; April 2, 1962; September 13, 1966.

Kansas City Times, December 15, 1964.

London, England, *Evening Standard,* September 24, 1944.

Louisiana State University, the *Reveille* and the *Daily Reveille,* July, 1930–March, 1973.

Montgomery (Ala.) *Advertiser-Journal,* May 16, 1955.

Nashville Banner, June 13, 1955.

New Orleans Item, August 1, 1943.

New Orleans States, September 25, 1953.

New Orleans *States-Item,* October 13, 1961; December 15, 1964; September 20, 21, 1966; December 1, 1967.

New Orleans *Times-Picayune,* August 22, 1943; April 1, 1951; August 20, 1961; October 18, 1961; February 24, 1963; September 3 and 30, 1965; October 22, 1972.

New York Times, February 19, 1959.

Philadelphia Inquirer, September 24, 1944.

Shreveport Times, April 12, 1958; February 28, 1960; August 28, 30, 1965; November 9, 1972.

Stars and Stripes, U.S. Army newspaper, September 26, 1944.

Washington *Evening Star,* August 5, 1943; February 19, 1959.

Washington Post, July 23, 1943.

Washington *Sunday Star,* July 25, 1943.

Index

411